D1356923

Home at Grasmere

The Cornell Wordsworth

General Editor: Stephen Parrish
Associate Editor: Mark L. Reed

Advisory Editors: M. H. Abrams, Geoffrey Hartman, Jonathan Wordsworth

---

The Salisbury Plain Poems, edited by Stephen Gill
The Prelude, 1798–1799, edited by Stephen Parrish
Home at Grasmere, edited by Beth Darlington

Home at Grasmere

Part First, Book First,
of *The Recluse*

by William Wordsworth

Edited by
BETH DARLINGTON

Cornell University Press | *Ithaca, New York*
The Harvester Press, Ltd. | *Hassocks, Sussex*

THIS BOOK HAS BEEN PUBLISHED WITH THE AID OF A GRANT FROM THE
HULL MEMORIAL PUBLICATION FUND OF CORNELL UNIVERSITY.

Copyright © 1977 by Cornell University

The Harvester Press Limited, *Publisher: John Spiers*
2 Standford Terrace, Hassocks, Sussex, England

First printing 1977

International Standard Book Number 0 85527 779 3
Printed in the United States of America by Vail-Ballou Press, Inc.

British Library Cataloguing in Publication Data
For library cataloguing purposes only

Wordsworth, William
    Home at Grasmere. (The Cornell Wordsworth)
    I. Title   II. Darlington, Beth   III. Series
    821'.7   PR5869.R/

    ISBN 0-85527-779-3

Contents

The Cornell Wordsworth

The individual volumes of the Cornell Wordsworth series, some devoted to long poems, some to collections of shorter poems, have two common aims. The first is to bring the early Wordsworth into view. Wordsworth's practice of leaving his poems unpublished for years after their completion, and his lifelong habit of revision—Ernest de Selincourt called it "obsessive"—have obscured the original, often the best, versions of his work. These original versions are here presented in the form of clean, continuous "reading texts" from which all layers of later revision have been stripped away. The second aim of the series is to provide, for the first time, a complete and accurate record of variant readings, from Wordsworth's earliest drafts down to the final lifetime (or first posthumous) publication. The most important manuscripts are shown in full transcription; on pages facing the transcriptions of the most complex and interesting of these manuscripts, photographs of the manuscript pages are also provided. Besides the transcriptions and the photographs, on which draft revisions may be seen, and an *apparatus criticus* in which printed variants are collected, a third device for the study of revisions is adopted: when two versions of a poem match sufficiently well, they are arrayed on facing pages so that the steps by which one was converted into the other become visible.

Volumes in the series are unnumbered, but upon publication are inserted into the list of volumes in print in the order in which the poems were written.

S. M. PARRISH

Ithaca, New York

Preface

Toward the end of his life Wordsworth returned to a number of poems he had written in his early years but left unpublished. He revised *Salisbury Plain*, *The Borderers*, and some Matthew poems—all composed in the 1790's—and published them in the 1842 volume, *Poems, Chiefly of Early and Late Years*. He also revised *The Prelude*, over the course of many years, and though he chose not to publish it he instructed his executors to do so; it appeared in July 1850, three months after his death. Only one important poem of any length he neither published himself nor instructed others to publish for him: *Home at Grasmere*.

Begun in 1800, *Home at Grasmere* was only slightly younger than the early pieces included in the 1842 volume and a close contemporary of *The Prelude*, and until the 1840's Wordsworth treated *The Prelude* and *Home at Grasmere* similarly: he revised both carefully on more than one occasion; he permitted selections from *The Prelude* to appear in Coleridge's *Friend* and among his own published poems, while he used extracts from *Home at Grasmere* in his *Guide to the Lakes*. Yet finally he arranged only for *The Prelude*'s appearance; *Home at Grasmere* he left abandoned. The final manuscript bears signs of extensive revision but no indication that Wordsworth even contemplated publication. He seemed reconciled, at the end, to allowing the poem to die a peaceful death.

When the poem was posthumously published, his Victorian readers were convinced that the reason for its abandonment was Wordsworth's recognition of serious deficiencies in the poem, but it seems doubtful that his critical judgment would have coincided with theirs. A more likely answer can be found in the title heading the final manuscript:

The *Recluse—Part first*
Book first
Home at Grasmere

In the 1814 Preface to *The Excursion*, Wordsworth explained that *The Recluse*, a "long and laborious Work," was to comprise three parts. *The Excursion* formed the second, but at its appearance the first and third parts were still unfinished—and unfinished they were destined to remain. All Wordsworth had completed of either part by 1814 was *Home at Grasmere*, the first book of the first part; by the 1840's, when he revised and sent his previously unpublished early poems to press, he had written no more. Hence he may have thought that to publish *Home at Grasmere* with *Guilt and Sorrow* and *The Borderers* would only advertise failure. In the Preface of 1814 Wordsworth had likened the position of *The Recluse* within the body of his work to that of a nave and chancel in a Gothic church. His "Anti-chapel," *The Prelude*, promised an awesome structure, as did collectively the "little Cells, Oratories, and sepulchral Recesses," his "minor Pieces." *The Prelude* (which was to introduce *The Recluse*), *The Excursion* (the second part of *The Recluse*), and the "minor Pieces" formed distinct wholes that could stand independent of the larger scheme. But *Home at Grasmere* represented only a beginning of the first part of the unexecuted plan. What architect would willingly draw attention to gaping holes in the structural core of his cathedral?

Wordsworth may also have conjectured that publishing the single book would leave a misleading conception of the larger poem he had planned. Parts I and II, he remarked in the 1814 Preface, were to "consist chiefly of meditations in the Author's own Person." *Home at Grasmere* depicts in joyous terms the poet's arrival among "his native Mountains," whither he retired in late 1799 with the "hope of being enabled to construct a literary Work that might live." He looked forward to a happy continuation of his new life and to its triumphant justification in the writing of *The Recluse*. "In this peaceful Vale," he exultantly vows,

> we will not spend
> Unheard-of days, though loving peaceful thoughts;
> A voice shall speak. . . .

Boldly it will discourse "On Man, on Nature, and on human Life," a subject as awe-inspiring as that of *Paradise Lost*. Wordsworth knew that he must pass the familiar landmarks of Milton's universe "unalarmed," since the "mind of Man, / My haunt, and the main region of my song," threatened greater "fear and awe" than the terrors of an anthropomorphic world; and in *Home at Grasmere* he completed his preparations for the monumental task ahead. In 1814, however, he had still to take up that task. How, then, could *Home at Grasmere*—itself no more than a prologue and a promise—adequately convey the character of the announced "meditations in the Author's own Person"? Would not publication mislead or disappoint the poem's readers, and embarrass its author?

Amid such doubts and questionings Wordsworth decided against publication. By leaving the poem in manuscript he avoided signaling his failure to complete *The Recluse* and giving a false notion of his purpose. But he made such gains at a price, a price we may regret. He did not destroy the manuscripts of the poem, and nearly forty years after his death it was published. Since Wordsworth had excluded it from his canon, however, publication in 1888 failed to win it an accepted place in later editions of his poetry. Macmillan held the exclusive copyright, and as *Home at Grasmere* was rarely reprinted, it remained somewhat inaccessible. While the poem was available in England in Macmillan's separate issues of *The Recluse* (1888 and 1891), in its Globe Edition of Wordsworth's poems (1888; reprinted several times thereafter), in the first edition of William Knight's biography of Wordsworth (1889), and in Knight's Eversley Edition (1896) published by Macmillan, other presses could not legally reprint it until the expiration of a fifty-year copyright.[1] Even since that period, however, editors have tended to exclude it from their collections. Not until 1949 was the first critical text of the poem published, by Helen Darbishire, as an appendix to the final volume of the Oxford Edition of Wordsworth's poetry begun by Ernest de Selincourt. Following the policy pursued throughout that edition, she adopted the text of Wordsworth's final version of the poem—that first printed in 1888. Save for a piecemeal appearance in her *apparatus criticus*, the earlier version has remained to this day in manuscript; it is now published for the first time in this volume.

This version is separated from that of the latest manuscript by several stages of revision, in which Wordsworth muted the openly personal tone of the original, altered the phrasing freely throughout, and—most important— abridged the poem by some three hundred lines. Among his excisions are passages central to an understanding of his first years at Grasmere, and central also to an understanding of the task he believed himself called upon to complete there. Publication of the earliest texts, therefore, retrieves and clarifies much that has been overlooked or misinterpreted.

But other reasons, no less cogent, prompt publication of these texts. Almost ignored by his editors, *Home at Grasmere*, with a few notable exceptions, has received scant and sometimes dismissive consideration from Wordsworth's critics. Editorial and critical neglect went hand in hand; and, reacting as they had toward the Vallon affair, admirers of Wordsworth seemed to regret that the poet had ever been entangled in his scheme for *The Recluse* and pretended that the waif, *Home at Grasmere*, had not indeed survived infancy. It is a harshly ironical fate for such fine poetry and for the first chapter of the grand project Wordsworth had deemed the chief work of his life. A full reassessment of *Home at Grasmere* and its place in the canon of Wordsworth's poetry is long overdue. To initiate such a reassessment is a major purpose of the present edition.

I am heavily indebted throughout this volume to John Finch's pioneering research on *Home at Grasmere*, terminated by his sudden death in 1967. Had he lived, this work would have appeared under his editorship, and I have

---

[1] In America, A. J. George included *Home at Grasmere* in his Cambridge Edition of Wordsworth's poems, published in 1904 by Houghton Mifflin Company; the firm has no record of permissions from Macmillan.

endeavored to meet the rigorous standards which I know Finch would have imposed upon himself. I must also express my thanks to the Trustees of Dove Cottage and to my fellow editors in this series, whose repeated assistance and encouragement have been invaluable; to Simon Nowell-Smith, George Kirkby, and John West, who kindly gave me information that had otherwise proved inaccessible; to Macmillan & Co. Ltd. and to the Houghton Mifflin Company, which helpfully supplied data concerning the early publication of *Home at Grasmere*; to the British Museum, for permission to quote from manuscripts in the Macmillan Archive; and to Vassar College, for its generous support of this project.

BETH DARLINGTON

Grasmere

Abbreviations

BL	British Library.
BWS	*Bicentenary Wordsworth Studies in Memory of John Alban Finch*, ed. Jonathan Wordsworth (Ithaca, 1970).
Chronology: EY	Mark L. Reed, *Wordsworth: The Chronology of the Early Years, 1770–1799* (Cambridge, Mass., 1967).
Chronology: MY	Mark L. Reed, *Wordsworth: The Chronology of the Middle Years, 1800–1815* (Cambridge, Mass., 1975).
DC	Dove Cottage.
DW	Dorothy Wordsworth.
Exc.	*The Excursion.*
EY	*Letters of William and Dorothy Wordsworth: The Early Years, 1787–1805*, ed. Ernest de Selincourt (2d ed.; rev. Chester L. Shaver; Oxford, 1967).
GW	Gordon Wordsworth.
Journals	*The Journals of Dorothy Wordsworth*, ed. Mary Moorman (Oxford, 1971).
LY	*Letters of William and Dorothy Wordsworth: The Later Years, 1821–1850*, ed. Ernest de Selincourt (3 vols.; Oxford, 1939).
Memoirs	Christopher Wordsworth, ed., *Memoirs of William Wordsworth* (2 vols.; London, 1851).
MH	Mary Hutchinson, later Mary Wordsworth.
Moorman	Mary Moorman, *William Wordsworth: A Biography* (2 vols.; Oxford, 1957, 1965).
Morley	*The Correspondence of Henry Crabb Robinson with the Wordsworth Circle*, ed. E. J. Morley (2 vols.; Oxford, 1927).
MW	Mary Wordsworth, earlier Mary Hutchinson.
MY	*Letters of William and Dorothy Wordsworth: The Middle Years, 1806–1820*, ed. Ernest de Selincourt (2 vols.; 2d ed.; Part I, 1806–1811, rev. Mary Moorman [Oxford, 1969]; Part II, 1812–1820, rev. Mary Moorman and Alan G. Hill [Oxford, 1970]).
Prel.	William Wordsworth, *The Prelude*, ed. Ernest de Selincourt (2d ed.; rev. Helen Darbishire; Oxford, 1959). All references are to the text of 1805 unless that of 1850 is specified.
Prose	*The Prose Works of William Wordsworth*, ed. W. J. B. Owen and Jane Worthington Smyser (3 vols.; Oxford, 1974).
PW	*The Poetical Works of William Wordsworth*, ed. Ernest de Selincourt and Helen Darbishire (5 vols.; Oxford, 1940–1949; rev. 1952–1959).
SH	Sara Hutchinson.
STC	Samuel Taylor Coleridge.

STCL   *Collected Letters of Samuel Taylor Coleridge*, ed. Earl Leslie Griggs
                (6 vols.; Oxford, 1956–1971).
STCNB   *The Notebooks of Samuel Taylor Coleridge*, ed. Kathleen Coburn
                (3 vols.; London, 1957–1973).
Vincent   *Letters of Dora Wordsworth*, ed. Howard P. Vincent (Chicago, 1944).
WW   William Wordsworth.

Home at Grasmere

Introduction

"I have written 1300 lines of a poem in which I contrive to convey most of the knowledge of which I am possessed," Wordsworth announced to James Tobin on 6 March 1798. "My object is to give pictures of Nature, Man, and Society. Indeed I know not any thing which will not come within the scope of my plan" (*EY*, p. 212). Five days later he disclosed a title to James Losh: "I have written 1300 lines of a poem which I hope to make of considerable utility; its title will be *The Recluse or views of Nature, Man, and Society*" (*EY*, p. 214). What the 1300 lines were is unclear; John Finch has persuasively conjectured that *The Ruined Cottage*, *The Discharged Soldier*, and *The Old Cumberland Beggar* made up the tally (*BWS*, pp. 14–15). But there can be no uncertainty about which project Wordsworth delineated here, about the grand scale of its proportions or the high seriousness of its purpose. *The Recluse* immediately became Wordsworth's artistic *raison d'être*, the justification for his friends' faith in his genius, and the summit of his own aspirations.

Wordsworth conceived his plan for *The Recluse* during the winter at Alfoxden in 1797–1798, when his friendship with Coleridge was its fullest and strongest, and from its conception *The Recluse* bears the stamp of Coleridge's influence. Reminiscing toward the end of his life, Coleridge summed up his own idea of the poem's design:

The plan laid out, and, I believe, partly suggested by me, was, that Wordsworth should assume the station of a man in mental repose, one whose principles were made up, and so prepared to deliver upon authority a system of philosophy. He was to treat man as man,—a subject of eye, ear, touch, and taste, in contact with external nature, and informing the senses from the mind, and not compounding a mind out of the senses; then he was to describe the pastoral and other states of society, assuming something of the Juvenalian spirit as he approached the high civilizations of cities and towns, and opening a melancholy picture of the present state of degeneracy and vice; thence he was to infer and reveal the proof of, and necessity for, the whole state of man and society being subject to, and illustrative of, a redemptive process in operation, showing how this idea reconciled all the anomalies, and promised future glory and restoration. Something of this sort was, I think, agreed on. It is, in substance, what I have been all my life doing in my system of philosophy.[1]

---

[1] 21 July 1832; *Specimens of the Table Talk of the Late Samuel Taylor Coleridge* (2 vols.; London, 1835), II, 70–71.

3

Upon this gigantic frame a mass of Wordsworth's blank-verse compositions was to be fitted: first *The Ruined Cottage*, *The Discharged Soldier*, and *The Old Cumberland Beggar*, and later *Michael*, *The Brothers*, *Home at Grasmere*, *The Tuft of Primroses*, and *The Excursion*. As Wordsworth shaped *The Prelude*, he regarded it, too, as a part of this structure—initially as an appendix, and subsequently as a prologue.

The mere bulk of the poem as Wordsworth and Coleridge projected it is overwhelming. In 1804, Wordsworth estimated that *The Recluse* would come to "10 or 12 thousand" lines (WW to Sir George Beaumont, 25 December; *EY*, p. 518), but the plan he outlined in the 1814 Preface to *The Excursion* promised a vaster work. Finch drew up a modest calculation: "*The Prelude* is to act as an introduction to a three-part poem of which *The Excursion* forms the second section; except for *Home at Grasmere*, Parts One and Three have still to be written. *The Prelude* (1850) approaches 8000 lines, *The Excursion* 9000; assuming comparable length in the unwritten Parts, *The Recluse* might have reached 33,000 lines—*Paradise Lost* has a mere 10,500" (*BWS*, p. 16). The comprehensiveness of the poem's subject matter is even more overwhelming. The grand design proposed to synthesize mankind's philosophical, scientific, historical, and political knowledge and experience in poetry that would move man to realize on earth the Utopian vision confined for centuries to his hopes and dreams. To this awesome task Wordsworth was to consecrate his full powers and energies; for this, he believed, he had been singled out by Nature, reared and schooled to be a poet. Two letters of 1804 reveal the depth of his commitment. To Beaumont he avowed that *The Recluse* "is the chief object upon which my thoughts have been fixed these many years," and he announced to Thomas De Quincey, "To this work I mean to devote the Prime of my life and the chief force of my mind" (25 December, *EY*, p. 518; and 6 March, *EY*, p. 454).

In the early years Coleridge's unbounded enthusiasm and his extravagant praise of Wordsworth's abilities nurtured Wordsworth's aspirations. He bombarded friends with reports of Wordsworth's progress on the *magnum opus*. To Joseph Cottle he effused in 1798, "The Giant Wordsworth—God love him! . . . has written near 1200 lines of a blank verse, superior, I hesitate not to aver, to any thing in our language which any way resembles it" (7 March; *STCL*, I, 391). And he rejoiced to Thomas Poole in 1803, "with a deep & true Joy, that he [Wordsworth] has at length yielded to my urgent & repeated—almost unremitting—requests & remonstrances—& will go on with the Recluse exclusively.—A Great Work, in which he will sail; on an open Ocean, & a steady wind; unfretted by short tacks, reefing, & hawling & disentangling the ropes——great work necessarily comprehending his attention & Feelings within the circle of great objects & elevated Conceptions."[2] Writing to Richard

---

[2] 14 October; *STCL*, II, 1013. See also *STCNB*, Entry 1546, which duplicates some of the thought and phrasing of this paragraph in the letters.

Sharp in 1804, Coleridge modulated his prose but not his admiration:

I dare affirm that he [Wordsworth] will hereafter be admitted as the first & greatest philosophical Poet—the only man who has effected a compleat and constant synthesis of Thought & Feeling and combined them with Poetic Forms, with the music of pleasurable passion and with Imagination. . . . and I prophesy immortality to his *Recluse*, as the first & finest philosophical Poem, if only it be (as it undoubtedly will be) a Faithful Transcript of his own most august & innocent Life, of his own habitual Feelings & Modes of seeing and hearing. [15 January; *STCL*, II, 1034]

Letters to Wordsworth also manifest Coleridge's faith in the poem and his solicitous concern for its growth. He wrote in September, 1799, "I am anxiously eager to have you steadily employed on 'The Recluse,'" and went on to suggest additional subject matter: "I wish you would write a poem, in blank verse, addressed to those, who, in consequence of the complete failure of the French Revolution, have thrown up all hopes of the amelioration of mankind, and are sinking into an almost epicurean selfishness, disguising the same under the soft titles of domestic attachment and contempt for visionary *philosophes*. It would do great good, and might form a part of 'The Recluse'" (*STCL*, I, 527). A month later Coleridge exuberantly declared:

I long to see what you have been doing. O let it be the tail-piece of 'The Recluse!' for of nothing but 'The Recluse' can I hear patiently. That it is to be addressed to me makes me more desirous that it should not be a poem of itself. To be addressed, as a beloved man, by a thinker, at the close of such a poem as 'The Recluse,' a poem *non unius populi*, is the only event, I believe, capable of inciting in me an hour's vanity. [12 October; *STCL*, I, 538]

The encouragement continued in a more subdued tone when Wordsworth's muse deserted him. "I grieve that 'The Recluse' sleeps," Coleridge wrote simply in February, 1800 (*STCL*, I, 575); but by early April, when Coleridge paid his first visit to the Wordsworths in Dove Cottage, *The Recluse* had wakened—perhaps in anticipation of his arrival. The creative outburst of that spring yielded a substantial body of *Home at Grasmere* composition, including many of the finest passages in the poem. Subsequently, however, Wordsworth made only halting progress toward the execution of his grand scheme.

Despite Coleridge's support and his own fervent commitment, Wordsworth's confidence waned as a method of systematizing his views repeatedly eluded him. The odd period of work after the creative burst of spring, 1800, would be followed by longer stretches of slack and depression; and the excuses and apologies for not getting on with composition—so frequently offered in the letters—betray Wordsworth's anxiety and that of his family as well.[3] For inspiration he appears to have depended entirely on Coleridge's ideas. In his presence, there were long, thought-provoking conversations; in his absence,

---

[3] For DW's early apologies on this subject, see *BWS*, p. 24, also *EY*, pp. 617, 650, 664, and *MY*, I, 2; for later excuses, see *MY*, II, 200 and 402.

Wordsworth begged for instruction to help him find his way. "I am very anxious to have your notes for the Recluse. I cannot say how much importance I attach to this, if it should please God that I survive you, I should reproach myself for ever in writing the work if I had neglected to procure this help" (6 March 1804; *EY*, p. 452). News of Coleridge's severe attack of diarrhea a few weeks later prompted a still more urgent request: "I cannot help saying that I would gladly have given 3 fourths of my possessions for your letter on The Recluse at that time. I cannot say what a load it would be to me, should I survive you and you die without this memorial left behind. Do for heaven's sake, put this out of the reach of accident immediately" (29 March; *EY*, p. 464).

At last, in Malta, Coleridge—so he said—did compile the long promised and eagerly awaited notes, but through a whim of fate they never reached Wordsworth in England. "My Ideas respecting your Recluse were burnt as a Plague-garment," Coleridge mournfully disclosed to the Wordsworths in 1805, "and all my long letters to you and Sir George Beaumont sunk to the bottom of the Sea!" (*STCL*, II, 1169; see also the editor's note to an earlier letter, pp. 1159–1160). One wonders if Coleridge's notes did in fact ever exist, and if they did, how much useful advice they might have contained. Even before his removal to Malta he had confessed incapacities to William Godwin: "Wordsworth . . . wished, & in a very particular manner expressed the wish, that I should write to him at large on a poetic subject, which he has at present sub malleo ardentem et ignitum—I made the attempt—but I could not command my recollections. It seemed a Dream, that I had ever *thought* on Poetry—or had ever written it—so remote were my Trains of Ideas from Composition, or Criticism on Composition" (10 June 1803; *STCL*, II, 950). Persistent illness and the concerns of his new environment must have further undermined his abilities.

The absence of Coleridge's notes itself, however, can hardly account for Wordsworth's difficulties. More fundamental reasons are not hard to find. From its inception, as Helen Darbishire remarked (*PW*, V, 368), there must have been some "divergence" between Wordsworth's and Coleridge's ideas of *The Recluse*: whereas Coleridge would have expected a philosophical discourse delivered by the poet *in propria persona*, Wordsworth would have inclined toward a narrative or dramatic work. No doubt one reason that Wordsworth came to depend so heavily upon Coleridge's assistance was simply that extensive philosophical discourse in the first person was alien to his own poetic instincts—though he may for a time have been deceived about the nature of those instincts by the ring of Coleridge's praise. In 1814, when Wordsworth published the only full Part of *The Recluse* he ever completed— nine books of *The Excursion*—Coleridge made known his disappointment, and Wordsworth wrote him to demand an explanation:

I have rather been perplexed than enlightened by your *comparative* censure. One of my principal aims in the Exn: has been to put the commonplace truths, of the human affections especially, in an interesting point of view; and rather to remind men of their knowledge, as it lurks inoperative and unvalued in their own minds, than to attempt to convey recondite or refined truths. Pray point out to me the most striking instances where I have failed. [22 May 1815; *MY*, II, 238]

Coleridge's reply, 30 May (*STCL*, IV, 574–575), reveals some of the burdens under which Wordsworth must have labored, for it most likely reflects advice given years earlier. Coleridge's general expectation was encouraging, if intimidating: "In the very Pride of confident Hope I looked forward to the Recluse, as the *first* and *only* true Phil[osophical] Poem in existence. Of course, I expected the Colors, Music, imaginative Life, and Passion of *Poetry*; but the matter and arrangement of *Philosophy*." But his specifications were staggering:

I supposed you first to have meditated the faculties of Man in the abstract, in their correspondence with his Sphere of action, and first, in the Feeling, Touch, and Taste, then in the Eye, & last in the Ear, to have laid a solid and immoveable foundation for the Edifice by removing the sandy Sophisms of Locke, and the Mechanic Dogmatists, and demonstrating that the Senses were living growths and developments of the Mind & Spirit in a much juster as well as higher sense, than the mind can be said to be formed by the Senses—. Next, I understood that you would take the Human Race in the concrete, have exploded the absurd notion of Pope's Essay on Man, Darwin, and all the countless Believers—even (strange to say) among Xtians of Man's having progressed from an Ouran Outang state . . . Fallen men contemplated in the different ages of the World, and in the different states—Savage—Barbarous— Civilized—the lonely Cot, or Borderer's Wigwam—the Village—the Manufacturing Town—Sea-port—City—Universities—and not disguising the sore evils, under which the whole Creation groans, to point out however a manifest Scheme of Redemption from this Slavery, of Reconciliation from this Enmity with Nature . . . and to conclude by a grand didactic swell on the necessary identity of a true Philosophy with true Religion, agreeing in the results and differing only as the analytic and synthetic process, as discursive from intuitive, the former chiefly useful as perfecting the latter— in short, the necessity of a general revolution in the modes of developing & disciplining the human mind by the substitution of Life, and Intelligence . . . for the philosophy of mechanism which in every thing that is most worthy of the human Intellect strikes *Death*. . . . In short, Facts elevated into Theory—Theory into Laws—& Laws into living & intelligent Powers—true Idealism necessarily perfecting itself in Realism, & Realism refining itself into Idealism.—
    Such or something like this was the Plan, I had supposed that you were engaged on—.

As S. M. Parrish has observed, it is hardly surprising that *The Recluse* foundered: "Wedding poetry to philosophy, at least in the way Coleridge envisioned, was something no mortal could have managed."[4]

---

[4] *The Art of the "Lyrical Ballads"* (Cambridge, Mass., 1973), pp. 57–58.

II

But when Wordsworth began writing *Home at Grasmere* in the early spring of 1800 he was free and unfettered, burdened neither by the magnitude of his own commitment nor by Coleridge's ambitious hopes. The beginnings were unpretentious, and hardly philosophical: they celebrate Wordsworth's arrival in the Lakes after many years of wandering, and his settling into Dove Cottage with Dorothy. Their tone is joyful and confident, matching the exuberance of his "glad preamble" to *The Prelude*. No manuscript survives from this period, but lines in the first complete version of the poem, MS. B (a reading text is given below), clearly express events and feelings of March and April, 1800:

> Thrice hath the winter Moon been filled with light
> Since that dear day when Grasmere, our dear Vale,
> Received us. [ll. 257–259][5]

> By a sullen storm,
> Two months unwearied of severest storm,
> It put the temper of our minds to proof,
> And found us faithful. . . . [ll. 269–272]

> But the gates of Spring
> Are opened; churlish Winter hath given leave
> That she should entertain for this one day,
> Perhaps for many genial days to come,
> His guests and make them happy. [ll. 277–281]

In lines composed at the same time, Wordsworth describes the cold December journey that brought him and Dorothy across England to Grasmere in 1799:

> Bleak season was it, turbulent and bleak,
> When hitherward we journeyed, and on foot,
> Through bursts of sunshine and through flying snows,
> Paced the long vales—how long they were, and yet
> How fast that length of way was left behind,
> Wensley's long Vale and Sedbergh's naked heights.
> The frosty wind, as if to make amends
> For its keen breath, was aiding to our course
> And drove us onward like two Ships at sea. [ll. 218–226]

The lines echo Wordsworth's letter to Coleridge, written just before and just after Christmas, chronicling the journey: "Twas a keen frosty morning, showers of snow threatening us but the sun bright and active" (*EY*, p. 278), and "we walked the next ten miles, by the watch over a high mountain road,

---

[5] Helen Darbishire calculated that the moon was full on 10 January, 9 February, and 10 March 1800. These lines thus date the earliest work on *Home at Grasmere* within the four weeks after 10 March.

thanks to the wind that drove behind us and the good road, in two hours and a quarter" (p. 280).

On grounds of content, a number of other passages appear to date from that first spring in Grasmere: the scattered evocations of the vale, of the cottage "where with me my Emma dwells" (l. 98), of Emma (Dorothy) herself—"She whom now I have, who now / Divides with me this loved abode" (ll. 107–108)—and of the "lonely pair / Of milk-white Swans," who

> came, like Emma and myself, to live
> Together here in peace and solitude,
> Choosing this Valley, they who had the choice
> Of the whole world. [ll. 322–323; 326–329]

The deeply felt happiness of the spring inspired Wordsworth to compose some of his tenderest love poetry. One lyrical outpouring reads as a moving hymn to Dorothy:

> Mine eyes did ne'er
> Rest on a lovely object, nor my mind
> Take pleasure in the midst of [happy] thoughts,
> But either She whom now I have, who now
> Divides with me this loved abode, was there
> Or not far off. Where'er my footsteps turned,
> Her Voice was like a hidden Bird that sang;
> The thought of her was like a flash of light
> Or an unseen companionship, a breath
> Or fragrance independent of the wind. [ll. 104–113]

Other lines become a love song directed to the Vale of Grasmere itself:

> Embrace me then, ye Hills, and close me in;
> Now in the clear and open day I feel
> Your guardianship; I take it to my heart;
> 'Tis like the solemn shelter of the night.
> But I would call thee beautiful, for mild
> And soft and gay and beautiful thou art,
> Dear Valley, having in thy face a smile
> Though peaceful, full of gladness. [ll. 129–136]

Wordsworth's verse captures the mood of the brief idyll which he and Dorothy shared during their first months in this valley—the unnamable sense

> Of majesty and beauty and repose,
> A blended holiness of earth and sky,
> Something that makes this individual Spot,
> This small abiding-place of many men,
> A termination and a last retreat,
> A Centre, come from wheresoe'er you will,
> A Whole without dependence or defect,
> Made for itself and happy in itself,
> Perfect Contentment, Unity entire. [ll. 162–170]

Toward the end of the poem a section of some fifteen lines plainly refers to John Wordsworth's sojourn at Dove Cottage (January to September, with a brief absence) and to the expected arrivals of Mary Hutchinson (she came at the end of February and stayed through March) and of Coleridge (who came in April and departed in May):

> we have enough within ourselves,
> Enough to fill the present day with joy
> And overspread the future years with hope—
> Our beautiful and quiet home, enriched
> Already with a Stranger whom we love
> Deeply, a Stranger of our Father's house,
> A never-resting Pilgrim of the Sea,
> Who finds at last an hour to his content
> Beneath our roof; and others whom we love
> Will seek us also, Sisters of our hearts,
> And one, like them, a Brother of our hearts,
> Philosopher and Poet, in whose sight
> These mountains will rejoice with open joy.
> Such is our wealth: O Vale of Peace, we are
> And must be, with God's will, a happy band! [ll. 860–874]

Their serenity marks these lines as early composition, for after the anguish of John's death in 1805 Wordsworth could never have written about the "happy band" in this tone.

Such evidence led early commentators to date *Home at Grasmere* with some confidence, and Helen Darbishire drew on received opinion when she declared that the earliest manuscripts all date from 1800 (*PW*, V, 475). But John Finch showed this date to be impossible, not least because two of the manuscripts are made of paper countermarked 1801, and he developed strong independent evidence that fixes 1806 as the date when Wordsworth shaped the poem into a finished work, joining the passages from 1800 with fresh composition (*BWS*, pp. 24–28). Finch's ingenious demonstration involved analysis of the poem's surviving manuscripts, and it is necessary to consider them closely to understand the growth of the poem. The latest of them, which Darbishire called MS. D and published in *PW*, V (Appendix A, pp. 313–338), is discussed below, in Sections IV and V of the Introduction, as much of it clearly postdates publication of *The Excursion* in 1814. Two others contain only copies of the Prospectus (*PW*, V, 3–6), and are described in Section III below. The remaining three manuscripts, to use Darbishire's nomenclature again, are as follows:

(1) MS. B (DC MS. 59) is the earliest full text, a fair copy, in the hands of William, Mary, and Dorothy Wordsworth, with some drafts interspersed, and later much revised. The manuscript is a small notebook, made by folding and tearing three folio sheets to convert each sheet into eight leaves; into this book three similar gatherings were inserted to make a total of forty-eight leaves, of

which three have been torn out, one of them containing lines 185–208 of the text. The summary line count at the end of the poem reads "1047," though in fact 1049 lines appear to be present in the fair copy. A full transcription of MS. B with facing photographs is given below.

(2) MS. A (DC MS. 58) is a single folio sheet of the kind used to construct MS. B. Folded in accordion style into three vertical panels, the sheet is filled, front and back (six columns in all), with lines equivalent to lines 192–457 of the B text but in a version earlier than B's, plus two additional lines not copied into B. The text is a fair copy mainly in Wordsworth's hand, with lines 278–321 in Mary's. The first summary line number in A is 215; thereafter, from line 220 onward, lines are numbered in twenties, except for a summary line number (377) before a separate sheet sewn onto the first column of A and another summary number marking the last line on the sheet itself (396). MS. A provides all but seven of the lines lacking in B where a leaf is missing. Full transcriptions of A with facing photographs may be found below.

(3) MS. R (DC MS. 28) is part of an interleaved copy of Coleridge's *Poems on Various Subjects* published in 1796. Over the pages of print and on the interleaves Wordsworth scrawled drafts and some fair copy of the three stories that constitute lines 469–860 of MS. B. "Though not systematic," John Finch observed, Wordsworth tended "to use interleaves and blank pages to receive the continuous text, pages with printed text to try out drafts and sketches" (*BWS*, p. 22). At least one of the *Home at Grasmere* entries, Finch showed, has to be later than entries for *The Waggoner* here, which can be independently dated January, 1806; this entry, however, is probably a revision of lines which formerly stood on the interleaf facing page 138 of MS. R, now removed. Although it must date from 1806, it does not help to date other composition in the manuscript. The MS. R drafts precede the version of *Home at Grasmere* in MS. B. A transcription of R, as full as the extremely illegible hand permits, faced with photographs, is given below.

Present evidence does not enable us to date the major composition in MS. R with certainty, but it is apparent that the work moves steadily toward the plan of *Home at Grasmere* in MS. B. Had Wordsworth completed this phase of work in 1800 or 1801, the poem would then have attained conceptually almost the final form of MS. B. It is difficult to believe that with such a clear design in mind Wordsworth would not have copied the poem out in proper sequence in a single manuscript after drafting MS. R. It is also difficult to believe that on 6 March 1804 he could have told De Quincey he had written only "one Book and several scattered fragments" of *The Recluse* (*EY*, p. 454). The completed book was *The Ruined Cottage*, and MS. R displays too great a coherence and awareness of the outline of an integral poem for Wordsworth to have described *Home at Grasmere* as mere scattered fragments once MS. R had been drafted.

Finch's assertion that MSS, B, A, and R all belong "to a single phase of work" (*BWS*, p. 23) seems correct. In addition to the evidence already summarized, Finch offered the findings of his search for other pieces of the 1801 paper used to make MSS. A and B. His premise was simple but intelligent: "The Wordsworths habitually used whatever stock of paper they had in the house to write both letters and manuscripts. At any given period the paper that appears in their letters will usually reappear in manuscripts contemporary with those letters" (*BWS*, p. 21). Finch counted sixteen letters using the 1801 paper, the earliest from Wordsworth to Beaumont on 20 February 1805, and the latest from Dorothy to Catherine Clarkson, 28 December 1807. He also discovered the paper in two other manuscripts: MS. Z of *The Prelude* (DC MS. 49), from the first half of 1805, and MS. 1 of *The White Doe of Rylstone* (DC MS. 61), from the autumn of 1807. Nowhere else could the 1801 paper be found.

Finch's research made it possible to consider a further piece of evidence of 1806 work on *Home at Grasmere*. Among the "miscellaneous jottings" from Dorothy's journals that William Knight found and published in his life of Wordsworth, he included an extract which he himself, apparently, titled "To the Evening Star over Grasmere Water, July 1806" (Wordsworth did not use the tautological phrase "Grasmere Water"):

> The Lake is thine,
> The mountains too are thine, some clouds there are,
> Some little feeble stars, but all is thine,
> Thou, thou art king, and sole proprietor.
>
> A moon among her stars, a mighty vale,
> Fresh as the freshest field, scoop'd out, and green
> As is the greenest billow of the sea.
>
> The multitude of little rocky hills,
> Rocky or green, that do like islands rise
> From the flat meadow lonely there.[6]

Since Knight quoted from it, this journal has disappeared, and Helen Darbishire, when she reprinted—and rearranged—the lines in *PW*, V, 347, thought that Knight must have got the date wrong; she changed it conjecturally to 1800, noting that the extract is made up of "jottings for the description of Grasmere, *Recluse*, i, 117–128, in which one of the lines, 'The multitude of little rocky hills,' appears intact" (at l. 139 of MS. B, *Home at Grasmere*). The first to point out that 1806 might after all be correct was James Butler, in his

---

[6] Knight's life takes up Volumes IX–XI of his eleven-volume *Poetical Works of William Wordsworth* (Edinburgh, 1882–1889); the "Evening Star" lines are in Volume IX, pages 389–390. Knight reprinted the lines, with some additions, in his 1896 *Poetical Works* (VIII, 263). In a more fragmented form they also appear in the second edition of his *The English Lake District as Interpreted in the Poems of Wordsworth* (Edinburgh, 1891), p. 77.

Cornell University Ph.D. dissertation, "'This Sublime Retirement': A Textual and Literary Study of Wordsworth's *Home at Grasmere*" (1971; pp. 25–26). Butler remarks that "there is no reason to question Knight's dating of the lines. Clearly, Wordsworth was working on *Home at Grasmere* in July, 1806, and Knight's passage indicates part of that work."

Supplemented by letters and journals, the evidence previously cited allows us to cobble together a rough history of the composition of *Home at Grasmere*. If we turn back to 1800, we can find no indication that Wordsworth did much work on the poem after making his jubilant start during his first spring at Dove Cottage. Manuscripts from this period, now lost, must have carried versions of most of lines 1 to 457 of MS. B; possibly a passage of uncertain length, the first two lines of which are preserved in MS. A, following line 457; and lines 859 to 874 of MS. B. The degree to which this composition was linked in sequence cannot be determined. Additionally these manuscripts may have contained odd fragments later incorporated in MS. B, lines 875 to 958, and fragments such as i and ii in Appendix B, VII, published by de Selincourt and Darbishire in *PW*, V, 347. It is conceivable but unlikely for the reasons already noted that lines 469 to 859 of MS. B were drafted in MS. R at this time. An early version of the Prospectus (MS. B, lines 959 to 1001 and 1015 to 1048) appears to date from this phase; whether Wordsworth regarded it as part of *Home at Grasmere* is uncertain, though there can be no doubt that he conceived of it as part of *The Recluse*. In the summer and autumn of 1800 Wordsworth was busy with preparation of the second volume of *Lyrical Ballads* for the press. It is possible that he resumed work on *Home at Grasmere* in 1801; John Wordsworth wrote to Dorothy, 28–29 March, that he was "glad to learn that Wm is *going on* with the recluse," but no further allusions to 1801 work exist.[7] In 1802, Dorothy's journal entry for 13 February teasingly records, "William read parts of his Recluse aloud to me" (*Journals*, p. 90), but which parts, or when they were composed, we cannot know. Two letters of Coleridge's in 1803 imply that Wordsworth is deep in the throes of composition. Besides telling Godwin on 10 June that Wordsworth has *The Recluse* "sub malleo ardentem et ignitum" (*STCL*, II, 950), on 14 October he announced to Poole that Wordsworth "has made a Beginning to his Recluse" and "will go on with the Recluse exclusively" (*STCL*, II, 1012–1013). Furthermore, Coleridge recorded in his notebooks at about this time in October that Wordsworth had "bidden farewell to all small Poems—& is devoting himself to his great work" (*STCNB*, Entry 1546). But the fact is that Wordsworth himself on

---

[7] *The Letters of John Wordsworth*, ed. Carl Ketcham (Ithaca, 1969), p. 110. Ketcham suggests that this reference may be to work on *Home at Grasmere* or more probably on the early *Prelude* (p. 209). Jonathan Wordsworth and Stephen Gill find the latter possibility unlikely in "The Two-Part *Prelude* of 1798–99," *JEGP*, LXXII (1973), 522.

14 October sent Beaumont three sonnets which he described as "the only Verses I have written since I had the [pl]easure of seeing you and Lady Beaumont," and the meeting to which he alludes occurred between 23 July and 9 August (*EY*, pp. 409, 406n; *Chronology: MY*, p. 217). Likewise, Dorothy's letters belie Coleridge's assertions. She informed Catherine Clarkson on 13 November that "William has not yet done any thing of importance at his great work" and on 21 November that he "has written two little poems on subjects suggested by our Tour in Scotland—that is all that he has actually done lately" (*EY*, pp. 421, 423).

Although it is conceivable that Wordsworth wrote some passages for *Home at Grasmere* during 1804 and 1805, there is no evidence beyond good intentions. In late January or early February, 1804, he told Francis Wrangham, in response to an inquiry, "I have great things in meditation but as yet I have only been doing little ones." The great projects meditated were "a Philosophical Poem and a narrative one," which "will employ me some I ought to say several years, and I do not mean to appear before the world again as an Author till one of them at least be finished" (*EY*, p. 436). The philosophical poem still sounds distant, and Wordsworth's decision in March, 1804, to expand *The Prelude* beyond the five-book work he had planned preserved the distance. The decision itself was in part the result of Wordsworth's anxiety about *The Recluse*, for the enlargement of *The Prelude* enabled him to compose poetry associated with *The Recluse* but to avoid direct confrontation with his sense of inadequacy to proceed with it. Letters of 1804 and early 1805 repeatedly allude to progress on *The Prelude* (see *EY*, pp. 440, 447, 451–452, 470, 489, 592, and 594), often explaining that the poet is laboring at his autobiographical poem rather than at the great work itself. These references indicate that Wordsworth deemed the poem on his own life an inferior work, deriving its significance primarily as the means of his approaching *The Recluse*.

Following John's death, 5 February 1805, Wordsworth attempted a "poem upon him" which Dorothy claimed was a "*part* of the Recluse" (DW to Lady Beaumont, 11 April 1805; *EY*, p. 576), but the attempt failed. By this time, however, Wordsworth had brought the "poem to Coleridge" close to completion, and he finished it about the middle of May. Some introductory lines in this account of the growth of his own mind confess his "favourite aspiration," a yearning

> towards some philosophic Song
> Of Truth that cherishes our daily life;
> With meditations passionate from deep
> Recesses in man's heart, immortal verse
> Thoughtfully fitted to the Orphean lyre. [*Prel.*, I, 229–234]

But from this "awful burthen" he took "refuge," assailed by fear and doubt, his capacities locked up "in blank reserve" (I, 235–236, 248). Only toward the end of the great confessional poem does Wordsworth allow his spirit to break free of these shackles, to contemplate

> making Verse
> Deal boldly with substantial things, in truth
> And sanctity of passion . . .
> 　　. . . . .
> . . . my theme
> No other than the very heart of man. [XII, 233–240]

Echoing—or adumbrating—the bravado of the Prospectus, Wordsworth exults that he shall

> follow with no timid step
> Where knowledge leads me; it shall be my pride
> That I have dared to tread this holy ground
> Speaking no dream but things oracular. [XII, 249–252]

At the conclusion of *The Prelude* he appears to have won peace of mind, confidence, and creative energy, and thus to have fulfilled his purpose in composing the poem:

> we have reach'd
> The time (which was our object from the first)
> When we may, not presumptuously, I hope,
> Suppose my powers so far confirmed, and such
> My knowledge, as to make me capable
> Of building up a work that should endure. [XIII, 273–278]

With the completion of *The Prelude*, the "portico to the Recluse" (*EY*, p. 594), Wordsworth must have faced the fact that procrastination was no longer defensible. If he was indeed to construct his proposed edifice, he must plan its structure and begin laying its foundations. Instead, however, of preparing him for this demanding assignment, *The Prelude* seems to have debilitated him. "I finished my Poem about a fortnight ago," he informed Beaumont on 3 June 1805:

I had looked forward to the day as a most happy one; and I was indeed grateful to God for giving me life to complete the work, such as it is; but it was not a happy day for me[.] I was dejected on many accounts; when I looked back upon the performance it seemed to have a dead weight about it, the reality so far short of the expectation; it was the first long labour that I had finished, and the doubt whether I should ever live to write the Recluse and the sense which I had of this Poem being so far below what I seem'd capable of executing, depressed me much. [*EY*, p. 594]

Several months later, Dorothy was still hoping that Wordsworth "may begin in good earnest with his important Task" (27 October; *EY*, p. 634), and on 29 November she confided to the same correspondent, Lady Beaumont, "My Brother has not yet begun fairly with his great work; but I hope he will after his return from Park house. We shall then in right earnest enjoy winter quiet and loneliness; besides starlight walks and winter winds are his delight—his mind I think is often more fertile in this season than any other" (*EY*, p. 650).

But winter's winds and starlight did not help, and the year 1806 began with more excuses. Dorothy reported to Lady Beaumont on 19 January, "my Brother though not actually employed in his great work, is not idle, for he almost daily produces something and his thoughts are employed upon the Recluse (*MY*, I, 2). As late as mid-June, Wordsworth was confessing his idleness (WW to Walter Scott; *MY*, I, 41), and urging himself onward—"I must to business"—in an unpromising fashion. But the following month he did at last settle down to concentrated composition on *Home at Grasmere*. Casually, Dorothy closed a letter to Lady Beaumont on 23 July, "He is going on with The Recluse," and on the same day wrote Catherine Clarkson, "William goes on rapidly with the Recluse" (*MY*, I, 58–61).

Wordsworth's own letters give fuller details. On 1 August he informed Beaumont, "Within this last month I have returned to the Recluse, and have written 700 additional lines. Should Coleridge return, so that I might have some conversation with him upon the subject, I should go on swimmingly" (*MY*, I, 64). In the middle of August he learned of Coleridge's return to England, and on 8 September he had further progress to announce: "You will be glad to hear that I have been busily employed lately; I wrote one book of the Recluse nearly 1000 lines, then had a rest, last week began again and have written 300 more; I hope all tolerably well, and certainly with good views" (*MY*, I, 79).

Wordsworth's figures enable us to reconstruct conjecturally the rough stages of *Home at Grasmere* composition in 1806. During July, he must have taken up the manuscripts containing the passages composed in 1800. Ordering them and perhaps filling them out with some new composition, he achieved the plan and substance of what was to become the first 457 lines of MS. B; these lines he probably copied into MS. A, only one leaf of which survives. The mid-sentence breakoff at the end of A suggests that Wordsworth had composed beyond this point, but how far cannot be determined. MS. A concludes:

> And as these lofty barriers break the force
> Of winds this deep vale as it doth in part
> Conceal us from the storm so here there is
> Or seems to be for it befits it yet
> Newcomer as I am to speak in doubt.

To try to reconstruct what MS. A might have comprised is tempting, but no conjectures concerning a hypothetical first or third sheet can be proved. The manuscripts provide no justification for assuming that the poem at this stage was a self-contained work, rounded to a conclusion. It is quite possible that Wordsworth made extensive revisions on sections of A no longer extant, and that the resulting messy state of the manuscript prompted the new copy, MS.

B, which Mary began. If similar to the surviving sheet, a lost first sheet could have held as many as 260 lines, while the numbering shows that only 191 lines were ultimately kept. But speculation of this sort grows highly tenuous; obviously the lost opening lines as well as any lines subsequent to those preserved in A could have been written on paper of a type different from the extant sheet.

Whatever the condition and contents of MS. A, Mary Wordsworth, with some help from William and Dorothy, copied the opening 457 lines of *Home at Grasmere* into MS. B and added 11 new lines to bring to a close the first main section of the poem, marked by the summary line number, 470, in Wordsworth's hand. The 11 new lines replace a false start; Mary began to copy the last 2 lines of MS. A, writing, "Or seems to be," then deleted the phrase and began again with the 11 lines for which no drafts survive. John Finch offered a speculation about this first section of *Home at Grasmere*, finding it "conceivable that Wordsworth may initially have thought of the poem as consisting simply of these 470 lines. They describe his and his sister's long-held desire to make a home together, their journey to Grasmere in December 1799, and their happiness in the scene before them heightened by returning spring. The lines conclude with the reflection that Grasmere offers a 'Power & a protection' against the world's 'languour or indifference or despair'" (*BWS*, p. 26).

One fact undercuts this hypothesis. As Mary finished copying this section of the poem, she spaced out the 11 added lines to fill up a page, as though her copy had been "cast off," and it is easy to see why she did this. Following this page fresh gatherings were inserted, onto which had already been copied the second section, or at least its beginning. This section comprises the three narrative accounts of Grasmere inhabitants and a summary reflection, which Wordsworth had drafted in MS. R. The opening line of the first story, "Yon Cottage would that it could tell a part" (MS. B, l. 469), is neatly entered in Wordsworth's hand at the very top of the first inserted page. (See the photographic reproduction on p. 324, below.) From this point onward in MS. B, Wordsworth entered line numbers in twenties, picking up the count from MS. A and even including the two lines of A dropped in favor of revisions where the 11 transitional lines were added. (This inclusion creates the disparity here between his line count and the editorial count.)

Except for the final verse paragraph, lines 859 to 874, the second section of the poem, lines 469 to 874, was drafted in MS. R. No early drafts survive for that paragraph, describing the "happy band" at Dove Cottage in the spring of 1800, but the lines clearly date from that spring itself. The MS. R work, as discussed above, appears to be 1806 composition. Wordsworth marks the end of this section of MS. B ("we are / And must be, with God's will, a happy band!") with a summary line count, 878, and again it is possible to speculate that the poem for a time ended here. But on inspection this hypothesis seems unsound, as lines 821 to 859 form the first sections of a bridge intended to link the Grasmere stories to the Prospectus. It seems probable that Wordsworth jotted down a summary line count here, as he had done at line 468 (his line 470), because he had completed a phase of transcription. After copying the extensive MS. R work, he closed this section with lines transcribed from a different manuscript, now lost. Before moving on, either to copy from yet another manuscript (no longer extant) or perhaps to draft the third section of the poem, Wordsworth made his tally.

When Wordsworth reported to Beaumont, first that he had written "700 additional lines," and later that he "wrote one book of the Recluse nearly 1000 lines, then had a rest," he could have been talking about these "878" (874, in fact) lines, as John Finch first conjectured, and it would have been some time after 8 September, the date of the second letter, that he went on to bring MS. B to its present conclusion by adding two final sections, made up in part of the "300 more" lines he said he had written after his rest. To be sure, Wordsworth's line counts in the letters do not match those in the manuscripts very closely, nor was much of the material he implied to be recent composition actually new. But two factors should be borne in mind: First, Wordsworth's statistics appear in letters to Sir George Beaumont, and some exaggeration might be expected in a poet's progress reports to a patron. Second, Wordsworth may have drafted additional lines toward *The Recluse* which he did not include in *Home at Grasmere*. Mark Reed suggests the "remote possibility" that some lines of *The Excursion*, Book II, could date from this period (*Chronology: MY*, p. 661). Other unidentified composition might date from the summer and early autumn of 1806, for which manuscripts are no longer extant.

The third section of the poem, lines 875–958, probably composed after Wordsworth had learned of Coleridge's return to England, shows an abrupt transition to the proper philosophical mode. The manuscript in which Wordsworth drafted most of this section does not survive. It is conceivable that some lines could date from an earlier period, but the tone has far more in common with that of the *Ode to Duty*, *The Character of the Happy Warrior*, and *Peele Castle* (all composed between 1804 and 1806) than with that of *Home at Grasmere* lines of 1800. Thus 1806 seems the more probable date. The section opens with a thoughtful reservation that counterpoints the satisfied contentment of the poem's earlier stopping place:

> But 'tis not to enjoy, for this alone
> That we exist; no, something must be done.
> I must not walk in unreproved delight
> These narrow bounds and think of nothing more,
> No duty that looks further and no care.
> Each Being has his office. . . .

The office that Wordsworth defines for himself as poet, in lines partially drafted on the last leaves of MS. B itself (see the transcription, leaves 47 and 48), is a quiet one, obliging him, at Nature's bidding, to outgrow the agitations and the "motions of savage instinct" (l. 914) that drove his youthful spirits. "Be mild and love all gentle things," Nature tells him; "Thy glory and thy happiness be there" (ll. 943–944). In the lines concluding this section Wordsworth eloquently renounces his dream of writing a narrative poem, which he had confided to friends as late as June, 1805 (*EY*, p. 594):

> Then farewell to the Warrior's deeds, farewell
> All hope, which once and long was mine, to fill
> The heroic trumpet with the muse's breath!
> Yet in this peaceful Vale we will not spend
> Unheard-of days, though loving peaceful thoughts;
> A Voice shall speak, and what will be the Theme? [ll. 953–958]

The answer is supplied by the great Prospectus, which constitutes the fourth and final section of *Home at Grasmere*, lines 959 to the end:

> On Man, on Nature, and on human Life,
> Thinking in solitude, from time to time
> I feel sweet passions traversing my Soul
> Like Music; unto these, where'er I may,
> I would give utterance in numerous verse.
> Of truth, of grandeur, beauty, love, and hope—
> Hope for this earth and hope beyond the grave—
> Of virtue and of intellectual power,
> Of blessed consolations in distress,
> Of joy in widest commonalty spread,
> Of the individual mind that keeps its own
> Inviolate retirement, and consists
> With being limitless the one great Life—
> I sing. . . . [ll. 959–972]

III

In September, 1806, *Home at Grasmere* was probably complete. But one especially stubborn problem of dating remains: that of the Prospectus itself.

In addition to the version contained in MS. B, there are two separate manuscripts of the Prospectus. The earlier is in DC MS. 45, the notebook known as the Green family account book, which Reed conjectures was bought in Calais in the summer of 1802 (*Chronology: MY*, p. 642). The accounts for taxes and for the orphaned Green children date from 1808 to 1828; an isolated prose fragment Reed dates "possibly c Mar–Apr 1804" (*Chronology: MY*, p. 663). This fair copy of the Prospectus is 77 lines. (A transcription and facing photographic reproductions may be found below.) It does not include the lines in the MS. B version which describe the wedding of the mind of man to Nature (lines 1002–1014). Only a single leaf of the second manuscript of the

Prospectus survives (DC MS. 24). It once belonged to a notebook that Wordsworth used for drafts and copies of poems between 1801 and 1815. (See *Chronology: MY*, p. 664.) Although a few other scattered leaves of the notebook have been found, it is impossible to place them in any significant relation to each other, or to derive from them information relative to the Prospectus. Only the last 30 lines of the Prospectus survive, on the recto of the single leaf; on the verso Wordsworth wrote his motto to his version of Chaucer's *Prioress' Tale*. Neither of these two Prospectus manuscripts is a draft, and though both clearly precede MS. B there is no way of dating them precisely. (Darbishire, by misleadingly labeling MS. 2 "MS. 3," confused the sequence of the manuscripts.)

For many years scholars dated the Prospectus 1798 because of the similarity of its opening phrases to Wordsworth's accounts of *The Recluse* in letters of March, 1798 (*EY*, pp. 212, 214). (See *PW*, V, 369, 372, and *Prel.*, pp. xlv–xlvi.) But this is shaky evidence on which to rest a case. First, the likeness is not exact; the letters promise a poem giving "pictures of Nature, Man, and Society," while the pertinent line reads, "On Man, on Nature, and on human Life." If Wordsworth was incapable of using the phrase "Nature, Man, and Society" without echoing some other composition, he might well have had in mind the subtitle of John Thelwall's *Peripatetic, or Sketches of the Heart, of Nature and Society* (1793); Thelwall visited Wordsworth and Coleridge in July, 1797 (*Chronology: EY*, p. 202), and may have spoken of this work. Alternatively, Coleridge may have been the inspiration behind the phrase in the letters; during Wordsworth's residence at Alfoxden Coleridge was planning a long poem called "The Brook," which according to his 1817 description was to comprise "impassioned reflections on men, nature and society."[8]

In his unpublished doctoral dissertation, "Wordsworth, Coleridge, and *The Recluse*, 1798–1814" (Cornell University, 1964), John Finch presented two strong additional arguments against the 1798 dating of the Prospectus (pp. 56–71). The first of them grows out of an observation of fact: Dorothy Wordsworth copied and recopied the poems her brother wrote in 1798 into the Alfoxden, the "Christabel," and the "Red Leather" notebooks (DC MSS. 14, 15, and 16), yet there is no trace of the Prospectus there, on extant pages or stubs. The second argument maintains, rightly, that the theme and language of the Prospectus bear far less similarity to writings from the spring of 1798 than to the body of *Home at Grasmere* itself. Acceptance of this argument is implicit in Jonathan Wordsworth's *Music of Humanity* (London, 1969), which examines Wordsworth's commitment to the idea of the One Life in the spring of 1798 (pp. 184–232); this view of the inherent unity of Man and

---

[8] *Biographia Literaria* (2 vols.; London, 1817), I, 189.

Nature fundamentally contradicts that of the Prospectus, where unity can be achieved only through the marriage of the mind of man to Nature.

Even if 1798 can be ruled out, the range of possible dates for composition of the Prospectus remains disquietingly broad. The spring of 1800, when *Home at Grasmere* was begun, is the period that Jonathan Wordsworth and Stephen Gill accept in their article, "The Two-Part *Prelude* of 1798–99," *JEGP*, LXXII (1973), 503–525. In ruling out an 1806 date, the authors refer to the preamble of *The Prelude* (I, 1–54), which has been dated 18 November 1799.[9] "Four months after writing the 'Preamble' it is credible that Wordsworth should go out of his way to brave his Christian predecessor and assert that his own humanist theme is inherently greater than Milton's epic narrative of Heaven and Hell. That he should do so after the death of John (February 1805), and after his acceptance in *Peele Castle* three months later of the 'new controul' of Christian orthodoxy, is too difficult to believe" (pp. 521n–522n). Jonathan Wordsworth pursues and develops this thesis more fully in "Secession at Grasmere," *TLS*, 26 March, 1976, pp. 354–355. With reference to specific lines he spells out the strong similarities of phrasing between the preamble and the Prospectus, the intense energy, and the Miltonic tone. On the grounds of this internal evidence he builds a persuasive argument in support of the 1800 date, "the moment of Wordsworth's greatest confidence" (p. 355). Jonathan Wordsworth is careful to point out that lines 1002 to 1014 of MS. B, elaborating the metaphor of the wedding of the mind of man with Nature, are a later addition to the Prospectus, and that their diction ("consummation," "spousal," exquisitely," "progressive," and "species") is uncharacteristic of Wordsworth's verse before 1805.

Mark Reed also draws heavily on internal evidence in his assessment of the dating of the Prospectus. In the second volume of his chronology he acknowledged that a 1798–1800 date "remains persistently appealing on the basis of content," but he accepted late April, 1800, to September, 1806, as the range of dates during which the Prospectus probably was composed, favoring the time after March, 1804, because the Prospectus was not included in MS. M (DC MS. 44), the collection of Wordsworth's poems transcribed for Coleridge before his departure for Malta (*Chronology: MY*, p. 665).[10] Subsequently Reed pushed the later limit forward to 1802, "probably before 4 April." He bases

---

[9] By John Finch, in "Wordsworth's Two-Handed Engine," *BWS*, pp. 1–13. Reed, *Chronology: MY*, p. 629, concludes that January, 1800, is a more reasonable date, but the difference is not significant in this context.

[10] See also *Chronology: MY*, pp. 624 and 663; and see Jonathan Wordsworth's "Secession at Grasmere," p. 355, for a different interpretation of MS. M evidence. I am indebted to Mr. Reed for his kind permission to summarize the following hypothesis from his manuscript notes.

this redating on an apparent interplay of subject, imagery, and diction be-
tween the Prospectus and Coleridge's verse letter to Sara Hutchinson, the first
version of *Dejection: An Ode*, written on 4 April 1802. Reed speculates that in
the letter Coleridge reacts to Wordsworth's prophetic declarations in the
Prospectus and transforms them into expressions of his own private needs and
failure. Reed further suggests that a reciprocal influence may have operated;
in lines Wordsworth added to the Prospectus (MS. B, ll. 1002–1014), for
example, Wordsworth may have responded to Coleridge's use of the wedding
metaphor in the verse letter.

Thus while it is not possible to pinpoint the exact date of composition of
the Prospectus, the period between spring, 1800, and early spring, 1802,
appears the likeliest time. Lines 1002 to 1014 were probably added in 1806,
but could conceivably be an 1805 revision.

IV

While he was still working on *Home at Grasmere* in mid-August, 1806,
Wordsworth received news of Coleridge's landing in England, and he may
have brought the poem to completion the following month in the happy
expectation of showing it to Coleridge. But Coleridge, reluctant to come home
to his family, postponed his return to the Lakes until later October. When the
two poets did meet at last, Coleridge's appearance and manner were pro-
foundly altered. "Never did I feel such a shock as at first sight of him." Dorothy
Wordsworth wrote to Catherine Clarkson (*MY*, I, 86). "We all felt exactly
in the same way—as if he were different from what we have expected to see;
almost as much as a person of whom we have thought much, and of whom we
had formed an image in our minds, without having any personal knowledge
of him." Wordsworth recorded his feelings of loss in the brief, moving poem
A Complaint: "There is a change—and I am poor . . ." (*PW*, II, 34). The old
intimacy was gone, and the conversations on which Wordsworth had banked
so much hope never took place. Coleridge's vision, enthusiasm, and practical
advice were essential to *The Recluse*, and without them Wordsworth's vast
building project was as doomed as Michael's sheepfold. On 6 November,
Dorothy expressed a hope to Catherine Clarkson that "Wm will soon get to
work," but a few days later Wordsworth himself confessed to Walter Scott,
in defeated tones, "the day when my long work will be finished seems farther
and farther off" (*MY*, I, 88 and 96).

Not until the spring of 1808 was Wordsworth able to return to the mode of
his great work, with the composition of nearly seven hundred lines of blank
verse. One piece of this verse he published in 1842, much revised, as *To the
Clouds* (*PW*, II, 316–320); most he left in manuscript—though he later incor-
porated some lines in *The Prelude* and *The Excursion*—and de Selincourt and

Darbishire published it in 1949 as *The Tuft of Primroses* (Appendix C, *PW*, V, 348–362). This verse, as James Butler has observed, reveals significant alterations in the natural environment at Grasmere, hence in Wordsworth's use of the vale as a symbol of mental repose. In contrasting past and present, he defines an incalculable loss:

> Then, Grasmere, then
> Thy sabbath mornings had a holy grace,
> That incommunicable sanctity
> Which Time and nature only can bestow
>   . . . . .
> While Trees and mountains echoed to the Voice
> Of the glad bells, and all the murmuring streams
> United their Soft chorus with the Song.
>   Now stands the Steeple naked and forlorn
> And from the Haven, the "last Central Home,"
> To which all change conducts the Thought, looks round
> Upon the changes of this peaceful Vale. [ll. 115–118, 124–131; *PW*, V, 351]

The unfinished poem of 1808 thus became an elegy for the joy, the sense of harmony, the fullness, and the promise celebrated in 1800.[11]

After breaking off work on *The Tuft of Primroses*, Wordsworth was for a time preoccupied with prose writings—the early version of *Guide to the Lakes*, *The Convention of Cintra*, the *Letter to Mathetes*, and the essays *On Epitaphs*—some of these contributions to Coleridge's short-lived periodical, *The Friend*. Despite his own activities Coleridge, resident again in Grasmere, helpfully continued to gather ideas for *The Recluse*. A notebook entry from July to September, 1809 suggests:

> A fine subject to be introduced in William's great poem is the Savage Boy of Aveyron in Itard's account—viz—his restless joy & blind conjunction of his Being with natural Scenery; and the manifest influence of Mountain, Rocks, Waterfalls, Torrents, & Thunderstorms—Moonlight Beams quivering on Water, &c on his whole frame—as instanced in his Behaviour in the Vale of Monmorency—his eager desires to escape, &c.[12] [*STCNB*, Entry 3538]

If the savage boy found his way into Wordsworth's poetry it was, as Kathleen Coburn believes, into *The Excursion* (see her note to *STCNB*, Entry 3538), on which Wordsworth began regular work in 1810. Letters of that year and the year after document steady progress (*MY*, I, 391–392, 399, 408, 490, 502,

---

[11] See James Butler, "The End of an Ideal," in " 'This Sublime Retirement': A Textual and Literary Study of Wordsworth's *Home at Grasmere*" (Cornell University Ph.D. dissertation, 1971), pp. 123–129, and Butler's article, "Wordsworth's *Tuft of Primroses*: 'An Unrelenting Doom,' " *Studies in Romanticism*, XIV (Summer, 1975), 237–248.

[12] E. M. Itard's account was published in English as *An Historical Account of the Discovery and Education of a Savage Man* (London, 1802).

and 527); the occasional pauses were followed by reapplication of effort to the poem announced on publication in 1814 as the second part of *The Recluse*.

During his years of work on *The Excursion*, 1810 to 1814, the manuscripts of *Home at Grasmere* were frequently before Wordsworth's eyes. The earliest *Excursion* manuscript from this phase of composition is a small blue-green notebook (DC MS. 70) identical to the Green family account book. Work in this notebook includes a fair copy by Mary Wordsworth of some lines initially drafted in MS. R for *Home at Grasmere* but not used in MS. B; they became *Excursion*, IV, 332–372. On the versos of MS. B itself two of the three stories in this version of *Home at Grasmere* were revised for incorporation as *Excursion*, VI, 1079–1191. Further pillage took place as Wordsworth prepared his texts of the *Guide to the Lakes*. He included lines 141–144 of MS. B in the first edition[13] to add vividness to his description of Lakeland cottages, and manuscript drafts for the *Guide* now in the Dove Cottage collection reveal that he considered inclusion of other *Home at Grasmere* lines as well. (See *Prose*, II, 271–273.)

This sacking of *Home of Grasmere* left Wordsworth in need of a new manuscript. To set the remnants in order and to accommodate major revisions in the opening of the poem Mary Wordsworth appears to have begun a fresh transcription sometime between 1810 and 1814; part of this transcription survives in MS. D (DC MS. 76), the final manuscript of *Home at Grasmere*. (A reading text of MS. D faces the text of MS. B below, and a full transcription may also be found below.) MS. D is a curious hybrid. A homemade notebook without covers, like MS. B, it is stitched together out of two kinds of paper of different sizes, representing two different versions of the poem, widely separated in years; one type of paper is countermarked "1810," the other "1828." Neither version of the poem was or is complete. The later one picks up where the earlier stops and also, apparently, replaces its opening sixty-odd lines. The earlier version was copied on the 1810 paper from the text of MS. B as revised after 1806. It survives on nine and one half leaves of MS. D (numbered 5 to 14) underneath a good deal of later revision and ends about a third of the way through the poem. The text on the remaining one and one half leaves of 1810 paper was probably copied much later, with the addition of the 1828 paper (leaves numbered 16 to 30). The first three leaves, evidently, were sewn on at this late date to incorporate extensive revision of the opening sixty-odd lines.[14]

Dating the earlier version in MS. D is again made possible by the Wordsworths' habits of paper usage. They employed the 1810 paper for

---

[13] WW, Introduction to Joseph Wilkinson, *Select Views in Cumberland, Westmoreland, and Lancashire* (London, 1810), p. xviii.

[14] Formerly the whole of MS. D was loosely sewn to the account book which contains MS. RV of *The Prelude*, now DC MS. 14; some late revisions of *Home at Grasmere* appear penciled in WW's hand in the account book; they are printed on pp. 446n–447n, below.

other manuscripts and letters only between 1812 and 1816. The earliest letter so far discovered is that from Dorothy Wordsworth to Catherine Clarkson, 5 January 1813; the latest that from Wordsworth to Thomas Hutton, 25 November 1816.[15] Furthermore, insertions in MS. P of *The Excursion* (DC MS. 71) are on the same paper; these bear the story of the Solitary's marriage, the death of his family, and his subsequent withdrawal from society (II, 39–319, and III, 352–423, 583–631, 793–930). Wordsworth composed these lines when his grief at the death of two of his own children was still fresh; Catharine died on 4 June 1812 and Thomas on 1 December. Dorothy may well have referred to the composition of these *Excursion* lines when she wrote to Catherine Clarkson on 5 January 1813: "William has begun to look into his poem the Recluse within the last two days and I hope he will be the better for it" (*MY*, II, 64).[16] One other rather slender piece of evidence helps to narrow down the range of dates. When Wordsworth published separately the *Water-fowl* lines from *Home at Grasmere* in his 1836 *Poetical Works* (II, 188)—they had been included since 1823 in *Guide to the Lakes*—he dated them 1812. They were in fact composed earlier, for they are in MS. B, but Wordsworth may well have remembered the year in which he extensively revised the lines for MS. D.

The years 1812 to 1814 thus appear to be the likeliest for resumption of work on *Home at Grasmere* and transcription of the earlier portion of MS. D. For after the publication of *The Excursion*, Wordsworth seems to have distanced himself from *The Recluse*. A letter to Robert Southey, January, 1815 (*MY*, II, 187), feigns indifference: "As to the Excursion I have ceased to have any interest about it, . . . let this benighted age continue to love its own darkness and to cherish it." The next month (18 February 1815) Dorothy wrote Sara Hutchinson, "William has had one of his weeks of rest and we now begin to wish that he was at work again, but as he intends completely to plan the first part of the Recluse before he begins the composition, he must read many Books before he will fairly set to labour again" (*MY*, II, 200).

But while engaged in this reading, Wordsworth received Coleridge's annihilating criticism of *The Excursion*, already quoted. This must have brought home to him at last the virtual impossibility of the task he had set himself—or that Coleridge had set him. To be sure, the dream of accomplishing it persisted, and *The Recluse* continued to prey on Wordsworth's mind. He could still for a time speak openly of his grand project, as to Benjamin Robert Haydon and

---

[15] I am indebted here to unpublished notes left by John Finch, to information supplied by Mark Reed, and to Butler, "'This Sublime Retirement,'" pp. 66–68.

[16] Helen Darbishire first pointed out the heavily autobiographical nature of *Excursion*, III, 539–679; she also noted that the draft of a letter from WW to Lord Lonsdale of 8 January 1813 bears draftings of lines toward *Excursion*, III, 584–598, thus helping to date the composition. See *PW*, V, 419, and *Chronology: MY*, pp. 676–677.

John Scott in 1815,[17] or to Henry Crabb Robinson in 1826.[18] As the years passed, however, he came to brood about it in silence, and he composed no new work upon it. Save for revisions, *The Recluse* had reached its full growth.

Through the years when Wordsworth published other poems—*Peter Bell, The Waggoner*, and sequences of sonnets—the poet's family and friends maintained their hopes for *The Recluse*, but increasingly they came to be tinctured with doubts and uneasiness. Late in 1819, Sara Hutchinson dubiously wrote to John Monkhouse, "*He says* he will never trouble himself with anything more but the *Recluse.*"[19] The unfinished poem dances like a will-o'-the-wisp through Dorothy's correspondence of the 1820's. To Catherine Clarkson she reported on 27 March 1821: "William is quite well, and very busy, though he has not looked at *The Recluse* or the poem on his own life; and this disturbs us. After fifty years of age there is no time to spare, and unfinished works should not, if it be possible, be left behind. This he feels, but the will never governs *his* labours" (*LY*, I, 28). Dorothy went on regretfully, and with some trace of envy, to add: "How different from Southey, who can go as regularly as clockwork, from history to poetry, from poetry to criticism, and so on to biography, or anything else." Several months later ill health returned, and Wordsworth was compelled to rest. Again Dorothy revealed concern to Catherine Clarkson: "He has now two works unfinished (the Recluse and the Sonnets) and you may believe that it often disturbs him that he is forced to spend so much of his time in idleness" (25 August 1821; *LY*, I, 44). The years relieved her anxiety about the sonnets, but *The Recluse* continued a source of worry, and her fear of time running out reappears in a letter to Robinson in December 1824, following Wordsworth's return from a junket in north Wales: "My brother has not yet looked at the Recluse; he seems to feel the task so weighty that he shrinks from beginning with it . . . yet knows that he has now no time to loiter if another great work is to be accomplished by him" (Morley, I, 132).

---

[17] In an unpublished letter in the DC papers, written 18 November 1816, Haydon recalls a talk with Wordsworth which his diary reveals took place on 13 June 1815 (*The Diary of Benjamin Robert Haydon*, ed. Willard Bissell Pope [5 vols.; Cambridge, Mass., 1960–1963], I, 450–451): "If you remember My dear Sir, at the time you breakfasted with me you gave [John] Scott and I an account of the scope of your intentions with regard to the Recluse—I yet remember how I was affected at your powerful description, and Scott and I have often talked of it, with great delight—You would do me the greatest favor if you would write me, what you then said. . . . now do not hesitate but let the next letter you write me, be a full exposition of your feelings, of your intentions, and a full developpement of your plan, with respect to that sublime Poem." It is perhaps needless to add that the post brought Haydon no précis of the sublime poem.

[18] Robinson's diary entry for 6 October 1826 notes, tantalizingly, that WW "pointed out to my notice the beautiful spring, a description of which is to be an introduction to a portion of his great poem—containing a poetical view of water as an *element* in the composition of our globe. The passages he read me appear to be of the very highest excellence" (*Henry Crabb Robinson on Books and Their Writers*, ed. Edith J. Morley [3 vols.; London, 1938], I, 339–340).

[19] *The Letters of Sara Hutchinson from 1800 to 1835*, ed. Kathleen Coburn (London, 1954), p. 165.

The sparseness of Wordsworth's own comments on the poem in records of the late years intimates that the topic was a tender one, which he preferred to avoid. Occasional references are laden with excuses. "From want of resolution to take up anything of length," he confided to Walter Savage Landor in April, 1822 (*LY*, I, 71), "I have filled up many a moment in writing Sonnets. . . . *The Recluse* has had a long sleep, save in my thoughts; my MSS. are so ill-penned and blurred that they are useless to all but myself; and at present I cannot face them. But if my stomach can be preserved in tolerable order, I hope you will hear of me again in the character chosen for the title of that Poem." It is significant that as *The Recluse* moved farther and farther beyond his grasp, Wordsworth turned increasing energy to writing sonnets, linking them in sequences. Despite the scanty plot of ground the sonnet offered him to work in, he attempted to build these sequences out of the sort of philosophical "meditations in the Author's own Person" which he had once declared would constitute *The Recluse*. (See the Preface to *The Excursion* of 1814, Appendix II, below.) Doubtless it was primarily sonnets to which the posthumous Advertisement to *The Prelude* (1850) alluded in noting that "the materials" which would have made up Part III of *The Recluse* have "been incorporated, for the most part, in the Author's other Publications, written subsequently to the EXCURSION."

Dora Wordsworth's letters of the late 1820's and early 1830's expose tense and sometimes embarrassing family attitudes toward the work that Wordsworth could not bring to birth. Mary nagged about it, Dora shook her head behind her father's back, and both plotted with Dorothy about strategies to rouse Wordsworth to proceed with his masterpiece. On 21 November 1829, Dora wrote Edward Quillinan: "Father bids me tell you that he has removed the 1*st* stanza of his 'Sound Poem' [*On the Power of Sound*] as I call it, with which you were pleased to a place where it tells more & has written another stanza which is a better introduction—We all think there is a grandeur in this Poem but it ought to have been in the 'Recluse' & Mother on that account but half enjoys it."[20] Another report followed only a month later: "I am sorry to say Father has not yet heard from Longman—Aunt & I are exceedingly anxious something were done towards forwarding the printing of these small Poems, for till they are out of the way we feel convinced, his great work will never be touched; every day he finds something to alter or new stanzas to add—or a fresh sonnet—or a fresh Poem growing out of one just finished— which he always promises shall be the last."[21] But Dora came to view the "great work" with a sternly realistic eye. "He promises that the Recluse shall be his winter employment," she confided to Maria Jane Jewsbury on 20 October 1831, "but entre nous I think his courage will fail him when winter really arrives" (Vincent, p. 91).

---

[20] Unpublished letter, DC papers.
[21] Unpublished letter to Edward Quillinan, 19 December 1829, DC papers.

V

Dora's prophecy proved a half-truth. In the winter of 1831–1832, Wordsworth turned again, briefly and ineffectually, to *The Recluse*. Dora reported the event in a hushed postscript of 3 December 1831: "Since I began this letter Father has taken up the Recluse with good earnest—Mother & he are both hard at work in this room—*but take no notice of this when you write [to me] or dont name it to any one*."[22] Dorothy's journal substantiates the fact a few days later, noting that Wordsworth was "now at work with the Recluse."[23] An additional confirming report came the following summer from William Rowan Hamilton, who wrote Aubrey de Vere about progress on *The Recluse*: "It also [apparently like *The Prelude*], I fear, is destined to be a posthumous work, but I heard at Cambridge from a nephew of Wordsworth, who is a fellow of Trinity, and who had spent much of the winter at Rydal Mount, that Wordsworth was so much occupied with it then as to forget his meals and even his politics."[24]

What occupied Wordsworth chiefly was *The Prelude*; there can be no doubt that major revision took place during this active winter. (See *Prel.*, p. xxiii.) On 17 February 1832, Dora reported her father "busier than 1000 bees" on it; "Mother and he work like slaves from morning to night."[25] Revision and new composition necessitated a new copy of *The Prelude*—MS. D (DC MS. Verse 23)—which was extensively revised shortly after transcription. But *Home at Grasmere* was also before Wordsworth. MS. R carries a prose passage in pencil in Mary Wordsworth's hand (on the interleaf facing p. 132) which seems to be the basis for *Prelude* (1850), IV, 354–370; these lines in their earliest verse form first appear in revisions of *Prelude* MS. D. MS. R also contains scattered drafts, in Mary's hand, of lines incorporated into MS. D of *Home at Grasmere*, and the evidence of paper usage helps to confirm that the winter of 1831–1832 was the period when MS. D was completed. The 1828 paper sewn onto the 1810 leaves of *Home at Grasmere* MS. D, making up leaves 1 to 3 and 16 to 30 of the notebook, cannot be found in any letters, but does appear in segments of the revised *Prelude* MS. D, in Books III, IV, and V, and these revisions seem to date from 1832. (See *Prel.*, p. xxiii, and *Chronology: MY*, pp. 685–686.)

MS. D of *Home at Grasmere* reveals what Wordsworth did to complete

---

[22] Letter to Maria Jane Jewsbury; Vincent, p. 94.

[23] Quoted from GW's transcript of DW's journal, DC papers; he excised and destroyed the pages that originally carried this entry. The precise date is unclear, but falls between 11 and 16 December 1831.

[24] Robert Perceval Graves, *The Life of Sir William Rowan Hamilton* (3 vols.; Dublin and London, 1882–1891), I, 585. The nephew was Christopher Wordsworth, Jr.

[25] Unpublished letter to Miss Kinnaird; quoted *Prel.*, p. xxiii, and Moorman, II, 501.

transcription and revision of the poem in 1831–1832; it is, however, not possible to say precisely where his work began, since it is not possible to say with certainty where the 1812–1814 work ended. On the next to last leaf of the 1810 paper (leaf 14), after line 258, the ink color changes, and the new ink appears to proceed continuously in the manuscript after the transition to 1828 paper. Before the change of ink color, Mary had used only the rectos of the notebook leaves; beginning with the last 1810 leaf and onward through the 1828 paper, she also filled the versos. This evidence suggests that Mary abandoned her 1812–1814 copying at line 258, in mid-sentence—right in the middle of Wordsworth's lament for the pair of milk-white swans that had disappeared from Grasmere during the hard winter months of storm in 1800—and resumed copying at line 259 nearly twenty years later. This inference is hard to accept, but hard to escape. Mary could have gone on in 1812–1814 through the change of ink, and perhaps stopped at the foot of the recto of the last leaf of 1810 paper, then resumed nearly twenty years later with an ink that looked the same; but the stopping place there, too, is in mid-sentence (l. 283). It is possible that she went on past this place on 1810 paper, then tore away the following leaves when she made a fresh start in 1831–1832; but the manuscript yields no clues.

In any event, once she had moved on to the 1828 paper, Mary resumed copying from MS. B as revised; there appears to be no intervening lost manuscript. Some of the more substantial revisions were drafted on blank versos in B itself, then copied into D; another major revision consisted of leaving out the Grasmere stories in B, which had by this time been transferred to *The Excursion*. MS. D ends with the lines that lead into the Prospectus, followed by a note telling where it could be found:

> A Voice shall speak, & what will be the Theme?
> On Man, on Nature, & on Human Life
> Musing
> ~~Thinking~~ in Solitude (see Preface to the Excursion to its conclusion)

Copying from MS. B in the last line above, Mary wrote "Thinking"; she subsequently corrected the word to "Musing," the reading of the published Prospectus.

Either before or after completion of the base text of MS. D, Wordsworth turned to the opening of the poem, in the earlier version of D, and revised it so heavily as to require the grafting in of a fresh transcription. Three leaves of the 1810 paper seem to have been removed (the stub of one remains) and three new leaves, of the 1828 paper, sewn in. Even this process went forward in two stages: In the first stage Mary Wordsworth added two leaves and subsequently numbered them. In the second phase she inserted an additional leaf, which remained unnumbered. The transcriptions and selected photographs of MS. D, below, show the several levels of this revision.

Wordsworth's chief concern in these alterations appears to have been the extent to which he should cut or condense passages in MS. B, at about lines 54–98. He wavered, reinstating lines in corrections which he had previously deleted.

Mary Wordsworth made numerous further revisions in *Home at Grasmere*, MS. D, after completing the base text. Most of these probably date from 1831–1832, but a few could conceivably be as late as 1840–1841, when Wordsworth worked compulsively over some of his old poems to prepare them for publication in the 1842 volume, *Poems, Chiefly of Early and Late Years*. Leaf 25 of MS. D, unnumbered and therefore inserted late, bears a revision that grows out of drafts copied by Mary in blank pages in MSS. R and B, which must have been reviewed and used again during a late bout of revising and correcting. Other revisions accumulated so thickly (as in MS. D, at lines 384–400, 474–483, and 609–622) that they had to be cleanly copied on separate slips of paper which were then stuck with sealing wax over the pages of the notebook.

In the end, Wordsworth had a version of *Home at Grasmere* which differed substantially from that which he had finished in 1806. Besides muting the intensely personal tone of the poem, he had dropped nearly a quarter of the original text and added dozens of lines. Most of the revision occurred in the first two sections of the poem (up to line 874 in MS. B, 663 in MS. D); much of the shortening, in the second section, by transfer of two of the Grasmere stories to *The Excursion*. In the third section, dwelling on the office of the poet, there were only light alterations. The fourth section, the Prospectus (not in fact copied into MS. D), Wordsworth scarcely touched after its publication in 1814. All the changes can be studied in the facing reading texts of MSS. B and D.

VI

The rest is epilogue. Wordsworth's family and friends continued to speak of *The Recluse* into the last decade of his life—sometimes wistfully, at other times despairingly. By 17 May 1833, Dora had frankly abandoned hope: "Father has written several 100 lines this spring but only 'tiresome small Poems' as Mother calls them who is vexed she cannot get him set down to his long work. *I* don't believe the 'Recluse' will ever be finished."[26] Mary apparently tried to temper her dissatisfaction, but maintained her hope. On 28 September 1836 she wrote Henry Crabb Robinson, as he and Wordsworth laid plans for another visit in Wales, "We hope . . . that the Poet may leave home with a perfect holiday before him—&, but, I dare not say so—return to *the Recluse*;—& let me charge you, not to encourage the Muse to *vagrant* subjects—but gently recur, upon such indications should they arise, to Rogers'

---

[26] Unpublished letter to Edward Quillinan, DC papers.

hint that 'jingling *rhyme* does not become a certain age.' entre nous.—"
(Morley, I, 318). Friends lamented their loss. Barron Field pleaded with the
poet in 1836, "Oh! continue *The Recluse*. I wish I was Moxon. I would make
you such an offer for it as could ruin me and enrich my children. . . . I really
think from what Murray said to me . . . he would give you £1,000 for the
rest of *The Recluse*."[27] In 1843, Catherine Clarkson sadly remarked to Henry
Crabb Robinson, "I was thinking in a very melancholy way the other day of
time past present & to come when of a sudden the thought darted into my
mind that if I could hope to see the conclusion of the Excursion [i.e., *The
Recluse*] it would be worth living for—I am sure that I should live longer if
I could only have the hope of seeing a portion of it" (12 January; Morley, I,
474).

Wordsworth's own hopes may have lingered on for awhile, but in the mid-
1830's he admitted, to himself and to others, that *The Recluse* would never
be finished. Up through the 1832 edition of his collected works he included
a subtitle to *The Excursion:* "Being a Portion of the Recluse." In the edition
of 1836 (the first he published after Coleridge's death) and subsequent
editions he dropped it. In 1838, George Ticknor, lately resigned from his
Harvard professorship, dined with the Wordsworths at Rydal Mount and
afterward in his journal adroitly summed up both the state of the family's
concern and the poet's final testament:

Mrs. Wordsworth asked me to talk to him about finishing the Excursion, or the
Recluse; saying, that she could not bear to have him occupied constantly in writing
sonnets and other trifles, while this great work lay by him untouched, but that she
had ceased to urge him on the subject, because she had done it so much in vain. I
asked him about it, therefore. He said that the Introduction [*The Prelude*], which is
a sort of autobiography, is completed. This I knew, for he read me large portions of
it twenty years ago. The rest is divided into three parts, the first of which is partly
written in fragments, which Mr. Wordsworth says would be useless and unintelligible
in other hands than his own; the second is the Excursion; and the third is untouched.
On my asking him why he does not finish it, he turned to me very decidedly and
said, 'Why did not Gray finish the long poem he began on a similar subject? Because
he found he had undertaken something beyond his powers to accomplish. And that
is my case.'[28]

The conversation left Ticknor with "no hope" that the great work would ever
be finished. As if in silent confirmation Wordsworth, the next year in revising
the final fair copy of *The Prelude* (MS. E), tellingly struck out a line which
had seemed to promise *The Recluse:* "But this is matter for another Song"

---

[27] 17 December; quoted *PW*, V, 368. Edward Moxon became WW's publisher in 1831. In
1825–1826, WW considered John Murray as publisher for a new edition of his poems; Murray
was then unenthusiastic. See Moorman, II, 445–448.

[28] *Life, Letters, and Journals of George Ticknor*, ed. George S. Hillard, (2 vols.; London, 1876),
II, 167.

(*Prelude*, XI, 185; see *Prel.*, p. xxiv). Wordsworth's statement to Aubrey de Vere in 1841 that "the Recluse has never been written except a few passages— and probably never will [be]" is without illusions.[29]

Wordsworth died on 23 April 1850, leaving no instructions regarding the unfinished *Recluse*. The following spring, nearly a year after publication of *The Prelude*, his nephew Christopher included in his *Memoirs* of the poet three brief extracts from *Home at Grasmere*, copied with minor changes from MS. D.[30] For nearly forty years afterward the poem slept on in obscurity. Finally, in December, 1888, the MS. D text appeared in print as *The Recluse: Book First, Part First, Home at Grasmere*, issued by Macmillan in a thin green volume of fifty-six pages bearing no editor's name. (For an account of the circumstances surrounding this publication, see Appendix I, below.) Simultaneously Macmillan published a one-volume collected edition of Wordsworth's poems, commonly known as the Globe Edition, which also contained the text of *Home at Grasmere*. Some ninety years after Wordsworth and Coleridge had conceived their grandest scheme, the world thus received its seemingly meager fruits and learned the full dimensions of its failure.

But to recognize that *The Recluse* was a failure is not to declare *Home at Grasmere* a failure, and to slight *Home at Grasmere* is to slight some of Wordsworth's finest verse and a central document in the history of the poet's mind. The poem stands securely on its own as Wordsworth's triumphant manifesto, conceived, in William Minto's words, "in the first heat and confidence of the enterprise, before the mirage that lured him on had faded, and glad anticipation had given place to despondency and a cheerless sense of impotence."[31] By 1806, when he finished the poem, Wordsworth had been tested in Grasmere not only by "two months unwearied of severest storm," but also by suffering through the physical and psychological illnesses of Coleridge, through growing doubts about his own poetic purposes, through the strain of a settlement with Annette Vallon and their daughter, through the new domestic responsibilities of marriage and fatherhood, and finally through the crushing blow of the death of his brother John, whom he loved profoundly. Despite these trials, however, and the more somber tone of the later composition, *Home at Grasmere* retains the character of a blissful effusion of one joyous spring season, a spontaneous paean celebrating the time when the glory and the dream were realities for Wordsworth in Grasmere.

---

[29] Quoted from a letter of 25 June from de Vere to his sister, in Wilfred Ward, *Aubrey de Vere: A Memoir Based on His Unpublished Diaries and Correspondence* (London, 1904), p. 66.

[30] Ll. 71–97 and 110–125 (*Memoirs*, I, 157–158) and ll. 152–167 (*Memoirs*, I, 155).

[31] William Minto, "Wordsworth's Great Failure," *Nineteenth Century*, XXVI (September, 1889), 435–451. This admirable essay has been reprinted in shortened form in *Wordsworth's Mind and Art*, ed. A. W. Thomson (Edinburgh, 1969), pp. 10–27.

Editorial Procedure

Like other volumes in this series, this edition of *Home at Grasmere* provides two kinds of texts: (1) reading texts, from which all textual complexities and variant readings are stripped away, and (2) transcriptions of manuscripts, usually facing photographic reproductions of the manuscripts. Editorial procedures have been adapted to the aims of these two styles of presentation.

In this edition the reading texts are based on fair copies of *Home at Grasmere*. The reading text of MS. B presents as closely as possible the earliest full version of the poem (some lines, within brackets, have had to be supplied from MS. A, and seven lines are lost); corrections were accepted only when an original reading was unclear or represented an error in transcription. The reading text of MS. D presents the final, revised version. The conclusion of the reading text of MS. D, the lines known as the Prospectus to *The Recluse*, is presented, within brackets, from the Preface to the first edition of *The Excursion* (1814). Punctuation and spelling have been modernized where appropriate, ampersands have been expanded, and obvious errors or false starts silently corrected. Line numbers are assigned serially to each reading text, in the outside margins; the reading text of MS. D further carries, in the inside margins, bracketed line numbers which correspond to those of MS. B. The *apparatus criticus* to the reading texts shows all variant readings in those sections of the poem which were extracted and published during Wordsworth's lifetime, except that variants in MS. B, lines 469–606, subsequently incorporated in *The Excursion*, Book VI, are not recorded in this volume (see p. 37, below).

Transcriptions of manuscripts are more complicated. Here the aim is to depict accurately everything in the manuscripts which could be helpful to a study of the poem's growth and development. Since even false starts and corrected letters can sometimes reveal the writer's intentions, they are recorded, though reinforced letters, overwritten partial letters, and random marks are normally not. Wordsworth's hand is discriminated from the hands of his amanuenses by representing his in roman type, theirs in italic. (Unless otherwise noted, all italic type here represents Mary Wordsworth's hand.) Revisions are shown in type of reduced size, just above or below the line to which they pertain, and an effort has been made to indicate deletion marks, spacing, and other such physical features so that they resemble those of the manuscript itself, though some minor adjustments have had to be made in the interest of clarity. In the numbering of leaves, stubs are counted, but not pasted-down end papers. Editorial line numbers in the transcriptions correspond to the line numbers in the reading texts, as indicated in separate headnotes to the transcriptions.

In the reading texts brackets enclose words or lines which have had to be supplied, sometimes conjecturally, and square brackets enclosing blank spaces mark gaps. In the transcriptions, the following symbols are used:

[?friends]	Conjectural reading.
[?]	Illegible word.
[? ? ?] or [?] [?] [?]	Illegible words.
[—?—]	Illegible word deleted, by cancellation or erasure.
mo {st / re	An overwriting; the original reading, "more," is converted to "most" by writing "st" over the "re".
s}	A short revision, sometimes only a mark of punctuation.
power of song	Words written over an erasure; the original reading is now illegible.

To avoid unnecessary elaboration in textual notes, all quotations from manuscripts are printed in roman type.

Home at Grasmere

Parallel Reading Texts of MSS. B and D

The textual notes for MS. D show all printed variants in the passages of the poem that Wordsworth published in England during his lifetime. There were three such passages:

1. A four-line description of Lakeland cottages, MS. D, ll. 122–125 (MS. B, ll. 141–144), which appeared in *Guide to the Lakes* from 1810 onward. Editions of the *Guide* are abbreviated as follows (unless otherwise noted, the place of publication is London):

1810G   Joseph Wilkinson, *Select Views in Cumberland, Westmoreland, and Lancashire* (1810; reissued 1821).

1820G   *The River Duddon . . . and Other Poems. To Which is Annexed, A Topographical Description of the Country of the Lakes . . .* (1820; 2d ed. of *Guide*).

1822G   *A Description of the Scenery of the Lakes . . .* (1822; 3d ed. of *Guide*).

1823G   *A Description of the Scenery of the Lakes . . .* (1823; 4th ed. of *Guide*).

1835G   *A Guide through the District of the Lakes . . .* (Kendal and London, 1835; 5th ed. of *Guide*).

1842G   *A Complete Guide to the Lakes . . . With Mr. Wordsworth's Description of the Scenery of the Country* (Kendal, London, Liverpool, and Manchester, 1842).

2. *Water-fowl*, 27 lines, MS. D, ll. 203–229 (MS. B, ll. 292–314), which appeared in *Guide to the Lakes* from 1823 onward and also among "Poems of the Imagination" in collected editions of the poems from 1827 onward; titles are abbreviated as below.

3. The Prospectus (MS. B, ll. 959–1048), published as part of the Preface to *The Excursion* from 1814 onward. Titles of the pertinent editions are abbreviated as follows (the place of publication is London):

1814   *The Excursion* (1st ed.; 1814).

1820Ex   *The Excursion* (2d ed.; 1820).

1827   *Poetical Works* (5 vols.; 1827). Vol. V, *The Excursion*, issued separately 1827.

1832   *Poetical Works* (4 vols.; 1832). Vol. IV, *The Excursion*, issued separately 1832.

1836   *Poetical Works* (6 vols.; 1836–1837; reissued 1840, 1841, 1843). Vol. VI, *The Excursion*, issued separately 1836, reissued 1841, 1844.

1845   *Poems* (1845; reissued 1847, 1849).

1846   *Poetical Works* (7 vols.; 1846; reissued 1849). Vol. VII, *The Excursion*, issued separately 1847.

1849   *Poetical Works* (6 vols.; 1849–1850).

Finally, the collations include all variants in the first published edition of *Home at Grasmere*, abbreviated as follows:

1888   *The Recluse* (London and New York, 1888).

No variants in any other posthumous editions are recorded. One passage of MS. B (ll. 469–606) was revised in subsequent manuscripts for inclusion in *The Excursion*; its variants are not recorded here but will be in *The Excursion*, a separate volume in The Cornell Wordsworth series.

MS. B: Reading Text

<blockquote>

Once on the brow of yonder Hill I stopped,
While I was yet a School-boy (of what age
I cannot well remember, but the hour
I well remember though the year be gone),
5   And with a sudden influx overcome
At sight of this seclusion, I forgot
My haste—for hasty had my footsteps been,
As boyish my pursuits—[and sighing said],
"What happy fortune were it here to live!
10   And if I thought of dying, if a thought
Of mortal separation could come in
With paradise before me, here to die."
I was no Prophet, nor had even a hope,
Scarcely a wish, but one bright pleasing thought,
15   A fancy in the heart of what might be
The lot of others, never could be mine.
The place from which I looked was soft and green,
Not giddy yet aerial, with a depth
Of Vale below, a height of Hills above.
20   Long did I halt; I could have made it even
My business and my errand so to halt.
For rest of body 'twas a perfect place;
All that luxurious nature could desire,
But tempting to the Spirit. Who could look
25   And not feel motions there? I thought of clouds
That sail on winds; of breezes that delight
To play on water, or in endless chase

</blockquote>

---

1   The hill that WW refers to here is Loughrigg Terrace, at the southern end of Grasmere Lake.
8   This line was left incomplete in the original transcription; it is printed here as revised.
9–16   The sensation that WW attributes to his younger self on first viewing Grasmere, and the special serenity he later claims for the vale, are not a unique response. As early as 1769, Thomas Gray found an unusual sense of "repose" in "this little unsuspected paradise," where "all is peace, rusticity, & happy poverty in its neatest most becoming attire" (*Correspondence of Thomas Gray*, ed. Paget Toynbee and Leonard Whibley [3 vols.; Oxford, 1935], III, 1099). Guide books echo and amplify this description, and private journals surpass them in subtlety and detail. See, for example, Daphne Foskett, *John Harden of Brathay Hall 1772–1847* (Kendal, 1974), p. 8. For WW's prose description of Grasmere, see *Prose*, II, 163, 271n–272n. WW abandoned a full description of Grasmere in composing his Introduction to Wilkinson's *Select Views*; see *Prose*, II, 126–127, for the probable reasons.

MS. D: Reading Text

Once to the verge of yon steep barrier came
A roving School-boy. What the Adventurer's age
Hath now escaped his memory; but the hour,
One of a golden summer holiday,
He well remembers, though the year be gone.   5
Alone and devious, from afar he came;

[5]   And with a sudden influx overpowered
At sight of this seclusion, he forgot
His haste—for hasty had his footsteps been,
As boyish his pursuits—and sighing said,   10
"What happy fortune were it here to live!

[10]   And," if a thought of dying, if a thought
Of mortal separation could intrude
With paradise before him, "here to die!"
No Prophet was he, had not even a hope,   15
Scarcely a wish, but one bright pleasing thought,

[15]   A fancy in the heart of what might be
The lot of others, never could be his.
        The Station whence he looked was soft and green,
Not giddy yet aerial, with a depth   20

[19]   Of Vale below, a height of hills above.
For rest of body, perfect was the spot;
All that luxurious nature could desire,
But stirring to the Spirit. Who could gaze

[25]   And not feel motions there? He thought of clouds   25
That sail on winds; of Breezes that delight
To play on water, or in endless chase

---

2   School-boy. What] school-boy; what   Adventurer's] adventurer's *1888*
3   memory;] memory— *1888*
5   gone.] gone— *1888*
6   devious,] devious *1888*
7   And] And, *1888*
9   haste—] haste,   been,] been *1888*
10 pursuits—] pursuits; *1888*
12 And," if] And, if *1888*
13 separation] separation, *1888*
14 "here] here *1888*
19 Station] station *1888*
21 Vale] vale *1888*
22 body,] body   spot;] spot, *1888*
23 desire,] desire; *1888*
24 Spirit. Who] spirit; who *1888*
26 winds;] winds: Breezes] breezes *1888*

39

Pursue each other through the liquid depths
Of grass or corn, over and through and through,
30   In billow after billow evermore;
Of Sunbeams, Shadows, Butterflies, and Birds,
Angels, and winged Creatures that are Lords
Without restraint of all which they behold.
I sate, and stirred in Spirit as I looked,
35   I seemed to feel such liberty was mine,
Such power and joy; but only for this end:
To flit from field to rock, from rock to field,
From shore to island, and from isle to shore,
From open place to covert, from a bed
40   Of meadow-flowers into a tuft of wood,
From high to low, from low to high, yet still
Within the bounds of this huge Concave; here
Should be my home, this Valley be my World.
    From that time forward was the place to me
45   As beautiful in thought as it had been
When present to my bodily eyes; a haunt
Of my affections, oftentimes in joy
A brighter joy, in sorrow (but of that
I have known little), in such gloom, at least,
50   Such damp of the gay mind as stood to me
In place of sorrow, 'twas a gleam of light.
And now 'tis mine for life: dear Vale,
One of thy lowly dwellings is my home!
    Yes, the Realities of Life—so cold,
55   So cowardly, so ready to betray,
So stinted in the measure of their grace,
As we report them, doing them much wrong—
Have been to me more bountiful than hope,
Less timid than desire. Oh bold indeed
60   They have been! Bold and bounteous unto me,
Who have myself been bold, not wanting trust,
Nor resolution, nor at last the hope
Which is of wisdom, for I feel it is.

---

58 "more" is an editorial correction of "less," an apparent error in transcription.

Pursue each other through the yielding plain
Of grass or corn, over and through and through,
[30] In billow after billow, evermore   30
Disporting. Nor unmindful was the Boy
Of sunbeams, shadows, butterflies, and birds;
Of fluttering Sylphs and softly gliding Fays,
Genii, and winged Angels that are Lords
Without restraint of all which they behold.   35
The illusion strengthening as he gazed, he felt
[35] That such unfettered liberty was his,
Such power and joy; but only for this end:
To flit from field to rock, from rock to field,
From shore to island, and from isle to shore,   40
From open ground to covert, from a bed
[40] Of meadow-flowers into a tuft of wood,
From high to low, from low to high, yet still
Within the bound of this huge Concave; here
Must be his Home, this Valley be his World.   45
    Since that day forth the Place to him—*to me*
(For I who live to register the truth
Was that same young and happy Being) became
[45] As beautiful to thought as it had been
When present to the bodily sense; a haunt   50
Of pure affections, shedding upon joy
A brighter joy, and through such damp and gloom
Of the gay mind, as ofttimes splenetic Youth
Mistakes for sorrow, darting beams of light
That no self-cherished sadness could withstand.   55
[52] And now 'tis mine, perchance for life, dear Vale,
Beloved Grasmere (let the Wandering streams
Take up, the cloud-capped hills repeat the name),
One of thy lowly Dwellings is my Home.

---

31 Disporting. Nor] Disporting—nor   Boy] boy *1888*
32 butterflies,] butterflies *1888*
33 Sylphs] sylphs   softly gliding] softly-gliding *1888*
34 Angels] angels *1888*
38 end:] end, *1888*
42 wood,] wood; *1888*
44 Concave] concave *1888*
45 Home] home   Valley] valley   World] world *1888*
49 thought] thought, *1888*
50 present] present, *1888*
52 joy,] joy; *1888*
53 Youth] youth *1888*
55 withstand.] withstand; *1888*
57 Wandering] wandering *1888*
58 capped] capt   repeat] repeat,   name] Name *1888*

And did it cost so much, and did it ask
65 Such length of discipline, and could it seem
An act of courage, and the thing itself
A conquest? Shame that this was ever so,
Not to the Boy or Youth, but shame to thee,
Sage Man, thou Sun in its meridian strength,
70 Thou flower in its full blow, thou King and crown
Of human Nature; shame to thee, sage Man.
Thy prudence, thy experience, thy desires,
Thy apprehensions—blush thou for them all.
But I am safe; yes, one at least is safe;
75 What once was deemed so difficult is now
Smooth, easy, without obstacle; what once
Did to my blindness seem a sacrifice,
The same is now a choice of the whole heart.
If e'er the acceptance of such dower was deemed
80 A condescension or a weak indulgence
To a sick fancy, it is now an act
Of reason that exultingly aspires.
This solitude is mine; the distant thought
Is fetched out of the heaven in which it was.
85 The unappropriated bliss hath found
An owner, and that owner I am he.
The Lord of this enjoyment is on Earth
And in my breast. What wonder if I speak
With fervour, am exalted with the thought
90 Of my possessions, of my genuine wealth
Inward and outward? What I keep have gained,
Shall gain, must gain, if sound be my belief
From past and present rightly understood
That in my day of childhood I was less
95 The mind of Nature, less, take all in all,
Whatever may be lost, than I am now.
For proof behold this Valley and behold
Yon Cottage, where with me my Emma dwells.
   Aye, think on that, my Heart, and cease to stir;
100 Pause upon that, and let the breathing frame
No longer breathe, but all be satisfied.
Oh, if such silence be not thanks to God
For what hath been bestowed, then where, where then
Shall gratitude find rest? Mine eyes did ne'er

---

98 Emma or Emmeline is the name by which WW occasionally refers to DW in his poems.

And was the cost so great, and could it seem   60
[66]   An act of courage, and the thing itself
        A conquest? Who must bear the blame? Sage Man,
        Thy prudence, thy experience, thy desires,
[73]   Thy apprehensions—blush thou for them all.
[54]   Yes, the realities of life—so cold,   65
        So cowardly, so ready to betray,
        So stinted in the measure of their grace,
        As we pronounce them, doing them much wrong—
[58]   Have been to me more bountiful than hope,
        Less timid than desire; but that is passed.   70
            On Nature's invitation do I come,
        By Reason sanctioned. Can the choice mislead
        That made the calmest, fairest spot of earth,
        With all its unappropriated good,
        My own; and not mine only, for with me   75
        Entrenched—say rather, peacefully embowered—
        Under yon Orchard, in yon humble Cot,
        A younger orphan of a Home extinct,
        The only Daughter of my Parents dwells.
            Aye, think on that, my Heart, and cease to stir;   80
[100]   Pause upon that, and let the breathing frame
        No longer breathe, but all be satisfied.
        Oh, if such silence be not thanks to God
        For what hath been bestowed, then where, where then
        Shall gratitude find rest? Mine eyes did ne'er   85

---

60   great,] great? *1888*
62   Who] who   Man] man *1888*
65   Yes,] Yes   life—] life *1888*
67   grace,] grace *1888*
68   wrong—] wrong, *1888*
70   desire;] desire— *1888*
71–97   *Christopher Wordsworth quoted these lines in* Memoirs (*I, 157*), *silently correcting* this loved Abode *to* that loved abode *in l. 89.*
72   mislead] mislead, *1888*
73   calmest,] calmest   earth,] earth *1888*
74   good,] good *1888*
76   Entrenched—] Entrenched,   rather,] rather   embowered—] embowered, *1888*
77   Orchard] orchard   Cot] cot *1888*
78   orphan] Orphan   Home] home *1888*
80   Aye,] Aye   Heart,] heart   stir;] stir, *1888*
81   that,] that *1888*
83   Oh] —Oh *1888*

---

78   The companion WW refers to here and in the lines following is DW.

105 Rest on a lovely object, nor my mind
Take pleasure in the midst of [happy] thoughts,
But either She whom now I have, who now
Divides with me this loved abode, was there
Or not far off. Where'er my footsteps turned,
110 Her Voice was like a hidden Bird that sang;
The thought of her was like a flash of light
Or an unseen companionship, a breath
Or fragrance independent of the wind;
In all my goings, in the new and old
115 Of all my meditations, and in this
Favorite of all, in this the most of all.
What Being, therefore, since the birth of Man
Had ever more abundant cause to speak
Thanks, and if music and the power of song
120 Make him more thankful, then to call on these
To aid him and with these resound his joy?
The boon is absolute; surpassing grace
To me hath been vouchsafed; among the bowers
Of blissful Eden this was neither given
125 Nor could be given—possession of the good
Which had been sighed for, ancient thought fulfilled,
And dear Imaginations realized
Up to their highest measure, yea, and more.
    Embrace me then, ye Hills, and close me in;
130 Now in the clear and open day I feel
Your guardianship; I take it to my heart;
'Tis like the solemn shelter of the night.
But I would call thee beautiful, for mild
And soft and gay and beautiful thou art,

---

106 "happy" was supplied to fill a gap left in transcription.

[105]   Fix on a lovely object, nor my mind
        Take pleasure in the midst of happy thoughts,
        But either She whom now I have, who now
        Divides with me this loved Abode, was there
        Or not far off. Where'er my footsteps turned,   90
[110]   Her Voice was like a hidden Bird that sang;
        The thought of her was like a flash of light
        Or an *unseen* companionship, a breath
        Or fragrance independent of the wind;
        In all my goings, in the new and old   95
[115]   Of all my meditations, and in this
        Favorite of all, in this the most of all.
        What Being, therefore, since the birth of Man
        Had ever more abundant cause to speak
        Thanks, and if favours of the heavenly Muse   100
[120]   Make him more thankful, then to call on verse
        To aid him and in song resound his joy?
        The boon is absolute; surpassing grace
        To me hath been vouchsafed; among the bowers
        Of blissful Eden this was neither given   105
[125]   Nor could be given—possession of the good
        Which had been sighed for, ancient thought fulfilled,
        And dear Imaginations realized
        Up to their highest measure, yea, and more.
          Embrace me then, ye Hills, and close me in;   110
[130]   Now in the clear and open day I feel
        Your guardianship; I take it to my heart;
        'Tis like the solemn shelter of the night.
        But I would call thee beautiful, for mild
        And soft and gay and beautiful thou art,   115

---

89   Abode] abode   there] there, *1888*
91   Voice] voice   sang;] sang, *1888*
92   light] light, *1888*
93   *unseen*] unseen *1888*
94   wind;] Wind. *1888*
97   Favorite] Favourite *1888*
98   What Being] —What being *1888*
100 heavenly] Heavenly *1888*
101 verse] Verse *1888*
106 given—] given, *1888*
108 realized] realized, *1888*
109 yea,] yea *1888*
110–125 *Quoted in* Memoirs, *I, 157–158.*
114 mild] mild, *1888*
115 soft] soft,   gay] gay,   art,] art *1888*

135   Dear Valley, having in thy face a smile
       Though peaceful, full of gladness. Thou art pleased,
       Pleased with thy crags and woody steeps, thy Lake,
       Its one green Island and its winding shores,
       The multitude of little rocky hills,
140   Thy Church and Cottages of mountain stone—
       Clustered like stars, some few, but single most,
       And lurking dimly in their shy retreats,
       Or glancing at each other cheerful looks,
       Like separated stars with clouds between.
145   What want we? Have we not perpetual streams,
       Warm woods and sunny hills, and fresh green fields,
       And mountains not less green, and flocks and herds,
       And thickets full of songsters, and the voice
       Of lordly birds—an unexpected sound
150   Heard now and then from morn to latest eve
       Admonishing the man who walks below
       Of solitude and silence in the sky?
       These have we, and a thousand nooks of earth
       Have also these; but nowhere else is found—
155   No where (or is it fancy?) can be found—
       The one sensation that is here; 'tis here,
       Here as it found its way into my heart
       In childhood, here as it abides by day,
       By night, here only; or in chosen minds
160   That take it with them hence, where'er they go.
       'Tis (but I cannot name it), 'tis the sense
       Of majesty and beauty and repose,
       A blended holiness of earth and sky,
       Something that makes this individual Spot,

---

138   Grasmere Lake has a single island; WW enjoyed rowing out to it, resting, and composing there.

141–144   These lines were first published in WW's Introduction to Wilkinson's *Select Views*, following a passage describing the Lakeland cottages: "They are scattered over the vallies, and under the hill sides, and on the rocks; and to this day in the more retired dales, without any intrusion of more assuming buildings" (p. xviii).

[135]   Dear Valley, having in thy face a smile
         Though peaceful, full of gladness. Thou art pleased,
         Pleased with thy crags and woody steeps, thy Lake,
         Its one green Island and its winding shores,
         The multitude of little rocky hills,   120
[140]   Thy Church and Cottages of mountain stone—
         Clustered like stars, some few, but single most,
         And lurking dimly in their shy retreats,
         Or glancing at each other chearful looks,
         Like separated stars with clouds between.   125
[145]   What want we? Have we not perpetual streams,
         Warm woods and sunny hills, and fresh green fields,
         And mountains not less green, and flocks and herds,
         And thickets full of songsters, and the voice
         Of lordly birds—an unexpected sound   130
[150]   Heard now and then from morn to latest eve
         Admonishing the man who walks below
         Of solitude and silence in the sky?
         These have we, and a thousand nooks of earth
         Have also these; but *no* where else is found—   135
[155]   No where (or is it fancy?) can be found—
         The one sensation that is here; 'tis here,
         Here as it found its way into my heart
         In childhood, here as it abides by day,
         By night, here only; or in chosen minds   140
[160]   That take it with them hence, where'er they go.
         'Tis (but I cannot name it), 'tis the sense
         Of majesty and beauty and repose,
         A blended holiness of earth and sky,
         Something that makes this individual Spot,   145

---

119   Island] island   shores,] shores; *1888*
121   Cottages] cottages   stone—] stone *1888*
122-125   *These lines were included in* Guide to the Lakes *from 1810 onward.*
122   Clustered] Cluster'd *1823G–1842G*   stars,] stars *1810G–1842G, 1888*
124   at] on *1810G–1842G*   chearful] cheerful *1810G–1842G, 1888*   looks,] looks *1888*
126   Have] have *1888*
127   woods] woods,
130   birds—] birds,
131   eve] eve, *1888*
135   these;] these,   *no* where] nowhere   found—] found, *1888*
136   No where] Nowhere   found—] found *1888*
142   'Tis (but] —'Tis but   it),] it, *1888*
143   majesty] majesty,   beauty] beauty, *1888*
145   Spot] spot *1888*

165   This small abiding-place of many men,
       A termination and a last retreat,
       A Centre, come from wheresoe'er you will,
       A Whole without dependence or defect,
       Made for itself and happy in itself,
170   Perfect Contentment, Unity entire.
         Long is it since we met to part no more,
       Since I and Emma heard each other's call
       And were Companions once again, like Birds
       Which by the intruding Fowler had been scared,
175   Two of a scattered brood that could not bear
       To live in loneliness; 'tis long since we,
       Remembering much and hoping more, found means
       To walk abreast, though in a narrow path,
       With undivided steps. Our home was sweet;
180   Could it be less? If we were forced to change,
       Our home again was sweet; but still, for Youth,
       Strong as it seems and bold, is inly weak
       And diffident, the destiny of life
       Remained unfixed, and therefore we were still

Lines 185–191 are missing.

       [We will be free, and, as we mean to live
       In culture of divinity and truth,
       Will choose the noblest Temple that we know.
195   Not in mistrust or ignorance of the mind
       And of the power she has within herself
       To enoble all things made we this resolve;
       Far less from any momentary fit
       Of inconsiderate fancy, light and vain;
200   But that we deemed it wise to take the help
       Which lay within our reach; and here, we knew,
       Help could be found of no mean sort; the spirit
       Of singleness and unity and peace.
       In this majestic, self-sufficing world,
205   This all in all of Nature, it will suit,
       We said, no other [   ] on earth so well,
       Simplicity of purpose, love intense,
       Ambition not aspiring to the prize]

192–208   These lines are supplied from MS. A to fill part of the gap left in MS. B.
208   WW wrote "prize" over "praise" in MS. A, apparently correcting an error in transcription.

[165]   This small Abiding-place of many Men,
          A termination and a last retreat,
          A Centre, come from wheresoe'er you will,
          A Whole without dependence or defect,
          Made for itself and happy in itself,   150
[170]   Perfect Contentment, Unity entire.

146   Abiding-place] abiding-place   Men] men *1888*
147   termination] termination, *1888*
148   Centre] centre *1888*
149   Whole] whole *1888*
150   for itself] for itself, *1888*
151   Contentment] contentment *1888*

Of outward things, but for the prize within—
210   Highest ambition. In the daily walks
Of business 'twill be harmony and grace
For the perpetual pleasure of the sense,
And for the Soul—I do not say too much,
Though much be said—an image for the soul,
215   A habit of Eternity and God.
      Nor have we been deceived; thus far the effect
Falls not below the loftiest of our hopes.
Bleak season was it, turbulent and bleak,
When hitherward we journeyed, and on foot,
220   Through bursts of sunshine and through flying snows,
Paced the long vales—how long they were, and yet
How fast that length of way was left behind,
Wensley's long Vale and Sedbergh's naked heights.
The frosty wind, as if to make amends
225   For its keen breath, was aiding to our course
And drove us onward like two Ships at sea.
Stern was the face of nature; we rejoiced
In that stern countenance, for our souls had there
A feeling of their strength. The naked trees,
230   The icy brooks, as on we passed, appeared
To question us. "Whence come ye? To what end?"
They seemed to say. "What would ye?" said the shower,
"Wild Wanderers, whither through my dark domain?"
The Sunbeam said, "Be happy." They were moved,
235   All things were moved; they round us as we went,
We in the midst of them. And when the trance
Came to us, as we stood by Hart-leap Well—
The intimation of the milder day
Which is to come, the fairer world than this—
240   And raised us up, dejected as we were
Among the records of that doleful place

218–256 For a more detailed description of the journey referred to here, see WW's letter to STC, 24 and 27 December 1799, *EY*, pp. 273–280. In her Grasmere journal for 4–6 October 1802, DW describes the journey she made with WW and MW, following their wedding, along the same route, and her account recalls incidents from the earlier journey; see *Journals*, pp. 157–161.

236–256 See WW's poem *Hart-Leap Well*, which has some similarities of phrasing; composed January–February, 1800, and published in the 1800 *Lyrical Ballads*, it bears this headnote: "Hart-Leap Well is a small spring of water, about five miles from Richmond in Yorkshire, and near the side of the road which leads from Richmond to Askrigg. Its name is derived from a remarkable Chace, the memory of which is preserved by the monuments spoken of in the second Part of the following Poem, which monuments do now exist as I have there described them."

Bleak season was it, turbulent and bleak,
When hitherward we journeyed, side by side,
[220]   Through burst of sunshine and through flying showers,
Paced the long Vales—how long they were, and yet   155
How fast that length of way was left behind,
Wensley's rich Vale and Sedbergh's naked heights.
The frosty wind, as if to make amends
[225]   For its keen breath, was aiding to our steps
And drove us onward like two Ships at sea,   160
Or like two Birds, companions in mid air,
Parted and reunited by the blast.
Stern was the face of Nature; we rejoiced
In that stern countenance, for our Souls thence drew
A feeling of their strength. The naked Trees,   165
[230]   The icy brooks, as on we passed, appeared
To question us. "Whence come ye? To what end?"
They seemed to say. "What would ye?" said the shower,
[233]   "Wild Wanderers, whither through my dark domain?"
The sunbeam said, "Be happy." When this Vale   170

152–167 *Quoted in* Memoirs *(I, 155), with three silent emendations:* bleak *at the end of l. 152 altered to* wild*;* bursts *in l. 154 altered to* burst*;* like *in l. 160 altered to* as
153   journeyed,] journeyed   side,] side *1888*
154   showers,] showers *1888*
155   Vales] vales   were,] were—*1888*
157   Vale] Vale, *1888*
159   steps] steps, *1888*
160   Ships] ships *1888*
161   Birds] birds   mid air] mid-air *1888*
163   Nature] nature *1888*
164   Souls] souls *1888*
165   Trees] trees *1888*
167   ye? To] ye, to *1888*
168   say.] say,   ye?"] ye," *1888*
170   Vale] vale *1888*

By sorrow for the hunted beast who there
Had yielded up his breath, the awful trance—
The Vision of humanity and of God

245   The Mourner, God the Sufferer, when the heart
Of his poor Creatures suffers wrongfully—
Both in the sadness and the joy we found
A promise and an earnest that we twain,
A pair seceding from the common world,

250   Might in that hallowed spot to which our steps
Were tending, in that individual nook,
Might even thus early for ourselves secure,
And in the midst of these unhappy times,
A portion of the blessedness which love

255   And knowledge will, we trust, hereafter give
To all the Vales of earth and all mankind.
   Thrice hath the winter Moon been filled with light
Since that dear day when Grasmere, our dear Vale,
Received us. Bright and solemn was the sky

260   That faced us with a passionate welcoming
And led us to our threshold, to a home
Within a home, what was to be, and soon,
Our love within a love. Then darkness came,
Composing darkness, with its quiet load

265   Of full contentment, in a little shed
Disturbed, uneasy in itself, as seemed,
And wondering at its new inhabitants.
It loves us now, this Vale so beautiful
Begins to love us! By a sullen storm,

270   Two months unwearied of severest storm,
It put the temper of our minds to proof,
And found us faithful through the gloom, and heard
The Poet mutter his prelusive songs
With chearful heart, an unknown voice of joy

275   Among the silence of the woods and hills,
Silent to any gladsomeness of sound
With all their Shepherds.
                  But the gates of Spring
Are opened; churlish Winter hath given leave

---

253   "these" is an editorial correction for "those," which fails to make sense in context.

257   In early 1800 the moon was full on 10 January, 9 February, and 10 March; these dates help to fix the period to which WW alludes here.

We entered, bright and solemn was the sky
[260]   That faced us with a passionate welcoming
And led us to our threshold. Daylight failed
Insensibly, and round us gently fell
Composing darkness, with a quiet load   175
[265]   Of full contentment, in a little Shed
Disturbed, uneasy in itself, as seemed,
And wondering at its new inhabitants.
It loves us now, this Vale so beautiful
Begins to love us! By a sullen storm,   180
[270]   Two months unwearied of severest storm,
It put the temper of our minds to proof,
And found us faithful through the gloom, and heard
The Poet mutter his prelusive songs
With chearful heart, an unknown voice of joy   185
[275]   Among the silence of the woods and hills,
Silent to any gladsomeness of sound
With all their Shepherds.
                              But the gates of Spring
Are opened; churlish Winter hath given leave

---

172   welcoming] welcoming, *1888*
176   Shed] shed *1888*
177   itself,] itself *1888*
180   By] by *1888*
185   Chearful] cheerful *1888*
186   hills,] hills; *1888*
188   Shepherds] shepherds *1888*
189   Winter] winter *1888*

That she should entertain for this one day,
280   Perhaps for many genial days to come,
His guests and make them happy. They are pleased,
But most of all, the birds that haunt the flood,
With the mild summons, inmates though they be
Of Winter's household. They are jubilant
285   This day, who drooped or seemed to droop so long;
They show their pleasure, and shall I do less?
Happier of happy though I be, like them
I cannot take possession of the sky,
Mount with a thoughtless impulse, and wheel there,
290   One of a mighty multitude whose way
And motion is a harmony and dance
Magnificent. Behold them, how they shape,
Orb after orb, their course, still round and round,
Above the area of the Lake, their own
295   Adopted region, girding it about
In wanton repetition, yet therewith—
With that large circle evermore renewed—
Hundreds of curves and circlets, high and low,
Backwards and forwards, progress intricate,

292–314 WW published a version of these lines in the fourth edition of his *Guide to the Lakes* (1823), with this introduction: "Wild-ducks in springtime hatch their young in the islands, and upon reedy shores;—the sand-piper, flitting along the stony margins, by its restless note attracts the eye to motions as restless:—upon some jutting rock, or at the edge of a smooth meadow, the stately heron may be described with folded wings, that might seem to have caught their delicate hue from the blue waters, by the side of which she watches for her sustenance. In winter, the lakes are sometimes resorted to by wild swans; and in that season habitually by widgeons, goldings, and other aquatic fowl of the smaller species. Let me be allowed the aid of verse to describe the evolutions which these visitants sometimes perform, on a fine day towards the close of winter" (pp. 19–20). The lines were republished as *Water-fowl* in *Poetical Works*, 1827, among "Poems of the Imagination," with the concluding sentence of the above quotation as an epigraph. The published versions appear to be based on the revisions of *Home at Grasmere* that WW made in 1812–1814; in 1836 he dated the lines 1812.

That she should entertain for this one day,   190
[280]   Perhaps for many genial days to come,
His guests and make them jocund. They are pleased,
But most of all, the Birds that haunt the flood,
With the mild summons, inmates though they be
Of Winter's household. They keep festival   195
[285]   This day, who drooped or seemed to droop so long;
They show their pleasure, and shall I do less?
Happier of happy though I be, like them
I cannot take possession of the sky,
Mount with a thoughtless impulse, and wheel there,   200
[290]   One of a mighty multitude whose way
Is a perpetual harmony and dance
Magnificent. Behold, how with a grace
Of ceaseless motion that might scarcely seem
Inferior to angelical, they prolong   205
Their curious pastime, shaping in mid air
(And sometimes with ambitious wing that soars
High as the level of the mountain tops)
A circuit ampler than the lake beneath,
Their own domain; but ever, while intent   210
On tracing and retracing that large round,
Their jubilant activity evolves
Hundreds of curves and circlets, to and fro,
[299]   Upwards and downwards, progress intricate

---

192   guests] guests,   jocund.] jocund.— *1888*
193   all,] all   Birds] birds   flood,] flood *1888*
194   summons,] summons; *1888*
195   household. They] household, they *1888*
196   droop] droop, *1888*
200   there,] there *1888*
201   multitude] multitude, *1888*
203–229   *These lines were included in* Guide to the Lakes *from 1823 onward and also, entitled* Waterfowl, *in collected editions of the poems, among "Poems of the Imagination," from 1827 onward.*
203   Behold,] Behold *1888*
203–205   Mark how the feather'd tenants of the flood,
            With grace of motion that might scarcely seem
            Inferior to angelical, prolong *1823G–1842G, 1827–1849 but* feather'd] feathered *1827–1849*
204   motion] motion, *1888*
206   pastime,] pastime! *1823G–1842G, 1827–1849*   mid air] mid-air, *1888*
207   (And] And *1888*
208   mountain tops)] mountain tops,) *1823G–1842G* mountain-tops) *1836–1849* mountain-tops, *1888*
209   beneath,] beneath— *1836–1849*
210   domain;] domain;—*1823G–1842G, 1888*
214   Upwards and downwards,] Upward and downward, *1823G–1842G, 1827–1849* Upwards and downwards; *1888*

300   As if one spirit was in all and swayed
       Their indefatigable flight. 'Tis done,
       Ten times, or more, I fancied it had ceased,
       And lo! the vanished company again
       Ascending—list again! I hear their wings:
305   Faint, faint at first, and then an eager sound,
       Passed in a moment, and as faint again!
       They tempt the sun to sport among their plumes;
       They tempt the water and the gleaming ice
       To show them a fair image. 'Tis themselves,
310   Their own fair forms upon the glimmering plain,
       Painted more soft and fair as they descend,
       Almost to touch, then up again aloft,
       Up with a sally and a flash of speed,
       As if they scorned both resting-place and rest.
315   Spring! for this day belongs to thee, rejoice!
       Not upon me alone hath been bestowed—
       Me, blessed with many onward-looking thoughts—
       The sunshine and mild air. Oh, surely these
       Are grateful; not the happy Quires of love,
320   Thine own peculiar family, Sweet Spring,

Yet unperplexed, as if one spirit swayed   215
Their indefatigable flight. 'Tis done,
Ten times, or more, I fancied it had ceased,
But lo! the vanished company again
Ascending—they approach—I hear their wings:
[305]   Faint, faint at first, and then an eager sound,   220
Passed in a moment, and as faint again!
They tempt the sun to sport among their plumes;
Tempt the smooth water or the gleaming ice
To show them a fair image. 'Tis themselves,
[310]   Their own fair forms upon the glimmering plain,   225
Painted more soft and fair as they descend,
Almost to touch, then up again aloft,
Up with a sally and a flash of speed,
[314]   As if they scorned both resting-place and rest.
This day is a thanksgiving; 'tis a day   230
Of glad emotion and deep quietness.
Not upon me alone hath been bestowed—
[317]   Me, rich in many onward-looking thoughts—
The penetrating bliss. Oh, surely these
Have felt it; not the happy Quires of spring   235
Her own peculiar family of love,

---

215   unperplexed] unperplex'd *1823G, 1835G* perplex'd *1842G*
216   flight. 'Tis done,] flight.—'Tis done—*1823G–1842G* flight. 'Tis done— *1836–1849*
217   times, or more,] times and more *1888*   ceased,] ceased; *1823G–1842G, 1827–1849*
218   vanished] vanish'd *1823G–1842G*
219   Ascending—] Ascending; *1823G–1842G* Ascending; *1836–1849* ascending, *1888*
approach—] approach. *1888*   wings:] wings *1823G–1842G, 1827–1846, 1888* wings, *1849*
220   Faint, faint at first,] Faint, faint, at first, *1823G–1842G* Faint, faint at first; *1827–1849,*
1888   sound,] sound *1823G–1842G, 1827–1846, 1888*
221   Passed . . . moment,] Past . . . moment— *1823G–1842G, 1827–1849* Passed . . . moment— *1888*
222   among] amid *1823G–1842G, 1827–1849*   plumes;] plumes: *1842G*
223   Tempt the smooth] They tempt the *1823G–1842G, 1827–1849*   water] water, *1827–*
1849, 1888   ice] ice, *1823G–1842G, 1827–1849, 1888*
224   show] shew *1823G–1842G, 1827*   image. 'Tis] image;—'tis *1823G–1842G* image;
'tis *1827–1849* image,—'tis *1888*
225   forms] forms, *1823G–1842G, 1827–1849*
226   descend,] descend *1823G–1842G, 1827–1849*
227   touch,] touch;— *1823G–1842G, 1827–1849* touch,— *1888*
229   scorned] scorn'd *1823G–1842G*   rest.] rest! *1823G–1842G, 1827–1849, 1888*
230   This] —This   thanksgiving;] thanksgiving, *1888*
231   quietness.] quietness; *1888*
232   bestowed—] bestowed, *1888*
233   Me,] Me   thoughts—] thoughts, *1888*
234   bliss. Oh,] bliss; oh *1888*
235   it;] it,   spring] spring, *1888*
236   love,] love *1888*

That sport among green leaves so blithe a train.
　　But two are missing—two, a lonely pair
Of milk-white Swans. Ah, why are they not here?
These above all, ah, why are they not here
325　To share in this day's pleasure? From afar
They came, like Emma and myself, to live
Together here in peace and solitude,
Choosing this Valley, they who had the choice
Of the whole world. We saw them day by day,
330　Through those two months of unrelenting storm,
Conspicuous in the centre of the Lake,
Their safe retreat. We knew them well—I guess
That the whole Valley knew them—but to us
They were more dear than may be well believed,
335　Not only for their beauty and their still
And placid way of life and faithful love
Inseparable, not for these alone,
But that their state so much resembled ours;
They also having chosen this abode;
340　They strangers, and we strangers; they a pair,
And we a solitary pair like them.
They should not have departed; many days
I've looked for them in vain, nor on the wing
Have seen them, nor in that small open space
345　Of blue unfrozen water, where they lodged
And lived so long in quiet, side by side.
Companions, brethren, consecrated friends,
Shall we behold them yet another year
Surviving, they for us and we for them,
350　And neither pair be broken? Nay, perchance
It is too late already for such hope;
The Shepherd may have seized the deadly tube

350　"be broken" was written over "divided" in transcription.

[321]   That sport among green leaves, a blither train.
              But two are missing—two, a lonely pair
          Of milk-white Swans. Wherefore are they not seen
[325]   Partaking this day's pleasure? From afar   240
          They came, to sojourn here in solitude,
          Choosing this Valley, they who had the choice
          Of the whole world. We saw them day by day,
[330]   Through those two months of unrelenting storm,
          Conspicuous at the centre of the Lake,   245
          Their safe retreat. We knew them well—I guess
          That the whole Valley knew them—but to us
          They were more dear than may be well believed,
[335]   Not only for their beauty and their still
          And placid way of life and constant love   250
          Inseparable, not for these alone,
          But that *their* state so much resembled ours;
          They having also chosen this abode;
[340]   They strangers, and we strangers; they a pair,
          And we a solitary pair like them.   255
          They should not have departed; many days
          Did I look forth in vain, nor on the wing
          Could see them, nor in that small open space
[345]   Of blue unfrozen water, where they lodged
          And lived so long in quiet, side by side.   260
          Shall we behold them, consecrated friends,
          Faithful Companions, yet another year
          Surviving, they for us and we for them,
[350]   And neither pair be broken? Nay, perchance
          It is too late already for such hope;   265
              The Dalesmen may have aimed the deadly tube

---

237   train.] train! *1888*
238   missing—] missing, *1888*
239   Swans. Wherefore] Swans; wherefore *1888*
246   retreat. We] retreat, we   well—] well, *1888*
247   Valley] valley   them—] them, *1888*
249   beauty] beauty, *1888*
250   life] life, *1888*
252   ours;] ours, *1888*
254   strangers;] strangers, *1888*
261   them,] them *1888*
262   Companions] companions *1888*
263   us] us,   *1888*
264   Nay,] nay *1888*
266   tube] tube, *1888*

And parted them, incited by a prize
Which, for the sake of those he loves at home
355   And for the Lamb upon the mountain tops,
He should have spared; or haply both are gone,
One death, and that were mercy given to both.
        I cannot look upon this favoured Vale
But that I seem, by harbouring this thought,
360   To wrong it, such unworthy recompence
Imagining, of confidence so pure.
Ah! if I wished to follow where the sight
Of all that is before my eyes, the voice
Which is as a presiding Spirit here
365   Would lead me, I should say unto myself,
They who are dwellers in this holy place
Must needs themselves be hallowed. They require
No benediction from the Stranger's lips,
For they are blessed already. None would give
370   The greeting "peace be with you" unto them,
For peace they have; it cannot but be theirs.
And mercy and forbearance—nay, not these;
There is no call for these; that office Love
Performs and charity beyond the bounds
375   Of charity—an overflowing love,
Not for the creature only, but for all
Which is around them, love for every thing
Which in this happy Valley we behold!
        Thus do we soothe ourselves, and when the thought
380   Is passed we blame it not for having come.
What if I floated down a pleasant stream
And now am landed and the motion gone—
Shall I reprove myself? Ah no, the stream

366   "in" was written over "of" in transcription.
375   "an overflowing" was written over "a heart delighting" in transcription.

And parted them; or haply both are gone,
[357] One death, and that were mercy given to both.
Recall, my song, the ungenerous thought; forgive,
Thrice favoured Region, the conjecture harsh 270
Of such inhospitable penalty,
Inflicted upon confidence so pure.
Ah! if I wished to follow where the sight
Of all that is before my eyes, the voice
Which speaks from a presiding Spirit here 275
[365] Would lead me, I should whisper to myself,
They who are dwellers in this holy place
Must needs themselves be hallowed. They require
No benediction from the Stranger's lips,
For they are blessed already. None would give 280
[370] The greeting "peace be with you" unto them,
For peace they have; it cannot but be theirs.
And mercy and forbearance—nay, not these;
Their healing Offices a pure good-will
Precludes and charity beyond the bounds 285
[375] Of charity—an overflowing love,
Not for the Creature only, but for all
That is around them, love for every thing
Which in this happy Region they behold!
　　Thus do we soothe ourselves, and when the thought 290
[380] Is passed we blame it not for having come.
What if I floated down a pleasant Stream
And now am landed and the motion gone—
Shall I reprove myself? Ah no, the stream

267　gone,] gone *1888*
271　penalty,] penalty *1888*
275　Spirit here] spirit here, *1888*
276　myself,] myself: *1888*
278　hallowed. They] hallowed, they *1888*
279　Stranger's] stranger's *1888*
280　already. None] already; none *1888*
282　theirs.] theirs, *1888*
283　mercy] mercy,　　nay, not these;] nay—not these— *1888*
284　Offices] offices *1888*
285　Precludes] Precludes, *1888*
286　love,] Love; *1888*
288　them,] them;　　every thing] everything *1888*
289　this] their *1888*
291　passed] passed, *1888*
292　What] —What　　Stream] stream, *1888*
293　landed] landed,　　gone—] gone, *1888*

Is flowing and will never cease to flow,
385   And I shall float upon that stream again.
By such forgetfulness the soul becomes—
Words cannot say how beautiful. Then hail!
Hail to the visible Presence! Hail to thee,
Delightful Valley, habitation fair!
390   And to whatever else of outward form
Can give us inward help, can purify
And elevate and harmonize and soothe,
And steal away and for a while deceive
And lap in pleasing rest, and bear us on
395   Without desire in full complacency,
Contemplating perfection absolute
And entertained as in a placid sleep.
    But not betrayed by tenderness of mind
That feared or wholly overlooked the truth
400   Did we come hither, with romantic hope
To find in midst of so much loveliness
Love, perfect love, of so much majesty
A like majestic frame of mind in those
Who here abide, the persons like the place.
405   Nor from such hope or aught of such belief
Hath issued any portion of the joy
Which I have felt this day. An awful voice,
'Tis true, I in my walks have often heard,
Sent from the mountains or the sheltered fields,
410   Shout after shout—reiterated whoop
In manner of a bird that takes delight
In answering to itself, or like a hound

Is flowing and will never cease to flow,   295
[385]   And I shall float upon that stream again.
By such forgetfulness the soul becomes—
Words cannot say how beautiful. Then hail!
Hail to the visible Presence! Hail to thee,
Delightful Valley, habitation fair!   300
[390]   And to whatever else of outward form
Can give us inward help, can purify
And elevate and harmonize and soothe,
And steal away and for awhile deceive
And lap in pleasing rest, and bear us on   305
[395]   Without desire in full complacency,
Contemplating perfection absolute
And entertained as in a placid sleep.
    But not betrayed by tenderness of mind
That feared or wholly overlooked the truth   310
[400]   Did we come hither, with romantic hope
To find in midst of so much loveliness
Love, perfect love, of so much majesty
A like majestic frame of mind in those
Who here abide, the persons like the place.   315
[405]   Not from such hope or aught of such belief
Hath issued any portion of the joy
Which I have felt this day. An awful voice,
'Tis true, hath in my walks been often heard,
Sent from the mountains or the sheltered fields,   320
[410]   Shout after shout—reiterated whoop
In manner of a bird that takes delight
In answering to itself, or like a hound

---

295   flowing] flowing, *1888*
297   becomes—] becomes, *1888*
298   beautiful. Then hail!] beautiful: then hail, *1888*
299   Presence! Hail] Presence, hail *1888*
302   purify] purify, *1888*
303   elevate] elevate,   harmonize] harmonise, *1888*
304   away] away, *1888*
307   absolute] absolute, *1888*
310   feared] feared,   truth] truth, *1888*
313   love,] love: *1888*
316   hope] hope,   belief] belief, *1888*
318   voice,] voice *1888*
319   true,] true *1888*
321   whoop] whoop, *1888*
323   itself,] itself: *1888*

Single at chase among the lonely woods—
A human voice, how awful in the gloom
415   Of coming night, when sky is dark, and earth
Not dark, not yet enlightened, but by snow
Made visible, amid the noise of winds
And bleatings manifold of sheep that know
That summons and are gathering round for food—
420   That voice, the same, the very same, that breath
Which was an utterance awful as the wind,
Or any sound the mountains ever heard.
    That Shepherd's voice, it may have reached mine ear
Debased and under prophanation, made
425   An organ for the sounds articulate
Of ribaldry and blasphemy and wrath,
Where drunkenness hath kindled senseless frays.
I came not dreaming of unruffled life,
Untainted manners; born among the hills,
430   Bred also there, I wanted not a scale
To regulate my hopes; pleased with the good,

[413]   Single at chase among the lonely woods,
          His yell repeating. Yet it was in truth   325
          A human voice—a Spirit of coming night,
          How solemn when the sky is dark, and earth
[416]   Not dark, nor yet enlightened, but by snow
          Made visible, amid a noise of winds
          And bleatings manifold of mountain sheep,   330
          Which in that iteration recognize
[419]   Their summons and are gathering round for food,
          Devoured with keenness ere to grove or bank
          Or rocky *bield* with patience they retire.
              That very voice—which in some timid mood   335
          Of superstitious fancy might have seemed
          Awful as ever stray Demoniac uttered,
          His steps to govern in the Wilderness;
          Or, as the Norman Curfew's regular beat
          To hearths when first they darkened at the knell—   340
[423]   That Shepherd's voice, it may have reached mine ear
          Debased and under profanation, made
          The ready Organ of articulate sounds
          From ribaldry, impiety, or wrath,
          Issuing when shame hath ceased to check the brawls   345
          Of some abused Festivity—so be it.
[428]   I came not dreaming of unruffled life,
          Untainted manners; born among the hills,
[430]   Bred also there, I wanted not a scale
          To regulate my hopes; pleased with the good,   350

---

325   repeating. Yet] repeating; yet *1888*
326   night,] night *1888*
331   recognize] recognise *1888*
332   summons] summons, *1888*
333   keenness] keenness, *1888*
334   *bield*] bield *1888*
335   voice—which] voice, which, *1888*
336   fancy] fancy, *1888*
337   Demoniac] demoniac *1888*
339   Or,] Or *1888*
340   knell—] knell: *1888*
341   Shepherd's] shepherd's *1888*
343   Organ] organ *1888*
350   good,] good *1888*

---

334   A *bield* is a shelter or refuge; the word is in general dialect usage throughout Scotland
and northern England.

I shrink not from the evil in disgust
Or with immoderate pain. I look for man,
The common creature of the brotherhood,
435   But little differing from the man elsewhere
For selfishness and envy and revenge,
Ill neighbourhood—folly that this should be—
Flattery and double-dealing, strife and wrong.
  Yet is it something gained—it is in truth
440   A mighty gain—that Labour here preserves
His rosy face, a Servant only here
Of the fire-side or of the open field,
A Freeman, therefore sound and unenslaved;
That extreme penury is here unknown,
445   And cold and hunger's abject wretchedness,
Mortal to body and the heaven-born mind;
That they who want are not too great a weight
For those who can relieve. Here may the heart
Breathe in the air of fellow-suffering
450   Dreadless, as in a kind of fresher breeze
Of her own native element; the hand
Be ready and unwearied without plea
From task too frequent and beyond its powers,
For languor or indifference or despair.
455   And as these lofty barriers break the force
Of winds—this deep vale as it doth in part
Conceal us from the storm—so here there is
A Power and a protection for the mind,
Dispensed indeed to other solitudes

I shrink not from the evil with disgust
Or with immoderate pain. I look for Man,
The common Creature of the brotherhood,
[435]   Differing but little from the Man elsewhere
For selfishness and envy and revenge,   355
Ill neighbourhood—pity that this should be—
Flattery and double-dealing, strife and wrong.
        Yet is it something gained—it is in truth
[440]   A mighty gain—that Labour here preserves
His rosy face, a Servant only here   360
Of the fire-side or of the open field,
A Freeman, therefore sound and unimpaired;
That extreme penury is here unknown,
[445]   And cold and hunger's abject wretchedness,
Mortal to body and the heaven-born mind;   365
That they who want are not too great a weight
For those who can relieve. Here may the heart
Breathe in the air of fellow-suffering
[450]   Dreadless, as in a kind of fresher breeze
Of her own native element; the hand   370
Be ready and unwearied without plea
From tasks too frequent or beyond its power,
For languor or indifference or despair.
[455]   And as these lofty barriers break the force
Of winds—this deep Vale as it doth in part   375
Conceal us from the Storm—so here abides
A power and a protection for the mind,
Dispensed indeed to other Solitudes

---

351   disgust] disgust, *1888*
353   Creature] creature *1888*
354   elsewhere] elsewhere, *1888*
358   gained—] gained, *1888*
359   gain—] gain *1888*
360   Servant] servant *1888*
361   fire-side] fireside *1888*
362   Freeman,] Freeman *1888*
364   wretchedness,] wretchedness *1888*
365   mind;] mind: *1888*
367   relieve. Here] relieve; here *1888*
370   element;] element, *1888*
371   plea] plea, *1888*
375   winds—] winds,—   Vale] Vale, *1888*
376   Storm—] storm, *1888*
378   Solitudes] solitudes *1888*

460 Favoured by noble privilege like this,
Where kindred independence of estate
Is prevalent, where he who tills the field,
He, happy Man! is Master of the field
And treads the mountain which his Father trod.
465 Hence, and from other local circumstance,
In this enclosure many of the old
Substantial virtues have a firmer tone
Than in the base and ordinary world.
    Yon Cottage, would that it could tell a part
470 Of its own story. Thousands might give ear,
Might hear it and blush deep. There few years past
In this his Native Valley dwelt a Man,
The Master of a little lot of ground,
A man of mild deportment and discourse,
475 A scholar also (as the phrase is here),
For he drew much delight from those few books
That lay within his reach, and for this cause
Was by his Fellow-dalesmen honoured more.
A Shepherd and a Tiller of the ground,
480 Studious withal, and healthy in his frame
Of body, and of just and placid mind,
He with his consort and his Children saw
Days that were seldom touched by petty strife,
Years safe from large misfortune, long maintained
485 That course which men the wisest and most pure
Might look on with entire complacency.
Yet in himself and near him were there faults
At work to undermine his happiness
By little and by little. Active, prompt,
490 And lively was the Housewife, in the Vale
None more industrious; but her industry
Was of that kind, 'tis said, which tended more
To splendid neatness, to a showy trim,
And overlaboured purity of house
495 Than to substantial thrift. He, on his part
Generous and easy-minded, was not free
From carelessness, and thus in course of time
These joint infirmities, combined perchance
With other cause less obvious, brought decay

469–605 WW transferred these tales to *The Excursion*, VI, 1080–1191.

[460]   Favored by noble privilege like this,
Where kindred independence of estate   380
Is prevalent, where he who tills the field,
He, happy Man! is Master of the field
[464]   And treads the mountains which his Fathers trod.

---

379   Favored] Favoured *1888*
382   Man] man   Master] master   field] field, *1888*

500 Of worldly substance and distress of mind,
    Which to a thoughtful man was hard to shun
    And which he could not cure. A blooming Girl
    Served them, an Inmate of the House. Alas!
    Poor now in tranquil pleasure, he gave way
505 To thoughts of troubled pleasure; he became
    A lawless Suitor of the Maid, and she
    Yielded unworthily. Unhappy Man!
    That which he had been weak enough to do
    Was misery in remembrance; he was stung,
510 Stung by his inward thoughts, and by the smiles
    Of Wife and children stung to agony.
    His temper urged him not to seek relief
    Amid the noise of revellers nor from draught
    Of lonely stupefaction; he himself
515 A rational and suffering Man, himself
    Was his own world, without a resting-place.
    Wretched at home, he had no peace abroad,
    Ranged through the mountains, slept upon the earth,
    Asked comfort of the open air, and found
520 No quiet in the darkness of the night,
    No pleasure in the beauty of the day.
    His flock he slighted; his paternal fields
    Were as a clog to him, whose Spirit wished
    To fly, but whither? And yon gracious Church,
525 That has a look so full of peace and hope
    And love—benignant Mother of the Vale,
    How fair amid her brood of Cottages!—
    She was to him a sickness and reproach.
    I speak conjecturing from the little known,
530 The much that to the last remained unknown;
    But this is sure: he died of his own grief,
    He could not bear the weight of his own shame.
        That Ridge, which elbowing from the mountain-side
    Carries into the Plain its rocks and woods,
535 Conceals a Cottage where a Father dwells
    In widowhood, whose Life's Co-partner died
    Long since, and left him solitary Prop
    Of many helpless Children. I begin
    With words which might be prelude to a Tale
540 Of sorrow and dejection, but I feel—
    Though in the midst of sadness, as might seem—

No sadness, when I think of what mine eyes
Have seen in that delightful family.
Bright garland make they for their Father's brows,
545   Those six fair Daughters budding yet, not one,
Not one of all the band a full-blown flower.
Go to the Dwelling: There Thou shalt have proof
That He who takes away, yet takes not half
Of what he seems to take, or gives it back
550   Not to our prayer, but far beyond our prayer,
He gives it the boon-produce of a soil
Which Hope hath never watered. Thou shalt see
A House, which at small distance will appear
In no distinction to have passed beyond
555   Its Fellows, will appear, like them, to have grown
Out of the native Rock; but nearer view
Will show it not so grave in outward mien
And soberly arrayed as for the most
Are these rude mountain-dwellings—Nature's care,
560   Mere friendless Nature's—but a studious work
Of many fancies and of many hands,
A play thing and a pride; for such the air
And aspect which the little Spot maintains
In spite of lonely Winter's nakedness.
565   They have their jasmine resting on the Porch,
Their rose-trees, strong in health, that will be soon
Roof-high; and here and there the garden wall
Is topped with single stones, a showy file
Curious for shape or hue—some round, like Balls,
570   Worn smooth and round by fretting of the Brook
From which they have been gathered, others bright
And sparry, the rough scatterings of the Hills.
These ornaments the Cottage chiefly owes
To one, a hardy Girl, who mounts the rocks;
575   Such is her choice; she fears not the bleak wind;
Companion of her Father, does for him
Where'er he wanders in his pastoral course
The service of a Boy, and with delight
More keen and prouder daring. Yet hath She
580   Within the garden, like the rest, a bed
For her own flowers, or favorite Herbs, a space

550–551   WW appears to have developed these lines in transcription from a single original line.

Holden by sacred charter; and I guess
She also helped to frame that tiny Plot
Of garden ground which one day 'twas my chance
585   To find among the woody rocks that rise
Above the House, a slip of smoother earth
Planted with goose-berry bushes, and in one,
Right in the centre of the prickly shrub,
A mimic Bird's-nest, fashioned by the hand,
590   Was stuck, a staring Thing of twisted hay,
And one quaint Fir-tree towered above the Whole.
But in the darkness of the night, then most
This Dwelling charms me; covered by the gloom
Then, heedless of good manners, I stop short
595   And (who could help it?) feed by stealth my sight
With prospect of the company within,
Laid open through the blazing window. There
I see the eldest Daughter at her wheel,
Spinning amain, as if to overtake
600   She knows not what, or teaching in her turn
Some little Novice of the sisterhood
That skill in this or other household work
Which from her Father's honored hands, herself,
While She was yet a Little-one, had learned.
605   Mild Man! He is not gay, but they are gay,
And the whole House is filled with gaiety.
　　From yonder grey stone that stands alone
Close to the foaming Stream, look up and see,
Not less than half way up the mountain-side,
610   A dusky Spot, a little grove of firs
And seems still smaller than it is. The Dame
Who dwells below, she told me that this grove,
Just six weeks younger than her eldest Boy,
Was planted by her Husband and herself

[609]   Not less than half way up *yon* mountain's side,

Behold a dusky spot, a grove of Firs   385

That seems still smaller than it is. This grove

Is haunted—by what ghost? A gentle spirit

Of memory, faithful to the call of love.

For, as reports the Dame whose fire sends up

Yon curling smoke from the grey cot below,   390

The trees (her first-born Child being then a babe)

[614]   Were planted by her husband and herself,

---

384 half way] halfway   *yon*] yon *1888*
386 is. This] is; this *1888*
387 A] a *1888*
388 memory,] memory   love.] love; *1888*
389 Dame] Dame, *1888*
391 Child] child *1888*

615 For a convenient shelter, which in storm
Their sheep might draw to. "And they know it well,"
Said she, "for thither do we bear them food
In time of heavy snow." She then began
In fond obedience to her private thoughts
620 To speak of her dead Husband. Is there not
An art, a music, and a stream of words
That shall be life, the acknowledged voice of life?
Shall speak of what is done among the fields,
Done truly there, or felt, of solid good
625 And real evil, yet be sweet withal,
More grateful, more harmonious than the breath,
The idle breath of sweetest pipe attuned
To pastoral fancies? Is there such a stream,
Pure and unsullied, flowing from the heart
630 With motions of true dignity and grace,
Or must we seek these things where man is not?
Methinks I could repeat in tuneful verse
Delicious as the gentlest breeze that sounds
Through that aerial fir-grove, could preserve
635 Some portion of its human history
As gathered from that Matron's lips and tell
Of tears that have been shed at sight of it
And moving dialogues between this Pair,
Who in the prime of wedlock with joint hands
640 Did plant this grove, now flourishing while they
No longer flourish; he entirely gone,

That ranging o'er the high and houseless ground
Their sheep might neither want, from perilous storm
Of winter nor from summer's sultry heat,   395
[616]   A friendly Covert. "And they knew it well,"
She said, "for thither as the trees grew up
We to the patient creatures carried food
In times of heavy snow." She then began
In fond obedience to her private thoughts   400
[620]   To speak of her dead Husband. Is there not
An art, a music, and a strain of words
That shall be life, the acknowledged voice of life?
Shall speak of what is done among the fields,
Done truly there, or felt, of solid good   405
[625]   And real evil, yet be sweet withal,
More grateful, more harmonious than the breath,
The idle breath of softest pipe attuned
To pastoral fancies? Is there such a stream,
Pure and unsullied, flowing from the heart   410
[630]   With motions of true dignity and grace,
Or must we seek that stream where Man is not?
Methinks I could repeat in tuneful verse
Delicious as the gentlest breeze that sounds
Through that aerial fir-grove, could preserve   415
[635]   Some portion of its human history
As gathered from the Matron's lips and tell
Of tears that have been shed at sight of it
And moving dialogues between this Pair,
Who in their prime of wedlock with joint hands   420
[640]   Did plant the grove, now flourishing while they
No longer flourish; he entirely gone,

---

394   want,] want *1888*
395   winter] winter, *1888*
396   Covert. "And] covert; "and *1888*
401   Husband. Is] husband; is *1888*
403   life?] life, *1888*
409   stream,] stream *1888*
410   unsullied,] unsullied *1888*
411   grace,] grace? *1888*
413   verse] verse, *1888*
415   fir-grove,] firgrove *1888*
417   lips] lips, *1888*
418   it] it, *1888*
420   wedlock] wedlock; *1888*
422   flourish;] flourish *1888*

She withering in her loneliness. Be this
A task above my skill; the silent mind
Has its own treasures, and I think of these,
645   Love what I see, and honour humankind.
      No, we are not alone; we do not stand,
My Emma, here misplaced and desolate,
Loving what no one cares for but ourselves.
We shall not scatter through the plains and rocks
650   Of this fair Vale and o'er its spacious heights
Unprofitable kindliness, bestowed
On Objects unaccustomed to the gifts
Of feeling, that were cheerless and forlorn
But few weeks past, and would be so again
655   If we were not. We do not tend a lamp
Whose lustre we alone participate,
Which is dependent upon us alone,
Mortal though bright, a dying, dying flame.
Look where we will, some human heart has been
660   Before us with its offering; not a tree
Sprinkles these little pastures, but the same
Hath furnished matter for a thought, perchance
To some one is as a familiar Friend.
Joy spreads and sorrow spreads; and this whole Vale,
665   Home of untutored Shepherds as it is,
Swarms with sensation, as with gleams of sunshine,
Shadows or breezes, scents or sounds. Nor deem
These feelings—though subservient more than ours
To every day's demand for daily bread,
670   And borrowing more their spirit and their shape
From self-respecting interests—deem them not
Unworthy therefore and unhallowed. No,
They lift the animal being, do themselves

---

671   WW may originally have written "these" for "them."

She withering in her loneliness. Be this
A task above my skill; the silent mind
Has her own treasures, and I think of these,   425
[645]   Love what I see, and honour humankind.
              No, we are not alone; we do not stand,
My Sister, here misplaced and desolate,
Loving what no one cares for but ourselves.
We shall not scatter through the plains and rocks   430
[650]   Of this fair Vale and o'er its spacious heights
Unprofitable kindliness, bestowed
On objects unaccustomed to the gifts
Of feeling, which were cheerless and forlorn
But few weeks past, and would be so again   435
[655]   Were we not here. We do not tend a lamp
Whose lustre we alone participate,
Which shines dependent upon us alone,
Mortal though bright, a dying, dying flame.
Look where we will, some human hand has been   440
[660]   Before us with its offering; not a tree
Sprinkles these little pastures, but the same
Hath furnished matter for a thought, perchance
For some one serves as a familiar friend.
Joy spreads and sorrow spreads; and this whole Vale,   445
[665]   Home of untutored Shepherds as it is,
Swarms with sensation, as with gleams of sunshine,
Shadows or breezes, scents or sounds. Nor deem
These feelings—though subservient more than ours
To every day's demand for daily bread,   450
[670]   And borrowing more their spirit and their shape
From self-respecting interests—deem them not
Unworthy therefore and unhallowed. No,
They lift the animal being, do themselves

---

424   skill;] skill— *1888*
427   alone;] alone, *1888*
428   Sister,] sister *1888*
431   Vale] Vale,   heights] heights, *1888*
435   past,] past *1888*
436   here. We] here; we *1888*
443   thought,] thought; *1888*
445   Joy spreads] Joy spreads, *1888*
446   Shepherds] shepherds *1888*
449   feelings—] feelings, *1888*
452   interests—] interests; *1888*
453   therefore] therefore,   unhallowed. No,] unhallowed—no, *1888*

By nature's kind and ever present aid
675　Refine the selfishness from which they spring,
Redeem by love the individual sense
Of anxiousness with which they are combined.
Many are pure, the best of them are pure;
The best, and these, remember, most abound,
680　Are fit associates of the [　　　] joy,
Joy of the highest and the purest minds;
They blend with it congenially; meanwhile,
Calmly they breathe their own undying life,
Lowly and unassuming as it is,
685　Through this, their mountain sanctuary (long,
Oh long may it remain inviolate!),
Diffusing health and sober chearfulness,
And giving to the moments as they pass
Their little boons of animating thought,
690　That sweeten labour, make it seem and feel
To be no arbitrary weight imposed,
But a glad function natural to Man.
　　　Fair proof of this, Newcomer though I be,
Already have I seen; the inward frame,
695　Though slowly opening, opens every day.
Nor am I less delighted with the show
As it unfolds itself, now here, now there,
Than is the passing Traveller, when his way
Lies through some region then first trod by him
700　(Say this fair Valley's self), when low-hung mists
Break up and are beginning to recede.

680　In leaving this gap WW apparently rejected "worthiest," the reading of MS. R.

By nature's kind and ever-present aid   455
[675]   Refine the selfishness from which they spring,
Redeem by love the individual sense
Of anxiousness with which they are combined.
And thus it is that fitly they become
Associates in the joy of purest minds;   460
They blend therewith congenially; meanwhile,
Calmly they breathe their own undying life,
[685]   Through this, their mountain sanctuary (long,
Oh long may it remain inviolate!),
Diffusing health and sober chearfulness,   465
And giving to the moments as they pass
Their little boons of animating thought,
[690]   That sweeten labour, make it seen and felt
To be no arbitrary weight imposed,
But a glad function natural to Man.   470
        Fair proof of this, Newcomer though I be,
Already have I gained; the inward frame,
[695]   Though slowly opening, opens every day
With process not unlike to that which chears
A pensive Stranger, journeying at his leisure   475
Through some Helvetian Dell, when low-hung mists
[701]   Break up and are beginning to recede.
How pleased he is, where thin and thinner grows
The veil or where it parts at once, to spy
The dark pines thrusting forth their spiky heads,   480
To watch the spreading lawns with cattle grazed,

---

455   ever-present] ever present *1888*
458   anxiousness] anxiousness, *1888*
460   minds;] minds: *1888*
461   congenially; meanwhile,] congenially: meanwhile *1888*
462   life,] life *1888*
463   this,] this   sanctuary (long,] sanctuary; long *1888*
464   inviolate!),] inviolate, *1888*
465   chearfulness,] cheerfulness, *1888*
467   thought,] thought *1888*
470   Man] man *1888*
471   Newcomer] newcomer *1888*
474   chears] cheers *1888*
475   Stranger,] stranger *1888*
476   Dell,] Dell; *1888*
477   recede.] recede *1888*
478   is,] is *1888*
479   veil] veil, *1888*
480   heads,] heads; *1888*
481   grazed,] grazed; *1888*

How pleased he is to hear the murmuring stream,
The many Voices, from he knows not where,
To have about him, which way e'er he goes,
705   Something on every side concealed from view,
In every quarter some thing visible,
Half seen or wholly, lost and found again—
Alternate progress and impediment,
And yet a growing prospect in the main.
710   Such pleasure now is mine, and what if I—
Herein less happy than the Traveller—
Am sometimes forced to cast a painful look
Upon unwelcome things, which unawares
Reveal themselves? Not therefore is my mind
715   Depressed, nor do I fear what is to come;
But confident, enriched at every glance,
The more I see the more is my delight.
Truth justifies herself; and as she dwells
With Hope, who would not follow where she leads?
720   Nor let me overlook those other loves
Where no fear is, those humbler sympathies
That have to me endeared the quietness
Of this sublime retirement. I begin
Already to inscribe upon my heart
725   A liking for the small grey Horse that bears
The paralytic Man; I know the ass
On which the Cripple in the Quarry maimed
Rides to and fro: I know them and their ways.
The famous Sheep-dog, first in all the vale,
730   Though yet to me a Stranger, will not be

---

727 The quarry cannot be identified; there are numerous slate quarries in the vicinity, some very small. In *An Unpublished Tour*, WW describes the dangers and frequent accidents suffered by local quarrymen; see *Prose*, II, 315–316.

Then to be greeted by the scattered huts
As they shine out; and *see* the streams whose murmur
Had soothed his ear while *they* were hidden; how pleased

[704]   To have about him, which way e'er he goes,   485
Something on every side concealed from view,
In every quarter something visible,
Half-seen or wholly, lost and found again—
Alternate progress and impediment,
And yet a growing prospect in the main.   490

[710]   Such pleasure now is mine, albeit forced—
Herein less happy than the Traveller—
To cast from time to time a painful look
Upon unwelcome things, which unawares
Reveal themselves. Not therefore is my heart   495

[715]   Depressed, nor does it fear what is to come;
But confident, enriched at every glance,
The more I see the more delight my mind
Receives, or by reflection can create.
Truth justifies herself; and as she dwells   500
With Hope, who would not follow where she leads?

[720]   Nor let me pass unheeded other loves
Where no fear is and humbler sympathies.
Already hath sprung up within my heart
A liking for the small grey horse that bears   505
The paralytic Man and for the brute
In scripture sanctified—the patient brute

[727]   On which the Cripple in the Quarry maimed
Rides to and fro: I know them and their ways.
The famous Sheep-dog, first in all the Vale,   510

[730]   Though yet to me a Stranger, will not be

---

485   him,] him   goes,] goes *1888*
487   visible,] visible *1888*
488   Half-seen] Half seen   again—] again, *1888*
491   forced—] forced, *1888*
492   Traveller—] Traveller, *1888*
494   things,] things *1888*
495   themselves. Not] themselves, not *1888*
499   create.] create: *1888*
500   herself;] herself, *1888*
503   is] is, *1888*
506   Man] man *1888*
507   scripture] Scripture *1888*
508   Cripple] cripple,   Quarry maimed] quarry maimed, *1888*
510   Sheep-dog] sheep-dog   Vale] vale *1888*
511   Stranger] stranger *1888*

A Stranger long; nor will the blind Man's Guide,
Meek and neglected thing, of no renown.
Whoever lived a Winter in one place,
Beneath the shelter of one Cottage-roof,
735   And has not had his Red-breast or his Wren?
I have them both; and I shall have my Thrush
In spring time, and a hundred warblers more;
And if the banished Eagle Pair return,
Helvellyn's Eagles, to their ancient Hold,
740   Then shall I see, shall claim with those two Birds
Acquaintance, as they soar amid the Heavens.
The Owl that gives the name to Owlet-crag
Have I heard shouting, and he soon will be
A chosen one of my regards. See there,
745   The Heifer in yon little Croft belongs
To one who holds it dear; with duteous care
She reared it, and in speaking of her Charge
I heard her scatter once a word or two,
[   ] domestic, yea, and Motherly,
750   She being herself a Mother. Happy Beast,
If the caresses of a human voice
Can make it so, and care of human hands.
    And Ye as happy under Nature's care,
Strangers to me and all men, or at least
755   Strangers to all particular amity,
All intercourse of knowledge or of love
That parts the individual from the kind;
Whether in large communities ye dwell
From year to year, not shunning man's abode,
760   A settled residence, or be from far,
Wild creatures, and of many homes, that come
The gift of winds, and whom the winds again

---

739   Helvellyn is one of the highest mountains in the Lakes, and in England (3118 feet); it stands in a dominant position north of Grasmere.

742   Owlet-crag has not been identified.

749   In leaving this gap WW apparently rejected "A term," the reading of MS. R.

A Stranger long; nor will the blind man's guide,
Meek and neglected thing, of no renown.
Soon will peep forth the primrose; ere it fades
[736]   Friends shall I have at dawn, blackbird and thrush   515
To rouse me, and a hundred Warblers more;
And if those Eagles to their ancient Hold
Return, Helvellyn's Eagles, with the Pair
From my own door I shall be free to claim
[741]   Acquaintance, as they sweep from cloud to cloud.   520
The Owl that gives the name to owlet-crag
Have I heard whooping, and he soon will be
A chosen one of my regards. See there,
[745]   The Heifer in yon little Croft belongs
To one who holds it dear; with duteous care   525
She reared it, and in speaking of her Charge
I heard her scatter some endearing words
Domestic and in spirit motherly,
[750]   She being herself a Mother. Happy Beast,
If the caresses of a human voice   530
Can make it so, and care of human hands.
      And Ye as happy under Nature's care,
Strangers to me and all men, or at least
[755]   Strangers to all particular amity,
All intercourse of knowledge or of love   535
That parts the individual from his kind;
Whether in large communities ye keep
From year to year, not shunning man's abode,
[760]   A settled residence, or be from far
Wild creatures, and of many homes, that come   540
The gift of winds, and whom the winds again

---

512   Stranger] stranger *1888*
513   renown.] renown! *1888*
514   primrose;] primrose, *1888*
516   Warblers more;] warblers more! *1888*
517   Hold] hold *1888*
518   Eagles,] Eagles! *1888*
521   owlet-crag] Owlet-Crag *1888*
523   there,] there *1888*
524   Heifer] heifer   Croft] croft *1888*
526   Charge] charge *1888*
528   Domestic] Domestic, *1888*
529   Mother. Happy] mother; happy *1888*
532   Ye] ye *1888*
536   kind;] kind. *1888*

Take from us at your pleasure—yet shall ye
Not want for this, your own subordinate place,
765 According to your claim, an underplace
In my affections. Witness the delight
With which ere while I saw that multitude
Wheel through the sky and see them now at rest,
Yet not at rest, upon the glassy lake.
770 They cannot rest; they gambol like young whelps,
Active as lambs and overcome with joy;
They try all frolic motions, flutter, plunge,
And beat the passive water with their wings.
Too distant are they for plain view, but lo!
775 Those little fountains, sparkling in the sun,
Which tell what they are doing, which rise up,
First one and then another silver spout,
As one or other takes the fit of glee—
Fountains and spouts, yet rather in the guise
780 Of plaything fire-works, which on festal nights
Hiss hiss about the feet of wanton boys.
How vast the compass of this theatre,
Yet nothing to be seen but lovely pomp
And silent majesty. The birch tree woods
785 Are hung with thousand thousand diamond drops
Of melted hoar-frost, every tiny knot
In the bare twigs, each little budding-place
Cased with its several bead; what myriads there
Upon one tree, while all the distant grove
790 That rises to the summit of the steep
Is like a mountain built of silver light!
See yonder the same pageant, and again

Take from us at your pleasure—yet shall ye
[765]   Not want for this, your own subordinate place
In my affections. Witness the delight
With which erewhile I saw that multitude   545
Wheel through the sky and see them now at rest,
Yet not at rest, upon the glassy lake.
[770]   They *cannot* rest; they gambol like young whelps,
Active as lambs and overcome with joy;
They try all frolic motions, flutter, plunge,   550
And beat the passive water with their wings.
Too distant are they for plain view, but lo!
Those little fountains, sparkling in the sun,
Betray their occupation, rising up,
[777]   First one and then another silver spout,   555
As one or other takes the fit of glee—
Fountains and spouts, yet somewhat in the guise
Of plaything fire-works, that on festal nights
Sparkle about the feet of wanton boys.
[782]   How vast the compass of this theatre,   560
Yet nothing to be seen but lovely pomp
And silent majesty. The birch-tree woods
[785]   Are hung with thousand thousand diamond drops
Of melted hoar-frost, every tiny knot
In the bare twigs, each little budding-place   565
Cased with its several bead; what myriads there
Upon one tree, while all the distant grove
[790]   That rises to the summit of the steep
Shows like a mountain built of silver light!
See yonder the same pageant, and again   570

542   pleasure—] pleasure; *1888*
543   this,] this *1888*
547   rest,] rest   lake.] lake: *1888*
548   rest;] rest—   whelps,] whelps; *1888*
549   lambs] lambs,   joy;] joy *1888*
550   motions,] motions; *1888*
554   up,] up *1888*
556   glee—] glee, *1888*
558   fire-works] fireworks *1888*
560   How] —How *1888*
562   majesty. The] majesty; the *1888*
566   bead] beads   there] these *1888*
567   grove] grove, *1888*
568   steep] steep, *1888*
569   light!] light: *1888*

Behold the universal imagery
At what a depth, deep in the Lake below.
795   Admonished of the days of love to come,
The raven croaks and fills the sunny air
With a strange sound of genial harmony;
And in and all about that playful band,
Incapable although they be of rest,
800   And in their fashion very rioters,
There is a stillness, and they seem to make
Calm revelry in that their calm abode.
I leave them to their pleasure, and I pass,
Pass with a thought the life of the whole year
805   That is to come—the throngs of mountain flowers
And lilies that will dance upon the lake.
      Then boldly say that solitude is not
Where these things are: he truly is alone,
He of the multitude, whose eyes are doomed
810   To hold a vacant commerce day by day
With that which he can neither know nor love—
Dead things, to him thrice dead—or worse than this,

[793]   Behold the universal imagery
Inverted, all its sun-bright features touched
As with the varnish and the gloss of dreams;
Dreamlike the blending also of the whole
Harmonious Landscape, all along the shore   575
The boundary lost—the line invisible
That parts the image from reality;
And the clear hills, as high as they ascend
Heavenward, so deep piercing the lake below.
[795]   Admonished of the days of love to come,   580
The raven croaks and fills the upper air
With a strange sound of genial harmony;
And in and all about that playful band,
Incapable although they be of rest,
[800]   And in their fashion very rioters,   585
There is a stillness, and they seem to make
Calm revelry in that their calm abode.
Them leaving to their joyous hours, I pass,
Pass with a thought the life of the whole year
[805]   That is to come—the throng of woodland flowers   590
And lilies that will dance upon the waves.
      Say boldly then that solitude is not
Where these things are: he truly is alone,
[809]   He of the multitude, whose eyes are doomed
To hold a vacant commerce day by day   595
With objects wanting life, repelling love;
He by the vast Metropolis immured,
Where pity shrinks from unremitting calls,
Where numbers overwhelm humanity,
And neighbourhood serves rather to divide   600
Than to unite. What sighs more deep than his
Whose nobler will hath long been sacrificed;
Who must inhabit under a black sky

---

573   dreams;] dreams. *1888*
575   Landscape,] landscape: *1888*
580   come,] come *1888*
581   croaks] croaks, *1888*
586   stillness,] stillness; *1888*
588   hours,] hours *1888*
590   come—] come: *1888*
594   multitude,] multitude *1888*
596   objects] Objects   life,] life— *1888*
601   unite. What] unite—what   his] his, *1888*

With swarms of life, and worse than all, of men,
His fellow men, that are to him no more
815   Than to the Forest Hermit are the leaves
That hang aloft in myriads—nay, far less,
Far less for aught that comforts or defends
Or lulls or chears. Society is here:
The true community, the noblest Frame
820   Of many into one incorporate;
That must be looked for here; paternal sway,
One Household under God for high and low,
One family and one mansion; to themselves
Appropriate and divided from the world
825   As if it were a cave, a multitude
Human and brute, possessors undisturbed
Of this recess, their legislative Hall,
Their Temple, and their glorious dwelling-place.
    Dismissing therefore all Arcadian dreams,
830   All golden fancies of the golden age,
The bright array of shadowy thoughts from times
That were before all time, or are to be
When time is not, the pageantry that stirs
And will be stirring when our eyes are fixed
835   On lovely objects and we wish to part

A city where, if indifference to disgust
Yield not to scorn or sorrow, living Men   605
[814]   Are ofttimes to their fellow-men no more
Than to the Forest Hermit are the leaves
That hang aloft in myriads? Nay, far less,
For they protect his walk from sun and shower,
Swell his devotions with their voice in storms,   610
And whisper while the stars twinkle among them
His lullaby. From crowded streets remote,
Far from the living and dead wilderness
Of the thronged World, Society is here:
A true Community, a genuine frame   615
[820]   Of many into one incorporate;
That must be looked for here; paternal sway,
One household under God for high and low,
One family and one mansion; to themselves
Appropriate and divided from the world   620
[825]   As if it were a cave, a multitude
Human and brute, possessors undisturbed
Of this Recess, their legislative Hall,
Their Temple, and their glorious Dwelling-place.
    Dismissing therefore all Arcadian dreams,   625
[830]   All golden fancies of the golden Age,
The bright array of shadowy thoughts from times
That were before all time, or are to be
Ere time expire, the pageantry that stirs
And will be stirring when our eyes are fixed   630
[835]   On lovely objects and we wish to part

---

604   city] city, *1888*
605   Men] men *1888*
607   Forest] forest *1888*
608   Myriads? Nay] myriads; nay *1888*
613   wildnerness] Wildnerness *1888*
614   World] world   here:] here *1888*
615   Community,] community— *1888*
616   incorporate;] incorporate. *1888*
617   here;] here: *1888*
618   household] household,   God] God, *1888*
620   Appropriate] Appropriate,   world] world, *1888*
623   Recess,] Recess— *1888*
626   Age] age *1888*
630   And] Or   stirring] stirring, *1888*
631   objects] objects, *1888*

---

628   The original "are" has been accepted over the correction "is," which does not make
grammatical sense.

With all remembrance of a jarring world—
Give entrance to the sober truth; avow
That Nature to this favourite Spot of ours
Yields no exemption, but her awful rights,
840   Enforces to the utmost and exacts
Her tribute of inevitable pain,
And that the sting is added, man himself
For ever busy to afflict himself.
Yet temper this with one sufficient hope
845   (What need of more?): that we shall neither droop
Nor pine for want of pleasure in the life
Which is about us, nor through dearth of aught
That keeps in health the insatiable mind;
That we shall have for knowledge and for love
850   Abundance; and that, feeling as we do,
How goodly, how exceeding fair, how pure
From all reproach is the aetherial frame
And this deep vale, its earthly counterpart,
By which and under which we are enclosed
855   To breathe in peace; we shall moreover find
(If sound, and what we ought to be ourselves,
If rightly we observe and justly weigh)
The Inmates not unworthy of their home,
The Dwellers of the Dwelling.
                                        And if this
860   Were not, we have enough within ourselves,
Enough to fill the present day with joy
And overspread the future years with hope—
Our beautiful and quiet home, enriched
Already with a Stranger whom we love
865   Deeply, a Stranger of our Father's house,
A never-resting Pilgrim of the Sea,
Who finds at last an hour to his content
Beneath our roof; and others whom we love
Will seek us also, Sisters of our hearts,
870   And one, like them, a Brother of our hearts,
Philosopher and Poet, in whose sight

---

864   The "Stranger" is John Wordsworth, who stayed with WW and DW in Grasmere from the end of January through September, 1800.

869–870   The "Sisters of our hearts" are MH, SH, and Joanna Hutchinson; the "Brother" is STC.

With all remembrance of a jarring world—
Take we at once this one sufficient hope
[845] (What need of more?) : that we shall neither droop
Nor pine for want of pleasure in the life   635
Scattered about us, nor through dearth of aught
That keeps in health the insatiable mind;
That we shall have for knowledge and for love
[850] Abundance; and that, feeling as we do,
How goodly, how exceeding fair, how pure   640
From all reproach is yon etherial vault
And this deep Vale, its earthly counterpart,
By which and under which we are enclosed
[855] To breathe in peace; we shall moreover find
(If sound, and what we ought to be ourselves,   645
If rightly we observe and justly weigh)
The Inmates not unworthy of their home,
The Dwellers of their Dwelling.
                                        And if this
[860] Were otherwise, we have within ourselves
Enough to fill the present day with joy   650
And overspread the future years with hope—
Our beautiful and quiet home, enriched
Already with a Stranger whom we love
[865] Deeply, a Stranger of our Father's House,
A never-resting Pilgrim of the Sea,   655
Who finds at last an hour to his content
Beneath our roof; and others whom we love
Will seek us also, Sisters of our hearts,
[870] And One, like them, a Brother of our hearts,
Philosopher and Poet, in whose sight   660

---

632 world—] world, *1888*
633 Take] —Take *1888*
634 (What] What   more?) :] more? *1888*
637 mind;] mind. *1888*
638 That] —That *1888*
639 Abundance;] Abundance,   that,] that   do,] do *1888*
641 etherial vault] ethereal vault, *1888*
647 Inmates] inmates *1888*
650 joy] joy, *1888*
651 hope—] hope, *1888*
653 Stranger] stranger *1888*
654 Stranger] stranger   House] house *1888*
657 roof; and] roof. And *1888*
659 One] one *1888*

These mountains will rejoice with open joy.
Such is our wealth: O Vale of Peace, we are
And must be, with God's will, a happy band!
875   But 'tis not to enjoy, for this alone
That we exist; no, something must be done.
I must not walk in unreproved delight
These narrow bounds and think of nothing more,
No duty that looks further and no care.
880   Each Being has his office, lowly some
And common, yet all worthy if fulfilled
With zeal, acknowledgement that with the gift
Keeps pace a harvest answering to the seed.
Of ill advised ambition and of pride
885   I would stand clear, yet unto me I feel
That an internal brightness is vouchsafed
That must not die, that must not pass away.
Why does this inward lustre fondly seek
And gladly blend with outward fellowship?
890   Why shine they round me thus, whom thus I love?
Why do they teach me, whom I thus revere?
Strange question, yet it answers not itself.
That humble Roof, embowered among the trees,
That calm fire side—it is not even in them,
895   Blessed as they are, to furnish a reply
That satisfies and ends in perfect rest.
Possessions have I, wholly, solely mine,
Something within, which yet is shared by none—
Not even the nearest to me and most dear—
900   Something which power and effort may impart.
I would impart it; I would spread it wide,
Immortal in the world which is to come.

---

885   WW corrected "to" to "unto," the reading accepted here to preserve the meter.

These Mountains will rejoice with open joy.
Such is our wealth: O Vale of Peace, we are
And must be, with God's will, a happy Band!
　　Yet 'tis not to enjoy that we exist,
[876] For that end only; something must be done.　　　665
I must not walk in unreproved delight
These narrow bounds and think of nothing more,
No duty that looks further and no care.
[880] Each Being has *his* office, lowly some
And common, yet all worthy if fulfilled　　　　　670
With zeal, acknowledgment that with the gift
Keeps pace a harvest answering to the seed.
Of ill-advised Ambition and of Pride
[885] I would stand clear, but yet to me I feel
That an internal brightness is vouchsafed　　　675
That must not die, that must not pass away.
Why does this inward lustre fondly seek
And gladly blend with outward fellowship?
[890] Why do *They* shine around me, whom I love?
Why do they teach me, whom I thus revere?　　680
Strange question, yet it answers not itself.
That humble Roof, embowered among the trees,
That calm fire-side—it is not even in them,
[895] Blest as they are, to furnish a reply
That satisfies and ends in perfect rest.　　　　685
Possessions have I that are solely mine,
Something within, which yet is shared by none—
Not even the nearest to me and most dear—
[900] Something which power and effort may impart.
I would impart it; I would spread it wide,　　690
Immortal in the world which is to come.

661　Mountains] mountains *1888*
662　Such]—Such　　　wealth:] wealth!　　　Peace,] Peace　*1888*
663　Band!] Band. *1888*
665　done.] done: *1888*
667　bounds] bounds, *1888*
668　further] further, *1888*
669　*his*] his *1888*
679　me,] me *1888*
682　Roof,] Roof *1888*
683　fire-side—] fireside, *1888*
687　within,] within　　　none—] none, *1888*
688　dear—] dear, *1888*
689　impart.] impart; *1888*
690　it;] it,　　　wide,] wide: *1888*
691　come.] come—*1888*

I would not wholly perish even in this,
Lie down and be forgotten in the dust,
905   I and the modest partners of my days,
Making a silent company in death.
It must not be, if I divinely taught
Am privileged to speak as I have felt
Of what in man is human or divine.
910   While yet an innocent little-one, a heart
That doubtless wanted not its tender moods,
I breathed (for this I better recollect)
Among wild appetites and blind desires,
Motions of savage instinct, my delight
915   And exaltation. Nothing at that time
So welcome, no temptation half so dear
As that which [urged] me to a daring feat.
Deep pools, tall trees, black chasms, and dizzy crags—
I loved to look in them, to stand and read
920   Their looks forbidding, read and disobey,
Sometimes in act, and evermore in thought.
With impulses which only were by these
Surpassed in strength, I heard of danger met
Or sought with courage, enterprize forlorn,
925   By one, sole keeper of his own intent,
Or by a resolute few, who for the sake
Of glory fronted multitudes in arms.
Yea, to this day I swell with like desire;
I cannot at this moment read a tale
930   Of two brave Vessels matched in deadly fight

917 "urged" was supplied to fill a gap left in transcription.

Forgive me if I add another claim,
And would not wholly perish even in this,
Lie down and be forgotten in the dust,
[905]   I and the modest Partners of my days,   695
Making a silent company in death.
Love, Knowledge, all my manifold delights—
All buried with me without monument
Or profit unto any but ourselves.
[907]   It must not be, if I divinely taught   700
Be privileged to speak as I have felt
Of what in man is human or divine.
[910]   While yet an innocent Little-one, with a heart
That doubtless wanted not its tender moods,
I breathed (for this I better recollect)   705
Among wild appetites and blind desires,
Motions of savage instinct, my delight
[915]   And exaltation. Nothing at that time
So welcome, no temptation half so dear
As that which urged me to a daring feat.   710
Deep pools, tall trees, black chasms and dizzy crags
And tottering towers—I loved to stand and read
[920]   Their looks forbidding, read and disobey,
Sometimes in act, and evermore in thought.
With impulses that scarcely were by these   715
Surpassed in strength, I heard of danger met
Or sought with courage, enterprize forlorn,
[925]   By one, sole keeper of his own intent,
Or by a resolute few, who for the sake
Of glory fronted multitudes in arms.   720
Yea, to this hour I cannot read a Tale
[930]   Of two brave Vessels matched in deadly fight

---

692   claim,] claim— *1888*
695   days,] days *1888*
696   death.] death; *1888*
697   Knowledge] knowledge   delights—] delights, *1888*
699   ourselves.] ourselves! *1888*
700   I] I,   taught] taught, *1888*
703   Little-one] little one *1888*
707   instinct,] instinct *1888*
710   feat.] feat, *1888*
711   chasms] chasms,   crags] crags, *1888*
712   towers—] towers: *1888*
714   act,] act *1888*
715   impulses] impulses, *1888*
717   courage, enterprize forlorn,] courage; enterprise forlorn *1888*
722   Vessels] vessels   fight] fight, *1888*

And fighting to the death, but I am pleased
More than a wise Man ought to be; I wish,
I burn, I struggle, and in soul am there.
But me hath Nature tamed and bade me seek
935   For other agitations or be calm,
Hath dealt with me as with a turbulent stream—
Some Nurseling of the Mountains which she leads
Through quiet meadows after it has learned
Its strength and had its triumph and its joy,
940   Its desperate course of tumult and of glee.
That which in stealth by nature was performed
Hath Reason sanctioned. Her deliberate Voice
Hath said, "Be mild and love all gentle things;
Thy glory and thy happiness be there.
945   Yet fear (though thou confide in me) no want
Of aspirations which have been—of foes
To wrestle with and victory to complete,
Bounds to be leapt and darkness to explore.
That which enflamed thy infant heart—the love,
950   The longing, the contempt, the undaunted quest—
These shall survive, though changed their office, these
Shall live; it is not in their power to die."
Then farewell to the Warrior's deeds, farewell
All hope, which once and long was mine, to fill
955   The heroic trumpet with the muse's breath!
Yet in this peaceful Vale we will not spend
Unheard-of days, though loving peaceful thoughts;

And fighting to the death, but I am pleased
More than a wise man ought to be; I wish,
Fret, burn, and struggle, and in soul am there.   725
But me hath Nature tamed and bade to seek
[935]   For other agitations or be calm,
Hath dealt with me as with a turbulent stream—
Some nursling of the mountains which she leads
Through quiet meadows after he has learnt   730
His strength and had his triumph and his joy,
[940]   His desperate course of tumult and of glee.
That which in stealth by Nature was performed
Hath Reason sanctioned. Her deliberate Voice
Hath said, "Be mild and cleave to gentle things;   735
Thy glory and thy happiness be there.
[945]   Nor fear (though thou confide in me) a want
Of aspirations that *have* been—of foes
To wrestle with and victory to complete,
Bounds to be leapt, darkness to be explored.   740
All that inflamed thy infant heart—the love,
[950]   The longing, the contempt, the undaunted quest—
All shall survive, though changed their office, all
Shall live; it is not in their power to die."
        Then farewell to the Warrior's schemes, farewell   745
The forwardness of Soul which looks that way
Upon a less incitement than the cause
Of Liberty endangered, and farewell
That other hope, long mine, the hope to fill
[955]   The heroic trumpet with the Muse's breath!   750
Yet in this peaceful Vale we will not spend
Unheard-of days, though loving peaceful thoughts;

---

726   tamed] tamed, *1888*
727   agitations] agitations,   calm,] calm; *1888*
728   stream—] stream, *1888*
730   meadows] meadows, *1888*
734   sanctioned. Her] sanctioned; her *1888*
735   said, "Be mild] said; be mild,   things;] things, *1888*
737   fear (though] fear, though   me) a] me, a *1888*
738   *have*] have *1888*
739   with] with, *1888*
740   explored.] explored; *1888*
741   heart—] heart, *1888*
742   quest—] quest, *1888*
744   live;] live,   die."] die. *1888*
745   schemes] Schemes *1888*
746   Soul] soul *1888*
747   cause] Cause *1888*
752   thoughts;] thought, *1888*

A Voice shall speak, and what will be the Theme?
    On Man, on Nature, and on human Life,
960 Thinking in solitude, from time to time
    I feel sweet passions traversing my Soul
    Like Music; unto these, where'er I may,
    I would give utterance in numerous verse.
    Of truth, of grandeur, beauty, love, and hope—
965 Hope for this earth and hope beyond the grave—
    Of virtue and of intellectual power,
    Of blessed consolations in distress,
    Of joy in widest commonalty spread,
    Of the individual mind that keeps its own
970 Inviolate retirement, and consists
    With being limitless the one great Life—
    I sing; fit audience let me find though few!
       Fit audience find though few—thus prayed the Bard,
    Holiest of Men. Urania, I shall need
975 Thy guidance, or a greater Muse, if such

959–1048 These lines were published with *The Excursion* in 1814 as a Prospectus to *The Recluse*. For helpful suggestions concerning WW's allusions here, see *Prose*, III, 11–12.

972–973 WW quotes from Milton's invocation to his muse, Urania, in *Paradise Lost*, VII, 30–31.

[958] A Voice shall speak, and what will be the Theme?
          On Man, on Nature, and on Human Life,
[960] Musing in Solitude, I oft perceive   755
          Fair trains of imagery before me rise,
          Accompanied by feelings of delight
          Pure, or with no unpleasing sadness mixed;
          And I am conscious of affecting thoughts
          And dear remembrances, whose presence soothes   760
          Or elevates the Mind, intent to weigh
          The good and evil of our mortal state.
          To these emotions, whencesoe'er they come,
          Whether from breath of outward circumstance,
          Or from the Soul, an impulse to herself,   765
[963] I would give utterance in numerous Verse.
          Of Truth, of Grandeur, Beauty, Love, and Hope,
          And melancholy Fear subdued by Faith,
          Of blessed consolations in distress,
          Of moral strength, and intellectual power,   770
[968] Of joy in widest commonalty spread,
          Of the individual Mind that keeps her own
          Inviolate retirement, subject there
          To Conscience only, and the law supreme
          Of that Intelligence which governs all—   775
[972] I sing; "fit audience let me find though few!"
             So prayed, more gaining than he asked, the Bard,
          Holiest of Men. Urania, I shall need
[975] Thy guidance, or a greater Muse, if such

---

753   Voice] voice   Theme] theme *1888*
754–860   *In the Preface to* The Excursion, *1814, these lines are printed in italics and enclosed in
quotation marks. All the editions here collated except 1845 (and its reprints) and 1849 adopt the italics, but
to avoid confusion all citations are printed in roman. The quotation marks have been deleted from the reading
text, but are shown in the collations.*
754   On] "On *1814–1832* 'On *1836–1849*   Life,] Life *1814, 1820* Lif *1827 but corrected
to* Life *in Vol. V, issued separately as* Excursion, *1827*
755   Solitude] solitude *1836–1849, 1888*
763   To]—To *1814–1849, 1888*
765   Soul,] Soul— *1814–1849, 1888*   herself,] herself— *1836–1849, 1888*
766   Verse] verse *1836–1849, 1888*
767   Of]—Of *1814*   Hope,] Hope— *1814–1832*
768   Faith,] Faith; *1814–1849, 1888*
769   blessed] blessed *1888*   distress,] distress; *1814–1849, 1888*
770   power,] power; *1814* Power; *1820Ex–1849, 1888*
771   spread,] spread; *1814–1849, 1888*
775   all—] all; *1814–1832*
776   sing;] sing:— *1814–1849, 1888*   *single quotes 1827–1849*
777   So] "So *1827, 1832*   Bard,] Bard— *1845–1849, 1888*
778   Men.] Men.— *1814–1836*   Holiest of Men.] In holiest mood. *1845–1849, 1888*

Descend to earth or dwell in highest heaven!
For I must tread on shadowy ground, must sink
Deep, and, aloft ascending, breathe in worlds
To which the Heaven of heavens is but a veil.
980   All strength, all terror, single or in bands,
That ever was put forth in personal forms—
Jehovah, with his thunder, and the quire
Of shouting angels and the empyreal throne—
I pass them unalarmed. The darkest Pit
985   Of the profoundest Hell, chaos, night,
Nor aught of [   ] vacancy scooped out
By help of dreams can breed such fear and awe
As fall upon us often when we look
Into our minds, into the mind of Man,
990   My haunt and the main region of my song.
Beauty, whose living home is the green earth,
Surpassing the most fair ideal Forms
The craft of delicate spirits hath composed
From earth's materials, waits upon my steps,
995   Pitches her tents before me when I move,
An hourly Neighbour. Paradise and groves
Elysian, fortunate islands, fields like those of old
In the deep ocean—wherefore should they be
A History, or but a dream, when minds
1000   Once wedded to this outward frame of things
In love, find these the growth of common day?
I, long before the blessed hour arrives,

Descend to earth or dwell in highest heaven!   780
For I must tread on shadowy ground, must sink
Deep, and, aloft ascending, breathe in worlds
To which the heaven of heavens is but a veil.
[980]   All strength, all terror, single or in bands,
That ever was put forth in personal form—   785
Jehovah, with his thunder, and the choir
Of shouting Angels and the empyreal thrones—
I pass them unalarmed. Not Chaos, not
[985]   The darkest pit of lowest Erebus,
Nor aught of blinder vacancy scooped out   790
By help of dreams can breed such fear and awe
As fall upon us often when we look
Into our Minds, into the Mind of Man,
[990]   My haunt and the main region of my Song.
Beauty—a living Presence of the earth,   795
Surpassing the most fair ideal Forms
Which craft of delicate Spirits hath composed
From earth's materials—waits upon my steps,
[995]   Pitches her tents before me as I move,
An hourly neighbour. Paradise and groves   800
Elysian, Fortunate Fields—like those of old
Sought in the Atlantic Main—why should they be
A history only of departed things,
Or a mere fiction of what never was?
For the discerning intellect of Man,   805
[1000]   When wedded to this goodly universe
In love and holy passion, shall find these
A simple produce of the common day.
I, long before the blissful hour arrives,

---

782   Deep,] Deep—*1814–1849, 1888*
784   strength,] strength—*1814–1849, 1888*
785   form—] form; *1814–1832*
786   Jehovah,] Jehovah—*1814–1849, 1888*
787   Angels] Angels, *1814–1849, 1888*   thrones—] thrones, *1814*
788   them] them, *1814*
790   vacancy] vacancy—*1814–1832* vacancy, *1836–1849, 1888*
791   dreams] dreams, *1814–1832* dreams—*1836–1849, 1888*
793   Man,] Man—*1836–1849, 1888*
794   haunt] haunt, *1814–1849, 1888*   Song.] song. *1836–1849* song *1888*
795   Beauty—]—Beauty—*1814–1849, 1888*
797   composed] compose *1845*
798   steps,] steps; *1814–1849, 1888*
800   Paradise] Paradise, *1814–1849, 1888*
802   Main—] Main, *1814–1832*
809   I,]—I, *1814–1849, 1888*

Would sing in solitude the spousal verse
Of this great consummation, would proclaim—
1005 Speaking of nothing more than what we are—
How exquisitely the individual Mind
(And the progressive powers perhaps no less
Of the whole species) to the external world
Is fitted; and how exquisitely too—
1010 Theme this but little heard of among men—
The external world is fitted to the mind;
And the creation (by no lower name
Can it be called) which they with blended might
Accomplish: this is my great argument.
1015 Such [   ] foregoing, if I oft
Must turn elsewhere, and travel near the tribes
And fellowships of men, and see ill sights
Of passions ravenous from each other's rage,
Must hear humanity in fields and groves
1020 Pipe solitary anguish, or must hang
Brooding above the fierce confederate storm
Of Sorrow, barricadoed evermore
Within the walls of cities—may these sounds
Have their authentic comment, that even these
1025 Hearing, I be not heartless or forlorn!
Come, thou prophetic Spirit, Soul of Man,
Thou human Soul of the wide earth that hast
Thy metropolitan Temple in the hearts

1010 WW appears to have omitted this line accidentally, then added it in transcription.
1015 In leaving this gap, WW rejected the reading of Prospectus, MS. 1: "pleasant haunts."

Would chaunt in lonely peace the spousal verse   810
Of this great consummation; and by words
Which speak of nothing more than what we are
Would I arouse the sensual from their sleep
Of Death, and win the vacant and the vain
To noble raptures; while my voice proclaims   815
[1006]   How exquisitely the individual Mind
(And the progressive powers perhaps no less
Of the whole species) to the external World
Is fitted; and how exquisitely, too—
[1010]   Theme this but little heard of among Men—   820
The external World is fitted to the Mind;
And the creation (by no lower name
Can it be called) which they with blended might
Accomplish: this is our high argument.
[1015]   Such grateful haunts foregoing, if I oft   825
Must turn elsewhere, to travel near the tribes
And fellowships of men, and see ill sights
Of madding passions mutually inflamed,
Must hear Humanity in fields and groves
[1020]   Pipe solitary anguish, or must hang   830
Brooding above the fierce confederate storm
Of sorrow, barricadoed evermore
Within the walls of Cities—may these sounds
Have their authentic comment, that even these
[1025]   Hearing, I be not downcast or forlorn!   835
Come, thou prophetic Spirit, that inspirest
The human Soul of universal earth,
Dreaming on things to come, and dost possess
A metropolitan Temple in the hearts

---

810   chaunt] chant *1827–1849*, *1888*
811   consummation; and] consummation:—and, *1814–1849*, *1888*
812   are] are, *1814–1849*, *1888*
819   fitted;] fitted:—*1814–1849*, *1888*   too—] too, *1814–1832*
820   Men—] Men, *1814–1832* men—*1836–1849*, *1888*
824   Accomplish:] Accomplish:—*1814–1849*, *1888*
825   Such]—Such *1814–1849*, *1888*
826   elsewhere,] elsewhere—*1814–1849*, *1888*
828   inflamed,] inflamed; *1814–1849*, *1888*
830   anguish,] anguish; *1814–1849*, *1888*
833   Cities—] Cities; *1814–1832* cities—*1836–1849*, *1888*
834   comment,] comment,—*1814–1832* comment; *1836–1849*, *1888*   that] that, *1814*
835   forlorn!] forlorn!—*1845–1849*, *1888*
836   Come, thou]—Come thou *1814–1820Ex*—Descend, *1827–1849*, *1888*   Spirit,]
Spirit *1820Ex* Spirit! *1827–1849*, *1888*   inspirest] inspir'st *1814*, *1827*, *1836–1849*, *1888*
838   come,] come; *1814–1849*, *1888*
839   Temple] temple *1836–1849*, *1888*

Of mighty Poets; unto me vouchsafe
1030   Thy guidance, teach me to discern and part
Inherent things from casual, what is fixed
From fleeting, that my verse may live and be
Even as a Light hung up in heaven to chear
Mankind in times to come! And if with this
1035   I blend more lowly matter—with the thing
Contemplated describe the mind and man
Contemplating, and who and what he was,
The transitory Being that beheld
This vision, when and where and how he lived,
1040   With all his little realities of life—
Be not this labour useless. If such theme
With highest things may [   ], then, Great God,
Thou who art breath and being, way and guide,
And power and understanding, may my life
1045   Express the image of a better time,
More wise desires and simple manners; nurse
My heart in genuine freedom; all pure thoughts
Be with me and uphold me to the end!

1042   WW appears to have rejected the reading of Prospectus, MS. 2, "[?mingle]," and left
a gap for the verb; instead of supplying a word, however, he subsequently revised the line.

[1029] Of mighty Poets; upon me bestow   840
        A gift of genuine insight, that my Song
        With star-like virtue in its place may shine,
        Shedding benignant influence, and secure
        Itself from all malevolent effect
        Of those mutations that extend their sway   845
        Throughout the nether sphere! And if with this
[1035] I mix more lowly matter—with the thing
        Contemplated describe the Mind and Man
        Contemplating, and who and what he was,
        The transitory Being that beheld   850
[1039] This Vision, when and where and how he lived—
        Be not this labour useless. If such theme
        May sort with highest objects, then, dread Power,
        Whose gracious favour is the primal source
        Of all illumination, may my Life   855
[1045] Express the image of a better time,
        More wise desires, and simpler manners; nurse
        My heart in genuine freedom; all pure thoughts
        Be with me; so shall thy unfailing love
        Guide, and support, and cheer me to the end!   860

---

840 Poets;] Poets: *1836–1849*
841 insight,] insight; *1814–1849, 1888*
842 shine,] shine; *1814–1832*
843 influence,] influence,—*1814–1832*   secure] secure, *1814–1832, 1845–1849*
844 Itself] Itself, *1814–1849*
846 sphere!] sphere!—*1814–1849, 1888*
847 matter—] matter; *1814–1849, 1888*
848 Contemplated] Contemplated, *1814–1849, 1888*   and] of *1820Ex–1827*
849 Contemplating,] Contemplating; *1814–1820Ex, 1836–1849, 1888*   who] who, *1814–1849, 1888*   was,] was—*1836–1849*
851 Vision,] Vision,—*1814–1832* Vision; *1836–1849* Vision;—*1888*   where] where, *1814–1849, 1888*   lived—] lived;—*1814–1849* lived; *1888*
853 then,] then—*1836–1849, 1888*   Power,] Power! *1836–1849, 1888*
855 illumination,] illumination—*1836–1849, 1888*
857 manners;] manners; *1814–1849, 1888*
858 freedom;] freedom:—*1814–1849, 1888*
859 me;] me;—*1814–1849, 1888*
860 end!] end!" *1814–1832* end!' *1836–1849*

The Early Manuscripts

Transcriptions and Photographic Reproductions

MS. A

MS. A (DC MS. 58) preserves a continuous fair copy of ll. 192–457 in a version earlier than that of MS. B; it is in Wordsworth's hand, except for ll. 278–321, in Mary Wordsworth's. A single sheet survives, measuring 41.3 by 32.7–33 centimeters; the paper is white wove, untrimmed folio, countermarked at the center 1801. A small piece of white laid paper, measuring 13.7 by 11.5 centimeters, has been stitched onto the left side of the sheet; it bears an incomplete watermark: part of a horn-in-shield over traces of elaborate cursive capitals *GR*, or possibly *GL*. (The only other examples of this paper among the manuscripts and letters of the Wordsworth circle appear to be letters from Thomas Clarkson to Wordsworth, 1 March 1805, and from his wife, Catherine, to Wordsworth, 15 March 1805; both letters are in the Wordsworth Library at Dove Cottage.) Wordsworth folded the large sheet accordion-style, forming three columns on each side. He wrote on both sides of the sheet, a total of six columns. The piece of stitched-on paper holds ll. 379–397, and beneath it the sheet is blank. Photographs of the entire sheet, recto and verso, are followed by photographs broken down to half columns of text, each with a facing transcription.

MS. A dates from the summer of 1806, and its writing marks the final stage of preparation of the MS. B text. Mary Wordsworth used the revised MS. A as her copy text when she began to transcribe the first part of MS. B. Originally MS. A may have contained an additional sheet or sheets, but how much of *Home at Grasmere* it carried cannot be conjectured.

Editorial line numbers in MS. A correspond to the numbering of MS. B; bracketed numbers denote lines not present in MS. B but assumed to be part of the B text.

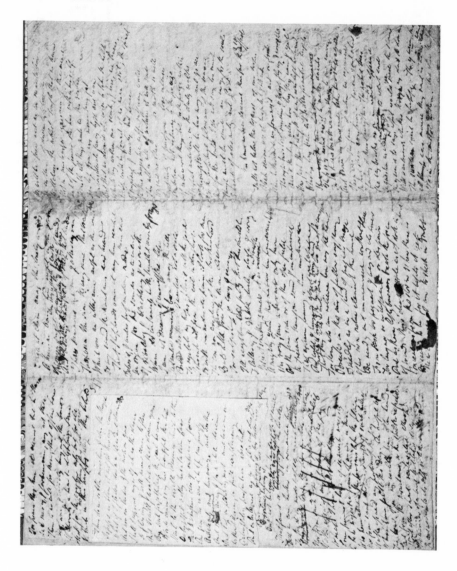

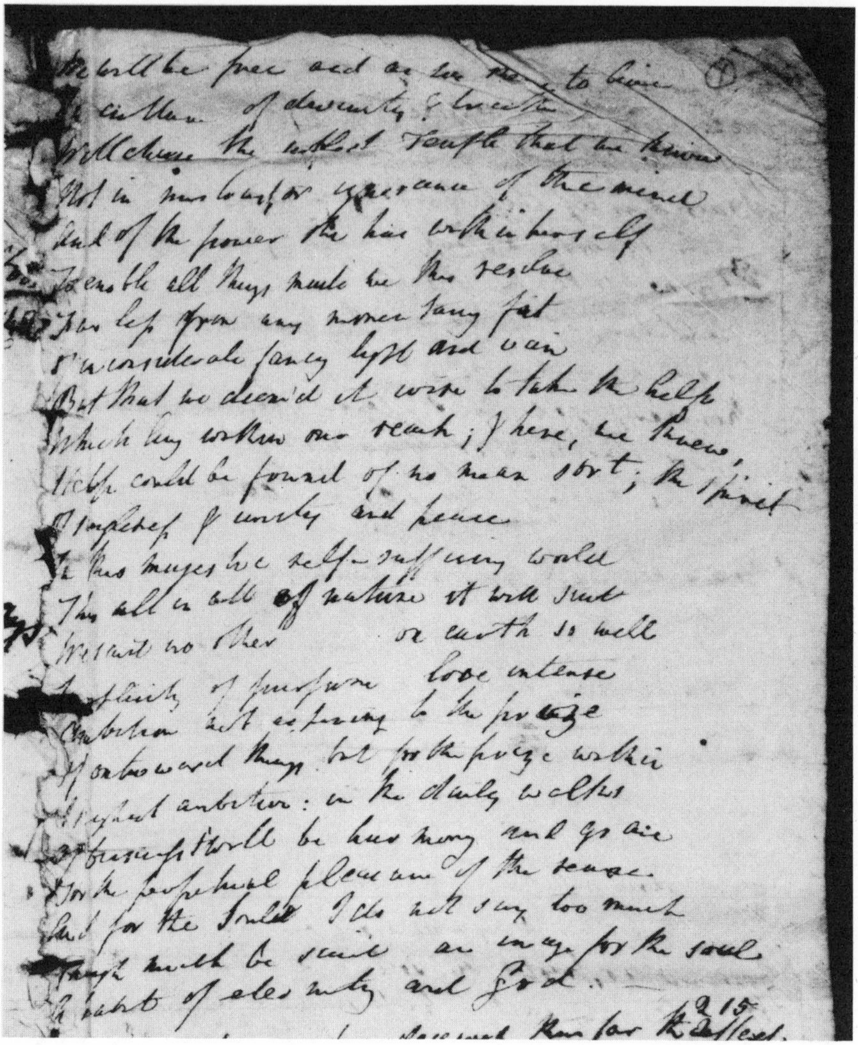

[192]   We will be free and as we mean to live
[193]   In culture of divinity & truth
[194]   Will chuse the noblest Temple that we know
[195]   Not in mistrust, or ignorance of the mind
[196]   And of the power she has within herself
[197]   To enoble all things made we this resolve

                       i ⎱

[198]   Far less from any momentary f[?]⎰t
[199]   Of inconsiderate fancy light and vain
[200]   But that we deem'd it wise to take the help
[201]   Which lay within our reach; & here, we knew,

      l ⎱

[202]   He[?]⎰p could be found of no mean sort; the spirit
[203]   Of singleness & unity and peace
[204]   In this majestic self-sufficing world

             of ⎱

[205]   This all in all [?]⎰ nature it will suit
[206]   We said no other   on earth so well
[207]   Simplicity of purpose love intense

                     ⎰ize

[208]   Ambition not aspiring to the pr⎰aise
209   Of outoward things but for the prize within
210   Highest ambition: in the daily walks
211   Of business t'will be harmony and grace
212   For the perpetual pleasure of the sense
213   And for the Sould I do not say too much
214   Though much be said an image for the soul

                    ⎰G

215   A habit of eternity and ⎰god. —   215

---

215   WW's line numbers in the right-hand margin are late; his count includes lines added in correction. Subsequent notes explain apparent discrepancies in numbering. The numbers at the tops of the columns of the MS., indicating their order, were probably entered by GW or another early editor.

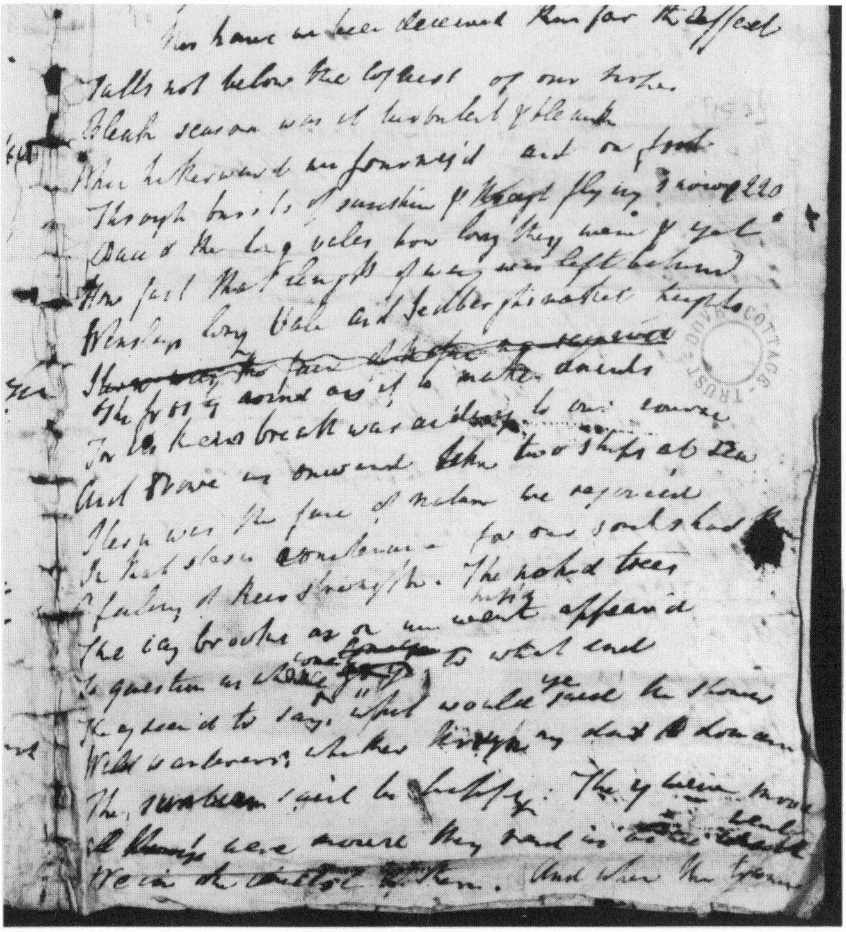

216   Nor have we been deceived thus far th effect
217   Falls not below the loftiest of our hopes
218   Bleak season was it turbulent & bleank
219   When hitherward we journey'd and on foot
220   Through bursts of sunshine & ~~through~~ flying snows   220
221   Paced the long vales how long they were & yet
222   How fast that length of way was left behind

        ⌠V
223   Wensleys long ⌡vale and Sedberghs naked heights
        Stern was the face of Nature we rejoiced
224   The frosty wind as if to make amends
225   For its keen breath was aiding to our course

                        li⌉
226   And drove us onward [?as]⌡ ke two ships at sea
227   ~~Stern was the face of nature we rejoiced~~
228   In that stern countenance for our souls had there
229   A feeling of their strength. The naked trees

                            pass'd
230   The icy brooks as on we went appear'd

                            ~~come ye~~
                        come [?y]
                        ⌠nce
231   To question us whe⌡re ~~go ye~~ to what end
                                    ye
232   They seem'd to say, "what would said the shower
233   Wild wanderers: whither through my dark domain
234   The sunbeam said be happy: They were mov'd

                                    went
                            ⌠ went
235   all things were movd they round us as we ⌡[?]
236   We in the midst of them. And when the trance

---

218   The penciled number in brackets at the end of the line, visible in the photographic reproduction, was added by an earlier editor, perhaps GW. This is l. 152 in previously published texts of the poem, based on MS. D.

220   The last letter of "snows" is obscured by an ink blot.

223/224   L. 227, entered here by mistake, was canceled at once.

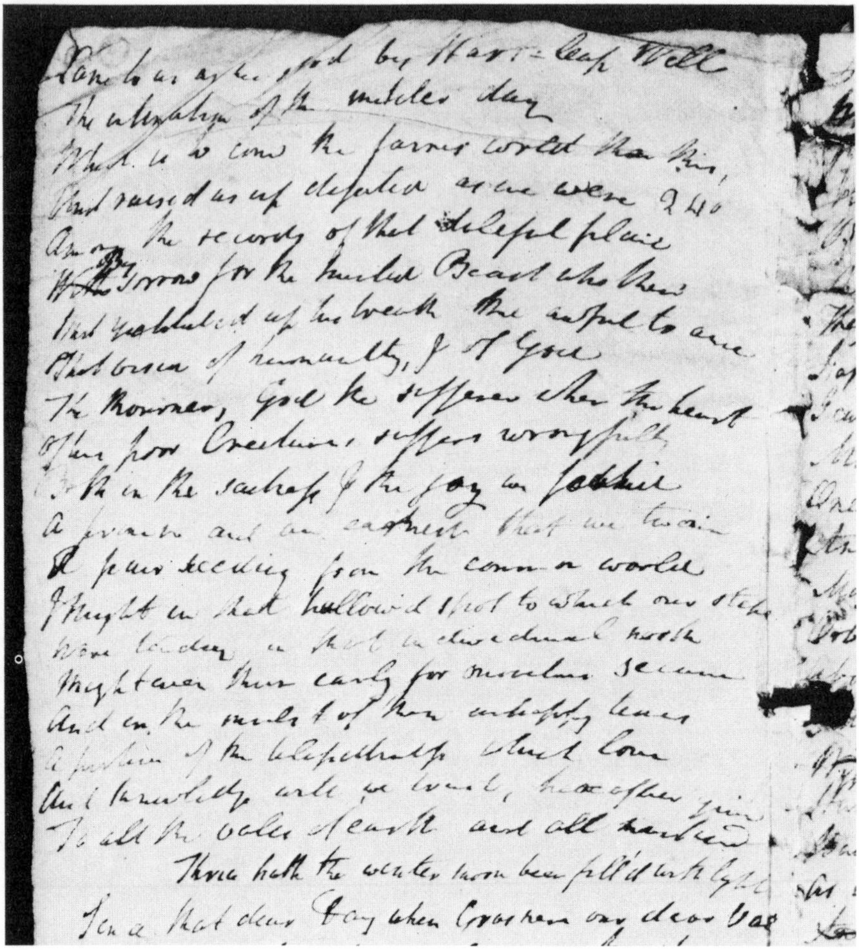

237   Came to us as we stood by Hart-leap Well
238   The intimation of the milder day
239   Which is to come the fairer world than this,
240   And raised us up dejected as we were   240
241   Among the records of that doleful place
          By
242   ~~With~~ sorrow for the hunted Beast who there
243   Had yieldeded up his breath the awful trance
244   That vision of humanity, & of God
245   The Mourner, God the sufferer when the heart
246   Of his poor Creatures suffers wrongfully
                            {ound
247   Both in the sadness & the joy we f{elt
                    rn}
248   A promise and an ea[?]}est that we twain
249   A pair seceding from the common world
250   Might in that hallow'd spot to which our steps
251   Were tending in that individual nook
252   Might even thus early for ourselves secure
253   And in the midst of those unhappy times
254   A portion of the blessedness which love
255   And knowledge will, we trust, hereafter give
256   To all the vales of earth and all mankind
257   Thrice hath the winter moon been fill'd with light
258   Since that dear Day when Grasmere our dear Vale

Received us, bright and solemn was the sky
That gladen'd with a perfect welcoming 2.
that led us to our threshold to our home
within a home, what was to be, and soon
Our love within a love then darkness came
composing darkness with its quiet load
of full contentment in a little shed
Disturb'd uneasy in its self so mild
And wondering at its new inhabitants
It loves us now this vale so beautiful
Begins to love us by a sullen storm

And found us faithful through the gloom I hear
The Poet mutter'd his prelusive songs
with cheerful heart an eager bird of joy
Away the silence of the woods & hills
Silent to any cheerfulness, nor tried
With all their shepherds—

                    But the gates of
Are open'd churlish .... given leave
That she should enter to one day
Perhaps for many several days to come 2.

259   Received us, bright and solemn was the sky
260   That [? faced] with a passionate welcoming   260
                                    a
261   And led us to our threshold to ~~our~~ home
262   Within a home, what was to be, and soon,
263   Our love within a love then darkness came
264   Composing darkness with its quiet load
265   Of full contentment in a little shed
266   Disturb'd uneasy in itself as seem'd
                            i }
267   And wondering at [?a]} ts new inhabitants
268   It loves us now this vale so beautiful
269   Begins to love us by a sullen storm
[270]   Two months unwearied of severest storm
       ~~It put us to the proof two months of storm~~
[271]   It put the temper of our minds to proof
272   And found us faithful through the gloom & heard
273   The Poet mutter his prelusive Songs
                        heart
274   With chearful‸an unknown voice of joy
275   Among the silence of the woods & hills
276   Silent to any gladsomeness of sound
                                    ⎰is
                        ~~But the storms~~ ⎱~~are [?over]~~
277   With all their Shepherds.—
                            But the gates of Spring
                    ⎰Winter
278   Are open'd churlish ⎱Spring hath given leave
                        this [?soft]
279   That she should entertain for‸one ~~sweet~~ day

280   Perhaps for many genial days to come   280

---

278   MW's hand begins, and runs through l. 321.

281   *His guests & make them happy. They are pleas'd*
      With the mild summons inmates tho' they be
282   *But most of all the birds that haunt the flood*
283   *With the mild summons inmates tho' they be*
284   *Of winter's household they are jubilant*
285   *This day who droop'd or seem'd to droop so long*
286   *They shew their pleasure & shall I do less*

           r
287   *Happie{st of happy tho' I be, like them*
288   *I cannot take possession of the sky*
289   *Mount with a thoughtless impulse & wheel there*
290   *One of a mighty multitude whose way*
291   *And motion is a harmony & dance*
292   *Magnificent behold them how they shape*
293   *Orb after orb their course still round & round*
           area
294   *Above the ~~circuit~~ of the lake their own*
295   *Adopted region girding it about*
    In   *yet therewith*
296   *~~With~~ wanton repetition ~~high & low~~*
        {that
297   With {[?] large circle evermore renew'd
298   *Hundreds of ~~lesser circles~~ high & low*
           curves & circlets
299   *Backwards & forwards progress intricate*
300   *As if one Spirit was in all & sway'd*   300
       {T   *tis done*
301   *~~And sway'd~~ {their indefatigable flight*
302   *Ten times or more I fancied it had ceased*
303   *And lo the vanish'd company again*

281/282   MW first skipped l. 282.
295   The MS. is worn away here, but parts of the missing letters can be seen.
297   Included in WW's line count.

And to the water's ...
... list again, clear their wings
faint, faint at first & then an eager ...
... in a moment & as faint again
they tempt the Sun to sport among their plumes
they tempt the water & the gleaming ice
to shew them a fair image of themselves
Their own fair forms upon the glimmering plain
... more soft & fair as they descend
... to touch them up again aloft
... as swiftly and ... a flash of speed
... if they scorn'd both resting place & rest
... for this day belongs to their rejoicing
Not upon one alone hath been bestow'd
the blessed with many onward looking thoughts
this sunshine & mild air Oh surely these
are grateful not the happy quires of love
Thine own peculiar favorites sweet spring 320
that sport among green leaves so blithe a train
But two are missing, two, a lonely pair
Of mute the like were a ... why are these not here
... down all ... why are they not here

304   *Ascending list again I hear their wings*
305   *Faint, faint at first & then an eager sound*
306   *Pass'd in a moment & as faint again*
307   *They tempt the Sun to sport among their plumes*
308   *They tempt the water & the gleaming ice*
                                    thems⎫
309   *To shew them a fair image 'tis ima⎰elves*
310   *Their own fair forms upon the glimmering plain*
311   *Painted more soft & fair as they descend*
312   *Almost to touch then up again aloft*
                        with a sally and
313   *Up ~~higher to the region with~~ a flash of speed*
314   *As if they scorn'd both resting place & rest*
315   *Spring! for this day belongs to Thee rejoice*
316   *Not upon me alone hath been bestow'd*
317   *Me blest with many onward looking thoughts*
318   *This sunshine & mild air oh surely these*
319   *Are grateful not the happy quires of love*
320   *Thine own peculiar family sweet spring*   320
321   *That sport among green leaves so blithe a train*
322   But two are missing, two, a lonely pair
323   Of milkwhite swans ah why are these not here
324   These above all ah why are they not here

---

320   The "l" of "family" has been crossed.

325	To share in this days pleasure. From afar
326	They came like Emmas & myself to live
327	Together here in peace and solitude
328	Chusing this valley they who had the choice
329	Of the whole world: we saw them ⎰day⎱ by by day
330	Through those two months of unrelenting storm
331	Conspicuous in the centre of the Lake
332	Their safe retreat we knew them well I guess
333	That the whole valley knew them but to us
334	They were more dear than may be well believed
335	Not only for their beauty and their still
336	And placid way of life & faithful love
337	Inseparable not for these alone
338	But ~~also~~ that ou⎰thei⎱r ⎰st⎱[?]ate‸resembled ours so much
339	They also having chosen this abode
340	They strangers & we strangers they a pair 340
341	And we a solitary pair like them.
342	They should not have departed: many days
343	Ive looked for them in vain nor on the wing
344	⎰H⎱have seen them nor ⎰in⎱on that small open space
345	Of blue unfrozen water where they lodg'd
346	And liv'd so long in quiet side by side
347	Companions partners consecrated Friends
348	Shall we behold them yet another year

---

339 Included in WW's line count.
347 Included in WW's line count.

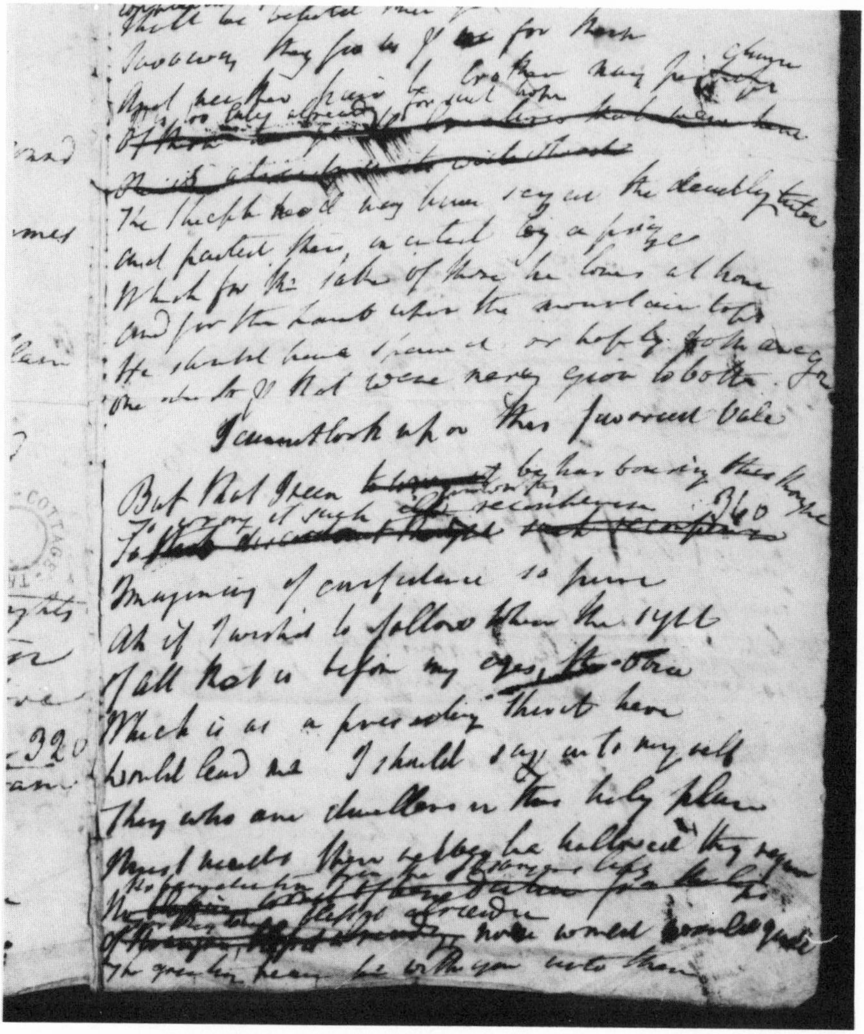

349   Surviving they for us & {we / us for them

                                chance

350   And neither pair be broken nay per~~haps~~

351   It is too late already for such hope

        ~~Of those two gentle Creatures that were here~~

        ~~One is already in its widowhood~~

               h }

352   The Sheeph[?]} erd may have seized the deadly tube

                      { by

353   And parted them incited }[?] a prize

354   Which for the sake of those he loves at home

355   And for the Lamb upon the mountain tops

356   He should have spared or haply both are gone

357   One death & that were mercy giv'n to both.

358   I cannot look upon this favoreed Vale

                         by harbouring this thought

359   But that I seem ~~to wrong it~~

             unworthy

      To wrong it such ~~ill~~ recompense   360

360   To ~~that discordant thought such recompense~~

361   Imagining of confidence so pure

362   Ah if I wish'd to follow Where the sight

363   Of all that is before my eyes, the voice

364   Which is as a presiding Spirit here

365   Would lead me I should say unto myself

366   They who are dwellers in this holy place

367   Must needs themselves be hallowed they require

368   No benediction from the Strangers lips

        No ~~blessing word of benediction from the lips~~

        For they are blessd already

369   Of ~~Strangers, blessd already~~, none would would give

370   The greeting peace be with you unto them

351, 351/352   The revision was made before WW's line count; new l. 351 is included in his count.

For peace they have it cannot but be theirs
And mercy, I forbear, ... may not there
There is no call for them; that office love
Performs ... priority beyond the bounds
Of ... a heart-delighting store
Not for the creature only but for all
Which in this happy valley they behold

Thus do we ... the miseries, & when the thought
Is passed we blame it not for having come
What if I floated down a pleasant stream
And now am landed & the motion gone
Shall I reprove myself ah no the stream
Is flowing & will never cease to flow
And I shall float upon that stream again
By such forgetfulness the soul becomes
Words cannot say how beautiful then how
Hail to the visible ... hail to thee
Delightful valley habitation fair
And to whatever else of outward form
Can give us inward help can purify
And elevate and harmonize and soothe
And ... away for a while dissever
And lap in pleasing rest and bear us on
Without ... in full complacency
Contemplating perfection absolute
And entertained as in a placid sleep

371   For peace they have it cannot but be theirs
372   And mercy, & forbearance; nay not these
373   There is no call for these; that office Love
374   Performs, & charity beyond the bonds
375   Of Charity a heart-delighting Love
376   Not for the creature only but for all
               {about them}
377   Which is {[?] [?]} them love for everything
                      Valley
378   Which in this happy   they behold
                 {o   377
379   Thus do we so {tthe ourselves & when the thought
380   Is pass'd we blame it not for having come
381   What if I floated down a pleasant stream   380
382   And now am landed & the motion gone
383   Shall I reprove myself ah no the stream
384   Is flowing, & will never cease to flow
385   And I shall flooat upon that stream again
        y}
386   B[?]} such forgetfulness the soul becomes
                              {i
387   Words cannot say how beautiful then ha{ l
388   Hail to the visible Presence hail to thee
389   Delightful valley habitation fair
390   And to whatever else of outward form
391   Can give us inward help can purify
392   And elevate and harmonize and soothe
             overcome
393   And ~~steal~~ away & for a while deceive
394   And lap in pleasing rest and bear us on
395   Without desire, in full complacency
396   Contemplating perfection absolute
397   And entertained as in a placid sleep   396
             betray'd by tenderness [?]

---

377   WW apparently did not include this line in his count at l. 378, but recognized his error and included it in the corrected count at l. 400.

379–397   These lines are written on a flap of paper, the top of which has been sewn to the folio sheet. The space beneath the flap, on the sheet itself, is blank.

                                      r⎫
                But neither lull'd nor lost nor l⎰apt away
                      ⎰D   l⎫
                  [? ⎱disso[?]⎰ved] betrayd
398   But not betray'd by tenderness of mind
                              wholly overlookd
399   That fear'd or ~~utterly forgot~~ the truth
400   Did we come hither in romantic hope   400
                                  majesty
401   To find in midst of so much loveliness   ~~400~~
                    Love purest
                ~~Nothing but~~ love the persons like the place
                Nor from such hope or aught of such belief
                Hath issu'd any portion of the joy
                Which I have feltt this day.
402   Love purest Love of so much majesty
403   A Like majestic frame of mind in those
404   Who here abide the persons like the place
405   Nor from such [?]hope or aught of such belief
406   Hath issued any portion of the joy
407   Which I have feltt this day. An awful Voice
408   Tis true I in my walks have often heard
409   Sent from the mountains or the shelter'd fields
410   Shout after shout reiterated whoop
411   In manner of a bird that takes delight
412   In answering to its self or like a Hound

400–401   The correction of the line count probably reflects the inclusion of l. 377.
401/402   These four lines were deleted directly after transcription and replaced by ll. 402–407.

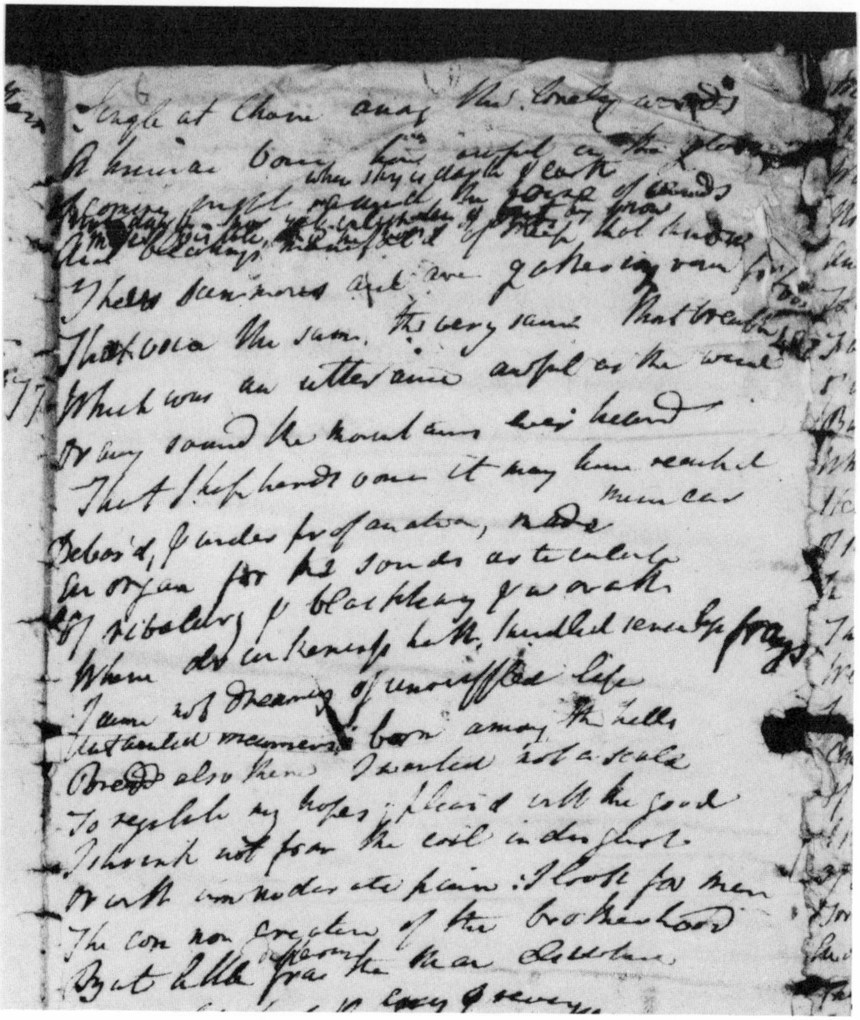

413 Single at Chace among the lonely woods
414 A human Voice how awful in the gloom
                 when sky is dark & earth
415 Of coming night amid the noise of winds
416   Not dark nor yet enlighten'd but by snow
417   Made visible amid the noise of winds
                           ow⎫
418 And bleatings manifold of sheep that kn[?]⎰
419 Their summons and are gathering round for food
420 That voice the same the very same that breath   420
421 Which was an utterance awful as the wind
422 Or any sound the mountains ever heard
423   That Shepherds voice it may have reachd
                       mine ear
424 Debas'd, & under profanation, made
425 An organ for the sounds articulate
426 Of ribaldry & blasphemy & wrath
                               ⎧frays
427 Where drunkenness hath kindled senseless ⎰[?]
428 I came not dreaming of unruffled life
429 Untainted manners: born among the hills
       ⎧d
430 Bre⎰ad also there I wanted not a scale
431 To regulate my hopes; pleas'd with the good
432 I shrink not from the evil in disgust
433 Or with immoderate pain: I look for man
434 The common creature of the brotherhood
          differing
435 But little from the Man elsewhere

416–417 Included in WW's line count.

436 For selfishness & envy & revenge
437 Ill neighbourhood pity that this should be
438 Flatterey & double dealing strife & wrong.

                                in truth
439   Yet is it something gained it is ~~indeed~~
440 A mighty gain that Labour here preserves   440
441 His rosy face a Servant only here
442 Of the fire side or of the open field
443 A Freeman therefore sound & unimpaired
444 That extreme penury is here unknowwn
445 And cold & hunger's abject wretchedness
446   Mortal to body & the heav'n born mind
447 That they who want are not too great a weight
448 For those who can relieve here may the heart
449 Breathe in the air of fellow suffering
450 Dreadless as in a kind of fresher breeze
451 Of her own native element the hand
452 Be ready and unwearied without plea
453 From task too frequent & beyond its power
454 For languor or indifference or despair
455 And as these lofty barriers break the force
456 Of winds this deep vale as it doth in part
457 Conceal us from the storm so here there is
     Or seems to be for it befits it yet
     Newcomer as I am to speak in doubt

457ff.   After l. 457 in MS. B, MW copied only "Or seems to be" then struck the words out, but these two lines were probably included in the MS. B line count; the first line number in MS. B is 470, at l. 468.

MS. R

MS. R (DC MS. 28) consists of three gatherings, K, L, and M, of an inter-leaved copy of Coleridge's *Poems*, 1796. The paper of the printed pages of the volume is white wove, watermarked J. WHATMAN; the interleaves are of white laid paper watermarked with the figure of Britannia enclosed in a circle surmounted by a crown, and countermarked COLES 1795. Pages of the printed book measure 16.1–16.7 by 10.2–10.5 centimeters; the interleaves measure 16.9 by 10.5 centimeters.

The only other gatherings of this particular volume to survive, gatherings D and E, constitute DC MS. 30, which contains a mass of blank verse from which Wordsworth drew for *Michael*, lines 73–77, 154–158, and 170–203, and for *The Prelude* (1805), VII, 698–704, VIII, 223–238, and XII, 185–203. (Much of this material Wordsworth transcribed in fair copy into the note-book that his sister subsequently used for her journal during 1802 [DC MS. 31]; de Selincourt printed most of it in *PW*, II, 479–482). Sections of a similar volume of Coleridge's 1796 *Poems* survive in the British Library's MS. Ashley 408, which comprises printed pages 141–176 and their interleaves; Coleridge used the volume for revisions toward his 1797 edition.

The three gatherings of MS. R are intact save for K, which lacks three leaves—pages 129–130, 133–134, and 139–140; the leaf bearing pages 173–174 has been partially torn away. The interleaves are conjugate, except for the single leaves tipped in at the middle of each gathering, at pages 130/131, 132/133 or 134/135, 138/139 or 140/141, and 142/143. The volume was inter-leaved before it was sewn together, and may originally have belonged to Coleridge, but the only fact that can be proved is that these gatherings were in Wordsworth's possession by 1800, the date of his earliest entries.

Wordsworth made three sets of entries, Mary Wordsworth two. His are: (1) a draft on page 131 and the recto of the succeeding interleaf of *The Waggoner*, II, 145–148 and 155–166, and III, 1–2; (2) drafts between pages 132 and 174 with interleaves of lines 471–859 of *Home at Grasmere*, in a version earlier than that of MS. B, and of lines which became *Excursion*, IV, 332–372; and (3) a draft on the interleaf facing page 175 and continued on page 176, a blank leaf, of part of the Preface to *Lyrical Ballads*, 1800 (see *Prose*, I, 186–187, and *Chronology: MY*, p. 626). Mary Wordsworth's entries are: (1) a prose passage on the interleaf facing page 132, below the *Waggoner* draft and with the leaf inverted, similar in meaning and phrasing to *The Prelude* (1850), IV, 354–370 (these lines first appear in verse in a revision of *The Prelude*, MS. D [Verse MS. 23, at Dove Cottage], dating from 1832 or later);

and (2) two drafts of lines incorporated into the MS. D text of *Home at Grasmere*:
along the outer edge of page 131, a version of MS. D lines 75–77; across the
interleaf facing page 167 and across page 167 itself, a version of MS. D, lines
597–606. The third of Wordsworth's drafts represents work from 1800 ante-
cedent to the second edition of *Lyrical Ballads*. His first draft supplies part of a
text of *The Waggoner* almost identical with that of the first full version of the
poem, which dates from 1806. His second set of drafts appears to be close in
date to MSS. A and B of *Home at Grasmere*; they belong with MS. A to the
final work of preparation for the MS. B text in 1806. (See the Introduction,
Section II, above.) Both Mary Wordsworth's entries probably date from
1831–1832, since they preserve revisions for *The Prelude* and *Home at Grasmere*
apparently of that period. It is, however, also possible that Wordsworth did
not initially regard the prose draft as work toward *The Prelude*; the impressions
of solitude it records are related to *Home at Grasmere*. Reed suggests that this
entry also dates from 1806 (*Chronology: MY*, p. 658).

MS. R is unusual among Wordsworth's extant manuscripts in that it
preserves so much of his early drafting. The transcription of it thus poses
special difficulty, for Wordsworth drafted rapidly and often illegibly here, on
absorbent paper with a bad pen, and he sometimes omitted parts of words
or whole words in his haste. It has not always been possible to decipher his
hand, but the facing photographs allow the reader to make his own attempts.

The photographs and transcriptions which follow reproduce only the pages
of MS. R carrying work toward *Home at Grasmere* and two passages originally
intended for the poem, one of which became *Excursion*, IV, 332–372, while
the other remained unpublished. The following list gives the contents of these
pages ("i" designates an interleaf):

131	MS. D, 75–77	145	MS. B, 698–700,
132	MS. B, 542–546		673–677, 693–698
132/135 i^r	MS. B, 533–541	146	MS. B, 697–708,
132/135 i^v	MS. B, 609–629		690–692
135	MS. B, 642–645	146/147 i^r	MS. B, 681–704
136	MS. B, 491–495	146/147 i^v	MS. B, 704–719
136/137 i^r	MS. B, 471–491	148	*Exc.*, IV, 338–341
136/137 i^v	MS. B, 490–511	148/149 i^r	MS. B, 745–752;
137	MS. B, 517–528		*Exc.*, IV, 332–345
138	MS. B, 512–532	148/149 i^v	*Exc.*, IV, 346–364
138/141 i^r	MS. B, 565–585	149	*Exc.*, IV, 355–359
138/141 i^v	MS. B, 586–606	150	*Exc.*, IV, 359–363
141	MS. B, 646–658	150/151 i^r	*Exc.*, IV, 332–356
142	MS. B, 652–660	150/151 i^v	*Exc.*, IV, 360–372;
143	MS. B, 659–667		MS. B, 722–733
144	MS. B, 647, 690–	151	MS. B, 720–722
	692, 673–677	152	MS. B, 807–811
144/145 i^r	MS. B, 646–667	152/153 i^r	MS. B, 734–752
144/145 i^v	MS. B, 668–690	152/153 i^v	MS. B, 807–818

154/155 i^r	MS. B, 753–776	162/163 i^v	Unpublished draft
154/155 i^v	MS. B, 777–798	163	Unpublished draft
155	MS. B, 786–789	164	Unpublished draft
156	MS. B, 803–806	164/165 i^r	MS. B, 829–848
156/157 i^r	MS. B, 799–819	164/165 i^v	MS. B, 849–850
156/157 i^v	MS. B, 820–853	165	Unpublished draft
157	MS. B, 838–841	166/167 i^v	MS. D, 597–606
160/161 i^v	MS. B, 764–781	167	MS. D, 601–602
161	MS. B, 838–839	172/173 i^v	Unpublished draft
162	Unpublished draft	174	Unpublished draft
162/163 i^r	MS. B, 854–859	174/175 i^r	MS. B, 829–858

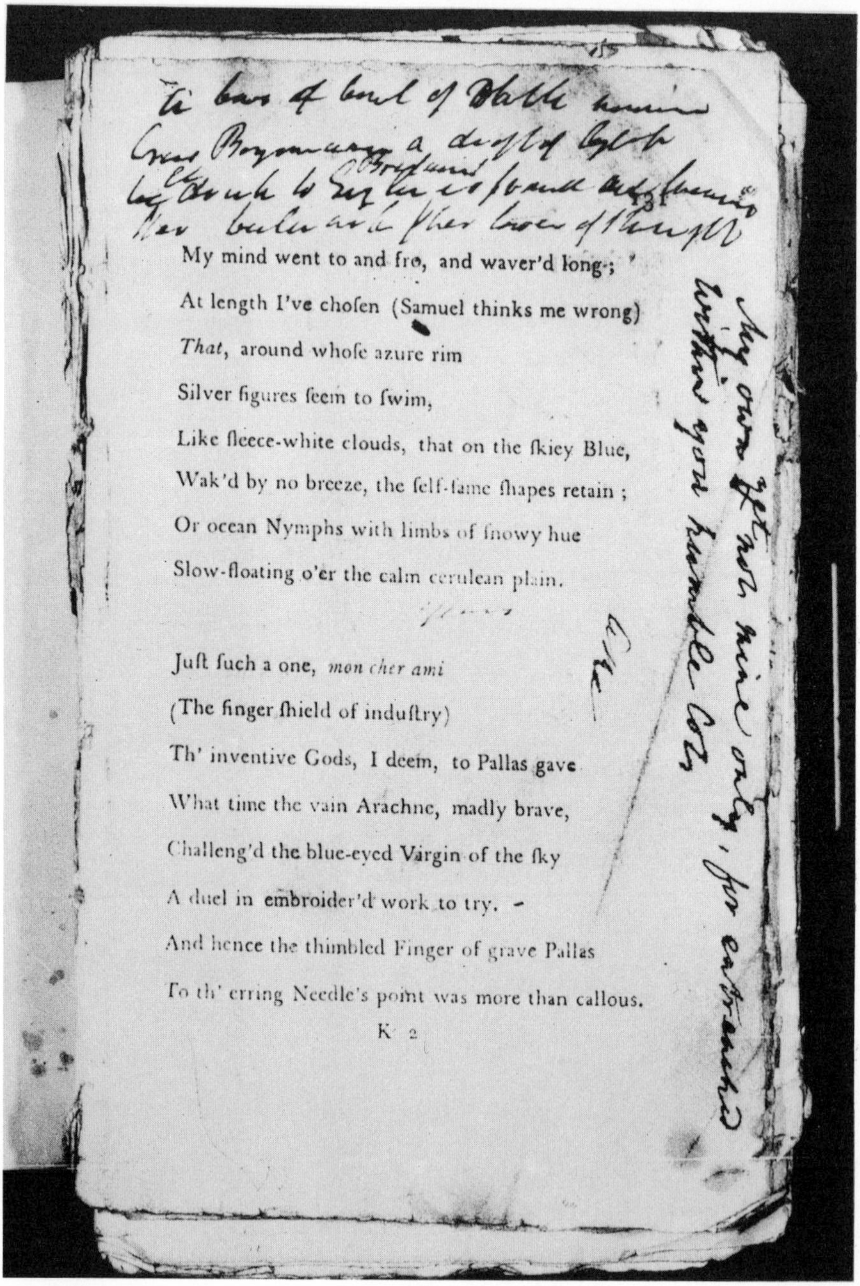

My mind went to and fro, and waver'd long;
At length I've chosen (Samuel thinks me wrong)
That, around whose azure rim
Silver figures seem to swim,
Like fleece-white clouds, that on the skiey Blue,
Wak'd by no breeze, the self-same shapes retain;
Or ocean Nymphs with limbs of snowy hue
Slow-floating o'er the calm cerulean plain.

Just such a one, *mon cher ami*
(The finger shield of industry)
Th' inventive Gods, I deem, to Pallas gave
What time the vain Arachne, madly brave,
Challeng'd the blue-eyed Virgin of the sky
A duel in embroider'd work to try.
And hence the thimbled Finger of grave Pallas
To th' erring Needle's point was more than callous.

K 2

[D, 75-77]

My own & not mine only, for entrenched
Within yon humble Cot
yet

  The draft at the top of the page is 1806 work for *The Waggoner*. The floating "amen" was probably written to test a new pen, as was frequently the Wordsworths' custom.

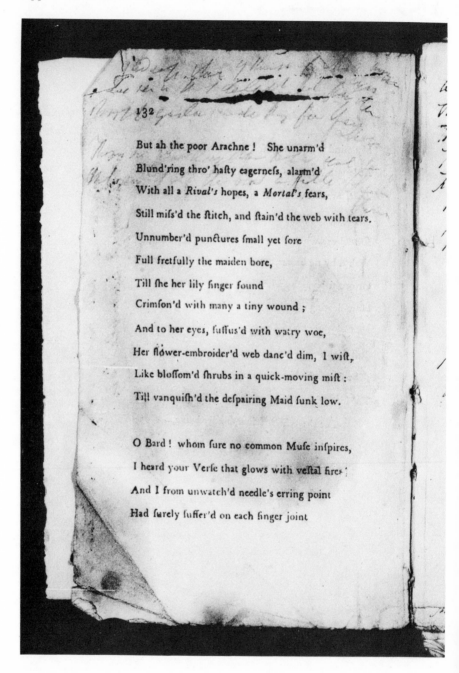

132

But ah the poor Arachne! She unarm'd

Blund'ring thro' hasty eagerness, alarm'd

With all a *Rival's* hopes, a *Mortal's* fears,

Still miss'd the stitch, and stain'd the web with tears.

Unnumber'd punctures small yet sore

Full fretfully the maiden bore,

Till she her lily finger found

Crimson'd with many a tiny wound;

And to her eyes, suffus'd with watry woe,

Her flower-embroider'd web danc'd dim, I wist,

Like blossom'd shrubs in a quick-moving mist:

Till vanquish'd the despairing Maid sunk low.

O Bard! whom sure no common Muse inspires,

I heard your Verse that glows with vestal fires:

And I from unwatch'd needle's erring point

Had surely suffer'd on each finger joint

[B, 542–546]

No sadness when I think of what mine
                              these
                      eyes
Have seen in that delightful family
Bright garland made they for their
                              fathers [?brow]
Those six [?fair] daughters budding yet not one
N)
Of ſot one of all the band a full blown
                              flower

   These lines in pencil appear to follow on from those WW drafted in pencil on the facing recto (the interleaf); the work is probably a revision of lines entered on the interleaf which formerly faced p. 138.

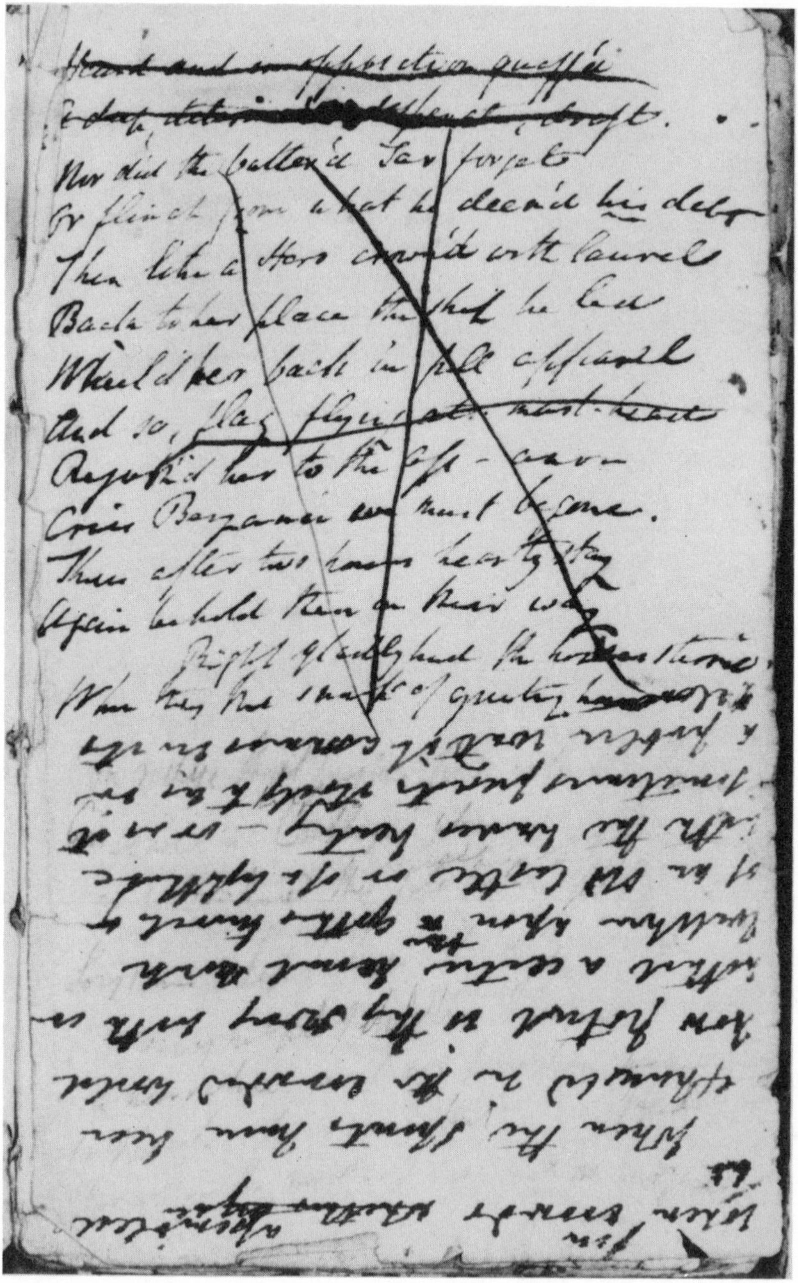

~~Heard and in affectation quaffd~~

~~...~~

Nor did the batter'd Tar forget

Or flinch from what he deem'd his duty

Then like a Hero crown'd with laurels

Back to his place the shed he led

Wheel'd her back in full apparel

And so, ~~Nay flying at next heat~~

Repok'd her to the ess — care

Cries Benjamin we must be gone.

Thus after two hours hearty stay

Again behold them on their way

Right gladly had the ...
When they had ... of greeting ...

[remaining lines inverted and illegible]

Yon ridge that [?shouldering ?into ? ?]
     [?]
Conceals a Cottage where
       [?his] [? ? ?]
In widowhood the [? ? ?]
Long since & left him solitary [?]
Of many helpless children I begin
[?In] words which [? ? ? ?]
[? ? ?] but   I [?feel]
Though in the midst of sadness as might

Only the penciled lines on this page relate to *Home at Grasmere*; they are partly obscured by an inverted prose draft for *The Prelude*, 1850, IV, 354–370, written over them in ink. The draft on the other half of the page is 1806 work on *The Waggoner*.

                                    half way up the mountain side
That rises from behind your cottage, see
A clustering grove of firs a little one
And [...] twelve [...] smaller than it is [...]
Who dwells within [...] ere he [...] this year
Just three years younger than her eldest
Was planted by her husband & herself
For a convenient shelter which in storm
Their sheep might draw to & they knew it
[...] she for further shelter bear them food
In time of heavy snows. She then [...] years
[...] obedience to [...]
To [...] of her dear husband. [...] were not
An [...] a music for a sleep of woods
That shall be [...] the [...] voice of life
Shall speak of what is done among the fields
Done truly there or felt of solid good
But will [...] yet be sweet to those
More [...] more [...] their own [...]
The idle breath of [...] pipe allure
To [...] fancies [...] there such a
[...] of [...] flowing from the heart

half way up the mountain side
That rises from behind yon Cottage, see
A dusky grove of firs a little one

                              [?grove]
   seems   :⎱   ⎰e   ⎰Dame
And looks still smaller than it is ⎰ th⎱is ⎱[?grove]
                           ⎰o
   This learned I from the Dame [?wh⎱at] dwells below
Who dwells below ~~me~~ told me that this grove
                  she
   [?one]
Just ~~three~~ years younger than her eldest Boy
Was planted by her husband & herself
⎰For
⎱[?A] a convenient shelter which in storms
Their Sheep might draw to & they know it
                              well
⎰Said
⎱[?] She for thither do we bear them food
In time of heavy snow. She then began
   In fond obedience to
~~Following~~   ~~of~~ her private
                    thoughts
     ⎰speak
To ⎱[?talk] of her dead Husband: Is there not
An art a music & a stream of words
            fe⎱   acknowledgd
That shall be like⎰ the ~~very~~ voice of Life
⎰S
⎱Thall speak of what is done among the fields
                f⎱
Done truly there or felt or⎰ solid good
           ⎰yet   [?]
And real evil ⎱& be sweet withal
      grateful
More ~~winning~~ more harmonious than the
                        breath
           sweetest
The idle breath of ~~pastoral~~ pipe attuned
To pastoral fancies? Is there such a
                stream
Pure & unsullied flowing from the heart

The underlining in the sixth line may be connected with the revision. The large X has soaked through from the recto.

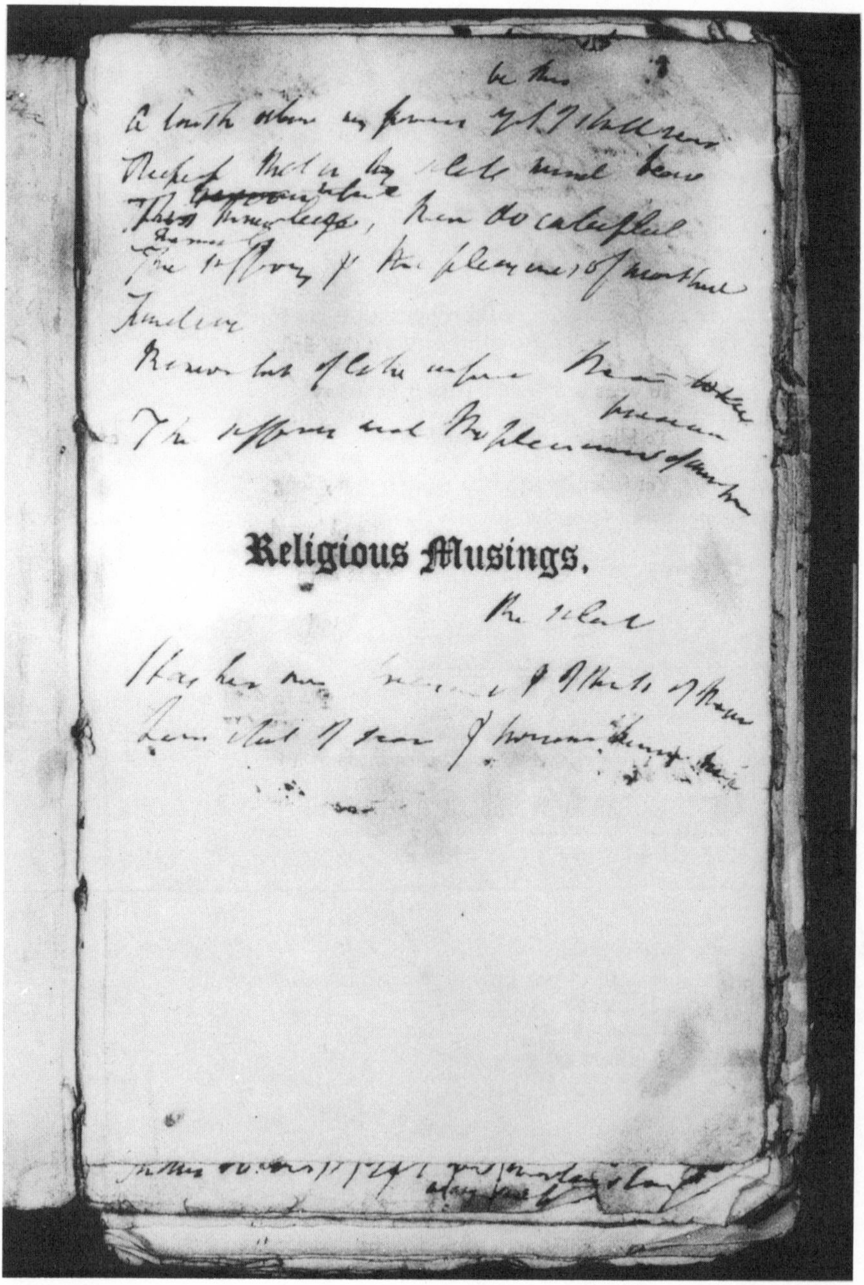
Religious Musings.

be this
A [?task] above my powers yet I shall [?rear]
        {th
Respect that in {my silent mind [?bears]
    human}
{[?These] [—?—]} [—?—]
{This [?knowledge], then do [?contemplate]
  [?Memorials]
The suffering & the pleasures of mankind
Finding
Renown but of like empire [?] ~~where~~
         presence
The suffering and the pleasures of mankind

    the silent
Has her own treasures & I think of them
          {kin
Love what I see & honour human{[?]d

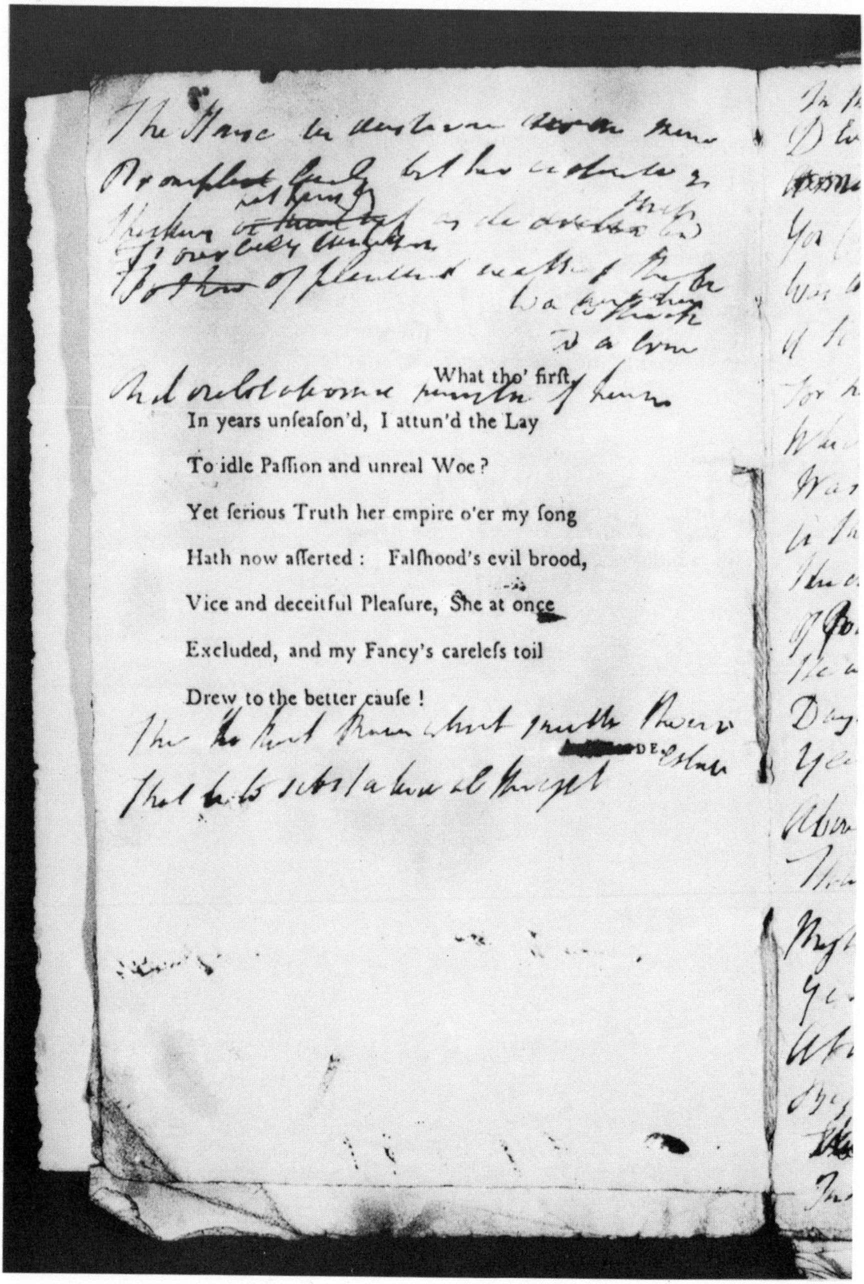
What tho' first,
In years unseason'd, I attun'd the Lay
To idle Passion and unreal Woe?
Yet serious Truth her empire o'er my song
Hath now asserted: Falshood's evil brood,
Vice and deceitful Pleasure, She at once
Excluded, and my Fancy's careless toil
Drew to the better cause!

                 no one⎫
The House industrious [?]⎬ [?more]
Prompt~~ed~~ lively but her industry
               [?that]
        not [?herself]
Shirking [~~?on~~ kindn~~e~~ss as [?do ?~~do~~ ?~~also~~] tend

  To over[?busy ?overlabour]   ⎧n
To ~~show~~ of [?pleasant] neatness tha⎨t
               to a neatness
             to thrift
               to a trim
And overlaboured purity of house

The the [?kind] [?known] which [?the ?oer]
               [?labour]
That to to substantial thrift

In his native valley dwelt

Dwelt and not long ago ... for I have heard

... the master of ... plot of hard ground

Yon Cottage with its tuft of sycamores

was his abode, a gentle natured ...

A scholar also ... the place where

for he found much delight in those few books

Which lay within his reach and ... their ...

Was by his fellow Dalesmen honour'd more

A shepherd and a tiller of the ground

Such was withal of health in his frame

Of body with a firm and ... course mind

... with his ... ... Child ...

Days that were seldom touch'd by ...

Years ... from large ... ...

... the common measure ... ...

That care ... men The wiser ... ...

... look on ... nature ... ...

Yet ... ...

... to understand its happiness

By little & by little ... ...

... ... Re ... ...

In his ... ...

[B, 471–491]

some few years past
~~within this Vale~~
In this his native valley dwelt a man
Dwelt and not long ago as I have heard
little ground
~~A man~~ the master of a^plot of Land
Yon Cottage with its tuft of sycamores
{his
Was {an abode, a gentle natur'd ~~M~~an
A Scholar also as the phrase is here
For he found much delight in those few books
Which lay within his reach and for this cause
Was by his Fellow-Dalesmen honour'd more
A Shepherd and a Tiller of the ground
{t {a
S{[?]udious withal & he{llthy in his frame
{B and of placid
Of {[?fr]ody ~~with a~~ just and ~~easy~~ mind
Consort & his saw
He with his ~~wife and~~ Children ~~livd~~
Days that were seldom touch'd by [~~?tribulation~~]
petty strife
safe
Years ~~free~~ from large misfortune, [~~?favored~~]
{~~long was~~ blessd
{[~~?~~]
was }
long [?]} blessd
Above the common measure & maintained
That course which Men the wisest and most
pure
Might look on with entire complacency
near }
in himself & [?him]} him weer there faults
Yet ~~were there faults & frailties~~ in
~~the hous~~e
At work to undermine its happiness
By little & by little. ~~On her part~~
Active prompt
{[~~?And~~]
{[~~?The~~] lively was the Huswife no
one more
Industrious, yet her industry
was such

And truly was the Housewife; in the scale
Were more industrious, yet her weakness lay
Was of that kind, tis said which tended more
To splendid rectitude, to a showy, even
And overlaboured purity of house
Than to substantial thrift. He, or his part
Perhaps of easy mixture was not free
From carelessness, & thus in course of time
There fault is far milder coloured part
With other care less obvious bigger
of worldly substance & distress of mind
Which to a thoughtful [...] had to them
And which he could not cure. O blessing
Few'd then, in haste of the heavy cloud!
Poor was in languid pleasure by sweet care
by thoughts of troubled [...] of the mind
[...]
[...]
[...]
Our work to effect
that what so had been weak enough to do
Was misery in remembrance he was born
By his inward thoughts & by the smile
of Wife and children then of his agony

[B, 490–511]

And lively was the Housewife; in the vale

None more industrious, &⌡ ᵉᵗ her industry

Was of that kind, tis ⌠said⌡ [?] which tended more

To splendid neatness to a shewy, trim

And overlaboured purity of house

Than to substantial thrift. He, on his part

Generous & easy minded was not free

From carelessness & thus in course of time

These joint infirmities combined perchance

With other cause less obvious brought

                decay

Of worldly substance & distress of mind

Which to a thoughtful man was hard to shun

                   ⌠o

And which he could not cure. A blo⌡mming Girl

             ⌠I

Serv'd them an ⌡inmate of the house, alas!

Poor now in tranquil pleasure he gave way

                  he became

To thoughts of troubled pleasure & the Maid

             the

A lawless suitor to the ~~Maid [?effect] was dire~~

         un ⌡

Yielded unworthily [?unhap]⌠happy Man

~~This did he without knowledg of himself~~

~~Dire was the effect~~

That which he had been weak enough to do

Was misery in remembrance: he was stung

        stung

By his inward thoughts & by the smils

Of Wife and children stung to agony

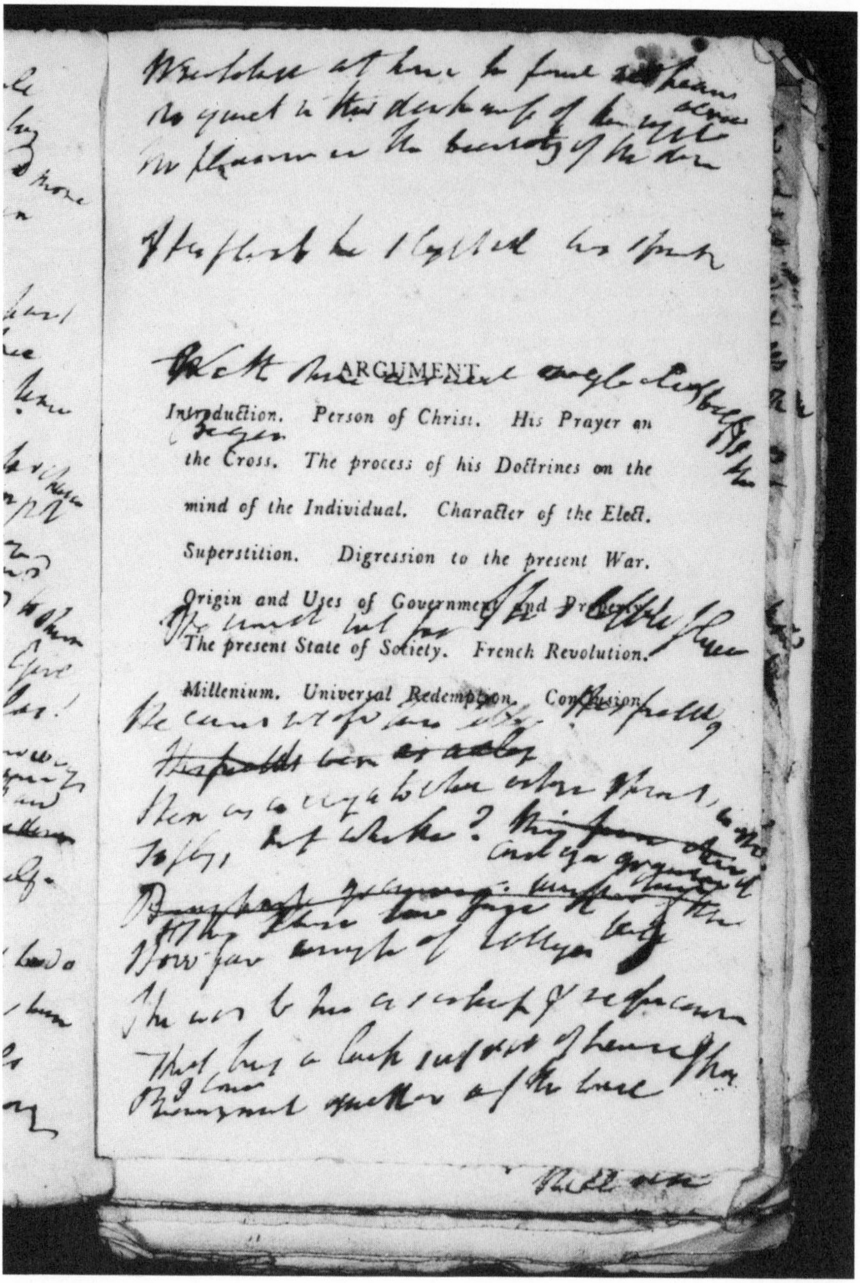

ARGUMENT

Introduction. Person of Christ. His Prayer on the Cross. The process of his Doctrines on the mind of the Individual. Character of the Elect. Superstition. Digression to the present War. Origin and Uses of Government and Property. The present State of Society. French Revolution. Millenium. Universal Redemption. Conclusion.

[B, 517–528]

Wretched at home he found no peace
                                    abroad
No quiet in the darkness of the night
No pleasure in the beauty of the day

His flock he slighted his spirit

⎰W
⎱[?In]ith [?shame] [?] neglected [?] & [?   ]
Began

He cared not for His little [?flock]
                         His field &
He cared not for his little
~~His fields were as a clog~~
Then as a clog a [?to ?whose] whose spirit wish
To fly, but whither? ~~this fair church~~
                    And yon gracious
                            church
~~Benignant gracious mother of the~~
                            Vale

   T⎰
   H⎱his [?Church] how fair
How [?pure] [?among ?h] of Cottages
She was to him a sickness & reproach
That has a look so full of peace & hope
      & love
Benignant mother of the Vale

These lines, which are drafts toward the version on 138, follow on from the work on 136/137 i, recto and verso.

His temper urg'd him not to seek re⌠l͏fief
Amid the noise of revellers nor from draught
Of lonely stupefaction, he himself
A rational   and suffering man
Was his own world without a resting-place
Wrecthed at home he had no peace abroad,
Rang'd through the mountains slept upon
                              the earth
Ask'd comfort of the open air & found
                  ⌠da
No quiet in the ⌡[?]rkness of the night
No pleasure in the beauty of the day
His flock he slighted his paternal fields
                            ⌠o
Were as a clog to him wh⌡[?]se Spirit wish'd
        but
To fly & whither? And yon gracious Church
                  ⌠so
That has a look ⌡of full of peace & hope
              ⌠beni   o ⌡
And love, ⌡[?deli]gnant M[?]⌡ther of the Vale
How fair amid her brood of Cottages
She was to him a sickness & reproach
I speak conjecturing from the little known
The much that to the last remained
                        unknown
But this is sure he died of his own grief
He could not bear the weight of
                        his own shame

These are revisions of drafts on 137.

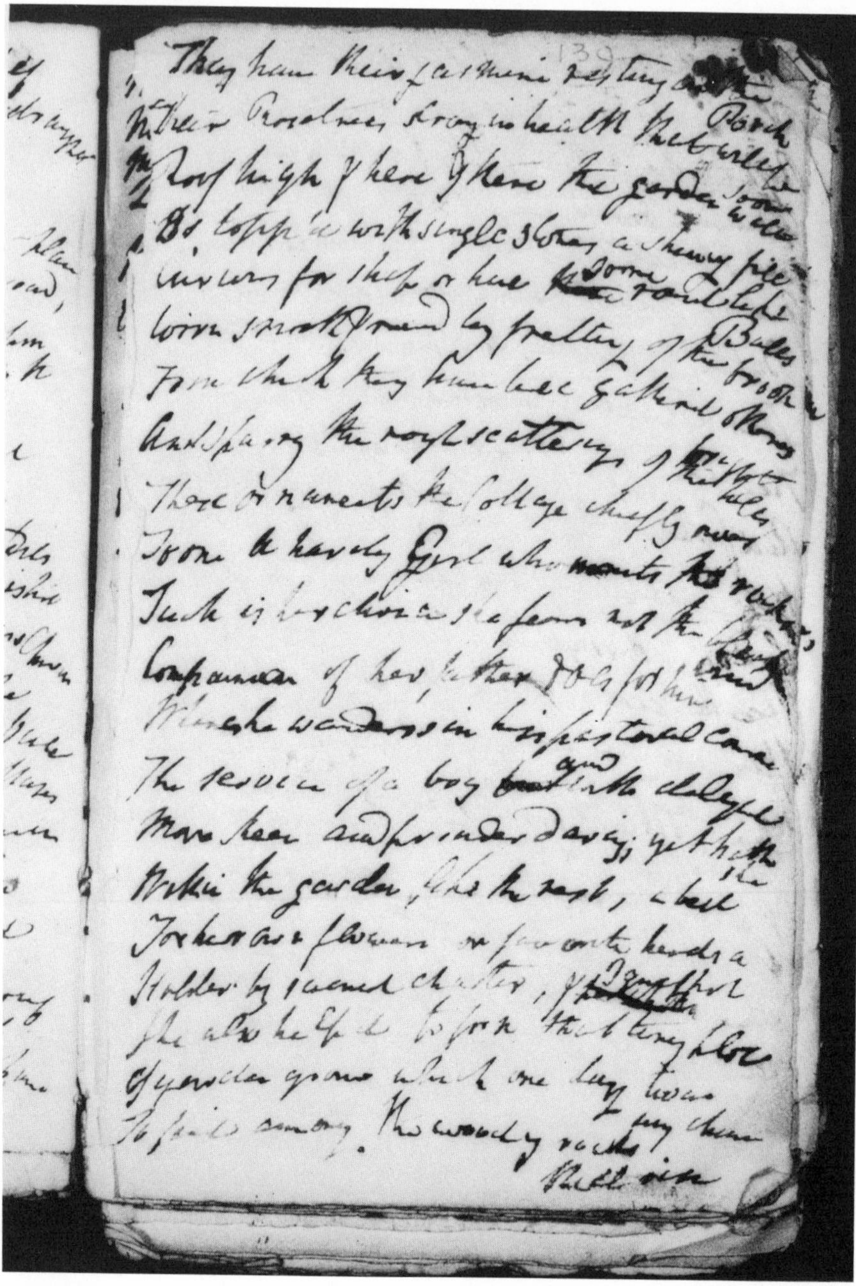
139
They have their jasmine resting on the
Their Rose-trees strong in health the Porch
Roof high & here & there the garden wall
Is topp'd with single stones a shewy file
Curious for shape or hue some round like
worn smooth & round by fretting of the brook
From which they have been gather'd others
And sparing the rough scattering of the hills
These ornaments the Cottage chiefly owes
To one a hardy Girl who mounts the rocks
Such is her choice she fears not the bleak wind
Companion of her father does for him
Where'er he wanders in his pastoral course
The service of a boy and with delight
More keen and prouder daring yet hath she
Within the garden like the rest a bed
For her own flowers or favorite herbs a
Holder by sacred charter & I guess that
She also help'd to frame that tiny plot
Of garden ground which one day 'twas my chance
To find among the woody rocks
that rise

[B, 565–585]

They have their jasmine resting on the
                                    Porch
Their Rosetrees strong in health that will be
                                        soon
Roof high & here & there the garden wall
  { I
  {[?T]s topp'd with single stones a shewy file
                        some
Curious for shape or hue ~~these~~ round like
                                        Balls
Worn smooth & round by fretting of the brook
From which they have been gather'd others
                                    bright
And sparry the rough scatterings of the hills
These ornaments the Cottage chiefly owes
                    {G
To one a hardy {girl who mounts the rocks
Such is her choice she fears not the bleak
                                    wind
Companion of her father does for him
        {er
Wher{e he wanders in his pastoral course
                        and
The service of a boy ~~but~~ with delight
More keen and prouder daring; yet hath
                                        she
Within the garden, like the rest, a bed
For her own flowers or favorite herds a
                                    spot
                        I guess
Holden by sacred charter, & ~~perchance~~
She also help'd to form that tiny plot
Of garden ground which one day twas
                                my chance
To find among the woody rocks
                        that rise

    The "139" penciled at the top of the page in an unidentified hand is misleading, as the page is an interleaf, rather than a leaf of the printed Coleridge volume; leaf 139–140 is lost. In the fifth line from the bottom, "herds" is a miswriting for "herbs."

[B, 586–606]

Above the house, a slip of smoother earth

Planted with ⎰G⎱gooseberry bushes & in one

Right in the Centre of ⎰the⎱⎰prickly⎱ shrub
                      ⎰[?]⎱⎰[?]⎱

A mimic birds nest fashiond by the hand
Was stuck, a staring thing of twisted hay
And one quaint fir tree towerd above the whole
But in the darkness of the night, then most
This Dwelling charms me, cover'd by the
                                    gloom
Then, heedless of good manners I stopp'd short

And,⎱ who could help it?⎰ feed by stealth
    ⎰   ⎰⎱
                                my sight
With prospect of the company within
Laid open through the blazing window: there
I see the eldest Daughter at her wheel
Spinning amain as if to overtake
She knows not what, or teaching in her turn
    Some little Novice of the Sisterhood
That skill, in this or other household work
Which from her honour'd fathers hand herself
While she was Yet a Little one, had Learn'd
Mild Man! he is not gay but they are gay
And the Whole House seems filled with
                            gaiety.

When all of Self regardless the scourg'd Saint

Mourns for th' Oppressor. O thou meekest Man! 25

Meek Man and lowliest of the Sons of Men!

Who thee beheld thy imag'd Father saw,

His Power and Wisdom from thy awful eye

Blended their beams, and loftier Love sate there

Musing on human weal, and that dread hour   30

When thy insulted Anguish wing'd the prayer

Harp'd by Archangels, when they sing of Mercy!

Which when th' ALMIGHTY heard, from forth his
Throne

Diviner light flash'd extacy o'er Heaven!

Heav'n's hymnings paus'd: and Hell her yawning
mouth   35

Clos'd a brief moment.

No {I {am}
   {we {are not alone we don

No I am not alone { I
                  {[?] do not stand
My Emma far [?divided] & alone
                  { cares
Loving what no one {[?cares] for but ourselves
We do not scatter through the fields & rocks
Of this fair Vale its groves & through
Its [? ?] in single [?] love
Unprofitable kindliness bestowed
On objects that were cheerless & forlorn
But few weeks past & would be so again
If we were not a dying joy a [?dead]
                    [?were] not [?dead] lamp
A mortal lamp
Mortal though bright, a dying dying
                              [?joy]

No I am not alone we do not stand
My Emma in a solitary world
{ Lov
{[?]ing   what no one cares for but
                              ourselves
                       [–?–]
We do not scatter through the fields
                              & rocks

       {f
Of this {Vair Vale & oer its spatious height
Unprofitable Kindless bestow'd

These are drafts toward the version on 144/145 iʳ. In the last line, "Kindliness" was doubtless intended.

Lovely was the Death
Of Him, whose Life was Love! Holy with power
He on the thought-benighted Sceptic beam'd
Manifest Godhead, melting into day   40
What Mists dim-floating of Idolatry
Split and misshap'd the Omnipresent Sire :
And first by TERROR, Mercy's startling prelude,
Uncharm'd the Spirit spell-bound with earthly lusts
Till of it's nobler Nature it 'gan feel
Dim recollections ; and thence soar'd to HOPE,   45
Strong to believe whate'er of mystic good

Th' ETERNAL dooms for his IMMORTAL Sons.

From HOPE and stronger FAITH to perfect LOVE

Attracted and absorb'd : and center'd there   50

GOD only to behold, and know, and feel,

Till by exclusive Consciousness of GOD

the ⎰ G
On objects unaccustom to ~~such~~ ⎱ gifts
Of feeling, that were cheerless & forlorn
But few past & would be so again
If we were not, we do not tend a lamp
Mortal though bright a dying dying joy
⎰ Lus
⎱ [?Lus]tre which we alone participate whose
Whose lustre we alone participate
That is dependent upon us alone
Mortal though bright a dying dying [?joy]
⎰ [?Look]
⎱ [?] where we will some human heart
                 has been
       ⎰ [?its]   its
before us [?in] ⎱ [?some] with some offering of delight
[?Pure] or with sickness mingled, [?selfish]
The [?sentiment ?pure] for [?such] must have
                   been
~~Far~~ different from [?ours] [?far ?different] [?]
                   [?still]

        ⎰ ~~tend a~~
~~We do not~~ ⎱ [?lamp]
         ⎰ ot
If we were [?n ⎱ t] we do not tend a lamp
Whose lustre we alone participate
That is dependent upon us alone
Mortal though bright a dying dying joy

These are further drafts toward 144/145 i[r]. In the third line, "weeks" was left out after "few." The X between the second and third lines signals that the revision at the foot of the page is to follow on.

All self-annihilated it shall make

We and our Father ONE !

                             And bleſt are they,

Who in this fleſhly World, the elect of Heaven,

Their ſtrong eye darting thro' the deeds of Men

Adore with ſtedfaſt unpreſuming gaze

Him, Nature's Eſſence, Mind, and Energy !   60

And gazing, trembling, patiently aſcend

Treading beneath their feet all viſible things

As ſteps, that upward to their Father's Throne

Lead gradual — elſe nor glorified nor lov'd.

THEY nor Contempt imboſom nor Revenge :   65

For THEY dare know of what may ſeem deform

The SUPREME FAIR ſole Operant : in whoſe ſight

[B, 659–667]

Look where we will some human heart has been
⎧B
⎨before us with its offering, ~~I possess~~
~~The sentiment [?must] oftentimes have~~ been
~~Far different from [?ours]~~   not a tree
Stand in thes [?little] pastures but the same
   Hath furnished [?hope]   ⎧a
To someone is ~~familiar~~ ⎨is a familiar
                    friend
Hath furnish'd matter for a thought
                   perchance
        ⎧as
To some is ⎨a a familiar friend
Joy spreads & sorrow spreading & this
                 whole
                 vale
             [?as]⎫
Home of [?untutord] Shepherd [?it]⎬ [?is]
Swarms with sensation [?as ?with ?morning]
                 mist
    ⎧or
Shadows ⎨br breezes scents or sounds

  These are further drafts toward the version on 144/145 i^r. In the fifth line from the bottom, "one" is omitted after "some."

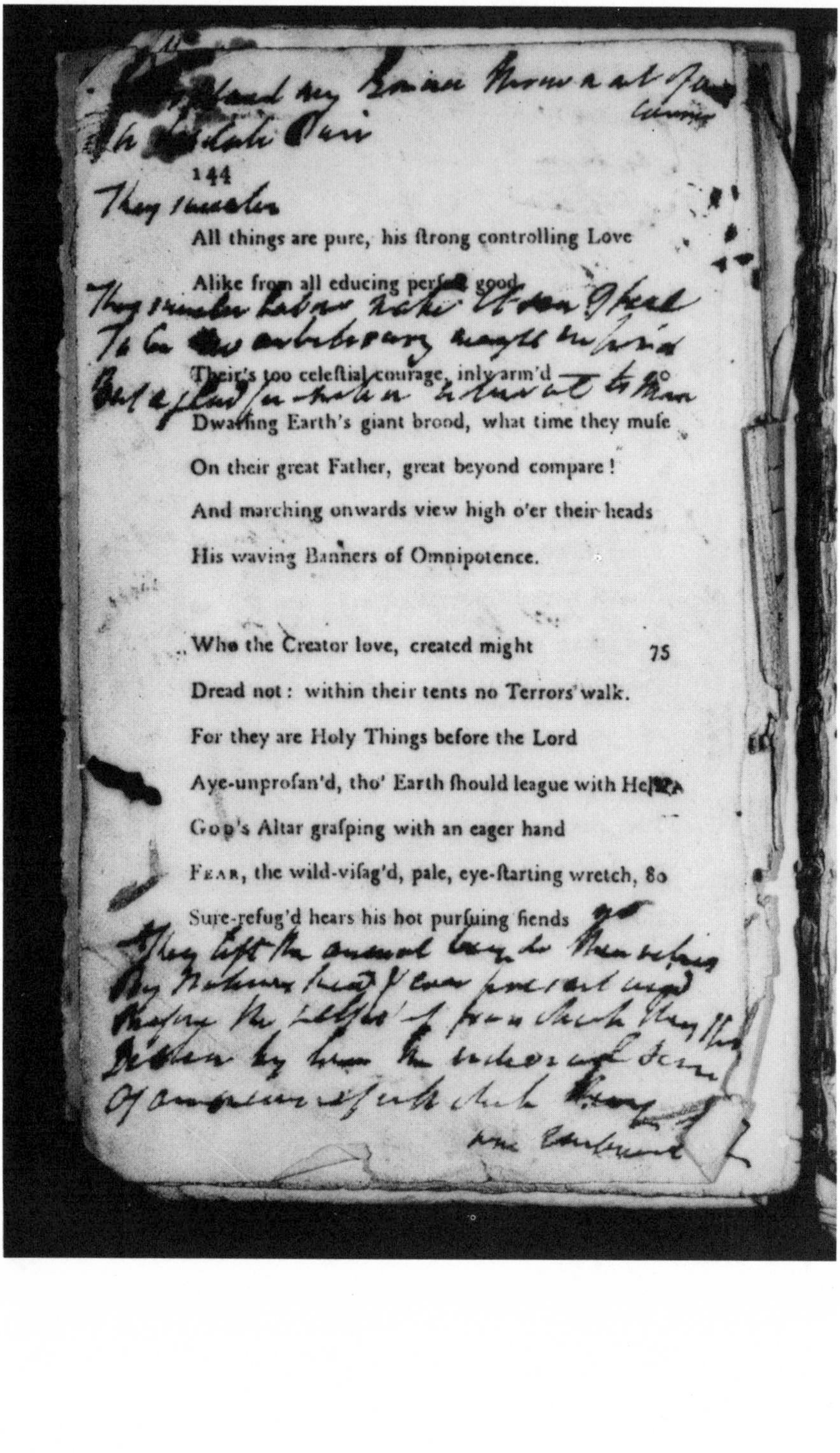

144

They number

All things are pure, his strong controlling Love

Alike from all educing perfect good

[handwritten lines]

Their's too celestial courage, inly arm'd

[handwritten line]

Dwarfing Earth's giant brood, what time they muse

On their great Father, great beyond compare!

And marching onwards view high o'er their heads

His waving Banners of Omnipotence.

Who the Creator love, created might   75

Dread not: within their tents no Terrors walk.

For they are Holy Things before the Lord

Aye-unprofan'd, tho' Earth should league with Hell

God's Altar grasping with an eager hand

FEAR, the wild-visag'd, pale, eye-starting wretch, 80

Sure-refug'd hears his hot pursuing fiends

[B, 647]

Misplaced my Emma thrown out of our
                              course
A desolate Pair
They sweeten

[B, 690–692]

They sweeten Labour make it seem & feel
To be no arbitrary weight impos'd
But a glad function natural to Man

[B, 673–677]

                              no
⎧ T
⎨[?]hey lift the animal being do themselves
By Natures kind & ever present aid
Refine the selfishness from which they spring
[?Declare] by love the individual sense
                         they ⎫
Of anxiousness with which [?]⎬
                      are combined

The third passage is a draft toward the version on 144/145 i^v.

No I am not alone we do not stand
　　　here misplac'd & desolate
My Emma ~~in a solitary world~~
Loving what no cares for but ourselves
We shall not scatter through the plains
　　　　　　　& rocks
Of this fair Vale & oer its spacious heights
Unprofitable kindliness, bestow'd
On objects unaccustom'd to the gifts
Of feeling that were cheerless and forlorn
　　　　　　⎧ w
But few weeks past & ⎨ sould be so
　　　　　　⎩
　　　　　　　　again
If we were not we do not tend a lamp
Whose lustre we alone participate
Which is dependent upon us alone
Mortal though bright a dying dying
　　　　　　　　flame
Look where we will some human heart
　　　　　　　　has been
Before us with its offering, not a tree
　　Sprinkles
~~Stands in~~ these little pastures but the
　　　　　　　　same
Hath furnished matters for a thought, perchance
To some one is as a familiar friend
Joy spreads & sorrow spreads & this
　　　　　　　whole Vale
Home of untutor'd Shepherds as it is
　　Teems
~~Swarms~~ with sensation as with gleams
　　　　　　　of light
Shadows or breezes scents or sounds
　　　　　　　nor deem

This page contains a version intermediate between the lines on 141–143 and MS. B, ll. 646–667. In the third line, "one" has been left out after "no."

                              servient
These feelings though submitted
                    more than ours
To the necessities of daily life
        To every day's demand for daily bread
And borrowing more their spirit & their [?shape]
From selfrespecting interests deem
                              them not
Unworthy therefore & unhallow'd, no—
Many are pure the best of them are pure
                      ⌠they
The best, & the ⌡se remember, most abound
                      worthiest
Are fit associates of the purest joy
Joy of the highest & the purest minds
                    n ⌠ n
They blend with it coge ⌡[?]ially
                      Meanwhile
⌠Labour   ⌠&
⌡They they [?sweeten] ⌡& they soften [?care]
            they
And calmly breathe their own undying
                          life
Lowly & unassuming as it is
Through this their mountain sanctuary,
                        long
Oh long may it remain inviolate
              innocence
Diffusing health,   & sober cheerfulness
And little boons   of animating thought
As faithfully   as   morning comes with
                              light
They lift the animal being do themselves
      [?They] by natures ever present [?aid] aid
Refine the selfishness from which they spring
[?Redeem] by love the individual [?sense]
Of anxiousness with which [?they]

This page incorporates the drafts at the foot of 144 and leads toward the version on 146/147 i^r.

Yell at vain diſtance, Soon refreſh'd from Heaven

He calms the throb and tempeſt of his heart:

His countenance ſettles : a ſoft ſolemn bliſs

Swims in his eye : his ſwimming eye uprais'd :   85

And Faith's whole armour glitters on his limbs !

And thus transfigured with a dreadleſs awe,

A ſolemn hush of ſoul, meek he beholds

All things of terrible ſeeming. , Yea, and there,

Enſhudder'd, unaghaſted, he ſhall view   90

E'en the SEVEN SPIRITS, who in the latter day

Will ſhower hot peſtilence on the ſons of men

For he ſhall know, his heart ſhall underſtand

That kindling with intenſer Deity

They from the MERCY-SEAT — like roſy flames, 95

From God's celeſtial MERCY-SEAT will flaſh,

And at the wells of renovating LOVE

[B, 698–700]

T}
The g {ravell[?er] [?groans] not if a mist
[?conceal]
~~I am stranger yet~~
A stranger am I yet have [?seen] [?]
[?]

[B, 673–677]

Add to the [?growth] of [?distress]
~~[?Enlarge ?the ?sha~~me] Of [?heart] ~~pur~~ify
The very selfish [?from] which they spring
Or which
Exalt the animal being do themselves
Refine the selfishness from which they
spring
Or [?other] [?]
Or [?Individual] anxiousness with which
They ~~are [?combining~~] the [?]
Or soften down [?By] love [?]
[?consecrating]
And soften down by ~~love~~ consecrating
love
[?T]
l}
And soften down [?a] [?by] [?] {ove
[?Redeem] by love the individual sense
~~of~~
~~This [?know] I [?]~~

[B, 693–698]

{O [?know]
{of this [?] little Stranger as I am
the inward
Already I have seen [~~?since] it is~~
frame
Though slowly opening opens every
day
{I
Nor am {l less delighted with
the shew
[?A]

These are drafts toward the version on 146/147 i^r.

Fill'd Seven Vials with salutary wrath,

~~The sickly~~ Nature more medicinal

That what soft balm the weeping good man pours 100

Into the lone despoiled trav'ller's wounds!

Thus from th' Elect, regenerate thro' faith,

Pass the dark Passions and what thirsty Cares

Drank up the spirit and the dim regards

Self center. Lo they vanish! or acquire 105

New names, new features — by supernal grace

Liv'd with Light, and naturaliz'd in Heaven.

As when a Shepherd on a vernal morn

Thro' some thick fog creeps tim'rous with slow foot,

Darkling he fixes on th' immediate road 110

His downward eye: all else of fairest kind

Hid or deform'd. But lo, the bursting Sun!

```
            alternate progress & impediment
[?The] [?traveller]
                        there
As it unfolds its self now here now
      is the
        pass⎫
Than trave∫ing traveller when his
            unpretending
                      way
Lies through some [?region] never [?trod]
This vale
When [?mists ?are] hu
This vale
                    f ⎫
Say this fair valley's sels∫, while mists
On all sides                    are hun
On every side & yet on every side
[?Low] [?hu]
On every side [?plaintively] [?plaintive] [?murmuring]
                                        streams
                    in time when mists
Low [?hung] are      [?or] [ ? ] [?gazes] [?round]
break up & are beginning to recede
How please he is to


Something on every side conceald
                        from view
In evry quarter some [?thing] visible
```

```
            make [?the ?burthen]
That sweeten labour [?make] it seem
                            & feel
      [?arbitrary] [?weight]
To be no weight [?imposed]
But a glad function natural
                to man
```

These are drafts toward the version on 146/147 i^r and 146/147 i^v.

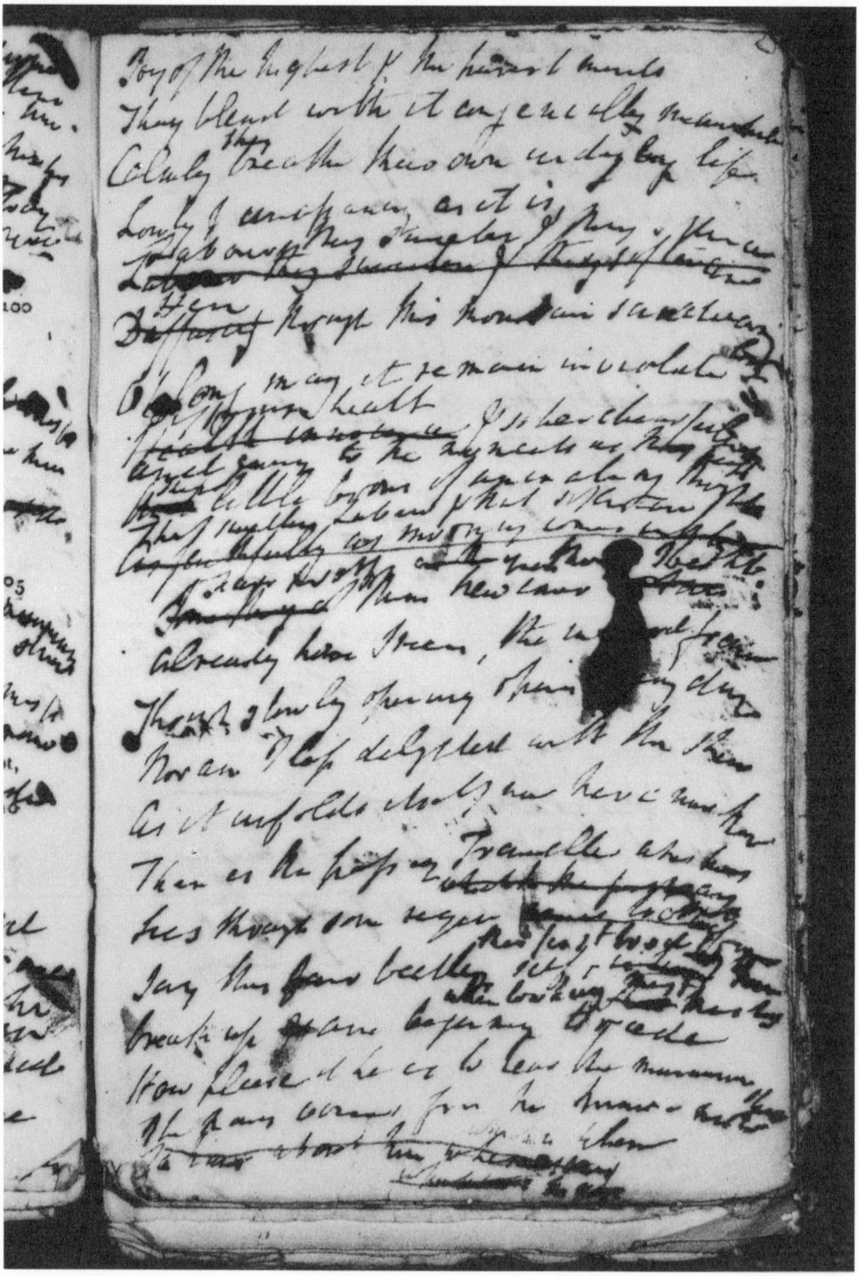
Joy of the highest & the purest minds
They blend with it congenially meanwhile
Calmly they breathe their own undying life
Lowly & unobtrusive as it is
[illegible]
[illegible]
[illegible] through this mountain sanctuary
O long may it remain inviolate
[illegible] health
[illegible]
[illegible]
[illegible]
[illegible]
[illegible]
[illegible]
Already have been, the [illegible]
Though slowly opening [illegible]
Nor are [illegible] delighted with the [illegible]
As it unfolds [illegible] here [illegible]
Then as the passing Traveller [illegible]
Sees through [illegible]
Say this fair [illegible]
Break up [illegible]
How pleased he is to hear the murmuring
Of [illegible]
[illegible]

Joy of the highest & the purest minds
They blend with it congenially meanwhile
     they   {y {ing
Calmly breathe their own und{ing{l life
Lowly & unassuming as it is
    Labour they sweeten & they soften car
~~Labour they sweeten & they soften cares~~
    Here   n}
~~Diffusing~~ through this mountain sa[?c]}ctuary
                        long

Oh long may it remain inviolate
    Diffusing healt
~~Health innocence~~ & sober chearfulness
    And giving to the moments as they pass

    Their
~~And~~ little boons of animating thought
    That sweetten Labour & that soften care
~~As faithfully as morning comes with light~~
    Fair proof ~~a Stranger~~ though I be
  ~~Something of~~ them Newcomer ~~as I am~~
Already have I seen, the inward frame
Though slowly opening opens every day
Nor am I less delighted with the shew
As it unfolds itself now here now there
Than is the passing Traveller when his
                way
      ~~which he the first~~
Lies through some region ~~never trod before~~
        then first trod by
             him
Say this fair Valleys self,—~~in time~~
        mists
    when low hung [–?–] misty
break up & are beginning to recede
How pleased he is to hear the murmuring
                streams
The many voices from he knows not w
         where
        which w
~~To have about him [?wheresoeer]~~
   ~~which [?ever] he goes~~

These lines replace and continue beyond the lines crossed out on 144/145 i^v and incorporate the work on 145–146.

    To have about him which way eer he goes
Something on every side conceald from
                    view
In every quarter something visibal
Half seen or wholly lost & found again
Alternate progress & impediment
And yet a growing prospect in the main
  u⎫   & ⎫
Ssu⎰ch pleasure now is mine [?]⎰ what if I
Herein less happy
Less happy than the Traveler in this
                  painful look
Am sometimes forced to cast a [?painful ?look]
                     unawares
Upon unwelcome things which [?unawares]
       or⎫
    n[?]⎰ therefore is
Reveal themselves is my mind thereby
Not [?damp'd] nor do I fear what is to come
              glance
But confident enriched at every step
The more I see the more is my delight
I see the growing prospect with delig
⎰Tr
⎱[?]uth justifies herself and as she
              dwells
With hope who would follow where
              she leads

These lines continue on from the preceding recto, and incorporate some of the work on 146.

Such honour, if that honour

148

This is indeed to dwell with the moſt High!

Cherubs and rapture-trembling Seraphim

Can preſs no nearer to th' Almighty's Throne.   130

But that we roam unconſcious, or with hearts

Unfeeling of our univerſal Sire,

And that in his vaſt family no Cain

Injures uninjur'd (in her beſt-aim'd blow

Victorious Murder a blind Suicide)   135

Haply for this ſome younger Angel now

Looks down on Human Nature : and, behold!

A ſea of blood beſtrew'd with wrecks, where mad

Embattling Interests on each other ruſh

With unhelm'd Rage,   140

The faculties

'Tis the ſublime of man,

Our noontide Majeſty, to know ourſelves

Such converse, if but fervent

[Exc., IV, 338–341]

       properties
The faculties that do to every class
Assign its several office & abod
Which they inherit but cannot step
               beyond
And cannot fall beneath

The line at the top of the page is unidentified. The lines at the foot are an addition to the passage on the lower half of 148/149 i[r]; they were rejected when that passage was recopied on 150/151 i[r].

The Heifer in yon little croft belongs
To one who holds it dear, with chains can
She received it of his speaking of her charge
There'd rather one a word or two

130   Domestic near the heart of motherly
She being herself a mother, happy while
Of the caresses of a human voice
Can make it so of some one heeds

─────────────────────────

135   Happy is he who lives to understand
Observes explores that he may find
The lines of which it is of whence begins
The union of discernment that which makes
all his
Degree or kind in every shape of being

140   The constitution powers & faculties
And habits of arguments that agree
To every class their office are abodes
Through all the might by common built
Up from the stone or plant to sovereign
Earth endeavours long
                                    Teaches how

[B, 745–752]

The Heifer in yon little Croft belongs
To one who holds it dear with duteous care
She reared it & in speaking of her charge
I heard scatter one a word or two
Domestic near the heart & motherly
She being herself a Mother, happy beast
If the comfort of a human voice
Can make it so & care of human hands

[Exc., IV, 332–345]

Happy is he who lives to understand
                    for this
Observes explores ~~to the end~~ that he
                              may find
The law & what it is & where begins
The union & disunion that which makes
                    all [?the]
Degree or kind in every shape of being
The constitution powers & faculties
                    ⸂o   do
And habits & enj⸃uyments that assign
                    its
To every class ~~their~~ offic or abode
Through all the mighty commonwealth
                              of things
Up from the stone or plant to sovereign
                              man
⸂S
⸃Cuch converse long   [?learns]
                    teaches love

    The lines following the enclosed passage form part of a passage never incorporated in MS. B
but taken into *The Excursion*. A version intermediate between these lines and the *Excursion* text
appears on 150/151 i^r. In the fourth line, "her" is left out after "heard," and "once" is telescoped
by the omission of a letter. The zig-zag interlining in the lower portion of the page is meant to
call attention to the revision on the facing verso.

For knowledge is delight & such delight
Is love yet suited as it rather is
To thought & to the climbing intellect
     adore⎱
It teaches less to love than to [?]⎰
If that be not indeed the highest love
And yet a something to our Nature
      cleaves
Which is not satisfied with this & he
Is still a happier Man who for the
      height
Of speculation not unfit descends
  [?~~Treads~~]
~~And often~~ walks in humbler ways
At Natures call & forgets seeks
   [?~~is ?refreshd~~]
[?Luxuriates ~~?seeks~~] ~~refreshment~~ & [?repose]
  universal   [?partial]
From general truth ~~in individ~~ual love
      [?partial] truth
Has individual objects of regard
Among the inferiour not mererely those
Which he may a call his own & which
     depend
Upon his care from [?them] he also looks
For signs & tokens of a mutual bond
  But [?other] far beyond the narrowness
    very
~~Which for the sake of love he loves~~
[?Or] ⎰T [?whereer]
And ⎱takes the after knowledge as it comes

The lines on this page follow on from the passage on the preceding recto; their history is the same. They are revised on 150/151 i^r–150/151 i^v. In the sixth main line from the bottom, "kinds" is left out after "inferiour."

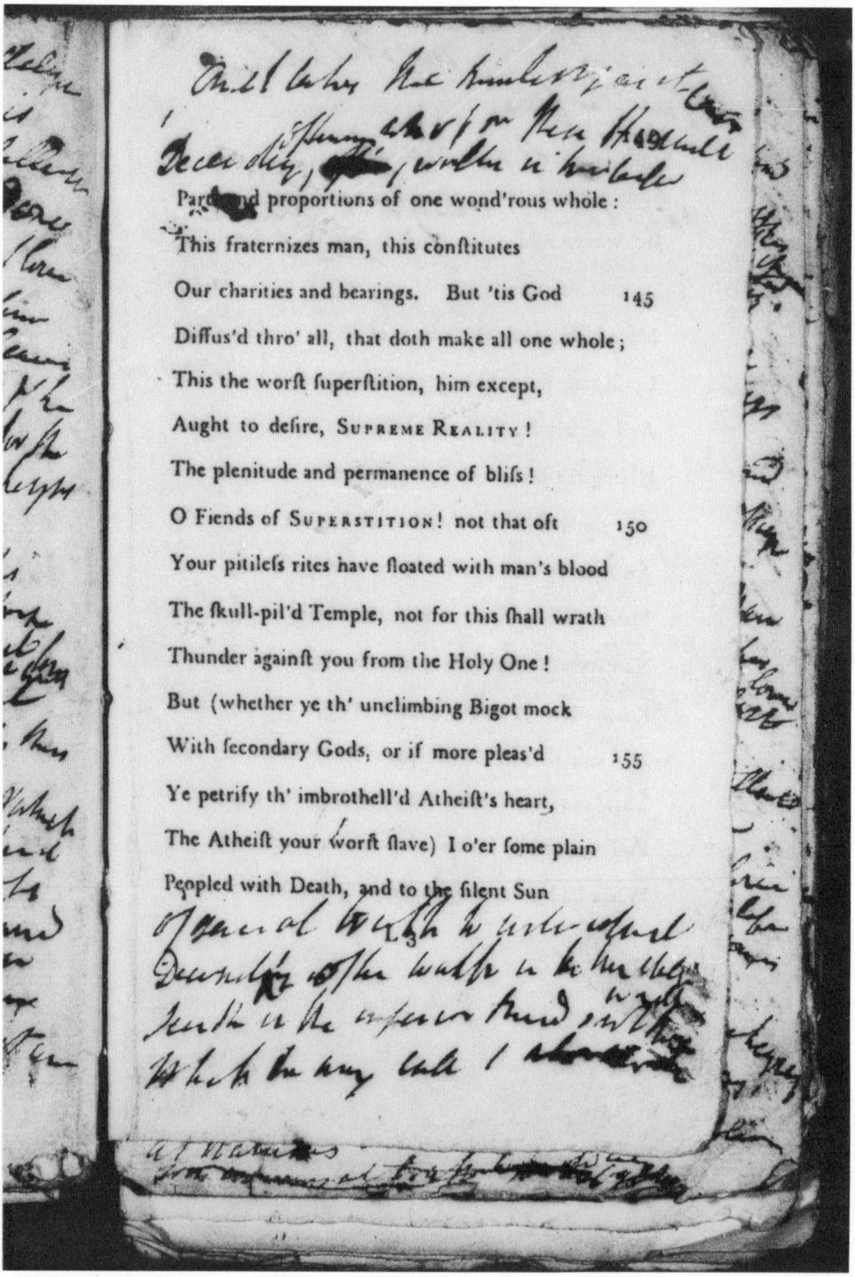

[handwritten lines, largely illegible]

Par[t] and proportions of one wond'rous whole :

This fraternizes man, this conſtitutes

Our charities and bearings.   But 'tis God   145

Diffus'd thro' all, that doth make all one whole ;

This the worſt ſuperſtition, him except,

Aught to deſire, SUPREME REALITY !

The plenitude and permanence of bliſs !

O Fiends of SUPERSTITION ! not that oft   150

Your pitileſs rites have floated with man's blood

The ſkull-pil'd Temple, not for this ſhall wrath

Thunder againſt you from the Holy One !

But (whether ye th' unclimbing Bigot mock

With ſecondary Gods, or if more pleas'd   155

Ye petrify th' imbrothell'd Atheiſt's heart,

The Atheiſt your worſt ſlave) I o'er ſome plain

Peopled with Death, and to the ſilent Sun

[handwritten lines, largely illegible]

[*Exc.*, IV, 355–359]

And takes that knowledg as it comes
                    who from these [?Heights]
        [oftimes]
Decending, ~~often~~, walks in [?humbler]

Of general truth to individual
        i   ⎰often
Decend̠ng ⎱[?in] walks in [?humbler]
        ∧   [?ways]
[?Seeks] in the inferior kinds [?not] [?those]
                    ~~alone~~ [?whi]

Which he may call

These lines are drafts toward the passage on 148/149 i^v. They precede the draft on 150/151 i^r–150/151 i^v.

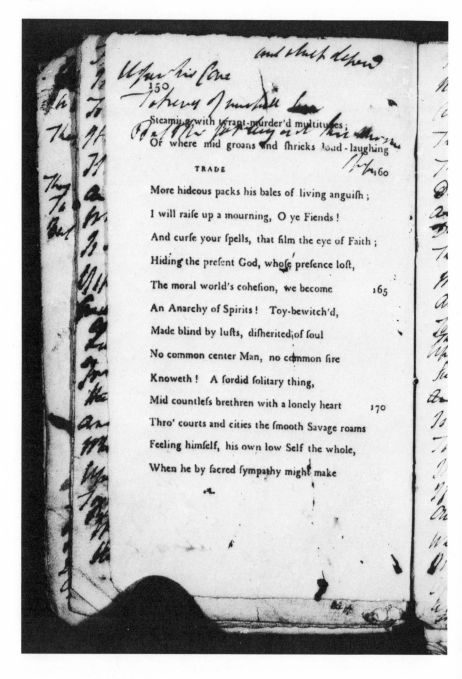

Steaming with tyrant-murder'd multitudes;

Or where mid groans and shrieks loud-laughing

TRADE 160

More hideous packs his bales of living anguish;

I will raise up a mourning, O ye Fiends!

And curse your spells, that film the eye of Faith;

Hiding the present God, whose presence lost,

The moral world's cohesion, we become 165

An Anarchy of Spirits! Toy-bewitch'd,

Made blind by lusts, disherited of soul

No common center Man, no common fire

Knoweth! A sordid solitary thing,

Mid countless brethren with a lonely heart 170

Thro' courts and cities the smooth Savage roams

Feeling himself, his own low Self the whole,

When he by sacred sympathy might make

[*Exc.*, IV, 359–363]

                    and which depend
Upon his [?Care]
Tokens of mutual love
But other far beyond this narrow
                    [?sphere]

These lines appear to be connected with the passages on 148/149 i^v and 150/151 i^v.

[*Exc.*, IV, 332–356]

Happy is he who lives to understand

                    u⌉
No human Nature only by⌠t explores
All Natures to the end that he may find
        w ⌉   ⌠[?ing]
The La[?]⌠, & what it is & where begin⌠s
              partition   makes
The union and disunion that which
                                makes
                          makes
⌠D   among all visible
⌊degree or kind on all the shapes of
Among all visible⌠s
Degree or kind among all visible
                          beings
The constitution powers & & faculties
              2   1
Which they inherit canot step beyond
And cannot fall beneath which do assign
        kind
To every class its station & its office
      Throughout the mighty Commonwealth of things
Up from the stone or plant to sovereign Man
Such converse, if but fervent, teaches
                                love

    For
And knowledge is delight and such delight
Is love, yet suited as it rather is
To thought and to the climbing Intellect
It teaches less to love than to adore
If that be not indeed the highest love
                    about our daily life
              ⌠thing hangs   cleaves
And yet a some ⌊to our
Which is not satisfied with this & he
Is a still happier Man Who for these heights
Of Speculation not unfit descends
At Nature's call to walk in humbler
                          [?ways]
[?From] universal truth to [?partial ?truth]

These lines revise the version on 148/149 iᵛ; they were not incorporated in MS. B but were taken into *The Excursion*. The lines of 150/151 iᵛ follow consecutively. The numbers under the ninth line suggest that WW considered transposing "powers" and "faculties."

Among the inferior things but merely
Which he may call his own & when
Upon his care, for which he also looks
For eyes & tokens of a mutual bond

That others far less in this narrow

Which for the origination of love

How is it a mean praise of rural life
And solitude that they the powers most
Most frequently call forth & best sustain
These milder pleasure affections & to the
How much do they endear the guiding
Of this sublime retirement. be you
Already to inscribe upon my heart
So asking for the small grey horse that bears
The grave & light Man: I know the Ass
On which the Cripple, in the journey
Plodies to & fro: I know him & his ways.
The famous sheep-dog, first in all the Vale
Though yet a stranger to me will not be
A stranger long, nor will the Blind mans
friends of neglected things of unrenown
whoso ever lived a winter in on
the one

[*Exc.*, IV, 360–372]

Luxuriates & [?finds] [?&] [/?] repose
From universal truth in [?partial ?]
Hath individual objects of regard
Among the inferior kinds not merely those
                 { h
Which he may call his own & whic{de depend
Upon his care, from which he also looks
             m{
For signs & tokens of a b{utual bond
But others far beyond this narrow
                 sphere
Which for the very sake of love he loves
   ſing
And tak{es the after knowledge as it comes
Nor is it a mean praise of rural life
And solitude that they do favour most
Most frequently call forth & best sustain
These mild & pure affections & to me
How much do they endear the quietness   [B, 722–733]
Of this sublime retirement. I begin
Already to inscribe upon my heart
A liking for the small grey horse that bears
The paralytic Man: I know the Ass
On which the Cripple, in the quarry
               maimed
Rides to & fro I know them & their ways.
         in
The famous Sheep-dog first ~~of~~ all the vale
      to me
Though yet ^a Stranger ~~to me~~ will not be
A Stranger, ^long, nor will the Blind man's
          ~~Dog~~
            guide
Meek & neglected thing of no renown
Who ever lived a winter in one
        place

The lines under the X revise versions on 148/149 i^v; they follow on from the lines on 150/151 i^r. The crossed-out lines were not incorporated in MS. B, but with the two lines immediately following them were taken into *The Excursion*.

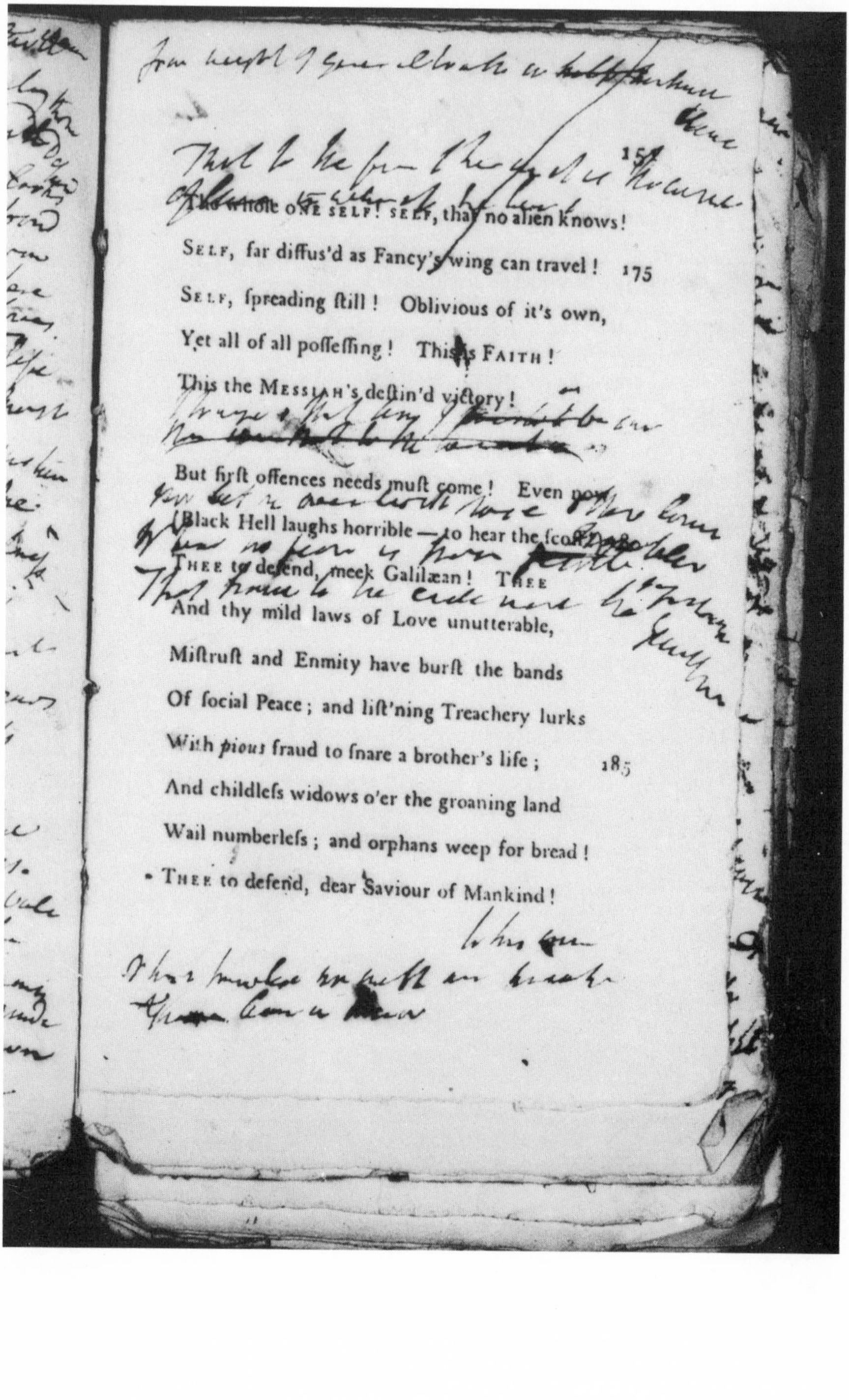
The whole ONE SELF! SELF, that no alien knows!
SELF, far diffus'd as Fancy's wing can travel!
SELF, spreading still! Oblivious of it's own,
Yet all of all possessing! This is FAITH!
This the MESSIAH's destin'd victory!

But first offences needs must come! Even now
(Black Hell laughs horrible—to hear the scoff!)
THEE to defend, meek Galilæan! THEE
And thy mild laws of Love unutterable,
Mistrust and Enmity have burst the bands
Of social Peace; and list'ning Treachery lurks
With *pious* fraud to snare a brother's life;
And childless widows o'er the groaning land
Wail numberless; and orphans weep for bread!
THEE to defend, dear Saviour of Mankind!

From aught of general truth or ~~help~~ [?partial]
                                            [?love]
That to [?the] [?forest ?hermit] is [?the ?]
[?Oftimes] [?] he [?hears]

                            [?]
[?Stranger] that [?am] & [—?—?]
~~Nor [?] [?that ?to ?the ?hermit ?is]~~

                                                    [B, 720–721]

        ⎰ 1
Nor ⎱[?]et me overlook those other loves
                    humbler
Where no fear is those ~~little~~ sympathies
That have to me endeared the quietness

                            to his own
[?] [?knowledge] [? ? ? ?]
[?Gives] [? ? ?]

   The lines at the top and foot of this page appear to be further revisions of the lines on 150/151 i^v.
Those in the middle draft a transition between MS. B, l. 718 and the lines on 150/151 i^v that WW
incorporated in MS. B.

THEE, Lamb of God! THEE, blameless Prince of Peace!

From all sides rush the thirsty brood of war! 190

AUSTRIA, and that foul WOMAN of the NORTH,

The lustful Murd'ress of her wedded Lord!

And he, connatural Mind! whom (in their songs

So bards of elder time had haply feign'd)

Some Fury fondled in her hate to man, 195

Bidding her serpent hair in tortuous folds

Lick his young face, and at his mouth inbreathe

Horrible sympathy! And leagued with these

Each petty German Princeling, nurs'd in gore!

Soul-harden'd barterers of human blood! 200

Death's prime Slave-merchants! Scorpion whips of Fate!

Nor least in savagery of holy zeal,

Apt for the yoke, the race degenerate,

Whom Britain erst had blush'd to call her sons!

[B, 807–811]

Is this then [?solitude], privation this
[?Is] this to [?be ?tru] alone he [?best] [?can ?tell]
He of the multitude whose eyes are doomd
To hold a vacant commerce day by
                              day
With [?that] which he can neither [?no] nor
                              [?]

What knows the hermit of the forests leaves
[?Or] aught that breathes & [?sings ?above]
But [?that] they screen him from the [?] of storms
And lull [?him] [?with] [?] [?music]

The lines at the top of the page are drafts toward the version on 152/153 iᵛ; those at the side are
unidentified.

Beneath the shelter of one cottage roof
We have not had his neighbour his
These then both & I shall have my
In spring-time of a hundred Warblers
And if the beauteous eagle pairs
With his mate
There shall I see I will dwell with these
two birds

Acquaintance as they near around that
The Owl that gives the name to
Have I heard shouting & in
A chosen one of my regards or see

The Heifer in yon little Croft below
To one who holds it dear with
She reared it & is breaking of his
I heard her scatter once a word or two
A term domestic yea & motherly
She being herself a mother, happy
Of the image of a human Voice
Can make at so & care of human

☩ Whenever I pursue my thoughts
When ever I look by some
That stops are mingling with my

[B, 734-752]

Beneath the shelter of one Cottage roof
And has not had his rebreast or his wren
&
I have them both [?] I shall have my
thrush
In spring-time & a hundred warblers
more
And if the banished eagle pair return
Helvellyn's eagles to their antient hold
Then shall I see shall claim with those
two birds
Acquaintance as they soar amid the
heavens
The Owl that gives the name to owlet
[?Crag]
Have I heard shouting & he soon will be
*
A chosen one of my reggrds. See there
The Heifer in yon little Croft belongs
To one who holds it dear with duteous
care
She reared it & in speaking of her charge
I heard her scatter once a word or two
A term domestic, yea & motherly
She being herself a mother, happy beast
If the caresses of a human voice
Can make it so & care of human hands
*
Wherever I pursue my studious walk
Where eer I look by something am I cross'd
That stops me mingling with my busy thought

In the second line, "redbreast" was intended. The asterisks may be intended to call attention
to the passage on 148/149 i^r; the lines at the foot of the page were not included in MS. B.

Then boldly say that solitude is not
Where these things are he truly is alone
He of the multitude whose eyes are doomed
To hold a vacant commerce day by day
With objects [...] he can neither know
[...]
[...] to the forest harness are the living
[...]
[...]
[...] what land
because as do his own

Then boldly say that solitude is not
Where these things are he truly is alone
He of the multitude whose eyes are doom'd
To hold a vacant commerce day by day
   that
    which⎞
With ~~things~~ of he⎰ he can neither know
 Dead things to him thrice dead or wors than this
       no love
A swarm of life that is to him no more
Than to the forest hermit are the leaves
That hang aloft in myriads oh far less
  f⎞
Far less a⎰or aught that comforts or defends
Or lulls or chears for what is like the weight
  vast [?burthen]   so like
Of that sad [?~~presence~~] what so [?beautifull]
     oh what hollowness
 [? ?] depth as [?]
~~With that [? ?]~~ what [?]
     [?]
[?beyond] as do [? ?]

153

THEE to defend the Moloch Priest prefers   205

The prayer of hate, and bellows to the herd

That Deity, ACCOMPLICE Deity

In the fierce jealoufy of waken'd wrath

Will go forth with our armies and our fleets

To fcatter the red ruin on their foes!   210

O blafphemy! to mingle fiendifh deeds

With bleffednefs! Lord of unfleeping Love,

From everlafting Thou! We fhall not die.

Thefe, even thefe, in mercy didft thou form,

Teachers of Good thro' Evil, by brief wrong   215

Making Truth lovely, and her future might

Magnetic o'er the fix'd untrembling heart.

In the primeval age a datelefs while

The vacant Shepherd wander'd with his flock

                              [?]
                        for [?hollow] [?]
[—?—]
          ⌠of
Asks ⎨h himself
          ⌡
                                [?]
                        [?for ? ?]
                            [?least ?the—?—]

              [?what] [?poverty] so [?poor]
        What depth of hollowness & void so deep

               ⌠at
Less by th⎨e dreary hollowness that
               ⌡   comes
[?   ?   ?—   ?—   ]

    These scraps are probably jottings for a revision of the conclusion of the passage on 152/153 i^v,
facing.

And ye as happy under Nature's care
Strangers to me and all mankind at least
Strangers to all particular amity
Whether in large communities ye keep
From year to year not shunny...
Your stationary homes or be from far
Wild creatures, old of many homes that
The gift of winds of whom the winds again come
...
Recording to your own an undist place
In my affections w... the delights
With which once while I saw the multitude
Wheel through the sky of ... how ... at rest
Yet not a rest when the glassy lake
They cannot rest they gambol like young
... as lambs of overcome with joy
They toss all frolic ... fluttter, plunge
And beat the puff in water with their w...
Too dis...ant are they for flight ... be...
Three little fountains sparkling in the ...
Who l... tell what they are doing whereof rose up

And ye as happy under Nature's care
{s
{strangers to me and all mankind at least
Strangers to all particular amity
Whether in large communities ye keep
From year to year not shunning man's
                                    abode
        a settled residence
Your stationary homes or be from far
                and}
Wild Creatures, o} of many homes that
                                come
The gift of winds, & whom the winds again
                    {will
                yet {wo ye
Take from us at your plan ~~ye would~~ have
        Not want for this your own subordinate [?place]
According to your claim an under place
                            l}
In my affections witness the dee}ight
With which ere while I saw that multitude
                        now}
Wheel through the sky & see them   [?not]} at rest
Yet not at rest upon the glassy lake
They cannot rest they gambol like young
                                whelps
Active as lambs & overcome with joy
They try all frolic motions, flutter, plunge
And beat the passive water with their wings
Too distant are they for plain view but Lo
Three little fountains, sparkling in the sun
Which tell what they are doing which rise up

This version of MS. B, ll. 753–776 comes later than that on 160/161 i^v.

First one & then another   spout
         glee

As one or other takes the fit of {g / joy

Fountains & Spouts yet rather in the gui {s / ze
Of plaything fireworks which on festal
         night
  {h   wanton
His {Hiss about the feet of ~~merry~~ boys
~~Look out where you wi~~ll throughtout this
        {[?aspect]
~~All [?Round ?through]~~ How vast the {[?] of this theatre
 ~~Throughout~~
Is nothing to be seen but lovely pomp
And silent majesty the birch tree woods
Are hung with thousand thousand diamond
         drops
 *   {fro every tiny knot
Of melted hoar {[?]st ~~see the myriads~~ there
 In the bare twigs each little budding-place
~~On that [?one] tree~~ while all the distant
         grove
 Cased with its several bead what myriads
That to the summit of the steep ascends
Is like a mountain built of silver light
  {yonder
See {the the same pageant & again
Behold the universal imagery
At what a depth, deep in the lake below
Admonish'd of the days of love to come
{The
{[?] Raven croaks & fills the sunny air
With a strange sound of genial harmony
And in and all about that playful
      band

  These lines are continued from 154/155 iʳ, overleaf; they extend and develop the version on 160/161 iᵛ. The asterisk near the left-hand margin indicates that the lines at the top of 155 are to be inserted here.

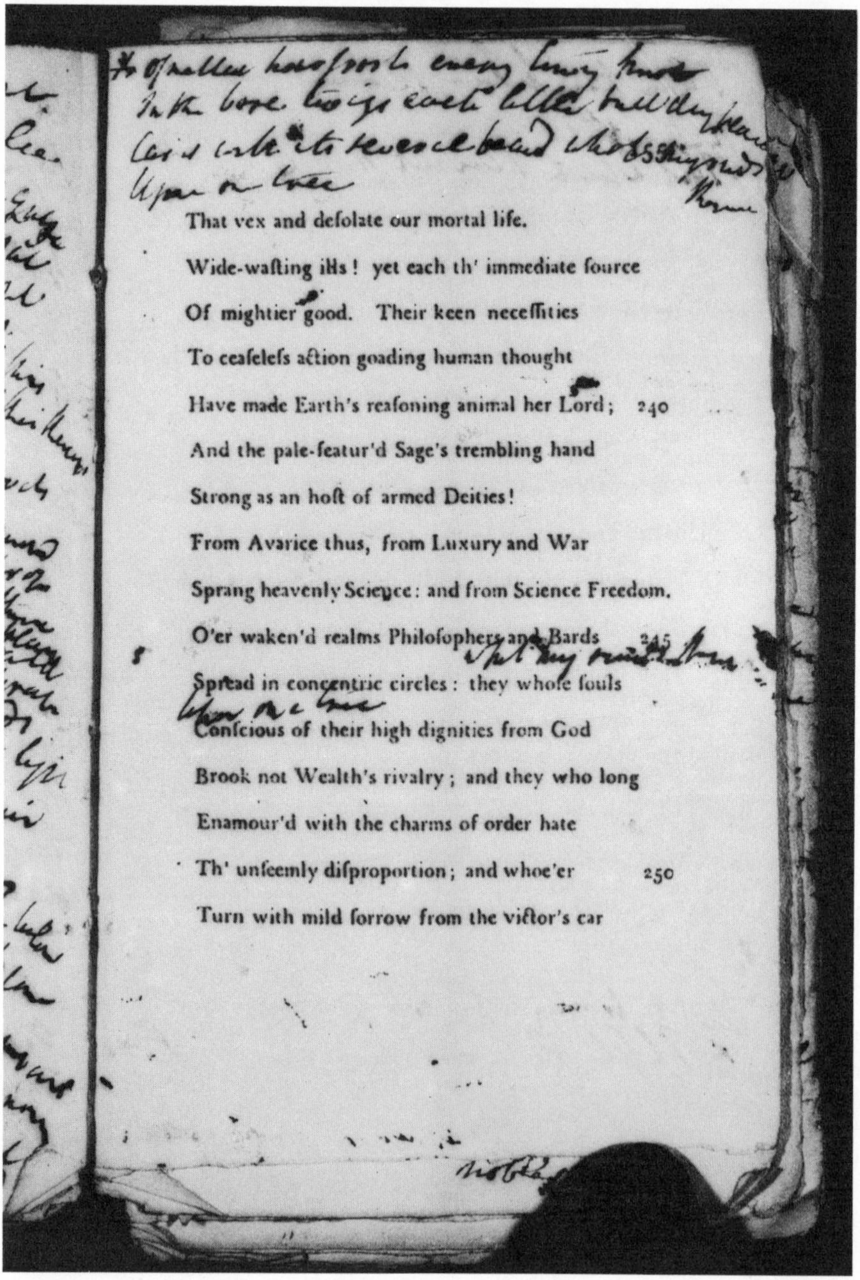

[handwritten marginal text at top:]

Of mallee horsfoorth every twig knot
In the bore twigs each little but dum
Cevis with its severest bend who styyn
Upon or tree

That vex and defolate our mortal life.

Wide-wafting ills ! yet each th' immediate fource

Of mightier good.   Their keen neceffities

To ceafelefs action goading human thought

Have made Earth's reafoning animal her Lord ;   240

And the pale-featur'd Sage's trembling hand

Strong as an hoft of armed Deities !

From Avarice thus, from Luxury and War

Sprang heavenly Science : and from Science Freedom.

O'er waken'd realms Philofophers and Bards   245

Spread in concentric circles : they whofe fouls

Confcious of their high dignities from God

Brook not Wealth's rivalry ; and they who long

Enamour'd with the charms of order hate

Th' unfeemly difproportion ; and whoe'er   250

Turn with mild forrow from the victor's car

[B, 786–789]

   *
Of melted hoarfrost every tiny knot
In the bare twigs each little budding place
Cas'd with its several bead what myriads
                       there
Upon one tree

               what myriads there
Upon one tree

The lines at the top of the page are to be inserted at the asterisk in the left-hand margin of 154/155 i^v. The half-lines at mid-page, correcting the version on 154/155 i^v, were probably written here before the lines at the top of the page were entered.

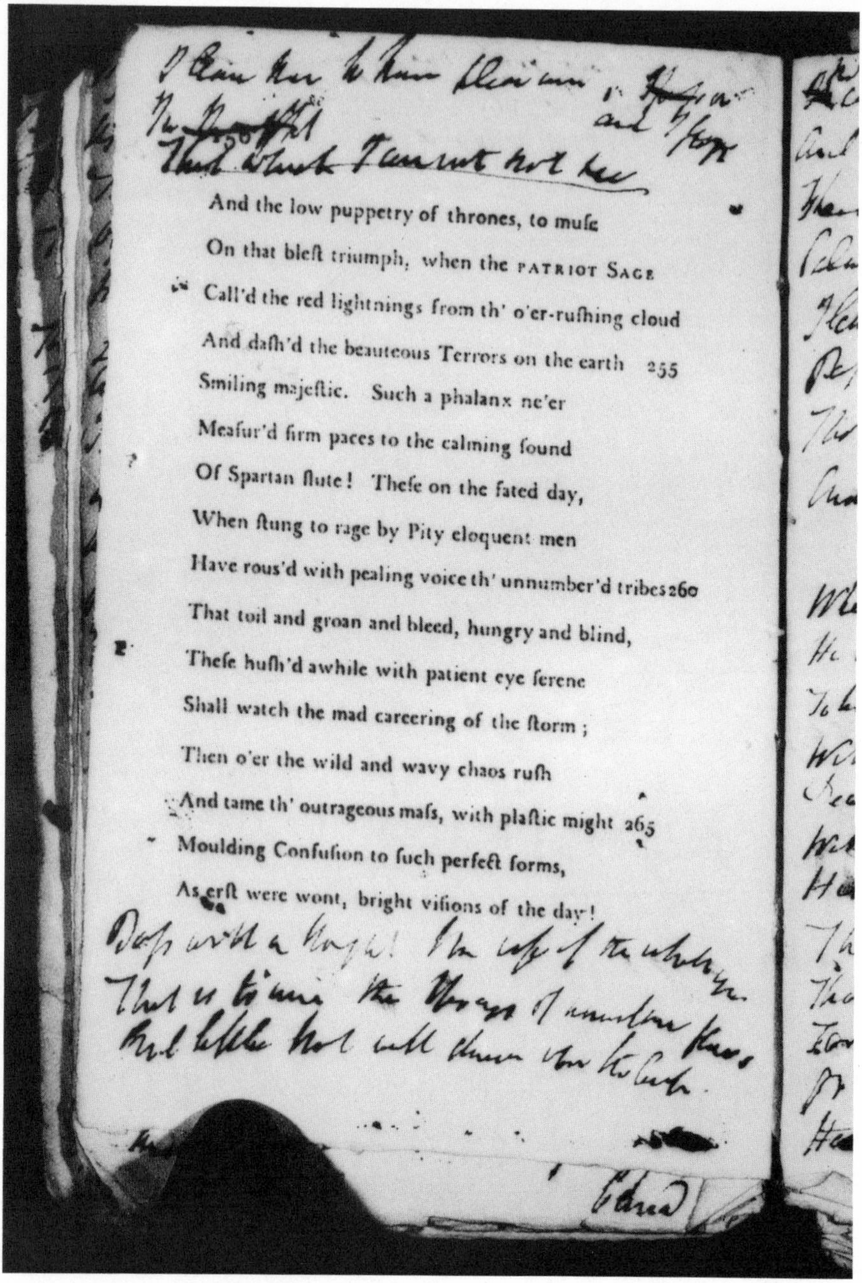

[handwritten, partly illegible]
O'Rin her to her claim or Prison and Hope
No hope left
That which I can not not be

And the low puppetry of thrones, to muſe

On that bleſt triumph, when the PATRIOT SAGE

Call'd the red lightnings from th' o'er-ruſhing cloud

And daſh'd the beauteous Terrors on the earth 255

Smiling majeſtic.   Such a phalanx ne'er

Meaſur'd firm paces to the calming ſound

Of Spartan flute! Theſe on the fated day,

When ſtung to rage by Pity eloquent men

Have rous'd with pealing voice th' unnumber'd tribes 260

That toil and groan and bleed, hungry and blind,

Theſe huſh'd awhile with patient eye ſerene

Shall watch the mad careering of the ſtorm ;

Then o'er the wild and wavy chaos ruſh

And tame th' outrageous maſs, with plaſtic might 265

Moulding Confuſion to ſuch perfect forms,

As erſt were wont, bright viſions of the day !

[handwritten lines, largely illegible]

[B, 803–806]

I leave them to their pleasure, ~~I pass~~ on
                                 pass⎫
                  and I [?leave]⎭
In ~~thought~~
~~That which I cannot not~~ [?]

Pass with a thought the life of the whole year
That is to come the throngs of mountain flowers
And lilllies that will dance upon the lake

These lines work toward the passage on 156/157 i^r.

     Not
~~Incapable~~ although they be of rest
And in their fashion ~~very~~ fashion very
              rioters
  ⎰Th
  ⎱Their is a stillness & they seem to [?~~mak~~]
             make
Calm revelry in that their calm abode
I leave them to their pleasure and I pass
Pass with a thought the life of the whole year
That is to come the throngs of mountain-flowers
And lillies that will dance upon the lake
    Then boldly say that solitude is not
Where these things are he truly is alone
He of the multitude whose eyes are doo
               m'd
To hold a vacant commerce day by day
With that which he neither knows nor loves
Dead things to him thrice dead or worse
             than this
With swarms of life, and worse than all, of ~~life~~
                men
His fellow men that are to him no more
Than to the Forest hermit are the leaves
That hung aloft in myriads, nay far less
Far less for aught that comforts or defends
Or lull or chears: socity is here
           ⎰T
[?~~Here~~] [?~~is~~] ⎱the true Community the
              noblest frame

Of many a ... to or incorporate
That must the looked for her ... pleasure
On these held under God ... the eye & love
Our family, our mansion, to themselves
appropriate, and the ... for the ...
... if it were a care; a ... but
... of brute possession ... a
... in this ... vale these ... Wall
Their length & their glorious dwelling ... them

  Distress therefore all Arcad... our dreams
All golden fancies, the ... join the trees
That were before all time. That perfect
How dear to think of when we ...
With all remembrance of a ...
... at once this one sufficient hope
... that feeling agree
How goodly her exceeding fair, how pure
From all reproach is his ethereal frame
And this ... pale Arcasker,
    ...

Of many in [?too] to one incorporate
That must be look'd for here paternal
            sway
One Household under God of high & low
One family & one mansion, to themselves
              world⎱
Appropriate, and divided from the [?Worl]⎰
As if it were a cave; a multitude
Human & brute possessors undisturbd
     recess
In this deep vale their legislative Hall
       p⎱
Their teml⎰le & their glorious dwelling-place
  Dismiss therefore all Arcadian dreams
         thoughts
All golden fancies, shadowy from the times
That were before all time that perfect
        age⎱
       [?]⎰
How dear to think of when we wish to
            part
With all remembrance of a jarring world
      once⎱
Take we at [?]⎰ this one sufficient hope
 What need of more
    ⎰[?consolation]
Un to ⎰[?ourselves] that feeling as we
            do
       [?as] we do
How goodly how exceeding fair how pure
          ⎰th
From all reproach is this e⎰atereal frame
   fair ⎰ V
And this deep ⎰[?]ale its earthly
            counterpart

This passage, which follows consecutively from that on 156/157 i^r, is later than the version on 174/175 i^r but precedes that on 164/165 i^r.

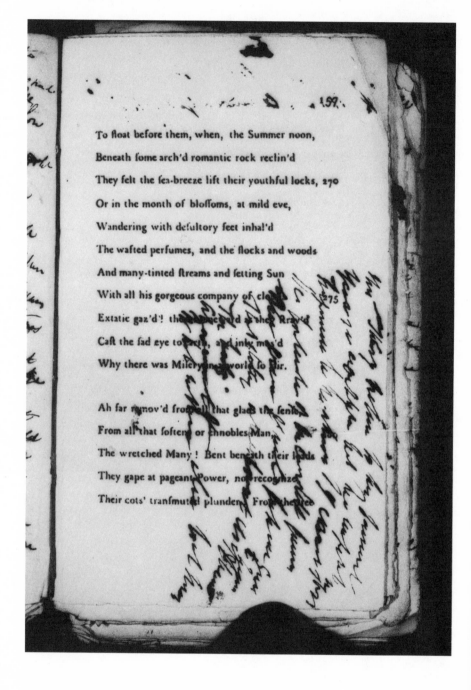

To float before them, when, the Summer noon,

Beneath some arch'd romantic rock reclin'd

They felt the sea-breeze lift their youthful locks, 270

Or in the month of blossoms, at mild eve,

Wandering with desultory feet inhal'd

The wafted perfumes, and the flocks and woods

And many-tinted streams and setting Sun

With all his gorgeous company of clouds 275

Extatic gaz'd! the ———————— they ———

Cast the sad eye to ———, and ——— mus'd

Why there was Misery ——— world so fair.

Ah far remov'd from all that glads the senses

From all that softens or ennobles Man,

The wretched Many! Bent beneath their loads

They gape at pageant Power, nor recognize

Their cots' transmuted plunder. From the tree

[B, 838–841]

[?thus] {[?Thus] Nature to her favourite
Yields no exemption but her [?imperial] rights
Enforces to the utmost & exacts
Her tribute of inevitable pain
[?The] vision & [?] passion gives
                                        to him
That [?sting] which [?] [?itself] & [?hence]
The [?]
[?Above] [?] &
What nature also [? ?]

Most of this passage is a later version of the jottings on 161; a fuller version of these lines is on 164/165 iʳ. The final lines on 157, however, are unidentified.

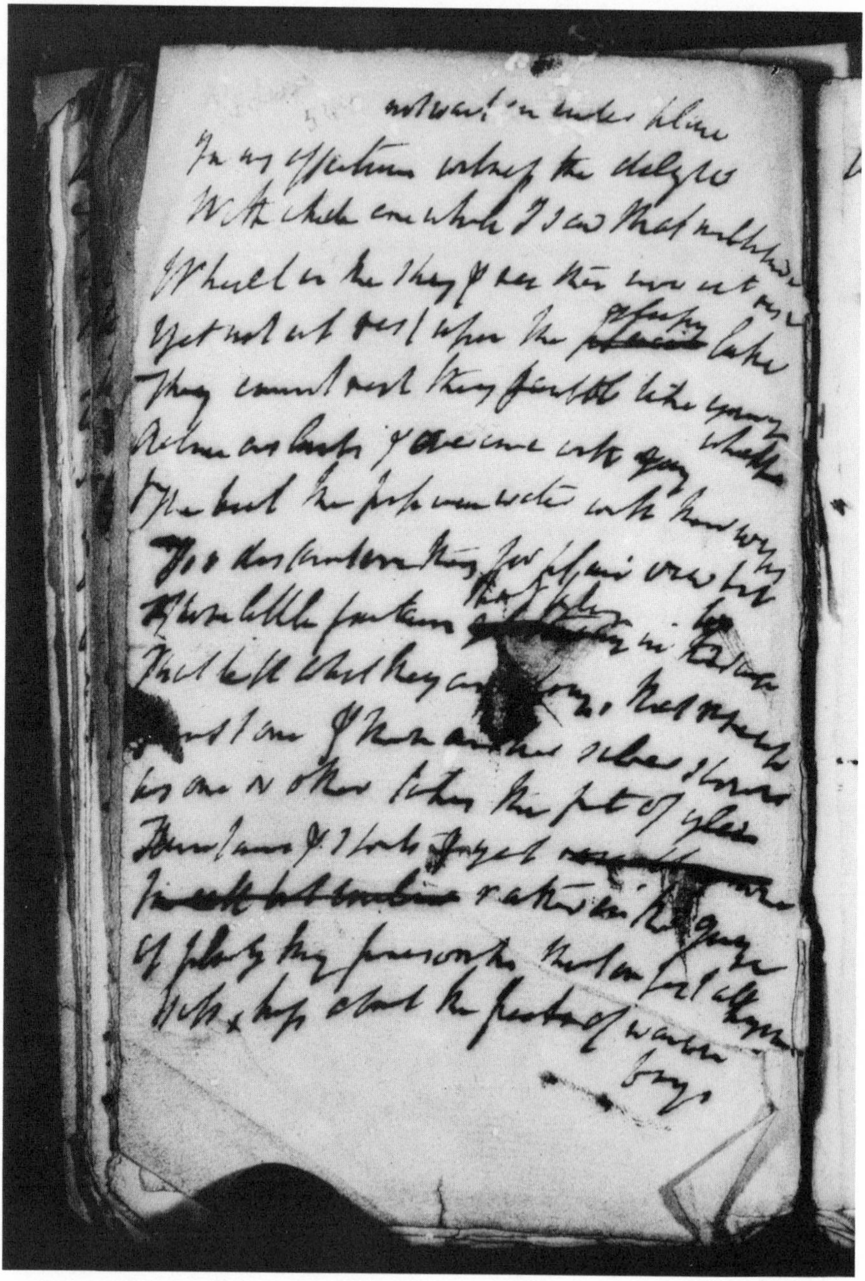

[B, 764-781]

                    not want an under place
In my affections witness the delight
With which ere while I saw that multitude
Wheell in the sky & see them now at rest
                        glassy
Yet not at rest upon the ~~placid~~ lake
                      ol⎞
They cannot rest they gamble⎠ like young
                              whelps
                      ⎧ o   ⎧ j
Active as lambs & ⎨[?]vercome with ⎨[?]oy
                      ⎩   ⎩
The beat the passive water with their wings
Too distant are they for plain view but
                                  lo
              sparkling
[?Those] little fountains ~~glittering~~ in [?the ?sun]
That tell what they are doing, that rise up
First one & then another silver spout
As one or other takes the fit of glee
⎧Fo
⎨[?]untains & spouts & yet resembling more
⎩
~~In all but [?contour]~~ rather in the guize
Of plaything fireworks that on festal nights
Hiss, hiss about the feet𝑠 of wanton
                        boys

The penciled note in the upper left-hand corner is in GW's hand; the first full line here cor-
responds to l. 544 of the published version of MS. D of *Home at Grasmere*. This version precedes
that on 154/155 iᵛ.

With all the fix'd on high like stars of Heaven

Shot baleful influence, shall be cast to earth

Vile and down-trodden, as the untimely fruit

Shook from the fig-tree by a sudden storm.

Ev'n now the storm begins: each gentle name,

Faith and meek Piety, with fearful joy

Tremble far-off — for lo! the Giant FRENZY

Uprooting empires with his whirlwind arm

Mocketh high Heaven; burst hideous from the cell

Where the old Hag, unconquerable, huge,   340

Creation's eyeless drudge, black RUIN, sits

Nursing th' impatient earthquake.

                              O return!

Pure FAITH! meek PIETY! The abhorred Form

Whose scarlet robe was stiff with earthly pomp,   345

Who drank iniquity in cups of gold,

                   M

[B, 838–839]

of which the water

[?One] mountain &

the [?chearful ?dome] of [?open]

And [? ?on ?the ?solemn ?thoughts]
That [?entrance] to this [?favour'd]

[?pass'd]
And   [?open] [?up]

Give entrance to this solemn [?sorrow]
[? ?]
That Nature to this favour'd spot
Yields no exemption

The jottings on this page antedate the lines on 157 and the fuller version on 164/165 i^r. The note visible above the tops of the photographs of pp. 161, 162/163 i^r, and 163 is no longer extant; it was inserted by GW to identify a passage.

Whose names were many and all blasphemous,

Hath met the horrible judgement! Whence that cry

The mighty army of foul Spirits shriek'd,

Disherited of earth! For She hath fallen

On whose black front was written MYSTERY;

She that reel'd heavily, whose wine was blood;

She that work'd whoredom with the DÆMON POWER

And from the dark embrace all evil things

Brought forth and nurtur'd: mitred ATHEISM;   355

And patient FOLLY who on bended knee

Gives back the steel that stabb'd him; and pale FEAR

Hunted by ghastlier terrors than surround

Moon-blasted Madness when he yells at midnight!

Return pure FAITH! return meek PIETY!   360

The kingdoms of the world are your's: each heart

Self-govern'd, the vast family of Love

Rais'd from the common earth by common toil

[?Can ?I ?omit]
~~Let us tr~~ust
That, it is not in the power of storms
Frost snow or hail or ~~[?blight~~ing ?wind]
                              to mar
                          ⎰ or
The external beauty that is here ⎱[?] [?]
                            [?]

⎰[?bu
⎱[?Tha]t rather as they [?a ?sublime]
But as they rather do exalt the
                          scene
                    to⎱
[?Without] give it⎰ itt a [?more ?affecting]
                        [?impassioned]
[?]   grace
                  neither [?frost]
Nor hail nor [?snow]
⎰C
⎱Tan mar the external beauty that is here

                  neither frost
Nor hail nor snow nor [?wind] [?might] [?here]
                  [?might] [?]
                        [?mar]
The external beauty that [?by ?far ?less]
That they [?]   which here

These lines appear to be jottings toward the passage on 172/173 i^v, revised on 162/163 i^r. None of the work on this page was incorporated in MS. B.

Recluse

By which & under which we are enclosed
To breathe in peac that we shall also find
　　　sound
If ~~pure~~ & what we ought to be ourselves
If rightly we observe & justly weigh
~~Unless the hindrance be within ourselves~~
　　　Enough of [? ? ?existence ?]
The innmates not unworthy of their home
　　　　　　　　And as
The dwellers of the dwelling ~~As in~~ storm
　　And change of [?season] neither can destroy
~~Snow frost or [?wind] though [?furious] is no [?power]~~
⎧Nor
⎩To mar the external beauty that is here
But as they rather do exalt the scene
And give to it a more impassiond grace
　　　Render
~~Making~~ what in itself was grand before
More grand more chearful when it
　　　　　　　　　　comes again
The native chearfulness and as the hawk
~~Though wheeling round upon the watch for~~
　　　　　　　　　　　prey
　　Prowling aloft
~~Incessantly~~ deteres not the small birds
　　　　warbling
From ~~singing~~ in their covert but him
Adds his own voice aeril with [?intent]
For so it might be thought by him
　　　　　　　who listens
To solemnize the general harmony

The passage which corresponds to MS. B, ll. 854–859 continues, to include lines not incorporated in MS. B. It is a later version of the lines on 162 and 172/173 i^v.

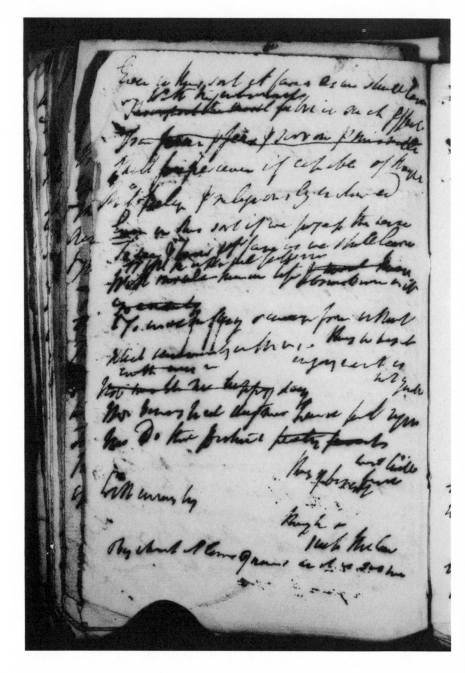

Even in this sort it fares as we shall [?learn]
  With the [?unbound]

~~Throughout the moral~~ fabric in such {[?f]ffect ⌠ e

    ⌠pain
From ~~{[?fear] & fear & sorrow & misrule~~

  ⌠[?we]
Shall {[?per] [?perceive] if capable of thought
And feeling & religiously [?endowed]
Even in this sort if we possess the [?sense]
To see & know it fares as we shall learn
  With [?mutual ?passions]
With ~~moral~~ human life & ~~moral~~ [?human]
      [?observations] [?with]

  ~~To [?enmity]~~
To unremitting [?ravage] from without
        though [?beset]
[?And ?]| within
      enjoyment is
        not [?quelld]
  ~~with [?ever ?]~~
~~Nor mirth nor happy days~~
Nor [?vanished] [?days ?nor] [?have ?fed ?upon]
Nor do these [?virtues ~~?piety~~ ~~?fervent~~]
      [? ?]
      [?find]
      [? ? ?]
[?With] [?]
    though [?]
      [?such] the [?law]
By which it [?lives] & [?moves] and is [?sustain]

These drafts appear to follow the passage on the recto; they were not incorporated in MS. B. An earlier version appears on 163, facing.

Preface

Enjoy the equal produce.   Such delights

As float to earth, permitted visitants!   365

When on some solemn jubilee of Saints

The sapphire-blazing gates of Paradise

Are thrown wide open, and thence voyage forth

Detachments wild of seraph-warbled airs,

And odors snatch'd from beds of amaranth,   370

And they, that from the chrystal river of life

Spring up on freshen'd wing, ambrosial gales!

The favor'd good man in his lonely walk

Perceives them, and his silent spirit drinks

Strange bliss which he shall recognize in heaven. 375

And such delights, such strange beatitude

Seize on my young anticipating heart

When that blest future rushes on my view!

looking out for
Nor can the [?hawk] [?though] frequently a
{I
{incessantly [?deter] the [?lighter] birds
From singing in their [?eagerness]

Like

Even in this sort it fares as we shall learn
With moral Beauty
                    such will be the
Upon our minds, if capable [?of] [?thought]
And [?religiously] [?composed]

Shall find in spite of suffering & distress
Inevitable &

The drafts at the top of the page are related to the passage on 172/173 i^v. The jottings at the foot are drafts toward or variants of some lines on 162/163 i^v, related to jottings on 165. The vertical lines on the right may relate to MS. B, l. 841.

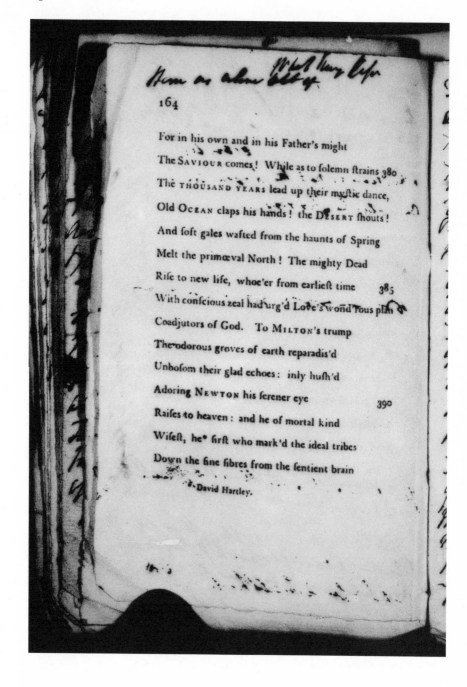

164

For in his own and in his Father's might

The SAVIOUR comes! While as to solemn strains   380

The THOUSAND YEARS lead up their mystic dance,

Old OCEAN claps his hands! the DESERT shouts!

And soft gales wafted from the haunts of Spring

Melt the primæval North! The mighty Dead

Rise to new life, whoe'er from earliest time   385

With conscious zeal had urg'd Love's wond'rous plan

Coadjutors of God.   To MILTON's trump

The odorous groves of earth reparadis'd

Unbosom their glad echoes: inly hush'd

Adoring NEWTON his serener eye
    390

Raises to heaven: and he of mortal kind

Wisest, he* first who mark'd the ideal tribes

Down the fine fibres from the sentient brain

* David Hartley.

What [?] [?life]
[?] [?as ?above ?all] [~~?~~]

These lines are unidentified.

Despising therefore all Arcadian dreams
All golden fancies of the golden age
The bright array of shadowy thoughts from
such were before all time — those
affections — by not the happiness
too — then — when our eyes are
And will be stir'd —
Oh lovely objects and the wish to part
With all remembrance of a passing world
Give entrance — & the solace to the —

That Nature & her favoured sha— of —
Yields no exception but her deepest —
Expose to the utmost and exact
Her tribute of insoluble pain,
And that the Slay is unabled means —
For ever busy to afflict himself
Yet temper him with no sufferings
What need of more That we shall —
Nor live through want of pleasure —
Which is about us nor through —
That keeps in health the —

Dismissing therefore all Arcadian dreams
All golden fancies of the golden age
The bright array of shadowy thoughts from
                                                times
                    or are to be
That were before all time ~~those~~ perfect days
          When time is not the pageantry that stir
~~How sweet to think of~~ when our eyes are fix'd
          And will be stirring
On lovely objects and we wish to part
                              ing⎫
With all remembrance of a jarr[?]⎬ world
Give entrance to the sober truth, avow
~~Alone with resolute & manly [?faith]~~
That Nature to this favoured spot of ours
Yields no exemption but her awful rights
Enforces to the utmost and exacts
Her tribute of inevitable pain,
And that the sting is [?added] man [—?—]
                              himself
For ever [?busy] to afflict himself
Yet temper this with one sufficient
                              [?hope]
                    faith
What need of more that we shall neither
                    [?droop]
Nor pine through want of pleasure in this
                    life
Which is about us nor through dearth
                              of aught
That keeps in health the insatiable
                    mind

This version of the lines is later than the versions on 156/157 iᵛ and 174/175 iʳ.

[B, 849–850]

          have for
That we shall of knowledge for love
Abundance & that feeling as we do

This passage continues consecutively from the draft on the recto.

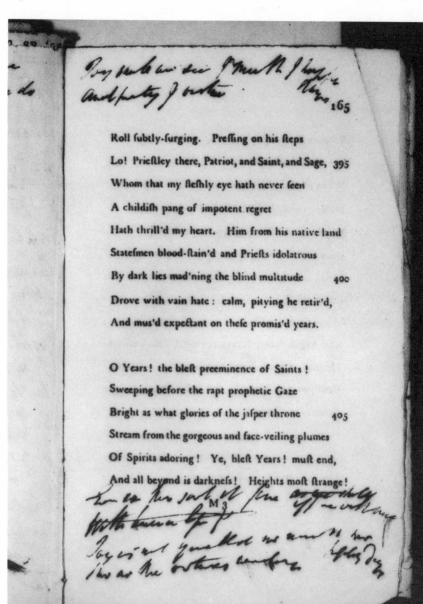

165

Roll ſubtly-ſurging. Preſſing on his ſteps
Lo! Prieſtley there, Patriot, and Saint, and Sage, 395
Whom that my fleſhly eye hath never ſeen
A childiſh pang of impotent regret
Hath thrill'd my heart. Him from his native land
Stateſmen blood-ſtain'd and Prieſts idolatrous
By dark lies mad'ning the blind multitude   400
Drove with vain hate: calm, pitying he retir'd,
And mus'd expeftant on theſe promis'd years.

O Years! the bleſt preeminence of Saints!
Sweeping before the rapt prophetic Gaze
Bright as what glories of the jaſper throne   405
Stream from the gorgeous and face-veiling plumes
Of Spirits adoring! Ye, bleſt Years! muſt end,
And all beyond is darkneſs! Heights moſt ſtrange!

Joy shall we see & mirth & happy
                                    days
And piety & virtue

Even in this sort it fares ~~as we~~ shall
                          it fares with us
~~With human life &~~
Joy is not quelld nor mirth nor
                            happy days
[?Nor ?are] the [?virtues] [?wanting]

These jottings are related to those at the foot of 163; a fuller version appears on 162/163 i^v.

[D, 597–606]

                by   the   d

He ~~whom~~ ~~some~~ vast Metropolis immures
Where pity shrinks from unremitting calls
Where numbers overwhelm humanity   *then*

And neighbourhood serves rather to divide
            to [?contain]

    H]   yes yes there is a weight
Than to unite { *[?on]e who inhabits, under a black sky*
    h]

  A
D world where if indifference do not yield
      disgust or sorrow
To scorn, ~~or fear~~ living Men
Are ofttimes to their fellow men no more

These two facing pages contain a very late revision of ll. 597–606 in MS. D. It was copied onto 25^v in MS. D.

167

And vice, and anguiſh, and the wormy grave,

Shapes of a dream ! The veiling clouds retire,   425

And lo ! the Throne of the redeeming God

Forth flaſhing unimaginable day

Wraps in one blaze earth, heaven, and deepeſt hell.

Contemplant Spirits ! ye that hover o'er

With untir'd gaze th' immeaſurable fount   430

Ebullient with creative Deity !

And ye of plaſtic power, that interfus'd

Roll thro' the groſſer and material maſs

In organizing ſurge ! Holies of God !

(And what if Monads of the infinite mind ?)   435

I haply journeying my immortal courſe

Shall ſometime join your myſtic choir ! Till then

I diſcipline my young noviciate thought

[D, 601–602]

Then to unite yes yes there is a weight
Of loneliness He can report of it
Whose nobler will ++ hath long been sacrificed

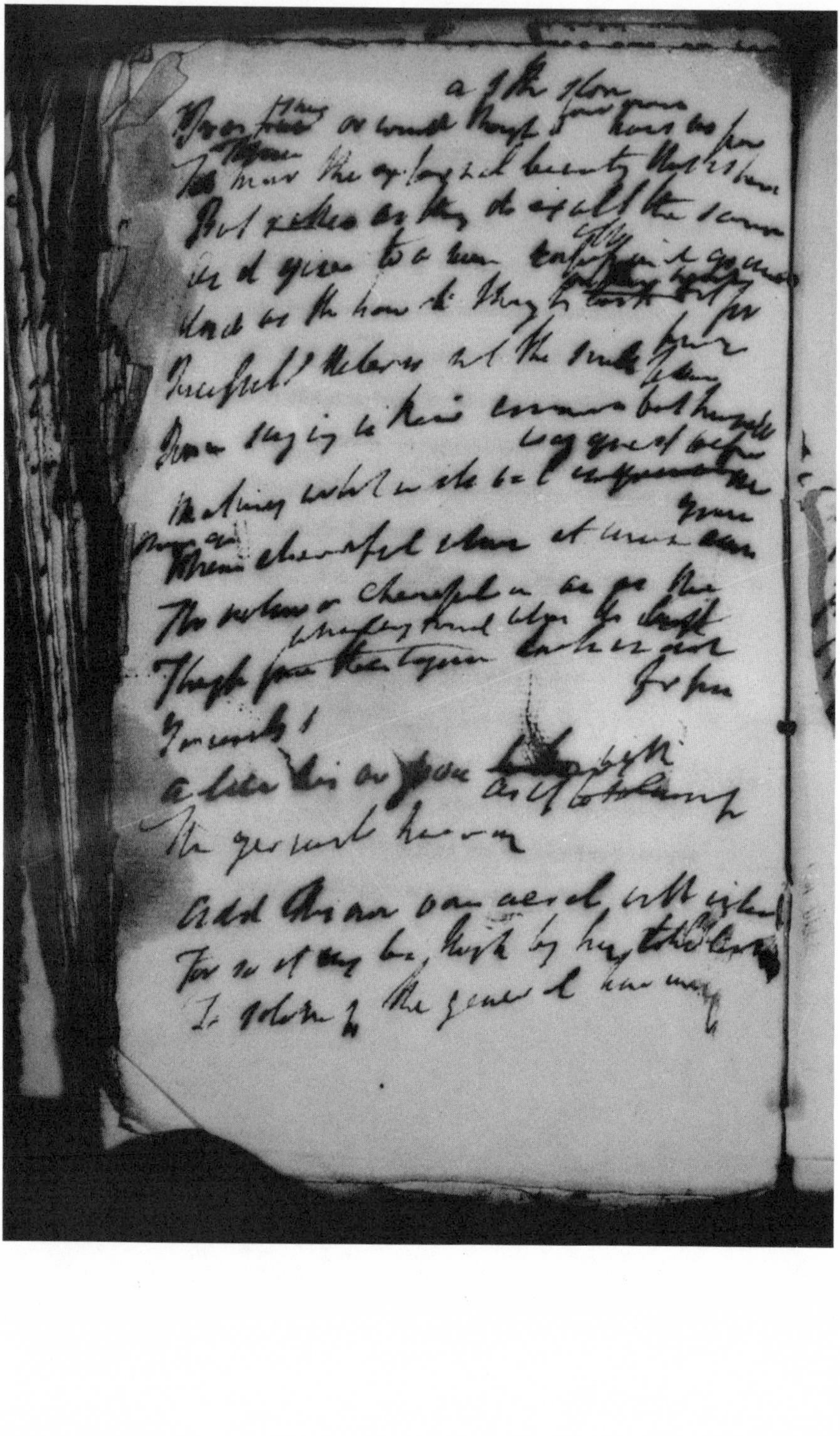

                          as the storm
⎰F   [?snow]   [?furious]
⎱Trost [?or] or wind though   [?hath ?no ?power]
       [?harm]
To mar the external beauty that is here
But rather as they do exalt the scene
                          [?oft]
And give to a more impassion'd grace
                     on the [?hunt]
And as the hawk though look out for
                          prey
Incessantl deteres not the [?small] [?]
From singing in their [?coverts] but himself
                    was grand before
Making what in itself is grand [?more]
                          grand
[?More] [?]
[?When] chearful [?when ?it ?comes ?]
The native [?] chearfuln [?as ?is ?the]
                                [?hawk]
               wheeling round [?upon ?the ?watch]
Though [?from ?this ?region ?looking ?out]
                          [?prey]
[?Incessnt]
                          [?with]
Adds his own voice [?to ?theirs]
                    as if to solemnize
The general harmony
          ⎰[?his]
Add ⎱[?] own voice aeril with intent
                          ⎰who
For so it may be though by him ⎱that listens
To solemnize the general harmony

  These lines are not incorporated in MS. B; this version is intermediate between the draft on
162 and the version on 162/163 iʳ.

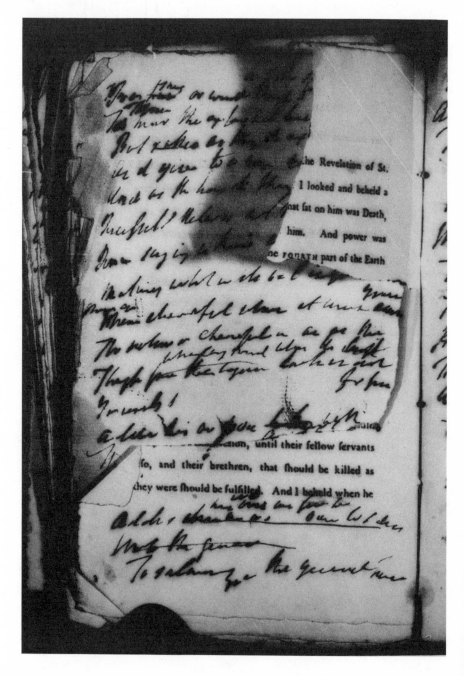

the Revelation of St.

I looked and beheld a

that sat on him was Death,

him. And power was

the FOURTH part of the Earth

until their fellow servants

so, and their brethren, that should be killed as

they were should be fulfilled. And I beheld when he

           [?is]
        his [?voice] [? ?]
Adds [?his ?own ?]   voice to solem
With the gener
To solemnize the general harm

   This page has been torn. The lines at the foot are a draft toward the passage on 172/173 i^v. WW, writing rapidly, failed to finish "solemnize," "general," and "harmony" at the ends of his lines.

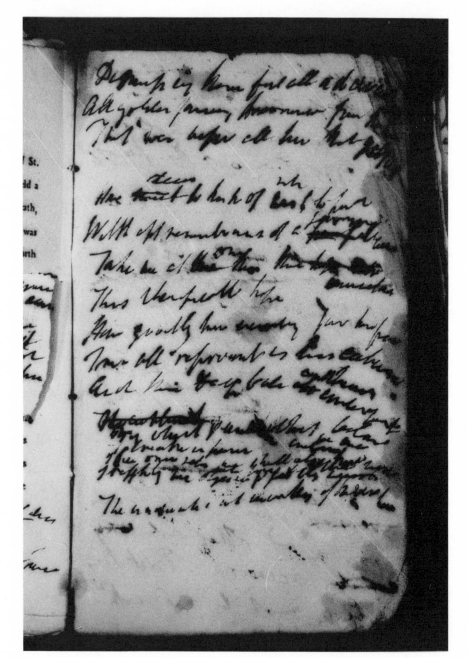

Dismissing therefore all [?all] arcadian
                                            d
                          bo⎱
All golden fancies, [?tomo⎰rrow] from the [?time]
                                perf⎱
That was before all time that gold⎰ age
            dear   wh
How ~~sweet~~ to think of [?wish] to part
                                        jarring
Witth all remembrance of a ~~painful~~ [?world]
                      once
            ⎧once
Take we at ⎨this this this hope unto
            ⎩   ourselves
This chearfull hope
How goodly how exceeding fair how pure
From all reproach is this [?aetherial]
                          [?frame]
              [?earthly]
And this deep Vale ~~its~~ counterpart
                              below
[?~~The~~] [?]
    By which & under which we are
                    enclosed
        To breathe in peace
        [?This] once [?] we shall also [?prove]
                  [?] [?free ?to ?choose] [?weigh]
I rightly we observe & justly [?]
The inmates not unworthy of their home

This draft precedes the versions on 156/157 iᵛ and 164/165 iʳ. Writing rapidly here, WW failed to finish some of his words: in l. 3, "perfect" and "golden" are incomplete, as is the phrase "when we wish" in l. 4, and the word "If" in the second line from the bottom.

The Prospectus to *The Recluse*:   MS. 1

MS. 1 of the Prospectus to *The Recluse* appears in the Green family account book (DC MS. 45). The notebook is a single gathering of sixty-four leaves, of which the first and last are stuck to the limp blue-green covers of the book; leaf 16 has been torn out, leaving a stub. The back cover has a flap through which a piece of string could be fitted so that the book could be secured for the pocket. The book measures 15.7 by 8.85 centimeters at the top, 9.35 centimeters at the foot. The paper is white laid, countermarked FD; the edges of the paper have been colored red. This notebook is similar to *Prelude* MSS. W, X, and Y (DC MSS. 38, 47, 48) and the former MS. Verse 58 (DC MS. 70) of *The Excursion*; Mark Reed conjectures that the books were bought in Calais in the summer of 1802 (*Chronology: MY*, p. 642).

On the verso of the first leaf in the book, Wordsworth signed his name; then on the rectos of leaves 2 to 5 he wrote a fair copy of the Prospectus to *The Recluse* in seventy-seven lines; he made corrections in his copy while writing, and on 3^v he revised two lines. This is the earliest extant version of the passage found in MS. B of *Home at Grasmere*, as the final lines of that poem, and excerpted in the 1814 Preface to *The Excursion*; the manuscript cannot be dated but can be shown to precede the versions in MS. 2 of the Prospectus and in MS. B.

The notebook contains no other verse. There is a prose fragment in the hand of Dorothy Wordsworth, which Reed describes as "seemingly psychological speculation about the daughter of a blind man" (*Chronology: MY*, p. 663). Starting from the back end, Mary Wordsworth used the notebook to record taxes paid on Allan Bank, the Wordsworth's second home in Grasmere, between 16 July 1808 and 23 April 1811 and to record payments made on behalf of the orphaned Green family between 15 October 1808 and 15 November 1828.

In the text of MS. 1 of the Prospectus line numbers at the left are serially assigned; bracketed line numbers at the right correspond to those of MS. B.

On Man, on Nature, and on human Life
Thinking in solitude, from time to time
I feel sweet passions traversing my soul
Like music: unto these, where'er I may
I would give utterance in numerous verse
Of Truth, of Grandeur, Beauty, Love, and
of joy in various commonalty spread; Hope,
of the individual mind that keeps its own
Inviolate retirement, and consists
With being limitless, the one great Life;
I sing; fit audience let me find though few.
          Fit audience find though few! Thus I prayed
                                        the Bard
Holiest of Men, Urania I shall need
Thy guidance, or a greater Muse, if such
Descend to earth or dwell in highest
                                        heaven
For I must tread on Shadowy ground,
Deep, and ascend aloft, and
So which the Heaven of heavens is but a veil.
All strength, all terror, single, or in bands
That ever was, put forth by personal Form
Jehovah, with his thunders, and the choir
Of shouting Angels, and th' empyreal
These then unalarm'd & the darkest
of the profoundest hell, night, chaos

1　On Man, on Nature, and on human Life
2　Thinking in solitude, from time to time　　　　[960]
3　I find sweet passions traversing my soul
4　Like music: unto these, where'er I may
5　I would give utterance in numerous verse
6　Of Truth, of Grandeur, Beauty, Love, and
　　　　　　　　　　　　　　Hope;
7　Of joy in various commonalty spread;
8　Of th'individual mind that keeeps its own
9　Inviolate retirement, and consists　　　　　　[970]
10　With being limitless, the one great Life;
11　I sing; fit audience let me find though few.
12　　'Fit audience find though few'! Thus prayd
　　　　　　　　　　　　　the Bard
13　Holiest of men. Urania I shall need
14　Thy guidance, or a greater Muse, if such　　　[975]
15　Desend to earth, or dwell in highest
　　　　　　　　　　　heaven.
16　For I must tread on Shadowy ground, must
　　　　　　　　　　　　　　sink
17　Deep, and ascend aloft, and　　　worlds
18　To which the Heaven of heavens is but a veil.
19　All strength, all terror, single, or in bands　[980]
20　That ever was put forth by personal Form
21　Jehovah, with his thunder, and the choir
22　Of shouting Angels, and Th'empyreal Thrones
23　I pass them unalarm'd. The darkest pit
24　Of the profoundest hell, night, chaos, death　[985]

Nor aught of blinder vacancy, scoop'd out
By help of dreams, can breed such fear
As fall upon me often when I look
Into my soul, into the soul of man
My haunt, and the main region of
Beauty, whose living home is the green earth
Surpassing far what hath by special craft
Of delicate Poets, been call'd forth, & shaped
From earths materials, waits upon my steps
Pitches her tents before as I move
My hourly neighbour. Paradise, & groves
Elysian, blessed island in the deep
Of choice seclusion, wherefore need they be
A history, or but a dream, when minds
Once wedded to this outward frame of things
In love, finds them the growth of common day
Such pleasant haunts foregoing, if my song
Thus turn elsewhere, & travel near the tribes
And fellow ships of men, and see ill sights
Of passions ravenous from each other
In want of injury, of wrong and strife
.... be these my guide, and ....
Their humanity in fields & groves
Pipe solitary anguish, or must hear
Brooding above the fierce confederate storm
Of sorrows, barricadoed evermore
Within the walls of Cities, to these sounds

25   Nor aught of blinder vacancy scoop'd out
26   By help of dreams, can breed such fear
                                    and awe
27   As fall upon me often when I look
28   Into my soul, into the soul of man
29   My haunt, and the main region of   [990]
                              my song
30   Beauty, whose living home is the green earth
31   Surpassing far what hath by special craft
32   Of delicate Poets, been cull'd forth, & shap'd
33   From earths materials, waits upon my steps
                                          ⌠ o
34   Pitches her tents before as I m⌡[?]ve   [995]
                    ⌠N
35   My hourly ⌡neighbour. Paradise, & groves
36   Elysian, blessed island in the deep
37   Of choice seclusion, wherefore need they be
38   A history, or but a dream, when minds
39   Once wedded to this outward frame of things   [1000]
40   In love, finds these the growth of common
                                      day.
41   Such pleasant haunts foregoing, if my Song   [1015]
42   Must turn elswhere, & travel near the tribes
43   And Fellowships of man, and see ill sights
44   Of passoons ravenous from each others rage,
45   Insult & injury & wrong and strife
46   ~~Wisdom be thou my Guide, and if so taskd~~
            Must
47   ~~I~~ hear humanity in fields & groves
48   Pipe solitary anguish, or must hang   [1020]
49   Brooding above the fierce confederate storm
50   Of sorrow, barricadoed ever more
51   Within the walls of Cities; to these sounds

---

34   Following "before" the word "me" was omitted.

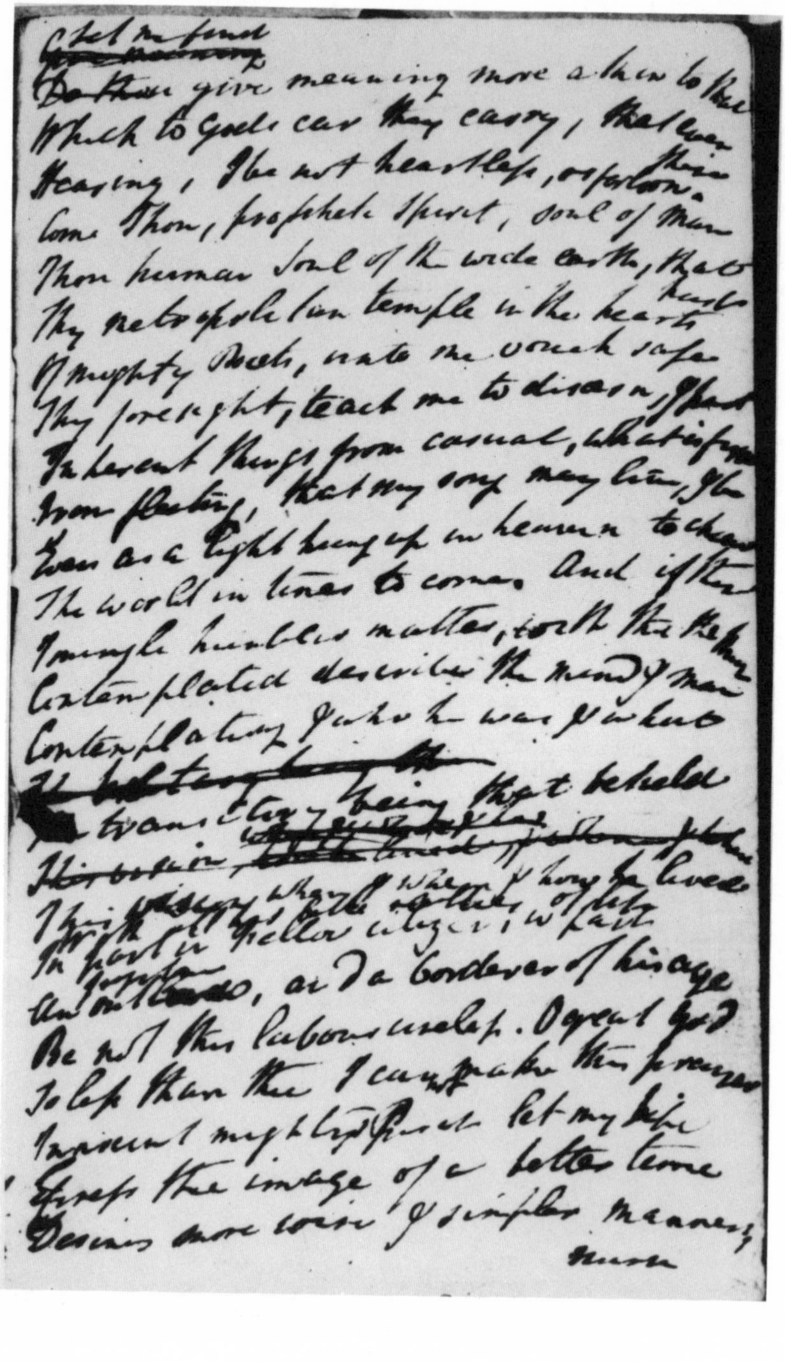
Let me find
~~Come meaning~~
~~Do thou~~ give meaning more akin to that
Which to God's ear they carry, that even these
Hearing, I be not heartless, or forlorn.
Come thou, prophetic Spirit, soul of Man
Thou human Soul of the wide earth, that hast
Thy metropolitan temple in the hearts
Of mighty Poets, unto me vouchsafe
Thy foresight, teach me to discern, & part
Inherent things from casual, what is fixed
From fleeting, that my song may live, & be
Even as a light hung up in heaven to chear
The world in times to come. And if with this
I mingle humbler matter, with the thing
Contemplated describe the mind & man
Contemplating & who he was & what
The transitory Being that beheld
This vision, when & where & how he lived
With all his little realities of life
In part a fellow citizen, in part
An outlaw, and a borderer of his age
Be not this labour useless. O great God
To less than thee I cannot make this prayer
Innocent mighty Spirit let my life
Express the image of a better time
Desires more wise & simpler manners, nurse

Let me find
~~Give meaning~~
52 ~~Do thou~~ give meaning more akin to that
53 Which to Gods ear they carry, that even
                                             these
54 Hearing, I be not heartless, or forlorn.   [1025]
55 Come Thou, prophetc Spirit, soul of Man
56 Thou human Soul of the wide earth, that
                                             hast
57 Thy metropolitan temple in the hearts
58 Of mighty Poets, unto me vouch safe
59 Thy foresight, teach me to discern, & part   [1030]
60 Inherent things from casual, what is fixd
61 From fleeting, that my song may live, & be
62 Even as a light hung up in heaven to chear
63 The world in times to come. And if this
64 I mingle humbler matter, with the the thing   [1035]
65 Contemplated describe the mind & man
66 Contemplating & who he was & what
                    ⌠ tr
The ⎨solitary being th
67 The transitory being that beheld
                    when & where & how
This vision, how he lived, & [?where] & [?when]
                    ⌠ visi
68 This ⎨[?when] on when & where & how he lived
                    With all his little realties of life   [1040]
69 In part a Fellow citizen, in part
            fugitive
                    aw ⎞
70 An outl[?]⎫, and a borderer of his age
71 Be not this labour useless. O great God
72 To less than thee I can   make this prayer
                            not
                    ⌠sp   ⌠li
73 Innocent mighty ⎨Pirit let my ⎨[?]fe
74 Express the image of a better time   [1045]
75 Desires more wise & simpler manners,
                            nurse

---

63 A preposition was omitted before "this."
71 Opposite this line, on the facing verso (3ᵛ), is the following draft:

                    such
                If ~~this~~ theme
        not unworthy
    Be ~~also~~ worthy then Eternal God

72 The word "not" was accidentally omitted in transcription and added later.

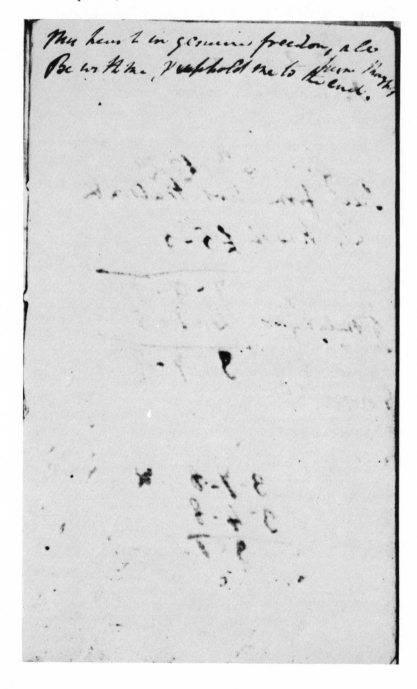

76   My heart in genuine freedom, all
                              pure thoughts
77   Be with me & uphold me to the end.

The Prospectus to *The Recluse*: MS. 2

MS. 2 of the Prospectus to *The Recluse* (in DC MS. 24) is a single leaf, measuring 22.2 by 14.4 centimeters; it belonged to a notebook which Wordsworth used for drafts and copies of poems from 1801 to 1815. The paper is blue-tinted, laid octavo, with a maker's name partially visible as a countermark, but not decipherable. De Selincourt and Darbishire refer to this manuscript as MS. 3 of the Prospectus and designate as MS. 2 the lines concluding MS. B. As their labels confuse the chronology, I have altered them.

On the recto of the leaf Wordsworth wrote the final thirty lines of the Prospectus in a version intermediate between the text of MS. 1 and that concluding MS. B of *Home at Grasmere*. The top left-hand corner of the leaf has been torn away, with the loss of part or all of the initial words in the top six lines. On the verso Wordsworth wrote the motto to his version of Chaucer's *Prioress' Tale*. Possibly when the leaf stood in the original the following leaves contained his modernization. A few other scattered leaves do survive from the notebook, but it is impossible to place them in significant relation to each other or to derive from them information relative to MS. 2 of the Prospectus. For a fuller discussion of the contents of this notebook and its possible dates of use, see *Chronology: MY*, 664–665.

In the text of MS. 2 of the Prospectus line numbers at the left correspond to those of MS. 1; bracketed line numbers at the right correspond to those of MS. B.

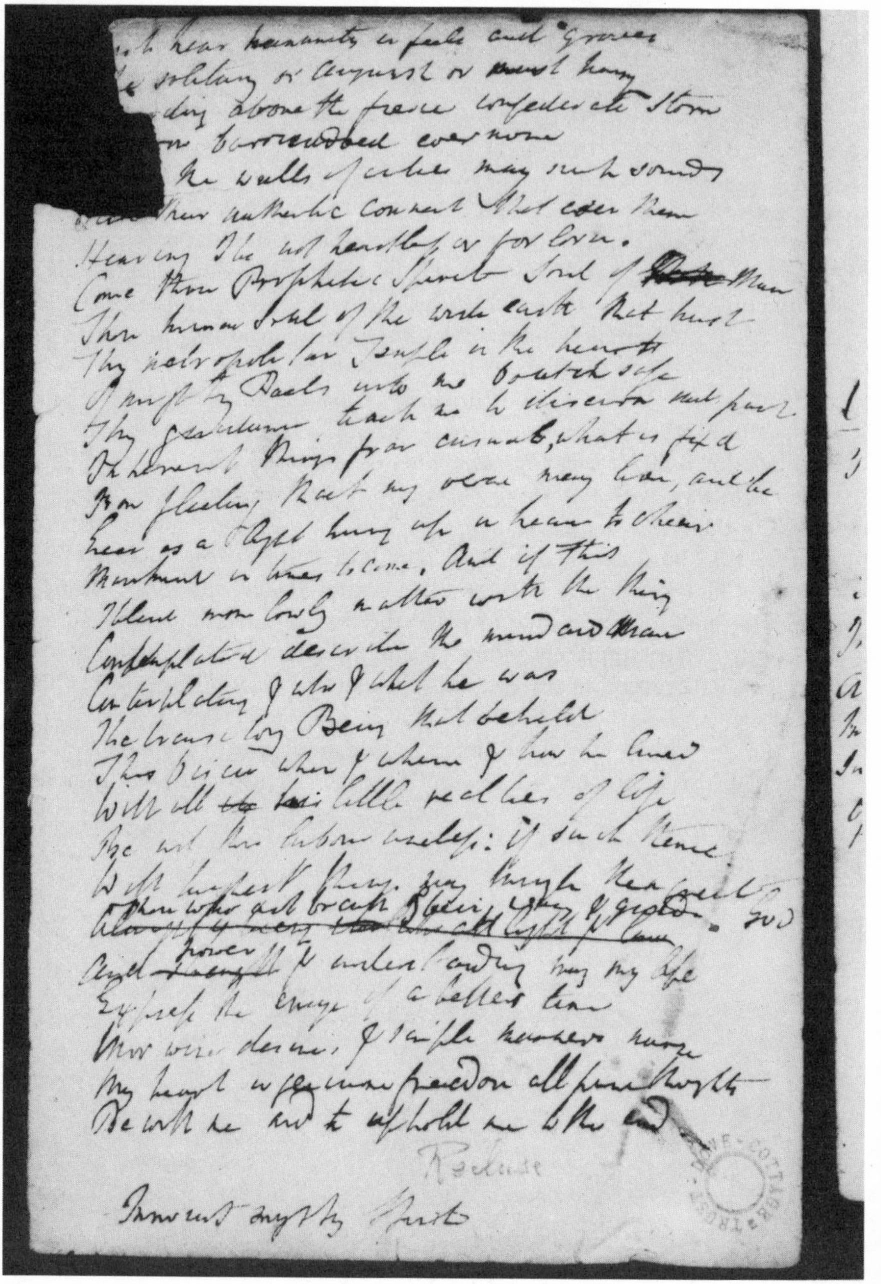

47　　[　　　]st hear humanity in feels and groves

　　　　　　　　　　　　　　⌠mus
48　　[　　　]e solitary or anguish or ⌡[?]t hang　　　　　[1020]
49　　[　　　]ding above the fierce confederate Storm
50　　[　　　]row barricadoed evermore
51　　[　　　] the walls of cities may such sounds

　　　　　　　　　　　　　　　　　　　　　　，
　　　[　　　] their authentic comment that even them
54　　Hearing I be not heartless or forlorn.　　　　　　[1025]

　　　　　　　　　　　　　　　　　　Man
55　　Come thou Prophetic Spirit—Soul of [?Earth]
56　　Thou human Soul of the wide earth that hast
57　　Thy metropolitan Temple in the hearts
58　　Of mighty Poets unto me voutchsafe
59　　Thy guidance teach me to discern and part　　　　[1030]
60　　Inherent things from casual, what is fixd
61　　From fleeting that my verse may live, and be
62　　Even as a light hung up in heaven to chear

　　　　　　　　　　　　　　　　⌠t
63　　Mankind in times to come. And if ⌡This
64　　I blend more lowly matter with the thing　　　　　[1035]

　　　　te ⌉　　　　　　　　　　　　⌠ M
65　　Con[?pl]⌡mplated describe the mind and ⌡[?]an
66　　Contemplating & who & what he was
67　　The transitory Being that beheld
68　　This Vision when & where & how he lived

　　　　　　　　⌠ h
　　　With all its ⌡[?]is little realties of life　　　　[1040]
71　　Be not this labour useless: if such theme
　　　With highest things may [?mingle] then great

　　　　　　　　　　　　　　　　　　　　　God
　　　Thou who art breath & being way & guide
　　　Almighty being [?whol] who art light & [?law]

　　　　power
　　　And strength & understanding may my life
74　　Express the image of a better time　　　　　　　[1045]
75　　Mor wise desires & simple manners nurse
76　　My heart in genuine freedom all pure thoughts
77　　Be with me and to uphold me to the end.

73　　Innocent mighty Spirit

47　WW wrote "feels" for "fields." The upper left-hand corner of this leaf has been torn off.
63　A preposition was omitted before "This."
77　The title, "Recluse," below this line is written in pencil in the hand of GW.

The Final Manuscripts

MS. B: Transcriptions and Photographic Reproductions

MS. B (DC MS. 59) is a small homemade notebook without covers. Forty-five leaves, measuring 16.9 by 10.4 centimeters, survive intact: 1–8, 10–15, 17–39, 41–48; three have been removed, leaving only stubs: 9, 16, 40. All leaves are conjugate in pairs, except 24 and 28; originally conjugate as 24 and 27, these have been separated and the second leaf moved back to its present position at 28. Initially the manuscript comprised three gatherings of eight leaves apiece; a second group of three gatherings was later inserted after leaf 21, the fifth leaf of the original third gathering. Gatherings were made by tearing and folding a total of six folio sheets into octavo leaves. These sheets were similar to the one preserved intact in MS. A. The paper is white wove, untrimmed, and countermarked 1801. The countermark appeared at the center of the folio sheet and is now at the top outer corners of the octavo leaves.

The original three gatherings contain a fair copy of the opening 468 lines written on the rectos primarily by Mary Wordsworth. (John Finch identified this hand as Sara Hutchinson's [*BWS*, p. 23], but Mary's neatest script is strikingly similar to Sara's.) Wordsworth's hand appears in ll. 91–171, his sister's in ll. 282–296 and ll. 385–417. The three added gatherings together with the final leaves of the original third gathering, 46–48, contain a fair copy of the rest of the poem, predominantly in Wordsworth's hand; Dorothy's hand appears in ll. 614–645 and ll. 759–804; Mary's in ll. 973–995 and ll. 1028–1048. Throughout, except where otherwise noted, italicized revisions are in Mary's hand. The addition of new gatherings and the changes in hand are related to the poem's expansion and eventual completion; their significance is discussed in the Introduction. Mary's spacing on page 20 suggests that Wordsworth had begun copying the text on the inserted gatherings (beginning on page 21) before she completed her transcription of the opening 468 lines of the poem. She was clearly aware that she had extra room as she approached the conclusion of the poem's first section and spaced out her lines. How far Wordsworth had proceeded in transcribing the second section before the new gatherings were sewn into the original is uncertain, but the first of the added gatherings also appears to have been "cast off." Dorothy Wordsworth, in concluding a block of her transcription on page 28, spaced out her lines, as Mary had earlier, before the second added gathering continues on page 29 in Wordsworth's most careful hand. The text occupies all the surviving rectos through 46^r and concludes on 46^v and 47^v; it lacks ll. 185–208, which stood on the missing leaf 9.

Four kinds of drafts and revisions appear in the manuscript in addition to the fair-copy text: (1) drafts of ll. 936–958 antecedent to the base text, in Wordsworth's hand on 47^v, 48^r, and 48^v; (2) revisions in the text with accompanying new drafts of ll. 469–613, in Wordsworth's hand on 21–27^r, 21–24^v, and 26^v; (3) new drafts running, intermittently, down to l. 945, in Wordsworth's hand on 1–2^v, 7–8^v, 14^v, 20^v, 27^v, 31–37^v, and 42^v; and (4) revisions in the text with a few accompanying new drafts, some in Wordsworth's but most in Mary's hand, continuous through the rectos and on 12^v, 18^v, 26^v, 30^v, 32^v, 34^v, 39^v, 43^v, 45^v, and 48^v. The base text of MS. B dates from 1806. The first set of drafts represents preparations for the completion of the MS. B text, probably accomplished by mid-September, 1806. The second set of revisions and drafts prepared ll. 469–606 for transfer to *The Excursion*, VI, 1080–1191; these entries date from 1809–1812. The third set of drafts points to a radical revision of the poem, in 1812–1814, which proved abortive. The fourth set of revisions and drafts prepared the way for the new text of the poem copied out in MS. D; the first of these (on 12^v) clearly dates from 1812–1814, as it is incorporated in the section of MS. D on 1810 paper. The remainder of this last group of revisions could date from 1812–1814 or alternatively from 1831–1832, prior to the copying of the final version of MS. D.

Pages 12^v, 18^v, 30^v, 39^v, and 45^v, carrying only very short, late revisions toward MS. D, and page 44^v, bearing only two letters, are not reproduced in photographs in the following text. Their contents, however, are transcribed in the appropriate notes.

7.   1

~~Tintern~~
Recluse

                    Book first   ~~propose~~
              to the brow of ~~yon~~ ~~steep~~ ~~which~~
Once on the ~~brow~~ ~~of~~ ~~yonder~~ Hill ~~I stopp~~
Jcame – a roving ~~School boy~~ (of what age
~~I forgot~~ a School boy (of what age
~~I~~ ~~hath~~ ~~how~~ ~~escaped~~ ~~my~~ ~~memory~~
~~I cannot well remember~~ but the hour
I well remember though the year be gone
And with a sudden influx overcome
At sight of this seclusion I forgot
My haste for hasty had my footsteps been
As boyish my pursuits ~~and~~ ~~yet~~ ~~how~~ ~~soon~~
~~as~~ ~~on~~ ~~the~~ ~~summit~~ ~~of~~ ~~the~~
What happy fortune were it here to live
                                              live
And if I thought of dying if a thought
                                              intrude
Of mortal separation could ~~come on~~
With paradise before me here to die.
I was no Prophet nor had even a hope
Scarcely a wish, but one bright pleasing thought
Afancy in the heart of what might be
The lot of others never could be mine.

1

Book first

    ~~grassy~~   grassy [?Hill]
    to the brow of yon~~der steep hill~~

1   *Once ~~on the brow of yonder Hill I stopp~~'d*
        I came — a roving

2   *~~While I was yet~~ a School-boy* ⸨ *of what age*

              ')
    Hath now escape∫d my memory
3   *~~I cannot well remember~~ but the hour*

4   *I well remember though the year be gone* ⸩
5   *And with a sudden influx overcome*
6   *At sight of this seclusion I forgot*
7   *My haste for hasty had my footsteps been*
                 and sighing said
8   *As boyish my pursuits*
     ~~As on the summit of the hill I stood~~
9   *What happy fortune were it here to*
                    live
10   *And if I thought of dying if a thought*
              intrude
11   *Of mortal separation could ~~come in~~*
12   *With paradise before me here to die.*
13   *I was no Prophet nor had even a hope*
14   *Scarcely a wish, but one bright pleasing thought*
15   *A fancy in the heart of what might be*
16   *The lot of other's never could be mine.*

  "Prelude" is written in the hand of John Carter, "Recluse" in the hand of GW. The penciled 7 in the upper left-hand corner refers to the former location of the MS. when exhibited in the Wordsworth Museum. Page numbers in ink in the upper right-hand corners are probably DW's or MW's. The portions of paper visible above the recto pages in photographs of MS. B formerly marked the position of lines incorporated in *The Excursion*; the hand is GW's.

Upon   my untired limbs
On the cool turf I stretchd ~~my limbs~~
                    ~~at eas~~
And halted long

~~at last,~~ the illullison strengthening
                as I gazed
~~The illusion~~ strengthening in me
~~The illusion~~
The illusion/strengthening as I gazd,
That lovely/prospect & those
        It seemed   [? ?]
{~~M~~
{[?]~~ethought,~~ the illusion strengthening
                as I gaze
That such unfetterd Liberty was
                    mine
Such power & joy

The lines at the top of the page are a revision of l. 20, on the facing recto; they were not incorporated into MS. D. The lines at the foot are a revision of ll. 34–36, facing; MS. D incorporates them with slight alteration.

C. VI. 1149

The Station whence

~~The place from which~~ I look'd was soft ~~soft~~

Not giddy yet aerial with a depth

Of Vale below a height of hills above

Long did I halt I could have made it even

My business & my errand so to halt

For rest of body ~~twas~~ a perfect place

All that luxurious nature could desire

But ~~stirring~~ to the spirit who could look

And not feel motion there? thought of Clouds

That sail on winds, of Breezes that delight

To play on water or in endless chase

Pursue each other through the liquid depths

Of grass or corn over & through & through

In billow after billow evermore;

Of ~~turbaing~~ Shadows, Butterflies & Birds

~~Speck, Elphs & ...~~

~~Angels & winged~~ creatures that are Lords

Without restraint of all which they behold

~~...~~ in short as I look'd

Seem'd to feel such liberty was mine.

Such power & joy but only for this end

To flit from field to ~~rock~~ from rock to field

From shore to island & from isle to shore

From open place to covert from a bed

Of meadow-flowers into a tuft of wood

2

	The station whence
17	~~The place from which~~ *I look'd was soft & green*
18	*Not giddy yet aerial with a depth*
19	*Of Vale below a height of Hills above*
20	*Long did I halt I could have made it even*
21	*My business & my errand so to halt*

                          was this

| 22 | *For rest of body 'twas a perfect place* |
| 23 | *All that luxurious nature could desire* |

                 stirring

24	*But* ~~tempting~~ *to the Spirit who could look*
25	*And not feel motions there? I thought of* {C / clouds
26	*That sail on winds, of* {B / breezes *that delight*
27	*To play on water or in endless chase*
28	*Pursue each other through the liquid depths*
29	*Of grass or corn over & through & through*
30	*In billow after billow evermore ;*
31	*Of Sunbeams Shadows Butterflies & Birds*

         Of aery Sylphs & sofly gliding Fays

| 32 | ~~Angels & winged~~ *Creatures that are Lords* |

         Genii & winged Angels

| 33 | *Without restraint of all which they behold* |

          moved   Fancy

| 34 | ~~I sate & stirr'd in Spirit~~ *as I look'd* |

         ~~[?did ?deem ?seem]~~

| 35 | *I seem'd to feel such liberty was mine* |
| 36 | *Such power & joy but only for this end* |

              {rock   {from

37	*To flit from field to* {field {to rock to field
38	*From shore to island & from isle to shore*
39	*From open place to covert, from a bed*
40	*Of meadow-flowers into a tuft of wood*

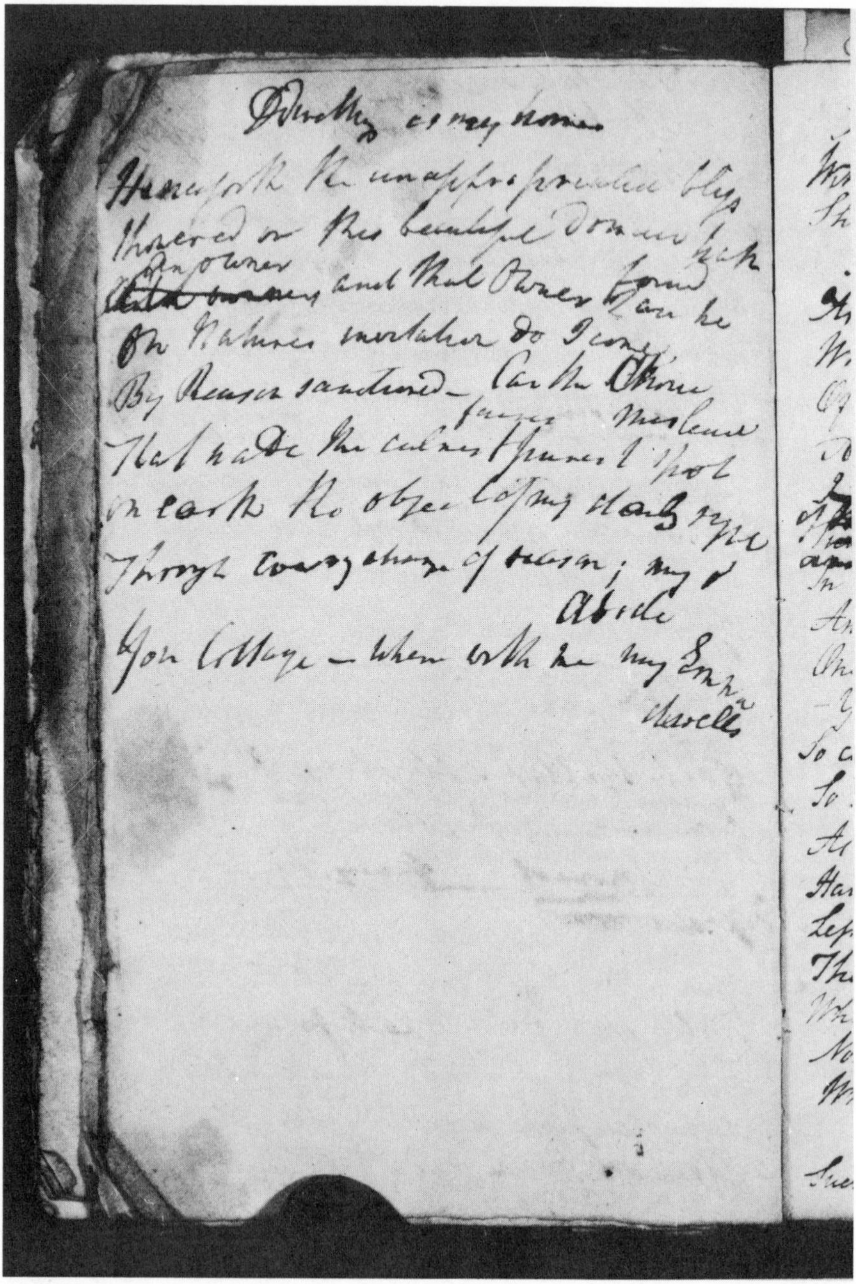
Henceforth the unappropriated bliss
Hovered on this beautiful domain
An owner and that Owner I am he
On Nature's invitation do I come
By Reason sanctioned— Can the choice mislead
That made the calmest fairest spot
on earth the object of my daily sight
Through every change of season; my abode
Yon Cottage—where with me my Emma dwells

        Ddwelling is my home
Henceforth the unappropriated bliss
Showered on this beautiful domain hath
                found
      An owner
⌠An
⌡At owner and that Owner I am he
On Natures invitation do I come
               ⌠ Choice
By Reason sanctioned— Can the ⌡[?]
                mislead
That made the calmest purest spot
on earth the object of my daily sight
Through every change of season; my [?]
            Abode
Yon Cottage — where with me my Emma
          dwells

  This draft was to follow l. 53 (ll. 54–98 are deleted). The lines were partially included in the earliest version of MS. D but later deleted.

C. VI 1149

From high to low from low to high yet still
Within the bounds of this huge Concave, here
Should be my home this Valley be my World

From that time forward was the place to me
As beautiful in thought as it had been
When present to my bodily eyes; a haunt
Of my affections oftentimes in joy
A brighter joy, ~~and in grief a~~ ~~that~~

~~I have known little~~ ~~in~~ ~~gloom at least~~
~~of the~~ ~~and~~ of the gay mind as ~~not~~ ~~Sometimes~~
~~and want,~~
In place of sorrow was a gleam of light
And now 'tis mine for life: dear Vale
One of the lowly dwellings is my home
— Yet the Realities of Life so cold
So cowardly so ready to betray
So stinted in the measure of their grace
As we report them doing them much wrong
Have been to me ~~less~~ more bountiful than hope
Less timid than desire oh bold indeed
They have been bold & bounteous unto me
Who have myself been bold not wanting ~~help~~
Nor resolution nor at last the hope
Which is of wisdom for I feel it is

And did it cost so much & did it ask
Such length of discipline & could it seem

3

41   *From high to low from low to high yet*
still
42   *Within the bounds of this huge Concave, here*
43   *Should be my home* this *Valley be my World*
44   *From that time forward was the place to me*
45   *As beautiful in thought as it had been*
46   *When present to my bodily eyes; a haunt*
47   *Of my affections oftentimes in joy*
and in such damp & gloom
48   *A brighter joy,* ~~in sorrow but of that~~
49   ~~I have known little in such gloom at least~~
Of ~~the gay mind such as stood to me in place~~
50   ~~Such damp~~ *of the gay mind as stood* ~~to me~~
and dark   ⌞sometimes
51   *In place of sorrow 'twas a gleam of light*
perchance
52   *And now 'tis mine for life: dear Vale*
53   *One of thy lowly dwellings is my home*ᴧ
54   —*Yes the Realities of Life so cold*
55   *So cowardly so ready to betray*
56   *So stinted in the measure of their grace*
57   *As we report them doing them much wrong*
more
58   *Have been to me* ~~less~~ᴧ*bountiful than hope*
59   *Less timid than desire oh bold indeed*
60   *They have been, bold & bounteous unto me*
⌠trust
61   *Who have myself been bold not wanting* ⌡[?*hope*]
62   *Nor resolution nor at last the hope*
63   *Which is of wisdom for I feel it is*
64   *And did it cost so much & did it ask*
65   *Such length of dicipline & could it seem*

---

53   The caret indicates the insertion of the lines on 2ᵛ.

C. VI. 1149

An act of courage & the thing itself
A conquest shame that this was ever so
Not to the Boy or youth but shame to thee
Sage Man thou Sun in its meridian strength
Thou flower in its full blow thou King & Crown
Of human nature shame to thee sage Man
Thy prudence thy experience thy desires
Thy apprehensions blush thou for them all
But I am safe, yes one at least is safe
What once was deem'd so difficult is now
Smooth easy, without obstacle that once
Did to my blindness seem a sacrifice
The same is now a choice of the whole heart.
If eer the acceptance of such dowry
                                        was deem'd
~~Appeard a condescension~~
~~Den made indulgence~~
A condescension or a weak indulgence
Of a sick fancy it is now an act
Of reason that exultingly aspires
This solitude is mine the distant thought
Is fetch'd out of the heaven in which it was
The unappropriated bliss hath found
An owner & that owner I am he
The Lord of this enjoyment is on Earth

4

66	An act of courage & the thing itself
67	A conquest shame that this was ever so
68	Not to the Boy or Youth but shame to thee
69	Sage Man thou Sun in its meridian strength
70	Thou flower in its full blow thou King & {C {crown
71	Of human Nature shame to thee sage Man
72	Thy prudence thy experience thy desires
73	Thy apprehensions blush thou for them all
74	But I am safe, yes, one at least is safe
75	What once was deem'd so difficult is now
76	Smooth, easy, without obstacle what once
77	Did to my blindness seem a sacrifice
78	The same is now a choice of the whole heart
79	If e'er the acceptance of such dower
	was deem'd
	Appeared a condecention
	Or a weak indulgence
80	A conde {s cention or a weak indulgence
81	{To {Of a sick fancy it is now an act
82	Of reason that exultingly aspires
83	This solitude is mine the distant thought
84	Is fetch'd out of the heaven in which it was.
85	The unappropriated bliss hath found
86	An owner & that owner I am he
87	The Lord of this enjoyment is on Earth

The long bracket in the left-hand margin indicates WW's decision to cut the lines it encloses. The draft on 2ᵛ incorporates ll. 85–86 and 98, and after composing it WW drew a slash down the center of 4ʳ and with a bracket on 5ʳ signaled the point at which the text was to continue.

79   The phrase "was deem'd" was written in after the deletion (probably in transcription) of the two subsequent defective lines.

C. VI. 1149

And in my breast. What wonder if I speak
With fervour, am exalted with the thought
Of my possessions of my genuine wealth
Inward & outward, what I keep have gain'd
Shall gain must gain if sound be my belief
From past & present rightly understood
That in my day of childhood I was less
The mind of Nature less take all in all
Whatever may be lost than I am now
For proof behold this valley and behold
Yon Cottage where with me my Emma dwells
     Aye think on that my Heart I cease to stir,
Pause upon that and let the breathing frame
No longer breathe but all be satisfied
Oh if such silence be not thanks to God
For what hath been bestow'd then where where
Shall gratitude find rest. Mine eyes did ne'er then
Rest on a lovely object nor my mind
Take pleasure in the midst of happy thoughts
But either She whom now I have, who now
Divides with me this lov'd abode, was there
Or not far off. Where'er my footsteps turn'd
Her voice was like a hidden Bird that sang

5

88   *And in my breast. What wonder if I speak*
89   *With fervour, am exalted with the thought*
90   *Of my possessions of my genuine wealth*
91   Inward & outward, what I keep have gain'd
92   Shall gain must gain if sound be my belief
93   From past & present rightly understood
94   That in my day of childhood I was less
95   The mind of Nature less take all in all
96   Whatever may be lost than I am now
         While I
97   For proof behold this Valley and behold
                                    Sister
98   Yon Cottage where with me my ~~Emma~~ dwells.
                              my Emma Dwell
99   Aye think on that my Heart & cease to stir
100   Pause upon that and let the breathing frame
101   No longer breathe but all be satisfied
102   Oh if such silence be noth thanks to God
103   For what hath been bestow'd then where where
                                              then
104   Shall gratitude find rest. Mine eyes did ne'er
105   Rest on a lovely object nor my mind
                        happy
106   Take pleasure in the midst of   thoughts
107   But either She whom now I have, who now
108   Divides with me this lov'd abode, was there
109   Or not far off. Where'er my footsteps turn'd
110   Her Voice was like a hidden Bird that sang

---

97   The partial bracket signals WW's intention to replace the lines preceding l. 98 with the
revision on 2ᵛ.

The thought of her was like a flash of light
Or an unseen companionship, a breath
Or fragrance independent of the wind;
In all my goings, in the new and old
Of all my meditations, and in this
Favorite of all, in this the most of all.
What Being, therefore, since the birth of Man
Had ever more abundant cause to speak
Thanks, and if music and the power of song
Make him more thankful, then to call on these
To aid him, and with these resound his joy.
The boon is absolute; surpassing grace
To me hath been vouchsafed; among the bowers
Of blissful Eden this was neither given
Nor could be given, possession of the good
Which had been sighed for, antient thought
And dear Imaginations realiz'd, fulfill'd
Up to their highest measure, yea, & more.
          Embrace me, then, ye Hills, & close me in
Now in the clear and open day I feel
Your guardianship; I take it to my heart
Tis like the solemn shelter of the night
But I would call thee beautiful, for mild
And soft and gay and beautiful thou art

6

111	The thought of her was like a flash of light
112	Or an unseen companionship a breath
113	Or fragrance independent of the wind
114	In all my goings in the new and old
115	Of all my meditations and in this
116	Favorite of all, in this the most of all.
117	What Being, therefore, since the birth of Man
118	Had ever more abundant cause to speak
119	Thanks, and if music and the power of song
120	Make him more thankful, then to call on these
121	To aid him and with these resound his joy.
122	The boon is absolute; surpassing grace
123	To me hath been voutchsaf'd; among the bowers
124	Of blissful Eden this was neither giv'n
125	Nor could be giv'n possession of the good
126	Which had been sigh'd for antient thought

                                    fulfilld

	⌠a
127	And dear Imaginations re⟨lliz'd
128	Up to their highest measure, yea, & more.
129	Embrace me, then, ye Hills & close me in
130	Now in the clear and open day I feel
131	Your guardianship; I take it to my heart
132	Tis like the solemn shelter of the night
133	But I would call thee beautiful, for mild
134	And soft and gay and beautiful thou art

Dear Valley having in thy face a smile
Though peaceful, full of gladness. Thou art pleas'd
Pleased with thy crags & woody steeps, thy Lake
Its one green Island and its winding shores
The multitude of little rocky hills
Thy Church and Cottages of mountain stone
Cluster'd like stars some few but single most
And lurking dimly in their shy retreats
Or glancing at each other chearful looks
Like separated stars with clouds between.
What want we have we not perpetual streams
Warm woods and sunny hills & fresh green fields
And mountains not less green and flocks & herds
And thickets full of songsters and the voice
Of lordly birds an unexpected sound
Heard now & then from morn to latter eve
Admonishing the man who walks below
Of solitude and silence in the sky
These have we & a thousand nooks of earth
Have also here but no where else is found
No where (or is it fancy) can be found
The one sensation that is here; tis here
Here as it found its way into my heart
In childhood, here as it abides by day
By night, here only, or in chosen minds
That take it with them here whereever they go.

7

135 Dear Valley having in thy face as smile
136 Though peaceful, full of gladness. Thou art pleas'd
137 Pleased with thy crags & woody steeps thy Lake
138 Its one green Island and its winding shores
139 The multitude of little rocky hills
140 Thy Church and Cottages of mountain stone
141 Cluster'd like stars some few but single most
142 And lurking dimly in their shy retreats
143 Or glancing at each other chearful looks
144 Like separated stars with clouds between.
145 What want we   have we not perpetual streams
146 Warm woods and sunny hills & fresh green fields
147 And mountains not less green and flocks & herds
148 And thickets full of songsters and the voice
149 Of lordly birds an unexpected sound
150 Heard now & then from morn to latest eve
151 Admonishing the man who walks below
152 Of solitude and silence in the sky
153 These have we & a thousand nooks of earth
154 Have also these but no where else is found
155 No where, (or is it fancy) can be found
156 The one sensation that is here; tis here
157 Here as it found its way into my heart
158 In childhood, here as it abides by day
159 By night, here only, or in chosen minds
160 That take it with them hence whereer they go.

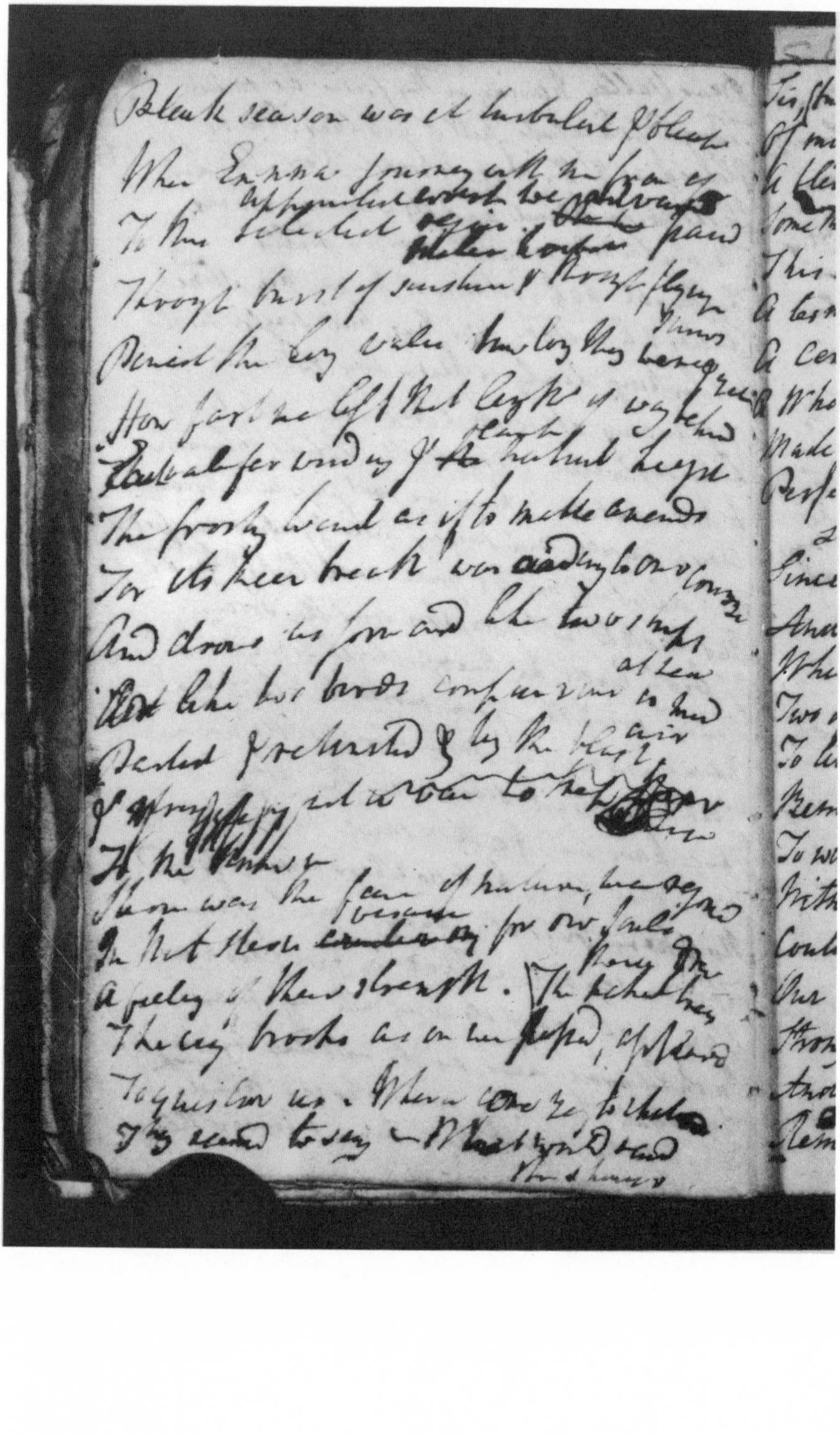

Bleak season was it turbulent & bleak
When Emma journey with me from afar
   appointed *covert we advanced*
To this selected region. O̶n̶ ̶w̶e̶ paced
   [?] [?harbour]
Through burst of sunshine & through flying
        snows
Paced the long vales how long they were & yet
How fast we left that length of way behind
⌠Each   each
⌡The vale far winding & t̶h̶e̶ naked height
The frosty Wind as if to make amends
     ⌠aid
For its keen breath was ⌡[?] ing to our course
And drove us forward like two ships
       at sea
⌠Or
⌡And like two birds companions in mid
      air
Parted & reunited & by the blast
& struggling not i̶n̶ ̶v̶a̶i̶n̶ ̶t̶o̶ ̶k̶e̶e̶p̶ ̶t̶h̶e̶i̶r̶
      [?wings]
To the [?tempest]
Stern was the face of nature, we rejoicd
     visage
In that stern [?c̶o̶u̶n̶t̶e̶n̶a̶n̶c̶e̶] for our Souls
      thence drew
A feeling of their strength/The naked trees
The icy brooks as on we passed, appeared
To question us. Whence come ye, to what [?end]
They seemd to say — What would said
     the shower

 This draft corresponds to ll. 218–232 on 10ʳ. The original text of MS. D follows this draft, but later corrections reinstate many of the readings of MS. B's base text.

'Tis that; I cannot name it,) 'tis the sense
Of majesty and beauty & repose
A blended holiness of earth & sky
Something that makes this individual Spot
This small Abiding-place of many men
A termination and a last retreat
A Centre, come from wheresoever you will
A Whole without dependence or defect
Made for itself and happy in itself
Perfect Contentment Unity entire. ✕

Long is it since we met, to part no more,
Since I and Emma heard each other's call
And were Companions once again like Birds
Which by the intruding Fowler had been scared
Two of a scatter'd brood that could not bear
To live in loneliness: 'tis long since we
Remembring much & hoping more found means
To walk abreast tho' in a narrow path
With undivided steps. Our home was sweet
Could it be less if we were forc'd to change
Our home again was sweet; but still for Youth
Strong as it seems & bold is inly weak
And diffident the destiny of life
Remain'd unfix'd & therefore we were still

8

161	Tis, (but I cannot name it) tis the sense
162	Of majesty and beauty & repose
163	A blended holiness of earth & sky
164	Something that makes this individual Spot
165	This small ⎰A ⎱abiding-place of many men
166	A termination and a last retreat
167	A Centre, come from wheresoe'er you will
168	A Whole without dependence or defect
169	Made for itself and happy in itsef
170	Perfect Contentment Unity entire. ✕
171	Long is it since we met, to part no more,
172	*Since I and Emma heard each other's call*
173	*And were Companions once again like Birds*
174	*Which by the intruding Fowler had been scar'd*
175	*Two of a scatter'd brood that could not bear*
176	*To live in loneliness : 'tis long since we*
177	*Remembring much & hoping more found*
	means
178	*To walk abreast tho' in a narrow path*
179	*With undivided steps. Our home was sweet*
180	*Could it be less if we were forc'd to change*
181	*Our home again was sweet; but still, for Youth*
182	*Strong as it seems & bold is inly weak*
183	*And diffident the destiny of life*
184	*Remain'd unfix'd & therefore we were still*

161–170 WW copied these lines into DC MS. Prose 25 for the first version of his *Guide to the Lakes*; they were never published in the *Guide*. (See *Prose*, II, 142–143, for a description of this manuscript and II, 271n, for the prose passage in which they occur.) The lines, here transcribed from MS. Prose 25, differ from the text of MS. B only in accidentals:

                    'tis the sense
Of majesty and beauty & repose
A blended holiness of earth & sky
Something that makes this individual spot
This small Abiding-place of many men
A termination & a last retreat
A Centre, come from wheresoeer you will
A Whole without dependence or defect
Made for itself & happy in itself
Perfect contentment unity entire

170 The X indicates that the text, in revision, was to skip to the draft on 7^v. The faint vertical line on the lower portion of 8^r may signal the deletion of the lines beneath it, for the draft on 7^v continues on 8^v, replacing MS. B ll. 171–268 in revisions for MS. D.

184 A blot has smeared from the opposite verso.

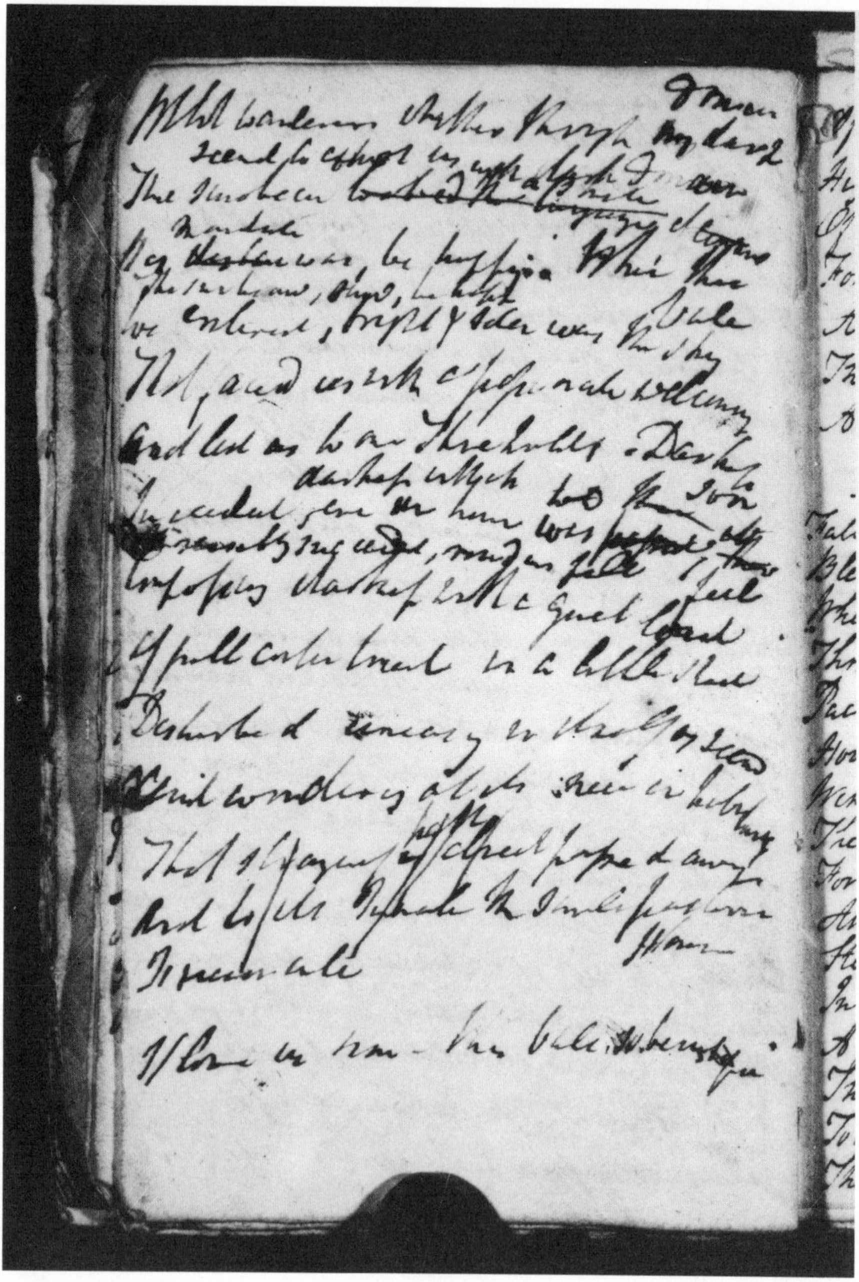

                        domain
Wild wanderers whither through my dark
                    dark domain
    seemd to exhort us with a smile
The sunbeam ~~looked the [?language]~~ [?of] [?content]
    mandate
Her [?dictat] was, be happy. When this
                     Vale
   The sunbeam, said, be happy
We entered, bright and solem was the sky
That faced us with a passionate welcoming
And led us to our Threshold. Darkness
               soon
      darkness which had [?then]   [?it]
Succeeded, ere an hour was ~~passed, there~~
               fell
   Insensibly succeeded, round us fell
Composing darkness with a quiet load
Of full contentment in a little [?shed]
Disturbed uneasy in itself as seemd
And wondering at its new inhabitants
        hath
That strangeness is/[?alred] passed away
And to its Inmate the [?small] [?pasture]
               It loves

[?Is] [?]
It loves us now — this Vale so beautiful

This draft toward MS. D follows on from that on 7ᵛ and corresponds to MS. B ll. 233–268.
    Following 8ᵛ a numbered leaf, 9, has been lost from the MS. The stub is too small to reveal any traces of writing; however, the page apparently carried twenty-four lines of text, ll. 185–208. The surviving sheet of MS. A provides ll. 192–208, but ll. 185–191 are irrecoverably lost.

Of outward things but for the prize within
Highest ambition: in the daily walks
Of business 'twill be harmony & grace
For the perpetual pleasure of the sense
And for the Soul I do not say too much
Though much be said an image for the soul
& habit of Eternity & God.

Nor have we been deceived thus far the effect
Falls not below the loftiest of our hopes
Bleak season was it turbulent & bleak
When hitherward we journey'd & on foot
Through bursts of sunshine & thro' flying snow
Pac'd the long Vales how long they were & yet
How fast that length of way was left behind
Wensley's long Vale & Sedbergh's naked heights
The frosty wind as if to make amends
For its keen breath was aiding to our course
And drove us onward like two Ships at sea
Stern was the face of nature we rejoiced
In that stern countenance for our souls had there
A feeling of their strength. The naked trees
The icy brooks as on we pass'd appear'd
To question us whence come ye to what end
They seem'd to say what would ye said the
                                        shower

209　　*Of outward things but for the prize within*
210　　*Highest ambition: in the daily walks*
211　　*Of business 'twill be harmony & grace*
212　　*For the perpetual pleasure of the sense*
213　　*And for the Soul I do not say too much*
214　　*Though much be said an image for the*
　　　　　　　　　　　　　　　　soul
215　　*A habit of Eternity & God.*

216　　　*Nor have we been deceived thus far the effect*
　　　　　　　　　　　　　⎰ *hopes*
217　　*Falls not below the loftiest of our* ⎱*[?thoughts]*
218　　*Bleak season was it turbulent & bleak*
219　　*When hitherward we journey'd & on foot*
220　　*Through bursts of sunshine & thro' flying snows*
221　　*Pac'd the long vales how long they were & yet*
222　　*How fast that length of way was left behind*
223　　*Wensley's long Vale & Sedbergh's naked heights*
224　　*The frosty wind as if to make amends*
225　　*For its keen breath was aiding to our course*
226　　*And drove us onward like two Ships at sea*
227　　*Stern was the face of nature we rejoiced*
228　　*In that stern countenance for our souls had*
　　　　　　　　　　　　　　　　　there
229　　*A feeling of their strength. The naked trees*
230　　*The icy brooks as on we passd appear'd*
231　　*To question us whence come ye to what end*
232　　*They seem'd to say what would ye said the*
　　　　　　　　　　　　　　　　　shower

Wild Wanderers whither thro' my dark domain
The Sunbeam said be happy: they were mov'd
All things were mov'd they round us as we went
We in the midst of them. And when the trance
Came to us as we stood by Hart-leap Well
The intimation of the milder day
Which is to come the fairer world than this
And raised us up dejected as we were
Among the records of that doleful place
By sorrow for the hunted beast who there
Had yielded up his breath the awful trance
The vision of humanity & of God
The Mourner, God the Sufferer when the heart
Of his poor creatures suffers wrongfully
Both in the sadness & the joy we found
A promise & an earnest that we twain
A pair seceding from the common world
Might in that hallow'd spot to which our steps
Were tending in that individual nook
Might even thus early for ourselves secure
And in the midst of those unhappy times
A portion of the blessedness which love
And knowledge, will we trust, hereafter give
To all the Vales of earth & all mankind
    Thrice hath the winter Moon been fill'd with light
Since that dear day when Grasmere our dear Vale

233 *Wild Wanderers whither thro' my dark domain*
234 *The Sunbeam said be happy : they were mov'd*
235 *All things were mov'd they round us as we went*
236 *We in the midst of them. And when the trance*
237 *Came to us as we stood by Hart-leap Well*
238 *The intimation of the milder day*
        be
239 *Which is to ~~come~~ the fairer world than this*
240 *And rais'd us up dejected as we were*
241 *Among the records of that doleful place*
242 *By sorrow for the hunted beast who there*
243 *Had yielded up his breath the awful trance*
244 *The vision of humanity & of God*
245 *The Mourner, God the Sufferer when the heart*
246 *Of his poor Creatures suffers wrongfully*
247 *Both in the sadness & the joy we found*
248 *A promise & an earnest that we twain*
249 *A pair seceding from the common world*
250 *Might in that hallow'd spot to which our steps*
251 *Were tending in that individual nook*
252 *Might even thus early for ourselves secure*
253 *And in the midst of those unhappy times*
254 *A portion of the blessedness which love*
255 *And knowledge, will we trust, hereafter give*
256 *To all the Vales of earth & all mankind*
257   *Thrice hath the winter Moon been fill'd with light*
258 *Since that dear day when Grasmere our dear Vale*

---

239   The correction is in pencil.

S. Kline

received us, bright & solemn was the sky
That fixed us with a passionate welcoming
And led us to our threshold to a home
Within a home, what was to be; & soon
Our love within a love then darkness came
Composing darkness with its quiet load
Of full contentment in a little shed
Disturbed, uneasy in itself as seem'd
And wondering at its new inhabitants
If loves us now this Vale so beautiful
Begins to love us by a sullen storm
Two months unwearied of severest storm
It put the temper of our minds to proof
And found us faithful thro' ~~the gloom~~ & heard
The Poet mutter his preclusive songs
With chearful heart an unknown voice of joy
Among the silence of the woods & hills
Silent to any gladness of sound
                          sound
With all their Shepherds

                    But the gates of Spring
                                              the
~~Nothing~~ Are open'd; churlish Winter hath giv'n
                                              leave
That she should entertain for this one day
Perhaps for many genial ~~days~~ to come
                              days
His guests & make them happy. They are pleas'd

12

259 *Received us, bright & solemn was the sky*
260 *That faced us with a passionate welcoming*
　　　　　　　ᵈ⎰
261 *And let⎱ us to our threshold to a home*
262 *Within a home, what was to be, & soon*
263 *Our love within a love then darkness came*
264 *Composing darkness with its quiet load*
265 *Of full contentment in a little shed*
　　　　　　　　ⁿ⎰
266 *Disturbed, uneasy it⎱ itself as seem'd*
267 *And wondering at its new inhabitants*
268 *It loves us now this Vale so beautiful*
269 *Begins to love us by a sullen storm*
270 *Two months unwearied of severest storm*
271 *It put the temper of our minds to proof*
272 *And found us faithful thro' the gloom & heard*
273 *The Poet mutter his preclusive songs*
274 *With chearful heart an unknown voice of joy*
275 *Among the silence of the woods & hills*
　　　　　　　　　some
276 *Silent to any gladness of sound*
277 *With all their Shepherds*
　　　　　　　　　　　　　　⎰*of Spring*
　　　　　　　　　　　　　　⎱of Spring
　　　　　　But the gates
　　　　　　⎰A　　　　⎰l
278 *Of Spring* ⎱*are open'd; chur*⎱*tish Winter hath giv'n*
　　　　　　　　　　　　　　　　　　　leave
279 *That she should entertain for this one day*
280 *Perhaps for many genial days to come*
　　　　　　　　　jocund
281 *His guests & make them happy. They are pleas'd*

277–278　The phrase "of Spring" and the "A" were written in pencil, probably by WW, then overwritten in ink.

13

ut most of all the birds that haunt
th the mild summer, inmates tho' the flood they be
Winter's household. they are jubilant
is day who droop'd or seem'd to droop so long
ey shew their pleasure, & shall I do less
ppier of happy tho' I be, like them
annot take possession of the sky
ount with a thoughtless impulse & wheel there
e of a mighty multitude whose way
nd motion is a harmony & dance
Magnificent. Behold them how they shape
b after orb their course still round & round
bove the area of the Lake their own
dopted region, girding it about
wanton repetition, yet therewith
ith that large circle evermore renew'd
undreds of curves & circlets high & low
backwards & forwards progress intricate
As if one spirit was in all & sway'd
Their indefatigable flight 'tis done
Ten times or more I fancied it had ceas'd
And lo the vanish'd company again
Ascending list again I hear their wings
Faint faint at first & then an eager sound
Pass'd in a moment & as faint again
They tempt the sun to sport among their plumes
They tempt the water & the gleaming ice

13

282   *But most of all the birds that haunt*
                            the flood
283   *With the mild summons, inmates tho' they be*
284   *Of Winter's houshold: they are jubilant*
285   *This day who droop'd or seem'd to droop*
                            so long
286   *They shew their pleasure, & shall I do less*
287   *Happier of happy tho' I be, like them*
288   *I cannot take possession of the sky*
289   *Mount with a thoughtless impulse & wheel*
                            there
290   *One of a mighty multitude whose way*
291   *And motion is a harmony & dance*
292   *Magnificent. Behold them how they shape*
293   *Orb after orb their course still round & round*
294   *Above the area of the Lake their own*
295   *Adopted region, girding it about*
                          meanwhile
296   *In wanton repetition, yet therewith*
297   *With that large circle evermore renew'd*
298   *Hundreds of curves & circlets high & low*
299   *Backwards & forwards progress intricate*
           dwelt [?in ?each] dwelt
300   *As if one spirit was in all & sway'd*
                    .⌉ ⌠T
301   *Their indefatigable flight* ⌡ ⌡*'tis done*
302   *Ten times or more I fancied it had ceas'd*
303   *And lo the vanish'd company again*
304   *Ascending list again I hear their wings*
305   *Faint faint at first & then an eager sound*
306   *Pass'd in a moment & as faint again*
307   *They tempt the sun to sport among their plumes*
                    or
308   *They tempt the water & the gleaming ice*

---

282   The text continues in DW's hand through l. 296.

14

To shew them a fair image 'tis themselves
Their own fair forms upon the glimmering
Painted more soft & fair as they descend   plain
Allured to touch them up again aloft
Up with a sally & a flash of speed
As if they scorn'd both resting-place & rest.
This day is a thanksgiving, 'tis a day
~~Of~~
Of glad emotion and deep quietness
        rich in
Not upon me alone hath been bestow'd
        rich in
He ~~blithe with~~ many onward-looking thoughts.
The ~~peaceful joy~~ oh surely these   ~~from~~
        than felt it
Are grateful not the happy Quires of ~~love~~
    Her
~~These~~ own peculiar family ~~forth bring~~   of love
That sport among green leaves so blithe a train

        But two are missing, two, a lonely pair
Of milk-white Swans ~~~~
~~~~ ah why are they not ~~here~~ seen
To share in this day's pleasure. From afar
They came like Emma & myself to live
Together here in peace & solitude
Chusing this Valley they who had the choice
Of the whole world: we saw them day by day
Through those two months of unrelenting storm
Conspicuous in the centre of the Lake
Their safe retreat we knew them well I guess
That the whole Valley knew them but to us

14

309 *To shew them a fair image 'tis themselves*
310 *Their own fair forms upon the glimm'ring*
                                        plain
311 *Painted more soft & fair as they descend*
312 *Almost to touch then up again aloft*
313 *Up with a sally & a flash of speed*
314 *As if they scorn'd both resting-place & rest.*
       This day is a thanksgiving, tis a day
315 ~~*Spring! for this day belongs to thee rejoice*~~
       Of glad emotion and deep quietness
316 *Not upon me alone hath been bestow'd*
              rich in
317 *Me ~~bless'd with~~ many onward-looking thoughts*
       ⌠is penetrating bliss
318 *Th⌡e ~~sunshine & mild air~~ oh surely these*
       have felt it   spring
319 *Are grateful not the happy Quires of ~~love~~*
       Her   of love
320 ~~*Thine*~~ *own peculiar family ~~Sweet Spring~~*
321 *That sport among green leaves so blithe a train*
322   *But two are missing, two, a lonely pair*
                           ~~I wish that~~   were
323 *Of milk-white Swans ~~ah why~~*ᴧ*are they*ᴧ*not here*
                                     seen
324 *~~These above all~~ ah why are they not ~~here~~*
       ~~have their share of~~
325 *To share in this day's pleasure. From afar*
326 *They came like Emma & myself to live*
327 *Together here in peace & solitude*
328 *Chusing this Valley they who had the choice*
329 *Of the whole world: we saw them day by day*
330 *Through those two months of unrelenting storm*
331 *Conspicuous in the centre of the Lake*
332 *Their safe retreat we knew them well I guess*
333 *That the whole Valley knew them but to us*

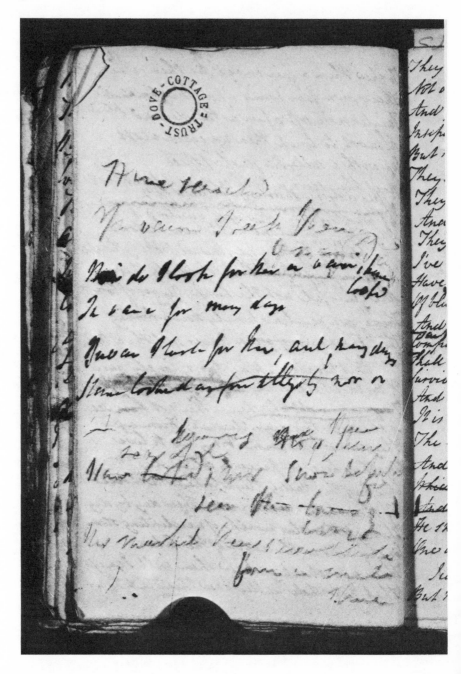

Have searched
In vain I seek them [?now]
          & many days

Now do I look for them in vain, have
                        lookd
In vain for many days
In vain I look for them, and, many days
Have looked as ~~fruitlessly~~ [?nor] [?on]

                 [?And]⎫ [?there]
     [?harmony]   [?Nor]⎭ [?their]
    [?seen] [?oft] [?oft]
Have ~~lookd~~, [?nor] [?snow] [?white]
                 [?fo]
        seen their [?lovely]
                [?wings]
Nor markd their snow white
      form in [?small]
          [?space]

   The drafts at the top and foot of the page are in pencil; all the drafts correspond to ll. 342–343, facing.

They were more dear then may be well believ'd

Not only for their beauty & their still

And placid way of life & faithful love

Inseparable not for these alone

But that their state so much resembled ours

They also having chosen this abode

They strangers & we strangers they a pair

And we a solitary pair like them

They should not have departed: many day

I've look'd for them in vain nor on the wing

Have seen them nor in that small open space

Of blue unfrozen water where they lodg'd

And liv'd so long in quiet side by side

Companions brethren consecrated friends

Shall we behold them yet another year

Surviving they for us & we for them

And neither pair be broken may perchance

It is too late already for such hope

The Shepherd may have siez'd the deadly tube

And parted them incited by prize

Which for the sake of those he loves at home

And for the lamb upon the mountain tops

He should have spared or haply both are gone

One death & that were mercy giv'n to both

I cannot look upon this favoured Vale

But that I seem by harbouring this Thought

15

	be
334	*They were more dear then may*ₐ*well believed*
335	*Not only for their beauty & their still*
	constant
336	*And placid way of life & faithful love*
337	*Inseparable not for these alone*
338	*But that their state so much resembled ours*
339	*They also having chosen this abode*
340	*They strangers & we strangers they a pair*
341	*And we a solitary pair like them*
342	*They should not have departed : many days*
343	*I've look'd for them in vain nor on the wing*
344	*Have seen them nor in that small open space*
345	*Of blue unfrozen water where they lodg'd*
346	*And liv'd so long in quiet side by side*
	Faithful
347	*Companions* ~~brethren~~ *consecrated friends*
348	*Shall we behold them yet another year*
349	*Surviving they for us & we for them*
	⎰be broken
350	*And neither pair* ⎱*divided nay perchance*
351	*It is too late already for such hope*
352	*The Shepherd may have seiz'd the deadly*
	tube
353	*And parted them incited by prize*
	her
354	*~~Which for the~~ sake of ~~those~~ he loves at home*
355	*~~And for the Lamb upon the mountain tops~~*
356	*He should have spared or haply both are gone*
357	*One death & that were mercy giv'n to both*
358	*I cannot look upon this favoured Vale*
	such
359	*But that I seem by harbouring ~~this~~ thought*

344/345   A blot has smeared from the facing verso.
347   No explanation for the marks under the line can be offered.
353   The line is short, "a" having been omitted before "prize."
358–362   On 12ᵛ is a revision written vertically in MW's hand, incorporated into MS.
D, then deleted:

⎰ould   ⎰harbour
And c⎱an a Poet ⎱imagine such a thought
Imagine such unworthy recompence ~~of Co~~
                          were it
Of confidence, so pure more natural ~~course~~
~~It were~~ to follow without scruple where the sight

Following 15ᵛ leaf 16, unnumbered, has been torn out; it was conjugate with leaf 9, and 9
was probably lost because of its removal.

16

~~The reward they recompence~~
To wrong it ~~such~~ ^not^ unworthy recompence
Imagining of confidence so pure
Ah! if I wish'd to ~~follow~~ where the sight.
Of all that is before ~~my~~ ^his^ eyes, the voice
Which ~~is~~ ^there is^ as a presiding Spirit ~~here in~~
~~would lead~~ him ~~it not wrong or~~ ~~the~~ ~~pair~~
~~these here~~ the
~~they~~ ~~are~~ dwellers ~~in~~ of this holy place
Must needs themselves be hallow'd they re-
                                        ^quire^
No benediction from the Stranger's lips
For they are bliss'd already none would give
The greeting peace be with you unto them
For peace they have it cannot but be theirs
And mercy & forbearance, nay not there
There is no call for these; that office Love
Performs & charity beyond the bounds of
Of charity an overflowing love
Not for the creature only but for all
Which is around them, love for every thing
Which in this happy ~~region~~ they behold

Thus ~~do~~ we soothe ourselves & when the thought
Pass'd we blame it not for having come
What if I floated down a pleasant stream
And now am landed & the motion gone
Shall I reprove myself ah no the stream

16

~~Such unworthy recompence~~

              so
360   *To wrong it ~~such~~ unworthy recompence*
361   *Imagining of confidence so pure*
362   *Ah! if I wish'd to follow where the sight*
                       his
363   *Of all that is before ~~my~~ eyes, the voice*
           speaks
364   *Which ~~is~~ as a presiding Spirit here*

                             e
          {him & not wronging th{is fair vale
365   *Would lead* {me ~~I should say unto myself~~
                          what he sees
       Whispers, the   {in
366   ~~They who are~~ *dwellers* {of *this holy place*
367   *Must needs themselves be hallow'd they re-*
                                  -quire
368   *No benediction from the Stranger's lips*
369   *For they are bless'd already none would give*
370   *The greeting peace be with you unto them*
371   *For peace they have it cannot but be theirs*
372   *And mercy & forbearance, nay not these*
373   *There is no call for these; that office Love*
374   *Performs & charity beyond the bounds ~~of~~*
               n}   over}   flow}
375   *Of charity a* { *heart*} *delight*{*ing love*
376   *Not for the creature only but for all*
377   *Which is around them, love for every thing*
                    region   {they
378   *Which in this happy ~~Valley~~* {*we behold*
                {do
379   *Thus* {[?] *we soothe ourselves & when the thought*
380   *Is pass'd we blame it not for having come*
381   *What if I floated down a pleasant stream*
382   *And now am landed & the motion gone*
383   *Shall I reprove myself ah no the stream*

A misplaced note of GW is visible in the photograph.
361/362   The mark may have signaled an intended revision.
374   The anticipatory "of" at the end of the line has been erased.

17

That ————— is flowing & will never cease to flow
And I shall float upon that stream again
By such forgetfulness the soul becomes
Words cannot say how beautiful: then hail
Hail to the visible Presence hail to thee
Delightful Valley habitation fair
And to whatever else of outward form
Can give us inward help, can purify
And elevate, & harmonize & soothe
And steal away & for a while deceive
And lap in pleasing rest & bear us on
Without desire in full complacency
Contemplating perfection absolute
And entertain'd as in a placid sleep.

But not betray'd by tenderness of mind
That fear'd or wholly overlook'd the truth
Did we come hither with romantic hope
To find in midst of so much loveliness
Love perfect love, of so much majesty
A like majestic frame of mind in those
Who here abide, the persons like the place
Nor from such hope or aught of such belief
Hath issued any portion of the joy
Which I have felt this day. An ample voice
Big time I in my walks have often heard
Sent from the mountains or the sheltered
                                        fields

17

384 ~~The stream~~ $\lbrace$ I is flowing & will never cease to flow

385 And I shall float upon that stream again

386 By such forgetfulness the soul becomes

387 Words can $\lbrace$ not t say how beautiful : then hail

388 Hail to the visible Presence hail to thee

389 Delightful Valley habitation fair

390 And to whatever else of outward form

391 Can give us inward help, can purify

392   Can   charm
~~And~~ elevate, & harmonize and soothe

393 And steal away & for a while deceive

394 And lap in pleasing rest & bear us on

395 Without desire in full complacency

396 Contemplating perfection absolute

397 And entertain'd as in a placid sleep

398   But not betray'd by tenderness of mind

399 That fear'd or wholly overlook'd the truth

400 Did we come hither with romantic hope

401 To find in midst of so much loveliness

402 Love perfect love, of so much majesty

403 A like majestic frame of mind in those

404 Who here abide, the persons like the place

405 Nor from such hope or aught of such belief

406 Hath issued any portion of the joy

407 Which I have felt this day. An awful voice

408 'Tis true I in my walks have often heard

409 Sent from the mountains or the shelter'd
                               fields

---

385   With the word "upon" the text continues in DW's hand through l. 417.

392   Revisions are in pencil.

Shout after shout reiterated whoop   78

In manner of a bird that takes delight

In answering to itself, or like a hound

single at chace among the lonely woods

His yelle repeating ... yet when wrought to mirth

... hue an voice ...

... of mirth & power now solemn to the ...

coming night when sky is dark ...

Not dark, not yet enlighten'd but by snow

Made visible amid the noise of wind

by bleatings manifold of mountain Sheep ...

... elevated, recognize

That ... summons, are gathering round for food.

... The upland ...

That ... breath

Which ...

... the ...

That Shepherds voice it may have reach'd mine

Debased & under prophanation, made   ear

In order for the sounds articulate

of ... impiety or

when shame with ... to check the ... brawl

of some abused festivity — to be ...

came not dreaming of unruffled life

Untainted manners; born among the hills

Bred also there I wanted not a Kale

To regulate my hopes; pleas'd with the good

I shrink not from the evil in disgust

Or with immoderate pain I look for man

The common creature of the brotherhood

But little differing from the man elsewhere

18

410   *Shout after shout reiterated whoop*
411   *In manner of a bird that takes delight*
412   *In answering to itself or like a hound*
413   *Single at chace among the lonely woods*
           His yell repeating yet ~~solemn~~ *was it in truth*
                      {*solemn mid*}
414   *A human voice* ~~how~~ {*awful in*} ~~the gloom~~
           Of spirit & power how solemn to the {*ear*
                                                  {*but*
           {*To*   *&*} *earth*
415   {*Of coming night when sky is dark*—}
416   *Not dark, not yet enlighten'd but by snow*
417   *Made visible amid the noise of winds*
                           mountain
418   *And bleatings manifold of sheep* ~~that know~~
           Which in that iteration recognize
419   ~~That know that~~ *summons, & are gathering round*
                                          for food.
           Their   ~~same the~~   {*that*
420   ~~That voice the~~*very same* {[*?the*] ~~breath~~
421   ~~Which was an utterance awful as the wind~~
422   ~~Or any sound the mountains ever heard~~
                                    since
423   *That Shepherds voice* ~~it may~~*have reachd mine*
                                                       ear
           {*b*
424   *De*{*pased & under prophanation, made*
425   *An organ for the sounds articulate*
                  or impiety or
426   *Of ribaldry &* ~~blasphemy &~~*wrath*
                                    brawls
           {*n*   *shame hath ceased to check the noisy*
427   *Whe*{*re* ~~drunkenness hath kindled senseless frays.~~
           Of some abused festivity— so be it
428   *I came not dreaming of unruffled life*
429   *Untainted manners; born among the hills*
430   *Bred also there I wanted not a scale*
431   *To regulate my hopes; pleas'd with the good*
432   *I shrink not from the evil in disgust*
433   *Or with immoderate pain I look for man*
434   *The common creature of the brotherhood*
           2   *1*
435   *But little differing from the man elsewhere*

414–415 Three lines of revision on the facing verso, in MW's hand, are incorporated in MS. D:

   His yell repeating yet was it in truth
   A human voice—a Spirit of coming
                                  night
   How solemn when the sky is dark &
                                    earth

418 MW's hand resumes here.
435 The numbers above "But" and "differing" indicate WW's intended change in word order.

19

For selfishness & envy & revenge
Ill neighbourhood that this should be
Flattery & double dealing strife & wrong
Yet is it something gain'd it is in truth
A mighty gain that Labour here preserves
His rosy face a Servant only here
Of the fire side or of the open field
A Freeman therefore sound & where
That extreme penury is here unknown
And cold & hunger's abject wretchedness
Mortal to body & the heaven-born mind.
That they who want are not too great a weight
For those who can relieve here may the heart
Breathe in the air of fellow-suffering
Dreadless as in a kind of fresher breeze
Of her own native element the hand
Be ready & unwearied without plea
From task too frequent & beyond its powers
For languor or indifference or despair.
And as these lofty barriers break the force
Of winds, this deep vale, as it doth in part
Conceal us from the storm, so here there is
                          abides

19

436	For selfishness & envy & revenge
	pity
437	Ill neighbourhood ~~folly~~ that this should be
438	Flattery & double dealing strife & wrong
439	Yet is it something gain'd it is in truth
440	A mighty gain that Labour here preserves
441	His rosy face a Servant only here
442	Of the fire-side or of the open field
	paird.
443	A Freeman therefore sound & ~~unenslaved~~
444	That extreme penury is here unknown
445	And cold & hunger's abject wretchedness
446	Mortal to body & the heaven-born mind.
	so
447	That they who want, are not to{ great a weight
448	For those who can relieve here may the heart
449	Breathe in the air of fellow-suffering
450	Dreadless as in a kind of fresher breeze
451	Of her own native element the hand
452	Be ready & unwearied without plea
453	From task too frequent & beyond its powers
454	For languor or indifference or despair.
455	And as these lofty barriers break the force
	{,—
456	Of winds{ this deep vale, as it doth in part
457	Conceal us from the storm, so here ~~there is~~
	abides ~~dwells~~

For conjectures about the spacing of lines on this page and 21^r, see Introduction, p. 17.
443   The intention was to revise "unenslaved" to "unimpaired."

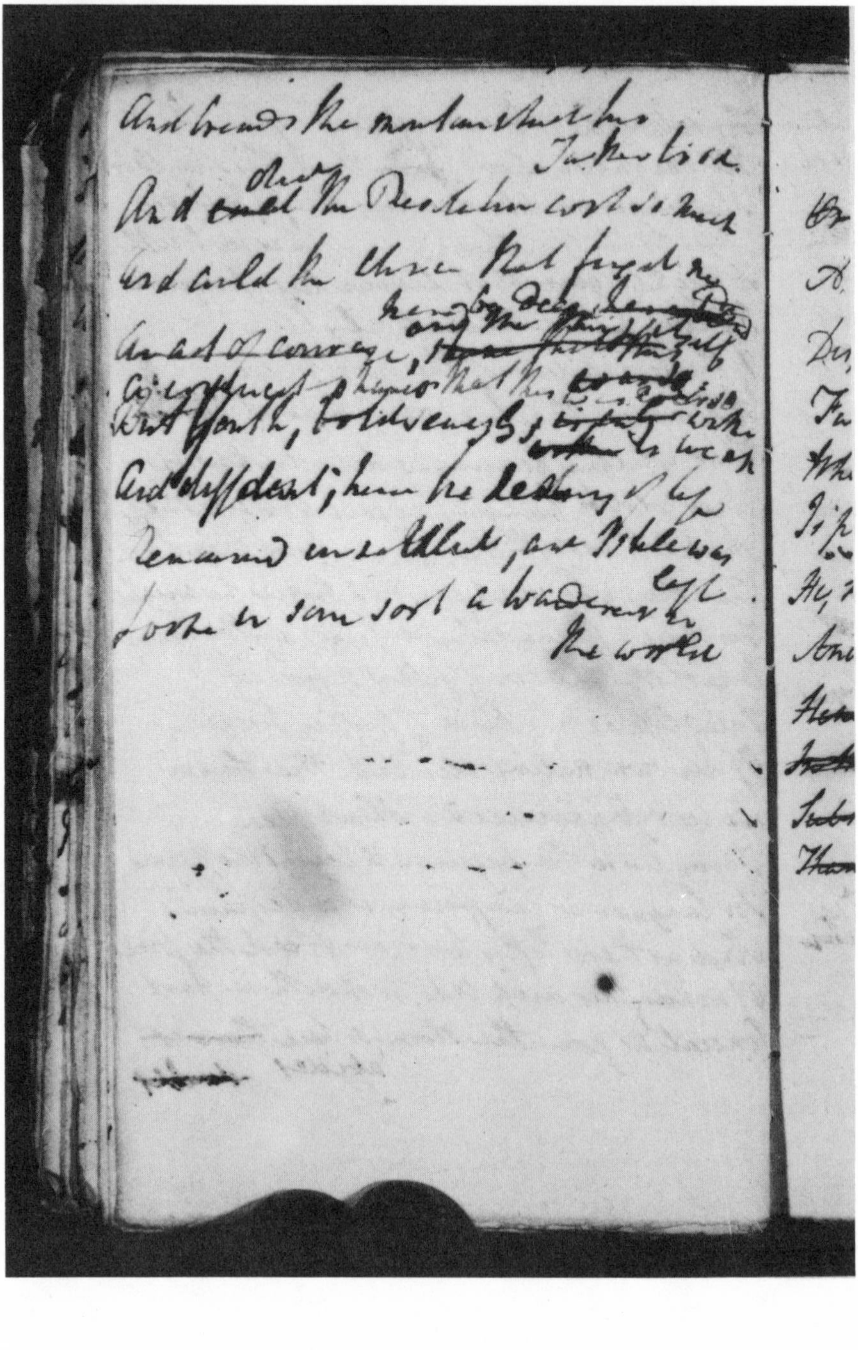

And treads the mountain which his
                              Father trod
              did
And ~~could~~ the Resolution cost so much
And could the choice that fixd me
                    ~~here [?]~~
              here be deemd
                    and the thing itself
~~An act of courage, shame that this~~
                    ~~was so~~
    A [?conquest]—[?shame] that this was ever so
      ⌠Y
But ⌡youth, bold [?seemingly], ~~is inly~~ within
                      ~~within~~ is weak
                    ⌠sti
And diffdent; hence the de⌡[?]ny of life
              ⌠t
Remained unse⌡ltled, and I still was
                    left
Lorne in some sort a Wanderer in
                    the world

"And treads . . . trod" corresponds to l. 464, on the facing recto; the remaining lines correspond to ll. 64, 66–67, and 181–183. The relationship between the lines is unclear; MS. D ll. 60–63 partially incorporate them.

20

~~Or some to be~~

A Power Is a protection for the mind
Dispensed indeed to other solitudes
Favoured by noble privilege like this
Where kindred independence of estate
Is prevalent where he who tills the field
A happy Man! is Master of the field
And treads the mountain which his Fathers
                                                    two
~~Herald from the trait circumstance~~
~~hither endwise envy of the old~~
Substantial ~~virtue have~~ a firmer tone
~~Than in the base tendency world~~
                                        470

20

Or seems to be
458 *A Power & a protection for the mind*
459 *Dispensed indeed to other solitudes*
460 *Favoured by noble privilege like this*
461 *Where kindred independance of estate*
462 *Is prevalent where he who tills the field*
463 *He, happy Man! is Master of the field*

                                     s⎫
464 *And treads the mountain which his Father* ⎰
                              -trod
465 *Hence, & from other local circumstance*
466 *In this enclosure many of the old*
467 *Substantial virtues have a firmer tone*
468 *Than in the base & ordinary world*

                             470

---

458   The four deleted words above the line are the beginning of a two-line passage at the end of MS. A not carried over here.

468   WW's line count begins where MS. A ends. (The last count reached there was 440.) It is presumably two over because the final two lines in MS. A, following l. 457, were omitted in MS. B.

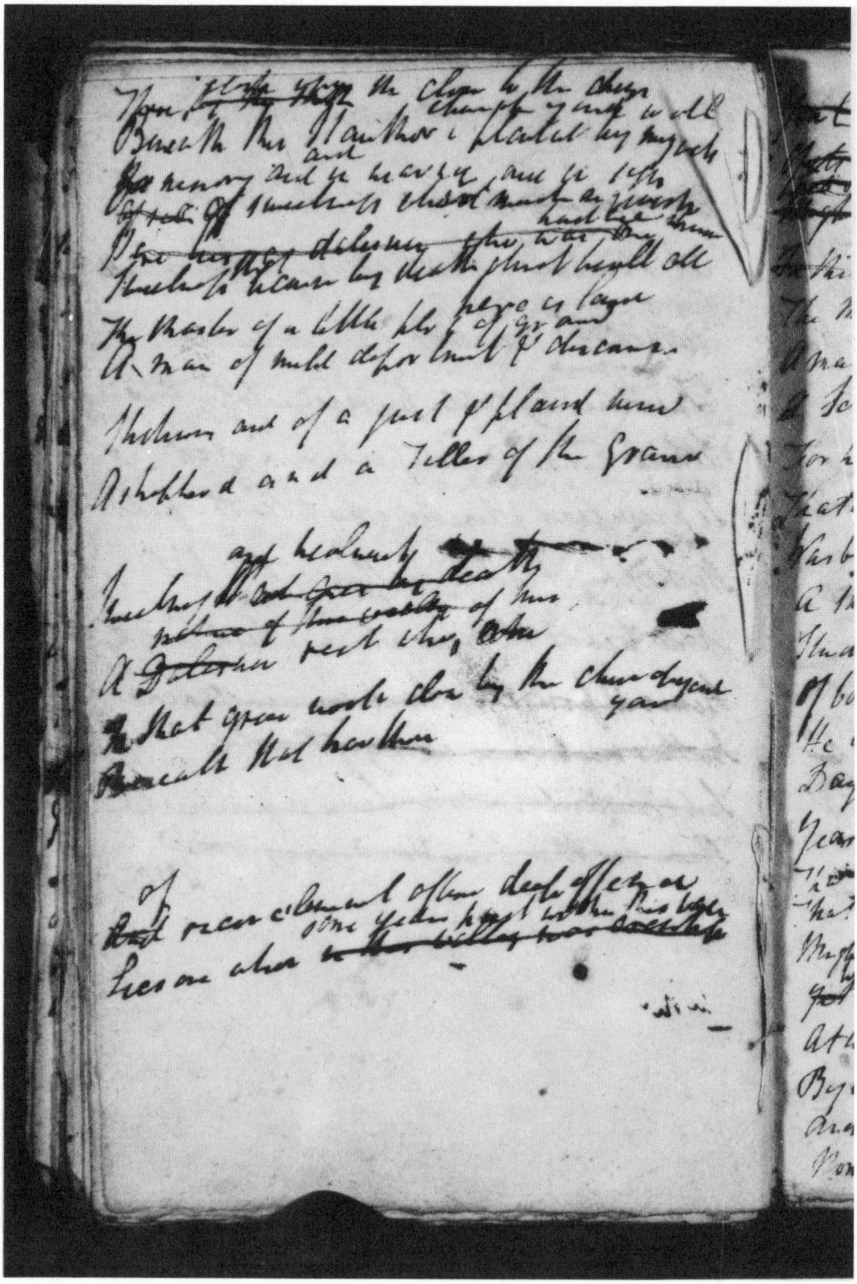

　　　　　above upon the close to the [?]
There, ~~by the [?path]~~　　church yard wall
Beneath this Hawthorn planted by myself
{[?For]　　　　　　and
{[?In] memory and in warning and in sign
~~Of [?swe]~~ Of sweetness where much anguish
　　　　　　　　　　　had been known
~~Here lies a dalesman who was one~~
　　　　　that
Sweetness because by death almost heald all
　　　　　　　here is laid
The Master of a little plot of ground
A Man of mild deportment & discourse
Studious and of a just & placid mind
A shepherd and a Tiller of the Ground

　　　　　and he almost [?]
　　　　{[?that]
Sweetness {[?which] ~~comes by~~ death
　　　　~~native of this valley~~ of this
A ~~Dalesman~~ rest who, [?]
In that green nook close by the churchyard
　　　　　　　　　　yar

Beneath that hawthorn

　　　of
~~And~~ reconcilement after deep offence
　　　　　some years past within this Vale
Lies one who ~~in this valley was erewhile~~

These lines are drafts toward the revision of ll. 472–481 made when WW was transferring *Home at Grasmere* lines to *The Excursion*; they correspond to *Excursion*, VI, 1080–1085.

21

~~In a Cottage ...~~
~~... our ...~~
~~... them ...~~
~~... them ...~~

had
In this our Native Valley dwelt a Man
The Master of a little lot of ground
A man of mild deportment & discourse
A Scholar also (as the phrase is here)
For he drew much delight from those few books
That lay within his reach and for this cause
Was by his fellow-dalesmen honoured more.
A thinker and a Teller o' the ground
Studious withal & healthy in his frame
Of body & of just and placid mind
He with his cares & of his Children saw
                          prosed
Days that were seldom touched by petty strife
Years safe from large misfortune long renewing
that overts which new the wisest & most pure
Might look on with ~~certain~~ confidence ...
... in himself & near him were there ...
At work to undermine his happiness
By little & by little. Action prompt
And lively was the Housewife in the Dale
None more laden to ... her understanding

21

469 Yon Cottage would that it could tell a part
470 Of its own story thousands might give ear
  Not one but tens of thousands might give ear
471 Might hear it & blush deep. There few years
            past
472 In this his Native Valley dwelt a Man
473 The Master of a little lot of ground
474 A man of mild deportment & discourse
  {A {S
475 {a {scholar also (as the phrase is here)
476 For he drew much delight from those few books
477 That lay within his reach and for this cause
478 Was by his Fellow-dalesmen honoured more.
479 A Shepherd and a Tiller of the ground
480 Studious withal & healthy in his frame
481 Of body & of just and placid mind
482 He with his consort & his Children saw
      cross'd
483 Days that were seldom touch'd by petty strife
484 Years safe from large misfortune long maintain'd
  Tha
485 That course which men the wisest & most pure
        And yet
486 Might look on with entire complacency.
  With
487 Yet in himself & near him were there faults
      peace of mind
488 At work to undermine his happiness
489 By little & by little. Active prompt
490 And lively was the Housewife; in the Vale
       yet but
      {yet
491 None more industrious {but her industry

475–481 These lines were crossed out when WW composed the draft on 21^v which replaces them in *Excursion*, VI, 1080–1085.

484/485 WW apparently decided to restart l. 485 lower down to avoid cramping from the line above.

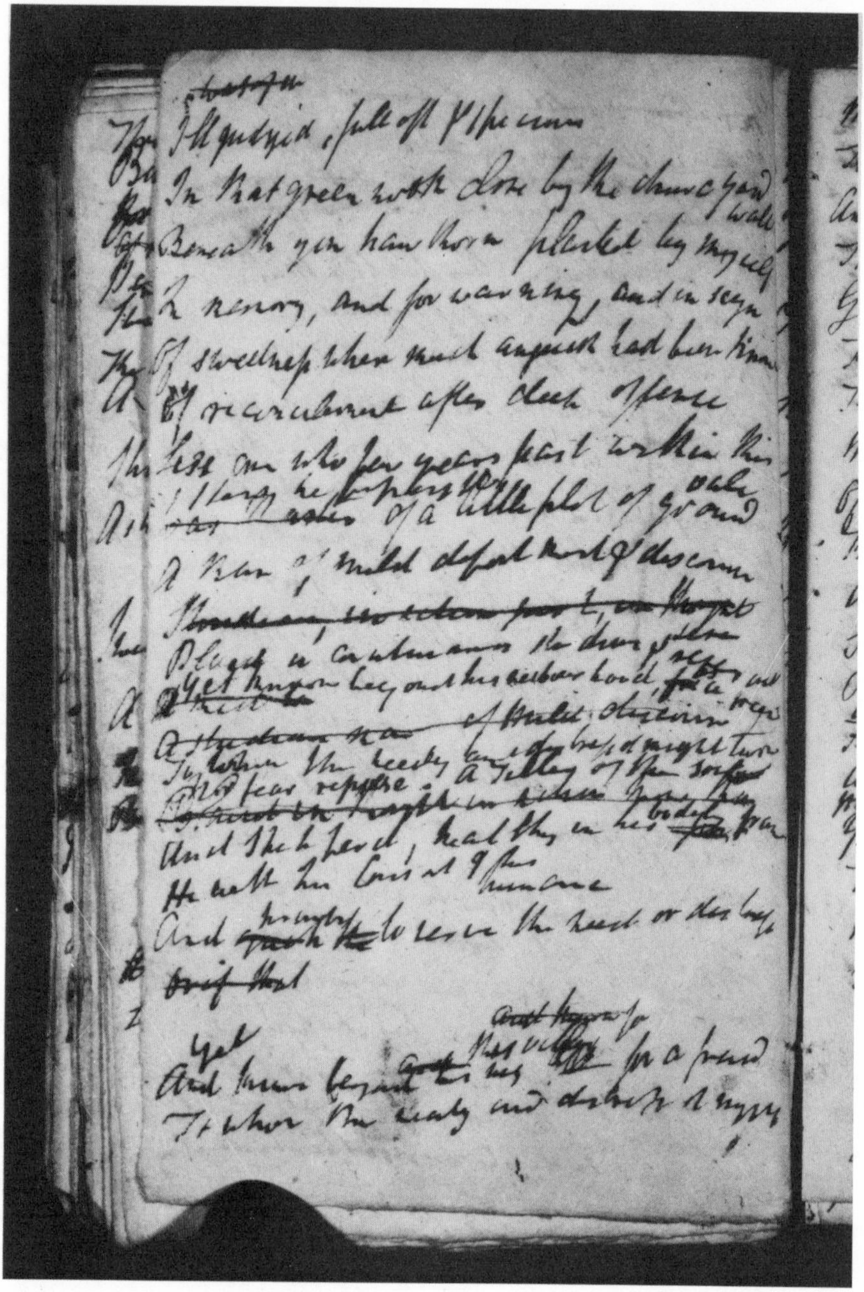

I'll gratified, full off & the own

In that green nook close by the church yard wall

Beneath yon hawthorn planted by myself

A memory, and for a warning, and in sign

Of sweetness where much anguish had been known

Of reconcilement after deep offence

Less one who for years past within this

I trust he [illegible] of a little plot of ground only

A Man of mild deportment and of discourse

[illegible line struck through]

Pleased in continuance the dear pleasure

Yet known beyond his neighborhood

[illegible struck through lines]

To restore the needy and the helpless might turn

Not fear repulse at a telling of his sorrow

And the h level, heal thy in his body

He will his own at & humane

And brought to serve the need or [illegible]

[illegible]

Yet

And knew beyond his his [illegible] for a friend

To whom the ready and [illegible]

was of a
Ill judge'd, full oft & specious
In that green nook close by the churcyard
                                    wall
Beneath yon hawthorn planted by myself
In memory, and for warning, and in sign
Of sweetness where much anguish had been known
Of reconcilement after deep offence
     ſies
L ſise one who few years past within this
                                    vale
   Here he [?possessd]
Was Master of a little plot of ground
A Man of mild deportment & discourse
Studious, in action just, in thought
                              sere
Placid in countenance studious & seren
                                    act
                                    as
   Yet known beyond his neibourhood, for a friend
A [?mast]
A studious man of mild discourse
   To whom the needy and distressd might turn
   Nor fear repulse. A Tiller of the soil
[?Placid] in [?mind] in riches more than
                              bodily frame
And Shepherd, healthy in his fra
He with his Consort & his
                    [?humane]
        prompt
And quick the to serve the need or distress
Or if that

                    and known for
   Yet   and this valley
And known beyond his neg [?]—for a friend
To whom the needy and distressd might

These revisions of ll. 492 and 472–482 were drafted after the lines on 21ᵛ. In the next to last line WW probably abbreviated "neighbourhood."

22

	specious
492	Was of that kind ~~tis said~~ which tended more
493	To splendid neatness to a shewy, trim,
494	And overlabour'd purity of house
495	Than to substantial thrift. He, on his part
496	Generous & easyminded was not free
497	From carelessness, & thus in course of time
498	These joint infirmities, ~~combined perchance~~

induced

500

499	With ~~other cause less obvious, brought~~ decay
500	Of worldly substance & distress of mind
501	Which to a thoughtful man was hard to shun
502	And which he could not cure. A blooming Girl
503	Serv'd them, an Inmate of the House, alas!

inclined

| 504 | Poor now in tranquil pleasure he gave way |

And sought for to thought

| 505 | ~~To thoughts of~~ troubled pleasure; he became |

f)

| 506 | A lawless Suitor or⟨ the Maid & she |

Nor is to be [?proud ?and] without [?shame]

| 507 | Yielded ~~unworthily~~. Unhappy Man |

⟍ to his desire

508	That which he had been weak enough to do
509	Was misery in remembrance; he was stung
510	Stung by his inward thoughts & by the smiles
511	Of Wife & children stung to agony.
512	His temper urg'd him not to seek relief
513	Amid the noise of revellers f nor from draught
514	Of lonely stupefaction, he himself

---

493   A blot has soaked through from the verso.

509–514   The faint vertical lines on the lower part of this page may be tentative marks of deletion.

Here rests A Mother; but of her no more
  Nor of the praise
Nor of the sorrow which she left behind
  Though to her honour much might be rehears'd
Turn from her grave, and halfway
                   up that ridge
             ing
That ridge which elbows from the mountain
                     side
  Carries into the plain its rocks & woods
Behold the Cottage where she dwellt, where
                    now
Her Husbad dwells in widowhood whom
                 she left,
Some few years past, the solitary prop

Here rests A mother— but no more
              of her
Or of the sorrow which she left behind
Turn from her grave
  Much to the last remained unknown—but this
  I sure, that through remorse and grief he died
The house where he who was her husband
                 dwells

  In widowhood   this
  Is sure   but sure
It is that of remorse & grief he died
Is sure, remorse consumed him & he died
     he perished by disease of mind
     absolved
H Bityd, by men, forgivn of God,
  Though pity'd among men absolvd by God
He could not find forgiveness in himself
He could not bear the weight of his
              thought
        own shame
Though pity among men absolved by god

Drafts toward revision of ll. 533–537 and 530–532 for *Excursion*, VI, 1110–1121. In the bottom
line and in the fifth from the bottom WW evidently miswrote "Pity'd."

A rational & suffering them trme'll 26
Was his own world, without resting place
Wretched at home, he & ah he peace abroad
Ranged through the mountains slept upon
Ask'd comfort of the open air & found
No quiet in the darkness of the night
No pleasure in the beauty of the day.
His flock he slighted: his paternal fields
Grew as a clog to him whose spirit wish'd
To fly, but whither? And ye gracious heaven
That wear a look so full of peace and hope
And love, benignant Mother of the Vale
How fair amid her brood of Cottages!
She was to him a sickness & reproach
I speak conjecturing from the little known
The much that to the last remain'd unknown
But this is sure he died of his own grief
He could not bear the weight of his own
                              shame
          That Ridge which elbowing from the mount
Carries into the Plain its rocky tum-side
Conceals a Cottage where this his
In widow hood, where Lefas & mother died
Long since, I left him solitary prop
Of many helpless Children Begin 540

23

515 A rational & suffering Man himself
516 Was his own world, without a resting-place
                found
              he gained
517 Wretched at home ~~he had~~ no peace abroad
518 Rang'd through the mountains slept upon the earth
                                              520
519 Ask'd comfort of the open air & found
520 No quiet in the darkness of the night
521 No pleasure in the beauty of the day.
522 His flock he slighted: his paternal fields
         Became ⌠C
523 ~~Were~~ as a ⌡clog to him whose Spirit wish'd
524 To fly, but whither? And yon gracious Church
525 That has a look so full of peace and hope
526 And love, benignant Mother of the Vale
527 How fair amid her brood of Cottages!
528 She was to him a sickness & reproach
529 ~~I speak conjecturing from the little known~~
530 The much that to the last remain'd unknown
                              ⌠own
531 But this is sure he died of his ⌡[?one] grief
532 He could not bear the weight of his own
                                    shame

                                        ⌠:
533   That Ridge which elbowing from the moun⌡ſ
                                    :tain-side
534 Carries into the Plain its rocks & woods
                    the husband
535 Conceals a Cottage where a ~~Father~~ dwells
536 In widowhood, whose Life's Copartner died
537 Long since, & left him solitary Prop
538 Of many helpless Children. I begin
                              540

Here rests a Mother but from her I turn
And from her grave — — look yonder — half
That village church elbowing upon the mountain
Comes into the plain its ranks & crowds
Behold the Cottage where she dwelt, where
Her Husband dwells in widowhood whom the
Before years past, he soledsey free life
Of his many helpless Children. The for

Here rests a Mother but from her I turn
And from her grave — — look yonder— half
                                   way up
That ridge which elbowing from the mountainside
Carries into the plain its rocks & woods
Behold the Cottage where she dwelt, where
                                 now
Her Husband dwells in widow-hood whom she
                                 left

   full eight
A few years past, the solitary prop
Of many helpless children, The [?]

These revisions of ll. 533–538 for *Excursion*, VI, 1115–1122, were written after those on 23ᵛ.

With words which might be prelude to a Tale
of sorrow & dejection, but I fail.
Though in the midst of sadness as might seem
In gladness when I think of what mine eyes
see daily in that ——— ful family
Bright garland make they for their Father's
those six fair Daughters budding yet; not one
not one of all the band a full-blown flower.
Go to the Dwelling: there shalt thou
that He who takes away yet takes withal
What he seems to take, or gives it back
not to our prayers, but ————
——— the poor ————— soul
Which Hope with tears watered . ——— shalt see
a House, which, at small distance, will
In no distinction to have passed beyond   appears
Its Fellows, will appear, like them, to have
Out of the native Rock but near our eyes   grown
& Will shew it not so grave in outward mien
And soberly array'd as for the most
are these rude mountain-dwellings,   560
mere friendless Nature, but a studious work   Nature's care
of many fancies & of many hands.
a play they ——— a ——— for such the air
And aspect which the little Spot maintains
In spite of lovely Counters nakedness.

24

539	With words which might be prelude to a Tale
540	Of sorrow & dejection, but I feel
541	Though in the midst of sadness as might seem
542	No sadness when I think of what mine eyes

     See daily   happy

543	H̶a̶v̶e̶ ̶s̶e̶e̶n̶ in that d̶e̶l̶i̶g̶h̶t̶f̶u̶l̶ family.
544	Bright garland make they for their Father's

                            brows

545	Those six fair Daughters budding yet, not one
546	Not one of all the band a full-blown flower.

                          ye
                              1̦

547	Go to the Dwelling: there T̶h̶o̶u̶ shalt⟨ have

                                    proof

548	That He who takes away yet takes not hallf
549	Of what he seems to take or gives it back
550	Not to our pray'r but far beyond our pray'r

                           ⟨s

551	G̶i̶v̶e̶s̶ ̶i̶t̶ ̶t̶h̶e̶ ̶b̶o̶o̶n̶ ̶&̶ ̶p̶r̶o̶d̶u̶c̶e̶ ̶o̶f̶ ̶a̶ ⟨s̶o̶i̶l̶

      He gives it the boon-produce of a soil

552	Which Hope hath never water'd. T̶h̶o̶u̶ shalt see

                              ye

553	A House, which, at small distance, will

                              appear

554	In no distinction to have passed beyond
555	Its Fellows, will appear, like them, to have

                            grown

556	Out of the native Rock but nearer view
557	Will shew it not so grave in outward mien
558	And soberly array'd as for the most

                         560

559	Are these rude mountain-dwellings,

                        Nature's care

560	Mere friendless Nature's, but a studious work
561	Of many fancies & of many hands
562	A play thing and a pride for such the air
563	And aspect which the little Spot maintains

      [?Even] with midst

564	In spite of lonely Winters nakedness.

550–551   WW's line count includes this revision, which must therefore have been made during the process of transcription.

They have their ~~woodbine~~ woodbine resting on the Porch
Their rose-trees, strong in health, that will be
Roof-high; & here & there the garden wall soon
Is topp'd with single stones, a showy file
Curious for shape or hue, some round, like Balls,
Worn smooth & round by fretting of the Brook
From which they have been gather'd, others bright
And sparry, the rough scatterings of the Hills.
These ornaments the Cottage chiefly owes
To one, a hardy Girl, who mounts the rocks
Such is her choice, she fears not the bleak wind
Companion of her Father, does for him
Wherever he wanders in his pastoral course
The service of a Boy, and with delight
More keen & prouder daring? yet hath she
Within the garden, like the rest, a bed
For her own flowers, or favorite Herbs, a space
Holden by sacred Charter; and I guess
She also help'd to frame that tiny Plot
Of garden ground which one day twas my chance
To find among the woody rocks that rise
Above the House, a slip of smoother earth
Planted with gooseberry bushes, & in one
Right in the centre of the prickly shrub

25

              wood-bine
565   They have their ~~jasmine~~ resting on the Porch
566   Their rose-trees strong in health that will be
                                 soon
567   Roof-high; & here & there the garden wall
        s
568   Is   topp'd with single stones a shewy file
569   Curious for shape or hue, some round, like Balls,
570   Worn smooth & round by fretting of the Brook
571   From which they have been gather'd, others bright
572   And sparry, the rough scatterings of the Hills.
        latter
573   These ornaments the Cottage ~~chiefly~~ owes
574   To one, a hardy Girl, who mounts the rocks
575   Such is her choice, she fears not the bleak wind
576   Companion of her Father, does for him
577   Whereer he wanders in his pastoral course
578   The service of a Boy and with delight
                             580
579   More keen & prouder daring: yet hath She
580   Within the garden, like the rest, a bed
581   For her own flowers, or favorite Herbs, a space
582   Holden by sacred charter; ~~and I guess~~
583   She also ~~framed~~ help'd to frame that tiny Plot
584   Of garden ground which one day twas my chance
585   To find among the woody rocks that rise
                     {S
586   Above the House, a {slip of smoother earth
587   Planted with goose-berry bushes, & in one
588   Right in the centre of the prickly shrub

---

588   A blot has soaked through from the verso.

And here fair eyes shall greet you, &c

Now hear ye not ever it good

For that the blessful tale which

prints, so God the Power man's friend

shall check the barque of innocence

where ere our was dire

both in doors & without; just the revered

Of conjugal

And fair house till ehen

Three happy her the Mosses may be deeme

The less who se the beneath

I turn'd, the eye on mead might which

And before her tears & heart eyes

Mark her

Not less their far away up your

Behold a dusky spot a grove of

and seems

this grove

                        thither go
And these fair sights shall [?greet] you for
                                your pains
Now have ye not receiv'd good recompense
                                last I told
For that distressful tale which ~~went before~~
        Thes
⌠[?This]
⌡[? ~~]~~ [?crops] fruits; so God the Poor mans friend
                                ordains
    ~~In [?lands]~~   ⌠of
Shall deck the bough ⌡[?] innocence and love
                        ⌠doth
Where æconomic wisdom ⌡[?] not fail
Within doors or without; such the reward
Of conjugal fidelity through life
                ⌠when   has   has
And partners help ⌡where death ~~hath~~ inter̶fer
                                interfered

[?Thris] happy then the Mother may be deemd
                within   grave
The wife who rests beneath this turf from which
        That ~~ye might see in fancy where~~
I ~~turnd [?aside] that ye might witness~~ how
    ~~And how~~
~~And where her tender Spirit yet survives~~
                                where
I turnd, that ye in mind might witness ~~how~~
        how
And ~~where~~ her ~~tender~~ spirit yet
                survives⎮
                ⌠on   ⌠earth
                ⌡[?in] ⌡[?]
~~Then wherefore should we grieve for her [?wherefor]~~
~~[?Must ? ? ?]~~ oftentime [?retain ?his] [?]

Not less than 1/2 way up yon Mountains
                        side
Behold a dusky spot a grove of
                        firs
And seems still smaller than it is
                        this grove

    The lines in WW's hand are drafts to follow l. 606, on the facing recto. Those at the top of the page were not incorporated in *The Excursion*; those in the middle became *Excursion*, VI, 1188–1191. The three lines at the foot of the page in MW's hand correspond to MS. B ll. 607–610, and were incorporated in MS. D.

342 MS. B

26

A minute Bird's-nest fashiond by the hand
Was there, a staring Thing of twisted hay
And one gigantic Firtree tower'd above the
But in the darkness of the night then Whole.
most
This Dwelling chear of spoil ~ cover'd by the gloom
Then in my ~~~ offee lines ~~~ stop short
And, (who could help it) feed by stealth my ~~~
With prospect of the company within
Laid open through the blazing windows: there
I see the elder Daughter at her Wheel
Spinning amain ~~~ as if to overtake
She knows not what, or leaking in her turn
Some little Novice of the sisterhood
That spell in this or that household work
Which from her Fathers hour ~~~ herself
While she was yet a little one, had learned
Child Man ! he is not gay but they are gay
And the whole House seem fill'd with gaiety

From yonder grey stone that stands alone
Close to the foaming Stream look up & see
Not less than half way up the mountainside
A dusky spot a little grove of firs
And seems the smyle ~~~ than it is: ~~~
~~~ ~~~
~~~ six weeks younger than her eldest Boy

26

589 A mimic Birds-nest fashion'd by the hand
590 Was stuck, a staring Thing of twisted hay
591 And one quaint Fir-tree tower'd above the
                                        Whole.
592 But in the darkness of the night then most
593 This Dwelling charms me: cover'd by the gloom
              in my walks I oftentimes
594 Then, ~~heedless of good manners,~~ I stop short
                                    {b
595 And, (who could help it) feed {my stealth my sight
596 With prospect of the company within
597 Laid open through the blazing window: there
598 I see the eldest Daughter at her wheel   600
599 Spinning amain as if to overtake
600 She knows not what, or teaching in her turn
601 Some little Novice of the sisterhood
602 That skill in this or other household work
603 Which from her Fathers honor'd hands, herself
604 While She was yet a Little-one, had learn'd.
605 Mild Man! he is not gay but they are gay
                        seems
606 And the whole House ~~is~~ fill'd with gaiety.
607   From yonder grey-stone that stands alone
608 Close to the foaming Stream look up & see
609 Not less than half way up the mountain-side
610 A dusky Spot a ~~little~~ grove of firs
                        ─[?]
611 And seems still smaller than it is: ~~The Dame~~
                              This grove
          As from the dame I learnd who dwells below
612 ~~Who dwells below she told me that this grove~~
          As from the dame I learnd who dwells below
613 Just six weeks younger than her eldest Boy

601–608 Blots have smeared from the facing verso.

A symbol of Eternity & heaven.
Nor have we [?been] deceivd—thus far
                          the Effect
Falls not below the loftiest of her hopes
Tis not in holy Nature to betray
                    votaries
Or disappoint her genuine [?followers]
My trembling Heart acknowleges
                        her power
To be divine—& therefore infinite.

This draft expands ll. 215–217 on 10^r. It precedes the draft on 31^v; neither was incorporated in MS. D.

Was planted by her Husband & herself 27

For a convenient shelter which in storm

Their sheep might draw to" & they knew

Said she, "for thither do we bear them food

In time of heavy snow. She then began

In pious obedience to her private thoughts

To speak of her dead Husband: is there not

An art, a music & a strain of words

That shall be life the acknowledged voice of life

Shall speak of what is done among the fields

Done truly there or felt, of solid good

And real evil yet be interfused

More grateful more harmonious than

The idle breath of sweetest pipe attuned

To pastoral fancies? Is there such a strain

Pure & unsullied flowing from the heart

With motions of true dignity & grace

Or must we seek these things where

man is not

27

614   *Was planted by her Husband & herself*
615   *For a convenient shelter which in storm*
616   *Their sheep might draw to "& they know*
                                    it well,
617   *Said she, "for thither do we bear them food*
618   *In time of heavy snow. She then began*
                           620
619   *In fond obedience to her private thoughts*
620   *To speak of her dead Husband: is there not*
                    strain   strain
                   ⸦strain
621   *An art, a music & a* ⸦stream⸧*of words*
622   *That shall be life the acknowledg'd voice*
                                  of life
623   *Shall speak of what is done among the fields*
624   *Done truly there or felt, of solid good*
                   ⸦And
625   *Of solid good* ⸦*& real evil yet be sweet*
                                  withal
626   *More grateful more harmonious than*
                             the breath
627   *The idle breath of sweetest pipe attuned*
628   *To pastoral fancies? Is there such a stream*
629   *Pure & unsullied flowing from the heart*
630   *With motions of true dignity & grace*
631   *Or must we seek these things where*
                      man is not?

---

614   The text continues in DW's hand through l. 645.
621   WW's "strain" is in pencil.
625   The correction is DW's.

28

Methinks I could repeat in tuneful verse
Delicious as the gentlest breeze that sound
through that aerial fir-grove could preserve
Some portion of its human history
As gather'd from that Matron's lips & tell
Of tears that have been shed at sight of it
And moving dialogues between this Pair
Who in their prime of wedlock with
did plant this grove, now flourishing while they
No longer flourish, he entirely gone
She withering in her loneliness. Be they
A task above my skill: the silent mind
Has its own treasures, & I think of these
Love what I see & honour human kind

28

632 *Methinks I could repeat in tuneful verse*
633 *Delicious as the gentlest breeze that*
                                    sounds
634 *Through that aerial fir-grove could*
                                preserve
635 *Some portion of its human history*
636 *As gather'd from that Matron's lips & tell*
637 *Of tears that have been shed at sight of it*
638 *And moving dialogues between this Pair*
                              640
          ir⎫
639 *Who in the* ⎬ *prime of wedlock with*
                              joint hands
          e
640 *Did plant this grove, now flourishing while*
                                    they
641 *No longer flourish, he entirely gone*
642 *She withering in her loneliness. Be this*
643 *A task above my skill: the silent*
                              mind
644 *Has its own treasures, & I think of these*
645 *Love what I see & honour hu-*
                        humankind

29

No we are not alone we do not stand
My Emma here misplac'd and desolate
Loving what no one cares for but ourselves,
We shall not scatter through the plains & rocks
Of this fair Vale and o'er its spacious heights
Vaps of table kindness bestow'd
On objects unaccustom'd to the gift
Of feeling, which were cheerless and forlorn
But few weeks past and would be so again
If we were not, we do not tend a lamp
Whose lustre we alone partticipate
Which is dependent upon us alone
Mortal though bright a dying, dying flame.
Look where we will some human heart has been
Before us with its offering; not a tree
Sprinkles these hills the pastures but the same
Hath furnish'd matter for a thought; perchance
To some one serves as a familiar friend.
Joy spreads and sorrow spreads & this whole Vale
Home of untutor'd shepherds as it is
Swarms with sensation as with gleams of sunshine
Shadows or breezes scents or sounds, Nor deem
These feelings though subservient more than
To every day's demand for daily bread
And borrowing more their spirit & their shape
From self respecting interests, deem them not
not

29

                    W⎤
646   No [?]]⎰e are not alone we do not stand
                                    ⎧s
647   My Emma here misplac'd and de ⎩lolate
648   Loving what no one cares for but ourselves
649   We shall not scatter through the plains & rocks
650   Of this fair Vale and oer its spatious heights
651   Unprofitable kindliness bestow'd
        ⎧O   ts⎤
652   ⎩on Objects unaccustomed to the gifs⎰
                    which
653   Of feeling, ~~that~~ were cheerless and forlorn
                            ,⎤
654   But few weeks past⎰ and would be so again
                        ;⎤
655   If we were not⎰ we do not tend a lamp
656   Whose lustre we alone participate
657   Which is dependent upon us alone
658   Mortal though bright a dying, dying flame
                                    660
659   Look where we will some human heart has been
660   Before us with its offering; not a tree
661   Sprinkles these little pastures but the same
662   Hath furnish'd matter for a thought; perchance
                serves
663   To some one ~~is~~ as a familiar Friend.
664   Joy spreads and sorrow spreads: & this whole Vale
665   Home of untutor'd Shepherds as it is
666   Swarms with sensation as with gleams of sunshine
                                    .⎤
667   Shadows or breezes, scents or sounds,⎰ Nor deem
668   These feelings though subservient more than
                                    ours
669   To every day's demand for daily bread
670   And borrowing more their spirit & their shape
                                    ⎧em
671   From selfrespecting interests; deem th⎩[?ese]
                        not

30

Unworthy therefore and unhallow'd, no,
They left the animal being, do themselves
By natures kind & wise provision are
Refine the selfishness from which they spring
Redeem by love the individual sense
Of anxiousness with which they are combin'd

~~Renewing have the best of being we prove~~
~~The best and the experience, most abound~~
~~are of approacher of the   ~~
~~Joy of the lightest of the pleasant of home~~

They blend with it congenially; meanwhile
Calmly they breathe their own undying life
~~Lonely and unseen unperceivd in~~
Through his their mountain sanctuary, (long
Along may it remain invisible)
Diffusing health & sober cheerfulness
And giving to the moments as they pass
Their little freces of animating thought
That sweeten labour make it seen & feel
To be no arbitrary weight impos'd
But a glad function natural to Man.
          Gain proof of this Newcomer though the
Already human Ideca; the inward frame
Though slowly opening opens every day
Nor am I less delighted with the show
As it unfolds ~~itself~~ itself now, here, there

30

672 Unworthy therefore and unhallow'd, no,
673 They lift the animal being, do themselves
674 By natures kind & ever present aid
675 Refine the selfishness from which they spring
676 Redeeem by love the individual sense
677 Of anxiousness with which they are combin'd*
678 ~~Many are pure the best of them are pure~~
                                              680
679 ~~The best, and these, remember, most abound~~
680 ~~Are fit associates of the   joy~~
681 ~~Joy of the highest & the purest minds.~~
682 They blend with it congenially: meanwhile
683 Calmly they breathe their own undying life
684 ~~Lowly and unassuming as it is~~
685 Through this their mountain sanctuary, (long
        h)
686 O { long may it remain inviolate)
687 Diffusing health & sober chearfulness
688 And giving to the moments as they pass
689 Their little booons of animating thought
690 That sweeten labour make it seem & feel
691 To be no arbitrary weight impos'd
692 But a glad function natural to Man.
693   Fair proof of this Newcomer though I be
694 Already have I seen; the inward frame
695 Though slowly opening opens every day
696 Nor am I less delighted with the show
697 As it unfolds [?itself] itself now here now
                                              there

---

677   The asterisk at the end of the line indicates that the draft on 30ᵛ is to follow:
      *And thus th̶r̶ it is that fitly they become
           (c
      Asso{siates in the joy of purest minds
      They blend therewith congenially

MS. D incorporates this revision.

A symbol of Eternity & heaven
Nor have we been deceived: thus far
                    the effect
Falls not below the loftiest of our hopes
Tis not in holy Nature to betray
Or disappoint her genuine Votary
My trembling Heart acknowledges
                    her Power
To be divine; & therefore infinite.
This Vale these mountains cease
                not to put forth
Fresh graces, new enjoyments to us here
Old to [?revere], the habitual to maintain.
      {t
The {[?]orrents [?murm] to my listening
      [?]   [—?—]
With unabated [?influence]. So it is
So must be, termination is not here
Tis not in holy Nature to betray
Or disappoint her genuine Votar[?ies]
      {ing
My trembl{[?y] heart acknowledges
                 her Power
To be divine & therefor infinite

This draft further develops that on 27ᵛ; none of it is incorporated in MS. D.

91

Than is the passing Traveller when his way
Lies through some ~~region~~ unknowing ~~where~~
~~(Say the fair valleys~~) when low-hung mists
Break up and are beginning to recede
How pleas'd he is to hear the murmuring stream
The many Voices ~~whence~~ he ~~cannot~~ ~~tell~~ plead
To have about which way he goes
Something on every side concealed from view
In every ~~quarter~~ some thing visible
Half seen or wholly, lost & found again
Alternate progress and impediments
~~And~~ Yet ~~gaining~~ a ~~prospect~~ ~~speed & speedy~~ the main.

        Such pleasure now is mine ~~& what if~~
~~Here~~ less happy than the Traveller
~~and obliged~~ from time to time
~~but to cast a painful look~~
Upon unwelcome things, which unawares,
Reveal themselves, not therefore is my heart
Deposs'd now does fear what it is to come
But confident enrich'd at every glance
The more I see the more is ~~delight~~
~~the grandeur or by reflection eye~~
With ~~joy~~ pursues herself and as she dwells
With Hope who would not follow where she leads,
~~Nor let me~~ ~~have unheeded~~ loves
When ~~so fear is~~ and humbler sympathies
~~to me endeared the ground~~

31

698 Than is the passing Traveller when his way
           700
    unknown vale
699 Lies through some ~~region~~ then ~~first trod by him~~
700 (~~Say this fair Valleys self~~) when low-hung mists
701 Break up and are beginning to recede
702 How pleas'd he is to hear the murmuring stream
        { *knows not*
    whence he { *does n*
703 The many Voices ~~from he knows not where~~
           pleasd

   him
704 To have about ᴀwhich way e'er he goes
705 Something on every side concealed from view
706 In every quarter some thing visible
707 Half seen or wholly, lost & found again
708 Alternate progress and impediment
   {ᵧ   *a prospect spred & spreding*
709 And {yet ~~a growing prospect in~~ the main.ᴀ
       {&   {*herein*
710 Such pleasure now is mine {& ~~what~~ if {I
          I am [?forced]
711 ~~Herein~~ less happy than the Traveller
  And frequently   *from time to time*
      {T
712 ~~Am sometimes forcd~~ {to castᴀa painful look
  not seldom forced
713 Upon unwelcome things which unawares
         heart
714 Reveal themselves/ not therefore is my ~~mind~~
    does it/
715 Depress'd nor ~~do I~~ fear what ~~it~~ is to come
716 But confident enrich'd at every glance
        my mind
717 The more I see the more ~~is my~~ delightᴀ
  Receives or by reflection can extract
718 Truth justifies herself and as she dwells
        720
719 With Hope who would not follow where she leads.
  pass unheeded [*?infin ?*]
720 Nor let me ~~overlook those other~~ loves
      and
721 Where no fear is ~~those~~ humbler sympathies,
722 ~~That have to me endeared the quietness~~

---

715 The extra "it" was underlined, as if queried, then deleted.

And for the simple [?form] frame of human
                                   life
Among thes hills established, on my sight
It opens [?As ?with]
Its composition opens by degrees
Nor am I delighted with the shew

            & for the brute
                    {*which*
In scripture glorified on {[?]
        the patient brute
                        patient [?brute]
On which the

And if Helvellyns eagle should
                            return
And occupy once more their antient
                            Hold

    Then duly

The draft at the top of the page corresponds to ll. 694–695; it is not incorporated in MS. D.
The second draft, in MW's hand, is a revision and expansion of l. 726; it is incorporated in MS. D.
The third draft revises ll. 738–740 and is not incorporated in MS. D.

32

Of this sublime retirement. They are
already inscribed upon my heart
A liking for the small grey Horse that bears
The paralytic Man the truant Boys
On which he crosses in the merry maze'd
Rides to & fro: I know them & their ways.
The famous Sheep-dog, first in all the vale;
Though yet to me a Stranger, will not be
a Stranger long; nor will the blind Man's Guide
Meek & neglected thing, of no renown.
Who lives here a winter in one place
Beneath the shelter of one Cottage-roof
And has not had his red-breast or his wren?
If there indeed they I shall have my Thrush
To rouse me a hundred Warblers more;
And if the banish'd Eagle Pair return   40
Llewellyn's Eagles to their ancient Hold
Then duly shall claim with those two Birds
Acquaintance as they soar amid the Heavens.
The Owl that gives the name to Owlet-crag
Have I heard shouting & he soon will be
A chosen one of my regards. See there
The Heifer in yon little Croft belongs
To one who holds it dear. with duteous care
He rear'd it & in speaking of his Charge
I heard her scatter some endearing words

32

723   Of this sublime retirement. ~~I begin~~

      is   ~~*have I*~~   *d*⎱

724   Already ~~to~~ inscribe ⎰ upon my heart

725   A liking for the small grey Horse that bears

                 [*?the ?brute*]

726   The paralytic Man ~~I know the ass~~

          & for the [*?meeker*] *brute* ✕

727   On which the Cripple, in the Quarry maim'd

728   Rides to & fro: I know them & their ways.

729   The famous Sheep-dog, first in all the vale—

730   Though yet to me a Stranger, will not be

731   A Stranger, long; nor will the blind Man's Guide

                ⎰T

732   Meek & neglected ⎱thing, of no renown⟂

733   Who ever liv'd a Winter in one ~~place~~

734   Beneath the shelter of ~~one~~ Cottage-roof

735   And has not ~~had his~~ Red-breast or his Wren?

      Ere fades the primrose

736   ~~I have them both~~; & I shall have my Thrush

      To rouse me   ⎰W

737   ~~In spring time~~ & a hundred ⎱warblers more;

738   And if the banish'd Eagle Pair return

                  740

739   Helvellyns Eagles to their antient Hold

      ~~in due season~~   *I*

740   Then ~~shall I see~~ shall⟨claim with those two

        duly   Birds

741   Acquaintance as they soar amid the Heavns.

742   The Owl that gives the name to Owlet-crag

743   Have I heard shouting & he soon will be

744   A chosen one of my regards. See there

745   The Heifer in yon little Croft belongs

746   To one who holds it dear: with duteous care

747   She rear'd it & in speaking of her Charge

748   I heard her scatter ~~once a word or two~~

              some endearing words

---

726   The X signals the insertion of the expansion of this line on 32^v.

That ~~multitude whose motions with~~ delight
~~My song pursued while~~
      lake
~~Behold it rest upon the~~ glassy
That multitude whose motions with delight
My song [?spurs ?on] which through the
      sunny [?vale]
  ~~day~~   ~~calm~~
Of the past day they wheeled upon
      the [?wing]
In wanton repetition like a band
Of [?aery] sylph obedient to their
      Queen,
~~Whose throne is centre to their~~ flight
That multitude which through the
      vernal calm
Of the past day were seen to soar aloft
     are reposing now
In wanton ~~repetition now repose~~
      lake
Upon the bosom of the glassy [?]
That here they settle from disturbance
      safe
But through the uneasy spirit of delight
They cannot rest, they gambol like
      young kids

These lines correspond to ll. 767–770, on the facing recto. Further drafts of this passage follow on 34ᵛ and 35ᵛ.

domestic yet in spring of the thistle

She being herself a Mother, happy Beast

If the caresses of a human voice

Can make it so and care of human hands,

And she as happy under Nature's care

Strangers to me and all men or at least

Strangers to all particular amity

All intercourse of knowledge or of love.

That parts the individual from the kind

Whether in large communities ye dwell

From year to year not shunning man's abode

A settled residence or be from far

Wild creatures, & of many homes that come

The gift of winds, & when the winds again

Take from us at your pleasure joy't shall ye

Not want for this your own subordinate

~~in my affections~~

In my affections witness the delight

With which ere while I saw that multitude

Wheel thro' the sky & see them now at rest

Yet not at rest upon the glassy lake

They cannot rest they gambol like young

Active as lambs & overcome with joy

They try all frolic motions, flutter plunge

And beat the passive water with their

wings

33

749 dome{s & in spirit
     {ttic∧yea∧& Motherly
750 She being herself a Mother, happy Beast
751 If the caresses of a human voice
752 Can make it so and care of human hands.

753 And Ye as happy {u
                    {ander Nature's care
754 Stranger's to me and all men or at least
                          each
755 Strangers to all particular amity
     And
756 All intercourse of knowledge or of love
757 That parts the individual from the kind
                                    nest
758 Whether in large communities ye d̶w̶e̶l̶l̶
                                    760
759 *From year to year not shunning man's*
                                    abode
760 *A settled residence or be from far*
761 *Wild creatures, & of many homes, that come*
                        &}   {om
762 *The gift of winds,* } *wh* {*en the winds again*
                              {s {ll
763 *Take from us at your pleasure yet* { *ha* {*ve ye*
                                    ,}
764 *Not want for this* } *your own subordinate place*
765 *A̶c̶c̶o̶r̶d̶i̶n̶g̶ ̶t̶o̶ ̶y̶o̶u̶r̶ ̶c̶l̶a̶i̶m̶ ̶a̶n̶ ̶u̶n̶d̶e̶r̶p̶l̶a̶c̶e̶*
766 *In my affections witness the delight*
767 *With which ere while I saw that mul-*
                                    -titude
768 *Wheel thro' the sky & see them now at rest*
769 *Yet not at rest upon the glassy lake*
770 *They cannot rest they gambol like young*
                                    whelps
771 *Active as lambs & overcome with joy*
772 *They try all frolic motions, flutter plunge*
77? *And beat the passive water with their*
                                    wings

755–756 The revisions are in pencil.
759 The transcription continues in DW's hand through l. 804. Corrections in ll. 762–763 are DW's.
763 The smudge before "yet" may be a smeared-out parenthesis.

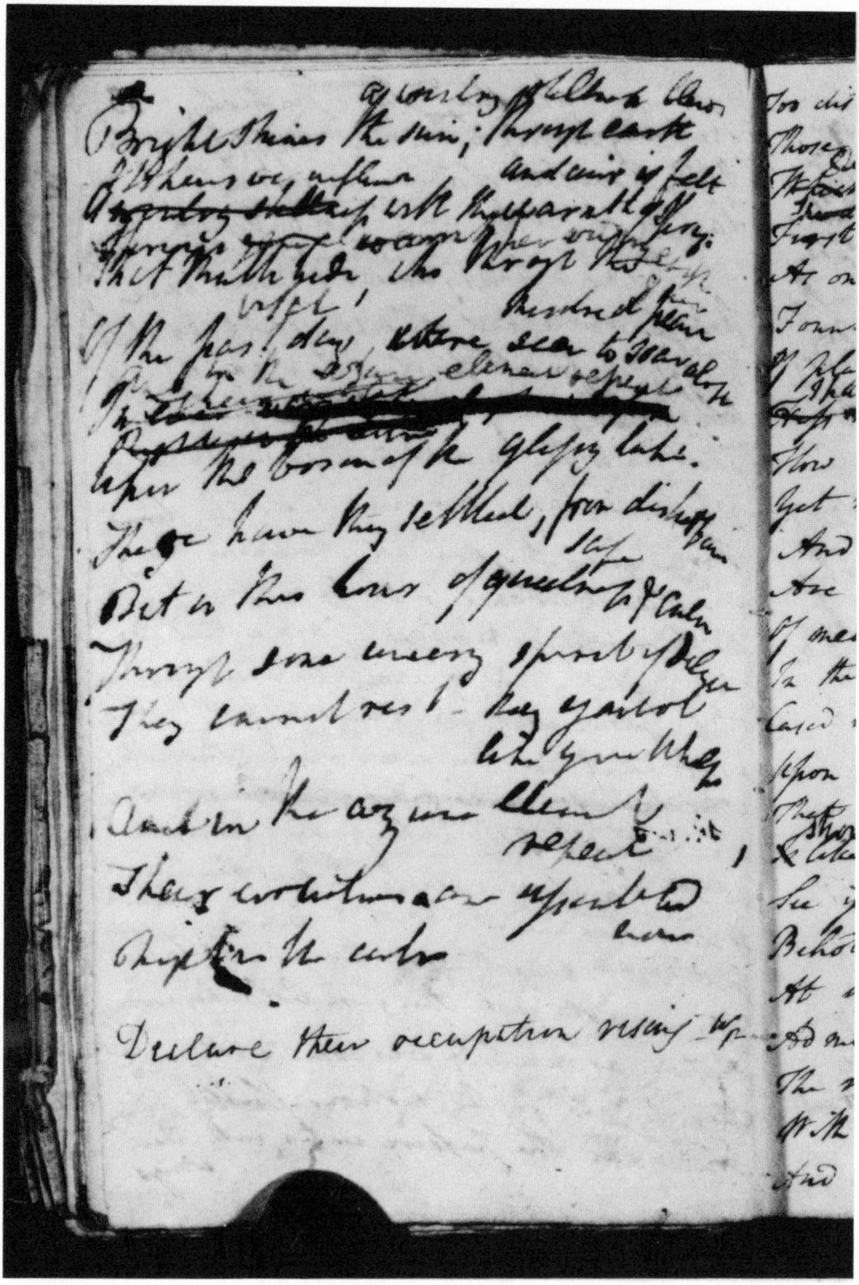

                    a wintry stillness blends
Bright shines the sun; through earth
    Its pensive influence   and air is felt
A ~~wintry still~~ness with the warmth of Spring:
    Spring's ~~genial~~ warmth pervading earth
                                    & air
That Multitude, who through the
                        kindred peace
            vital   w⎰
Of the past days, wh⎰ere seen to soar aloft
    And in the azure element repeat
    Their [?vary]
~~In ever varying circles [?near ?& ?far]~~
    ~~Right in [?the] centre~~
Upon the bosom of the glassy lake.
            ⎰re
The⎰y have they settled, from disturbance
                        safe
But in this hour of quietness & calm
Through some uneasy spirit of delight
They cannot rest—they gambol
                    like young Whelps
And in the azure element
                repeat
Their evolutions are assembled
                        now
Right in the centre

Declare their occupation rising up

   This page contains further drafts for the expansion of ll. 767–771 intermediate between drafts on 33ᵛ and 35ᵛ. Above the sixth full line, "vital" was probably intended to replace "genial" in the revision of l. 4. Blots on the lower portion of the page have smeared from the facing recto. The last line on the page is in MW's hand.

Too distant are they for plain view but lost
Those little fountains sparkling in the sun
Which tell ... ye ... what they are doing ...
... their ... one ... another silver spout
First one & then another silver spout
As one or other takes the fit of glee
Fountains & spouts yet rather in the guise
Of ... fire-works which on festal nights
... about the feet of wanton boys
How vast the compass of this theatre
Yet nothing to be seen but lovely pomp
And silent majesty the birch tree woods
Are hung with thousand thousand diamond
Of melted hoar-frost every tiny knot
In the bare twigs, each little bidding-place
... with its several bead, what myriads
Upon one tree while all the distant grove
That rises to the summit of the steep
... like a mountain built of silver light
See yonder the same pageant & again
Behold the universal imagery
At what a depth deep in the ... below
Admonish'd of the days of love to come
The raven croaks & fills the sunny air
With a strange sound of genial harmony
And in & all about that playful band

34

774　*Too distant are they for plain view but lo :*
775　*Those little fountains sparkling in the sun*
　　　　　　　　　　　　　　　rising⎫
　　　Declare their occupation　　　[?]⎰up
776　*Which tell what they are doing, ~~which rise~~ up*
　　　　　　　　　　　　　　780
　　　~~Thence their short lives appear & disappear~~
777　*First one & then another silver spout*
778　*As one or other takes the fit of glee*
779　*Fountains & spouts yet rather in the guise*
780　*Of plaything fire-works which on festal nights*
　　　　Sparkle
781　*~~Hiss hiss~~ about the feet of wanton boys*
782　*How vast the compass of this theatre*
783　*Yet nothing to be seen but lovely pomp*
784　*And silent majesty. the birch tree woods*
785　*Are hung with thousand thousand diamond*
　　　　　　　　　　　　　　　　drops
786　*Of melted hoar-frost every tiny knot*
　　　　　　　　　　　　⎰i
787　*In the bare twigs, each l⎱ttle budding-place*
788　*Cased with its several bead, what myriads*
　　　　　　　　　　　　　　　　　there
789　*Upon one tree while all the distant grove*
790　*That rises to the summit of the steep*
　　　　shows
791　*~~Is~~ like a mountain built of silver light*
792　*See yonder the same pagaent & again*
793　*Behold the universal imagery*
　　　　　　　　　　　Lake
794　*At what a depth deep in the ~~vale~~ below*
795　*Admonish'd of the days of love to come*
796　*The raven croaks & fills the sunny air*
　　　　　　　　　　　　　800
797　*With a strange sound of genial harmony*
798　*And in & all about that playful band*

776　WW's count jumps ahead by an additional two lines; the confusion probably resulted
from the preceding revisions.
787, 794　Corrections are DW's.

Bright shines the Sun; a wintry stillness
                                    blends
Its pensive influence with the warmth of
                                    spring
Springs vital warmth pervading earth &
                                    air
And chearingly reflected from the folds
And flecy skirts of clouds, that keeping
                                    each
Their form & station decorate the front
Of the clear sky; and from the naked rocks
And strong Hills imbued with tender light
                        which
That multitude ~~who~~ through the kindred
                                    peace
Of the past day were seen to soar aloft
And in the azure element repeat
Their evolutions are assembled now
Right at the centre of the glassy
                        lake
There have they settled from disturbance
                                    safe
But through the uneasy spirit of delight
They cannot rest—they gambol like
                            young whelps
Active as lambs &c

This page contains additional revisions of ll. 767–771; it follows the work on 33ᵛ and 34ᵛ. The apparent apostrophe in "Springs" in the third line is a flaw in the paper. Under the seventh line the penciled "naked r" visible in the photograph appears to be GW's.

35

Inaccessible altho' they be of rest
And in their fashion very riotous
There is a stillness & they seem to make
Calm revelry in that their calm abode
I leave them to their pleasure & I pass
Pass with a thought the life of the whole
                                        year
That is to come; the throngs of mountain flowers
And lilies that will dance upon the lake

   Then boldly say that solitude is not
Where these things are: he truly is alone
He of the multitude whose eyes are doomed
To hold a vacant commerce day by day
With that which he can neither know nor love
Dead things, to him thrice dead, or worse than this
With swarms of life, & worse than all, of men
His fellow men that are to him no more.
Than to the Forest Hermit are the leaves
That hang aloft in myriads, nay far less   820
Are less for aught that comforts or defends
Or lulls or cheers. Society is here:
The true community the noblest Friends?
Of many into one incorporate
That must be looked for here; paternal sway
The House hold, under God, for high & low

35

799 *Inca ⎰p ⎰b*
  ⎱ba⎱pable altho' they be of rest
800 *And in their fashion very rioters*
801 *Their is a stillness & they seem to make*
802 *Calm revelry in that their calm abode*
803 *I leave them to their pleasure & I pass*
804 *Pass with a thought the life of the whole*
        year

805 That is to come; the ⎰T
       ⎱ throngs of mountain flowers
806 And lillies that will dance upon the lake
807 Then boldly say that solitude is not
808 Where these things are: he truly is alone
809 He of the multitude whose eyes are doom'd
810 To hold a vacant commerce day by day
811 With that which he can neither know nor love
812 Dead things, to him thrice dead, or worse than this
813 With swarms of life, & worse than all, of men
814 His fellow men that are to him no more
815 Than to the Forest Hermit are the leaves
816 That hang aloft in myri ⎰ad
        ⎱dss, nay far less
          820
817 Far less for aught that comforts or defends
818 Or lulls or chears. Society is here:
819 The true community the noblest Frame
820 Of many into one incorporate
821 That must be lookd for here; paternal sway
822 One Household, under God, for high & low

---

799 The correction is DW's.
812–814 MW copied a revision of these lines on 45ᵛ, as follows:

    ⎰[?with]
    ⎱[?worse] with swarms of
      worse
Dead things, or ~~worse~~ living men
Who to his overwhelmed humanity
 If by
~~From~~ ambition or the thirst of gain
His mind be free are no~~thing~~ more
 From that bright day the Pla

The last line may possibly be a revision of l. 44 on 3ʳ. Still another revision of ll. 812–814, probably earlier, is on 48ᵛ; neither revision was incorporated in MS. D.
817 The mark under "Far" may be an underlining for emphasis.

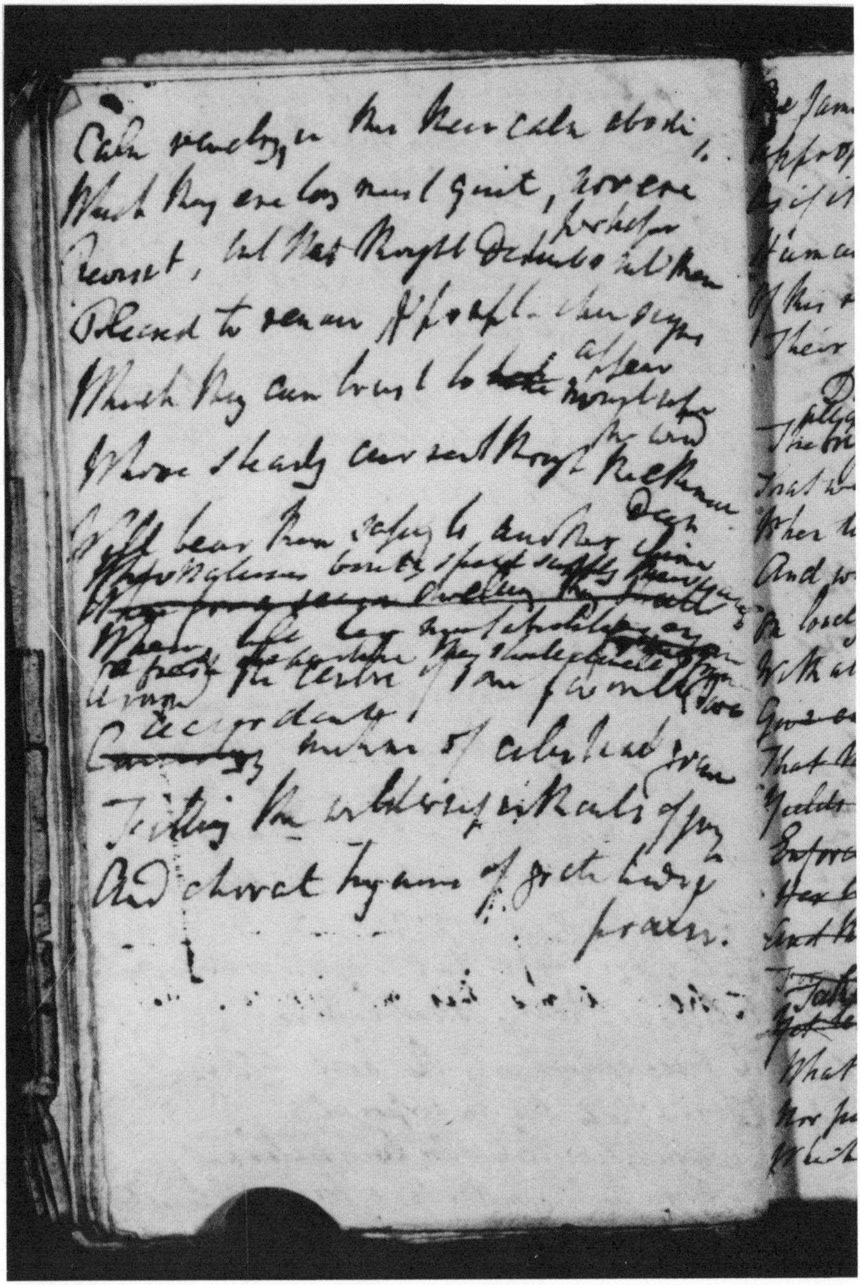

Calm revelry, in this their calm abode,
Which they ere long must quit, nor ere
                              perhaps
          [?is]⎫
Revisit, but that⎰ thought disturbs not them
Pleased to remain, & prompt when signs
                              appear
Which they can trust to ~~take~~ mount upon
                              the wind
Whose steady current through the ethereal
                              deep
Will bear them safely to another clime
    Where Natures bounty shall supply their [?wants]
~~Where for a season dwelling they shall~~
                              [?frame]
    Where life her mutabilities again
    A fresh departure they shall dwell & [?frame]
Around the centre of some favorite [?Place]
    Accordant
[?Cascading] motions of celestial grace
Filling the wilderness with [?cries] of joy
And choral hymns of gratitude &
                    praise.

These lines are an insertion to follow l. 802, which corresponds to the first line of this passage;
they are not incorporated in MS. D.

36

the family & one mansion, to themselves
appropriate & divided from the world
as if it were a cave; a multitude
Human & brute, possessors under turb is
of this recess their legislative Hall
their Temple, & their glorious dwelling place

Dismissing therefore, all Arcadian dreams
the golden fancies of the golden age
The bright array of shadowy thought for times
That were before all time or are to be
When time is not the pageantry but stern
And wholesome strife when our eyes are fixed
the lovely objects & we wish to part
With all remembrance of a jarring world 40
Give entrance to the stars to life, were
that Nature to this present spot of ----
Yields us every hour but her awful ----
Enforces to kind ---- ----
Her tribute of ---- pain

What need of more? That we shall ----
Nor pain for want of pleasure in the life
Which is about us nor through dearth of
aught

36

823   One family & one mansion, to themselves
824   Appropriate & divided from the world
825   As if it were a cave; a multitude
826   Human & brute, possessors undisturb'd
827   Of this recess their legislative Hall
828   Their Temple, & their glorious dwelling-place
                           {A
829   Dismissing therefore all {arcadian dreams
830   All golden fancies of the golden age
831   The bright array of shadowy thoughts from times
832   That were before all time or are to be
833   When time is not the pageantry that stirs
834   And will be stirring when our eyes are fix'd
835   On lovely objects & we wish to part
836   With all remembrance of a jarring world
                                  840
837   Give entrance to the sober truth; avow
838   That Nature to this favourite Spot of ours
839   Yields no exemption but her awful rights
840   Enforces to the utmost & exacts
841   Her tribute of inevitable pain
                       {ng
842   And that the sti{g sting is added, man himself
843   For ever busy to afflict himself
        Take we at once this one sufficient hope
844   Yet temper this with one sufficient hope
845   What need of more? that we shall neither droop
846   Nor pine for want of pleasure in the life
847   Which is about us nor through dearth of
                                aught

---

830   This line was inadvertently omitted in transcription: it is included in MS. R, where WW drafted the passage.

837–844   The first cross deleting this passage is in pencil, the second in ink. The correction of l. 844 was first written in pencil, then overwritten in ink.

<pre>
                      if this
Were not, our habitation will be sought
By kindred spirits Sisters of our hearts
                   ⌠they
And Brothers of our love ⌡[?] [?who] inspire
[?whose]⌡
By [?]⌡ example aided we shall strive
To make our minds as lovely as those
                            scenes
Which we behold, as fit as fair
                      above

      ⌠Dwellers
The ⌡owners of the Dwelling—& if this
               Desire within ourselves
Were otherwise, a Power in ourselves
Must needs exist
    The Dwellers of the Dwelling—
                      and if this
Were otherwise; Desire must needs
                            exist
            souls
            [?]⌡
To make our [?]⌡ as lovely as the
                            scene
            fair
Which we behold, as fit as [?fit ?above]
If heaven formed of Happiness joy
</pre>

These drafts are a revision of ll. 859–?874. WW apparently considered radically cutting the passage recalling John's visit to Grasmere, which must have evoked painful reflections after the breaking of the "happy band." The revision was rejected, however, in the transcription of MS. D.

That keeps in health the insatiable mind
                                    yes
That ~~we~~ she shall have for knowledge & for love
Abundance & that, feeling as we do
How goodly how exceeding fair how pure
                                   you
From all reproach is ~~the~~ ætherial frame
                                            unde
And this deep vale its earthly counterpart
By which and under which we are enclosd
To breathe in peace, we shall not ever find
         what
If sound if we ought to be ourselves & 860
If rightly we observe & justly weigh
The Inmates not unworthy of their home
The Dwellers of the Dwelling.

                              And if this
were not, we have enough within ourselves
Enough to fill the present day with joy
And overspread the future years with hope,
Our beautiful and quiet home, enriched
Already with ~~the~~ stranger whom we love
Deeply, a Stranger of our Father's house
A never-resting Pilgrim of the Sea,
Who finds at at last an hour to his content
Beneath our roof. And others whom
                             we love

37

848   That keeps in health the insatiable mind
     Yes
849   ~~That~~ we shall have for knowledge & for love
850   Abundance & that, feeling as we do
                        re⎱
851   How goodly how exceeding fair how pu[?]⎰
              yon   *vault*
852   From all reproach is ~~the~~ ætherial frame
                          ⎰o
853   And this deep vale its earthly c⎱[?]unterpart
854   By which and under which we are enclos'd
                 we⎱
855   To breathe in peace the⎰ shall moreover find
          what
856   (If sound &ᴧwe ought to be ourselves
                         860
857   If rightly we observe & justly weigh)
858   The Inmates not unworthy of their home
859   The Dwellers of the Dwelling.
                      And if this
860   Were not, we have enough within ourselves
861   Enough to fill the present day with joy
862   And overspread the future years with hope,
863   Our beautiful and quiet home, enrich'd
864   Already with a Stranger whom we love
865   Deeply, a Stranger of our Father's house
866   A never-resting Pilgrim of the Sea,
867   Who finds at at last an hour to his content
868   Beneath our roof: and others whom
                      we love

864–865   Blots have smeared from the facing verso.

Will seek us also, Sisters of our hearts
And one, like them, a Brother of our hearts
Philosopher and Poet in whose sight
These Mountains will rejoice with open joy
Such is our wealth; O Vale of Peace we are
And must be, with Gods will, a happy band

Yet it is no enjoy that we being
~~But this without enjoy for~~ that
for that end only
~~Neither exist we~~ something must be done
I must not walk in unreprov'd delight
These narrow bounds I think of nothing more
No duty that looks further & no care
Each Being has his office, lowly some
And common yet all worthy if fulfill'd
With zeal, acknowledgement that with
the gift
Keeps pace a harvest answering to the seed.
If ill, deliverd ~~ambition~~ &c
I would stand clear; yet to me I feel
that an unusual brightness is vouch safed
that must not yet be but must not pass away
Why does this inward lustre fondly seek
And gladly blend with outward fellowship

38

869   Will seek us also, Sisters of our hearts
870   And one, like them, a Brother of our hearts
871   Philosopher and Poet in whose sight
             ⌠M
872   These ⎨mountains will rejoice with open joy
873   Such is our wealth : O Vale of Peace we
                                  are
874   And must be, with Gods will, a happy band
                            878

              s⌉
        Yet it⌡ *it no enjoy that we exist*
875   ~~But tis not to enjoy for this alone~~
        For ⌠*that end only :*
            ⎨*man*
876   ~~That we~~ₐexist, ~~no~~, something must be done
877   I must not walk in unreprov'd delight
878   These narrow bounds & think of no thing more
879   No duty that looks further & no care
880   Each Being has his office, lowly some
881   And common yet all worthy if fulfill'd
882   With zeal, acknowledgement that with
                          the gift
883   Keeps pace a harverst answering to the seed.
                ⌠ m   ⌠pride
884   Of ill, advis'd a⎨[?]bition & of ⎨[?]
                un
885   I would stand clear yetₐto me I feel
886   That an internal brightness is voutchsafed
887   That must not die that must not pass away
888   Why does this inward lustre fondly seek
889   And gladly blend with outward fellowship

---

874   The summary line count, 878, is the only one in MS. B between the 470 on 21^r and the 1047 at the end of the poem.

876   The word "man" (replacing "we") and the caret are in pencil.

885   The revision and the caret are in pencil.

886–887   There are illegible pencil markings above the initial letters of both lines. The crowding of the lines suggests that WW may have left a gap here in his transcription with space for one line, then later squeezed two lines into it, but a new error in his count at l. 902 makes it impossible to tell how he numbered these lines.

Between 39^v and 41^r there is a stub from leaf 40. Scraps of letters visible on it indicate that the recto carried eighteen lines, beginning with l. 890; the initial letters seem to match only down through l. 896, as on 41^r. It seems probable that WW was unsatisfied with the lines on the missing leaf, destroyed it immediately after transcription, and composed a new passage for 41.^v. There is evidence of writing on the verso of the stub, but no letters survive intact.

Why shine they round me thus whom thus...
Why do they teach me whom I thus...
Strange question yet it answers...
that humble Roof embower'd among...
That calm fire side it is not seen in them
Bless'd as they are to...to reside...
that satisfies & ends in perfect rest
Possessions have I that are solely mine
Something within which yet is hardly...
Between the nearest to me & most dear
Something which power & effort may impart
I would impart it, I would spread it wide
Immortal in the world which is to come
Forgive me if I told any...claim...
...not wholly perish even in this
life dear, & be forgotten in the dust
...the most...of my days
Making a silent...in death
Love knowledge, all my manifold delight
All buried with me without monument

39

             whom I [?fondly]

890   Why shine they round me thus whom thus
                               I love
            my [?soul]

891   Why do they teach me whom I thus revere

892   Strange question yet it answers not itself

893   That humble Roof embower'd among the [?tre]
                                  trees

894   That calm-fire side it is not even in them

895   Bless'd as they are to furnish a reply
                      Which
       {[?Which]

896   {That satisfies & ends in perfect rest
                     that are

897   Possessions have I ~~wholly~~, solely, mine

898   Something within which yet is shar'd by
                            none

899   Not even the nearest to me & most dear

900   Something which power & effort may impart
                   ;}

901   I would impart it} I would spread it wide

902   Immortal in the world which is to come
                           900
      Forgive me if I add another claim
      {&

903   {I would not wholly perish even in this,

904   Lie down, & be forgotten in the dust
      I ~~with~~ modest

905   I & the most partners of my days

906   Making a silent company in death
      Love knowledge, all my manifold delights
      All buried with me without monument

890–891   These lines are revised on 39ᵛ by WW and recopied there by MW; the second draft
is incorporated in MS. D.

     Why do they shine around me whom I
                           love
   Why do they teach me whom my soul
                       reveres

   Why do they shine around me
                whom I love
   Why do the teach me whom I thus
               revere

896   The revisions are in pencil.
901   The added punctuation is in pencil.
902   WW introduces a new error in his line count, probably because he misread his 878 at
l. 874 as 872 or 873. It is not possible to tell whether he counted one or two lines for ll. 886–887
or whether his 900 refers to l. 902 or l. 902/903.

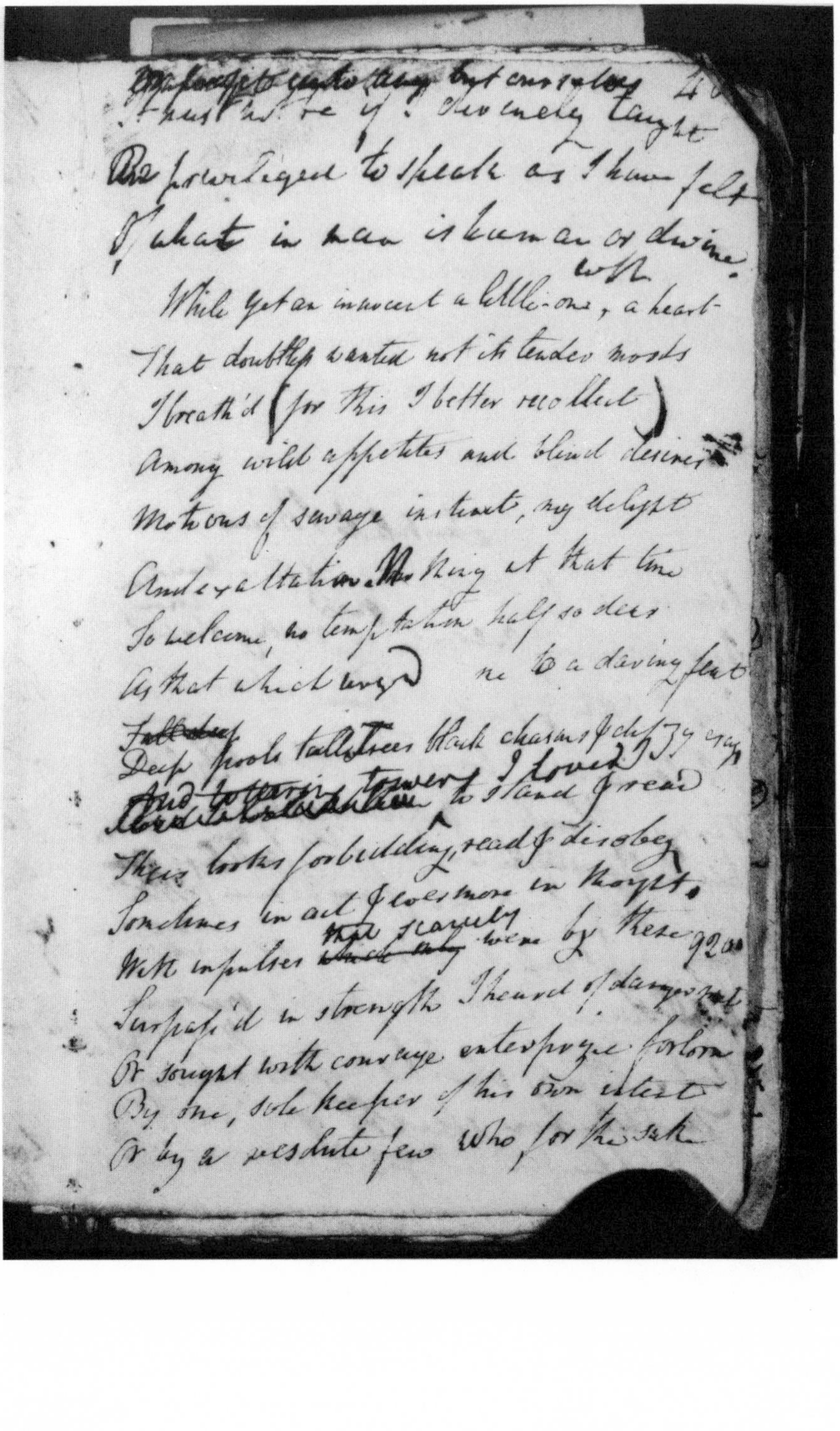

[Handwritten manuscript draft]

~~...~~ ... ... but ourselves

... ... if heavenly taught

Are privileged to speak as I have felt

Of what in man is human or divine.

While yet an innocent a little-one, a heart

That doubtless wanted not its tender moods

I breath'd (for this I better recollect)

Among wild appetites and blind desires

Motions of savage instinct, my delight

And my attention. Nothing at that time

So welcome, no temptation half so dear

As that which urged ... me to a daring feat

~~Fall deep~~

Deep pools tall trees black chasms & dizzy crags

~~And tottering towers~~ I loved

~~... ...~~ to stand & read

Their looks forbidding, read & disobey

Sometimes in act & evermore in thought.

With impulses that scarcely were by these

Surpass'd in strength I heard of danger met

Or sought with courage enterprize forlorn

By one, sole keeper of his own intent

Or by a resolute few who, for the sake

40

~~Or profit unto any~~ but ourselves
907 It must not be if I divinely taught
⌠Be
908 ⌡Am privileged to speak as I have felt
     t ⎱
909 Of wha[?]⎰ in man is human or divine.
                          with

910   While yet an innocent little-one—⎰a heart
911 That doubtless wanted not its tender moods
         ⌠(   )⎱
912 I breath'd ⎰for this I better recollect⌡
913 Among wild appetites and blind desires
914 Motions of savage instinct, my delight
             .⎱ ⌠N
915 And exaltation⌡ ⎰no thing at that time
916 So welcome, no temptation half so dear
              urged
917 As that which   me to a daring feat
~~Full deep~~
               ⌠T
918 Deep pools tall ⎰trees black chasms & dizzy crags
          And tottering towers I loved
919 ~~I lovd to look in them~~ᴧto stand & read
920 Their looks forbidding, read & disobey
                       .⎱
921 Sometimes in act & evermore in thought⌡
           that scarcely
922 With impulses ~~which only~~ were by these
                       920
923 Surpass'd in strength I heard of danger met
924 Or sought with courage enterprize forlorn
925 By one, sole keeper of his own intent
926 Or by a resolute few who for the sake

t ⎫
a turbulen [?]⎰ Stream
Nursed in the darkness of some moutain
cave
mid
And trained & exercise in rocky straits
who
And headlong steeps, ~~where~~ after it has
run
⎧ntly
Its desperate course triumpha⎨tly , she leads
quiet
Through ~~flowers~~ meadows & embowering ~~groves~~
Well [?pleased] to listen to its [?groves ?]
faintest voice
Yet apprehend not, though henceforth to
me
[?There ?do ?confide] a [?feature] or a [?word]
~~Ple~~ Pleased with the faintest murmur
that it makes
And soothd, while listening to its humblest
song
That which in stealth &
Yet apprehend not &c

These lines expand ll. 936–942, on the facing recto; they are not incorporated in MS. D.

of glory proudest multitudes in as was. 4)
Yea to this day I swell with like desire
your
Himself—at this moment read a tale
Of two brave vessels matchit in deadly fyre
And fighting to the death but I am pleas'd
More than a wise Man ought to be, I wish
I burn I struggle & in soul am there
But me hath Nature tamed & bade me seek
Than other agitations or be calm
Hath dealt with me as with a turbulent
Some Nursling of the Mountains which she
Through great meadows after hey I leads
my strength & had its triumph & its joy
His desperate course of tumult & of glee
That which in stealth by Nature was
Hath Reason sanctioned: her performd
Hath said be mild & love all gentle things
Thy glory, & thy happiness be there.
Yet fear though thou confide in me,
Of aspirations that have been of foes
To wrestle with & victory to complete
Bounds to be leapt & darkness to

41

927	Of glory fronted multitudes in arms.
928	Yea to this day I swell with like desire
	Nor I
929	~~I cannot~~ at this moment read a tale
930	Of two brave Vessels match'd in deadly fight
931	And fighting to the death but I am pleas'd
932	More than a wise Man ought to be, I wish
933	I burn I struggle & in soul am there
934	But me hath Nature tamed & bade me
	seek

   or⎰

935	Far⎰ other agitations or be calm
936	Hath dealt with me as with a turbulent
	stream

          ⎰om

937	Some Nurseling of the Mountains wh⎰ich she
	leads

       he

938	Through quiet meadows after ~~it~~ has learn'd
	⎰His his
939	⎰Its strength & had its triumph & ~~its~~ joy
	⎰His
940	⎰Its desperate course of tumult & of glee

       ⎰N

941	That which in stealth by ⎰nature was
	perform'd

        ⎰b

942	Hath Reason sanction'd: her deli⎰verate
	Voice

       940

943	Hath said be mild & love all gentle things
944	Thy glory, & thy happiness be there.
	Nor a
945	~~Yet~~ fear (though thou confide in me, ~~no want~~
	want
	that
946	Of aspirations ~~which~~ have been—of foes
947	To wrestle with & victory to complete
	be ⎰ored
948	Bounds to be leapt & darkness to ᴧexpl⎰ore

---

945 The apparent comma after "me" may be intended as a parenthesis. For earlier draft versions of ll. 936–958 see 47^v, 48^r, and 48^v.

The
frowardness of soul which looks that
upon a less incitement than the cause
of liberty endanger'd, and farewell
that other hope which long was mine to feel

Delightful passions traversing

And therewi[e]er the notion be received
Whether a breath of outward circumstance
Or from the soul an impulse to herself

[?I ?Of]
The
                         { d
All forwardness of soul ~~that~~ which look{ s that
                                way
Upon a less incitement than the cause
Of liberty endanger'd, and farewell
                          the hope
That other hope ~~which~~ long ~~was~~ mine ₐto fill

                I often feel
Delightful passions traversing

              {oe
And whences {e'e 'er the motion be receiv'd
Whether from [?breath] of outward circumstance
Or from the soul an impulse to herself

  The asterisk at l. 953 indicates that the four lines drafted at the top of this page were to be inserted at that point in the text. The lines are incorporated in MS. D. The two center lines revise ll. 960–961. Those at the foot became MS. D ll. 763–765.

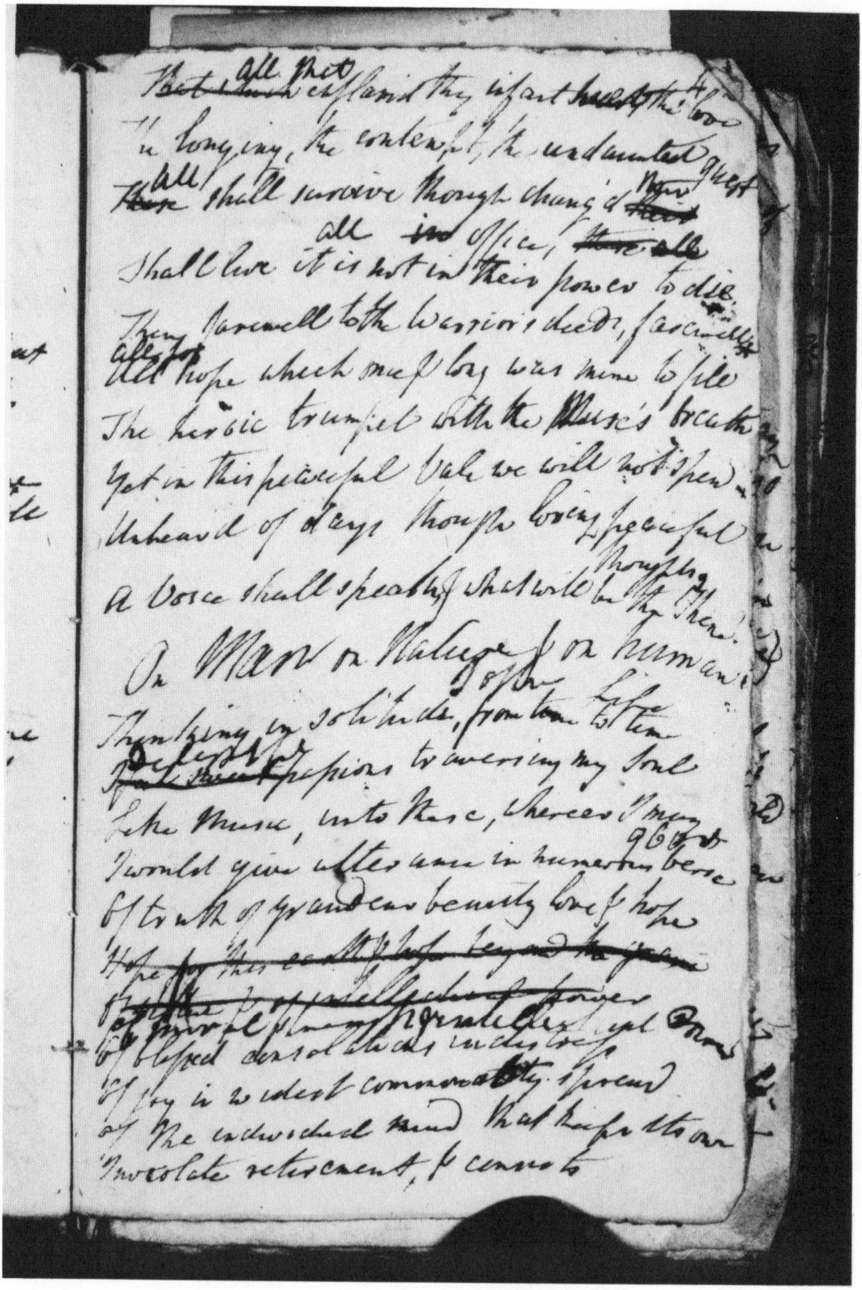
All that explain'd thy infant heart the love
The longing, the contempt, the undaunted quest
All shall survive though chang'd their office all
Shall live it is not in their power to die.
Then farewell to the Warrior's deeds, farewell
All hope which once & long was mine to fill
The heroic trumpet with the Muse's breath
Yet in this peaceful Vale we will not spend
Unheard of days though loving peaceful thoughts
A Voice shall speak & what will be the Theme?
On Man on Nature & on human Life
Thinking in solitude, from time to time
Deep felt passions traversing my Soul
Like Music, unto these, where'er I may
I would give utterance in numerous verse
Of truth of grandeur beauty love & hope
~~Hope for this earth & hope beyond the grave~~
~~Of virtue & of intellectual power~~
Of moral strength & intellect yet more
Of blessed consolations in distress
Of joy in widest commonalty spread
Of the individual mind that keeps its own
Inviolate retirement, & consents

42

949	All that ⌠heart That which enflam'd thy infant ⌡[?soul ?] the love
950	The longing, the contempt, the undaunted quest
951	All their These shall survive though chang'd their office, these
952	all in all Shall live it is not in their power to die.
953	Then farewell to the Warrior's deeds, farewell *
954	All for All hope which once & long was mine to fill
955	⌠M The heroic trumpet with the ⌡muse's breath
956	Yet in this peaceful Vale we will not spend
957	Unheard of days though loving peaceful thoughts,
958	A Voice shall speak, & what will be the Theme?
959	On Man on Nature & on human Life
960	I often Thinking in solitude, from time to time
961	Delightful I feel sweet passions traversing my Soul

962	Like Music, unto these, whereer I may
	                              [?]
	                    960

963	I would give utterance in numerous verse
964	Of truth of grandeur beauty love & hope
965	Hope for this earth & hope beyond the grave
966	Of virtue & of intellectual power
967	Of moral strength & intellectual Power Of blessed consolations in distress
968	nalty⌡ Of joy in widest commo[?]⌠spread
969	Of the individual mind that keeps it own
970	Inviolate retirement, & consists

---

953   The asterisk and the interlining at 954–955 signal the insertion of the draft at the top of 43^v.

With being limitless the one great life

[...] fit audience let me find though few

To [...] of, more [...]

[...] find the fed thus may'd

Holiest of Men Urania I shall need   the Bard

Thy guidance or a greater Muse if such

Descend to earth or dwell in highest heaven

For I must tread on shadowy ground must sink

Deep, & aloft ascending breathe in worlds

To which the Heaven of heavens is but a veil

[...] strength all terror single or in bands

That ever was put forth in personal forms

Jehovah with his thunder & the quire

Of shouting angels & the empyreal [...]

I pass them unalarm'd [...]

[...]

Nor aught of   vacancy scoop'd out

By [...] of dreams can breed such fear & awe

As fall upon us often when we look

Into our minds into the mind of Man

My haunt & the main region of my song

Beauty [...]   a living Presence of the earth

Surpassing the most fair ideal Forms

Which

The craft of delicate spirits hath compos'd

From earths materials waits upon my steps

Pitches her tents before me where I move

43

971 With being limitless the one great Life
972 I sing fit audience let me find though few
    ask'd
  pray'd, more gaining than was [–?–]
So
973 *Fit audience find tho' few thus pray'd*
     the Bard
974 *Holiest of Men Urania I shall need*
     ſe
975 *Thy guidance or a gr⎰aater Muse if such*
976 *Descend to earth or dwell in highest heaven*
977 *For I must tread on shadowy ground must sink*
978 *Deep, & aloft ascending breathe in worlds*
979 *To which the Heaven of heavens is but a veil*
980 *All strength all terror single or in bands*
981 *That ever was put forth in personal forms*
982 *Jehovah with his thunder & the quire*
       980
983 *Of shouting angels & the empyreal thron*
    .⎱ Not chaos not
984 *I pass them unalarmed* ⎰ *the darkest Pit*
  The darkest Pit of the profoundest hell
985 *Of the profoundest Hell chaos night*
  The lowes darkest Pit of lowest Erebus
986 *Nor aught of*   *vacancy scoop'd out*
987 *By help of dreams can breed such fear & awe*
988 *As fall upon us often when we look*
989 *Into our minds into the mind of Man*
990 *My haunt & the main region of my song.*
   a living Presence of the Earth
991 *Beauty whose living home is the green earth*
992 *Surpassing the most fair ideal Forms*
   Which
993 *The craft of delicate spirits hath compos'd*
994 *From earth's materials waits upon my steps*
     ſre
995 *Pitches her tents before me whe⎰n I move*

At the top of 44ᵛ, facing, WW wrote "Br" apparently to begin a line.

972/973 This line was first left incomplete; its completion probably accompanied the deletion in l. 973. WW may have intended the new line to read "So pray'd, more gaining than was ask'd the Bard." The transcription continues in MW's hand from l. 973 through l. 995.

983 The line runs off the edge of the page, and the terminal "e" or "es" is missing.

An hourly Neighbour, Paradise, & groves
Elysian fortunate islands, fields like those of
In the ocean wherefore should they be
A History or but a dream when men
Are wedded to this outward frame of things
In love find there the growth of common day
I say before the blessed hour arriving 1800
Would I say in solitude the special verse
Of this great consummation would proclaim
Speaking of nothing more then what we are
How exquisitely the individual Mind
And the progressive powers perhaps no less
Of the whole species to the external world
Is fitted: & how exquisitely too
Theme this but little heard of among men
The external world is fitted to the mind
And the creation (by no lower name new
Can it be call'd) which they with blended might
Accomplish: this is my great argument.
Such foregoing if I oft
must turn elsewhere & travel near the
tribes

44

996 An hourly Neighbour. Paradise, & groves
997 Elysian fortunate ~~islands~~, fields like those of
                                                     old
                     main
998 In the ~~deep~~ₐocean wherefore should they be
999 A History or but a dream when minds
1000 Once wedded to this outward frame of things
1001 In love find these the growth of common day
                ,⎫
1002 I ⎬ long before the bless'd hour arrives
                                            1000
             ~~chant~~
1003 Would sing in solitude the spousal verse
1004 Of this great consummation, would proclaim
1005 (Speaking of nothing more than what we are)
1006 How exquisitely the individual Mind
1007 And the progressive powers perhaps no less
1008 Of the whol species to the external world
1009 Is fitted; & how exquisitely too
1010   Theme this but little heard of among men
1011 The external world is fitted to the
                                        mind
1012 And the creation (by no lower name
1013 Can it be call'd) which they with
                              ⎧ight
                 blended m ⎨[?]
                              ⎩

1014 Accomplish: this is my great argument
1015 Such   foregoing if I oft
1016 Must turn elswhere & travel near the
                                        tribes

---

997 This line was originally long; the deletion corrects the meter.
1005 The parentheses may be a later addition.
1010 WW may have omitted this line inadvertently in copying from an earlier draft, for it is
included in his line count.

45

And fellowships of men & see ill sights
Of passions ravenous from each other; rage
Must hear humanity in fields & groves
Pipe solitary anguish or must hang
Brooding above the fierce confederate
Storm
Of sorrow barricadoed evermore 1020
Within the walls of cities may these sounds
Have their authentic comment that even these
Hearing, I be not heartless or forlorn.
here
Come thou prophetic Spirit, Soul of Man
thou human soul of the wide earth that
hast
Thy metropolitan Temple in the hearts
Of mighty Poets unto me vouchsafe
Thy picture teach me to discern & part
Inherent things from casual what is fixed
From fleeting that my verse may live & be
Even as a light hung up in heaven to cheer
Mankind in times to come. And if this
with this
I blend more lowly matter with the thing
Contemplated describe the mind & man
Contemplating & who & what he was
The transitory Being that beheld

45

1017	And fellowships of men & see ill sights
1018	Of passions ravenous from each other's rage
1019	Must hear humanity in fields & groves
1020	Pipe solitary anguish or must hang
1021	Brooding above the fierce confederate

storm

1022	Of Sorrow barricadoed evermore

1020

⌠C

1023	Within the walls of ⌡cities may these sounds
1024	Have their authentic comment that even

these

1025	Hearing, I be not heartless or forlorn.
1026	Come thou prophetic Spirit, Soul of Man
1027	Thou human Soul of the wide earth that

h⌉ t⌉
th⌡as⌡

1028	Thy metropolitan Temple *in the hearts*

⌠[Of]

1029	⌡[*?Oh*] *mighty Poets unto me vouchsafe*

succour   ⌠discern ⌠ &

1030	*Thy ~~guidance~~ teach me to* ⌡[?] ⌡[?] *part*
1031	*Inherent things from casual, what is fixed*
1032	*From fleeting that my verse may live & be*
1033	*Even as a light hung up in heaven to chear*

with

1034	*Mankind in times to come. And if ∧this*
1035	*I blend more lowly matter with the thing*
1036	*Contemplated describe the mind & man*
1037	*Contemplating & who & what he was*
1038	*The transitory Being that beheld*

1017–1020   Blots have smeared from the facing recto.
1028   The transcription continues in MW's hand through l. 1048.

C. VI. 1149

This vision when & where & how he lived
With all his ~~little~~ realities of life
Be not this labour useless: if such theme
~~may sort with highest things~~ then may I ~~speak~~
~~With suitable thoughts~~

Thou who art breath & being way & guide
And power & understanding may my life
Express the image of a better time
More wise desires & simple manners nurse
My heart in genuine freedom all pure thoughts
Be with me & uphold me to the end

1047

That my ~~verse~~ may live
Both in its ~~simple~~ tenderness
Replenished by the emulation of the world
That the body of my verse
By the revolution of the world unknown
And by its passionate understanding may
Even ~~on~~ a happy language ever to heaven be
then

46

1039   *This vision when & where & how he lived*
        ~~His joys & sorrows & his hopes & fears~~
1040   *With all his ~~little~~ realties of life*
                        small
1041   *Be not this labour useless : if such theme*
                        1040
        May sort with highest things, then gratious ~~god~~
                                    Power
1042   *~~With highest things may~~   ~~then Great~~ God*
                            way & guide
1043   *Thou who art breath & being*
                    soul
1044   *And ~~power~~ & understanding may my life*
1045   *Express the image of a better time*
1046   *More wise desires & simple manners nurse*
1047   *My heart in genuine freedom all pure thoughts*
1048   *Be with me & uphold me to the end*
                                1047

                verse a [?frame ?endued]
            that my ~~verse may live & shine~~
        With undecaying properties may [?live]
        Un⎱
        By ⎰touched by the mutation of the words
                        that the body of my verse
            Untouch
                            ⎰l
        By the mutation of the wo ⎱ rd untouchd
        And by its ferments undisturbed—may shine
                as a
        Even ~~like~~ a light hung up in heaven to
                                    chear

The draft at the foot of the page is a revision for ll. 1032–1033.

Hath dealt with me as with a turbulent stream
Some nursling of the mountains whom she leads
Through quiet medows after it has learned
Its strength & had its triumph & its joy
Its desperate course of tumult & of glee

Antecedent to the text of MS. B, these lines were incorporated in B at ll. 936–940.

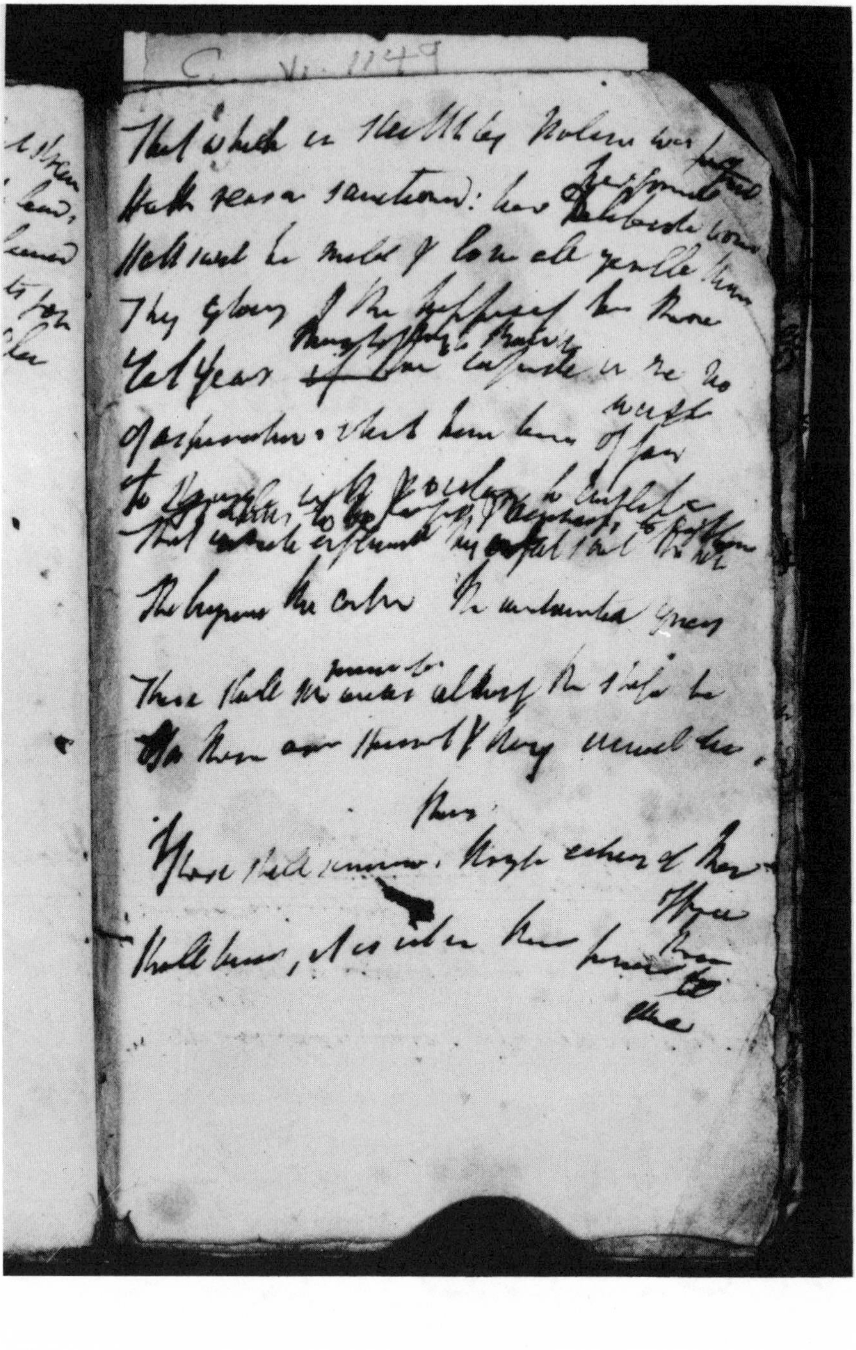

                                                     ⌠c
That whi⟨ h in stealth by Nature was [?performd]
                                                     ⟨c
                         performd
                                      ⌠D
Hath reason sanctioned: her ⟨deliberate voice
Hath said be mild & love all gentle things
Thy glory & the happiness be there
              [?though ?thou ?though]
Yet fear if thou confide in me no
                        [?want]
Of aspirations whih have been of [?foes]
To struggle with & victory to complete
    Bounds to be leapt & darkness to explore
        which⟩   ⌠[?infat]
That [?]⟨ enflamed thy ⟨[?] soul the [?hope]
The longing the [?contem] the undaunted quest
                [?survive ?]
These shall survive [?although] the strife be
⌠[?For]
⟨[?Of] there [?are ?spirit] & they [?immortal]
T   [?these]
    These shall survive, though [?changd] their
                                            office
                                            these
Shall live, it is not in their power to
                              die

This draft toward ll. 941–952 continues from that on 47ᵛ.

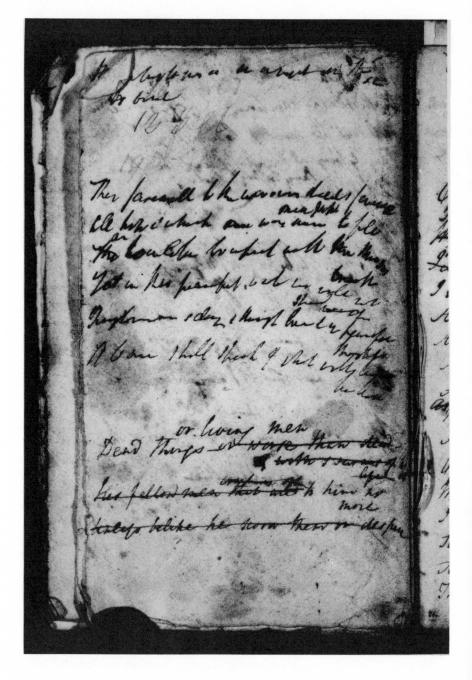

Turbulent as is a mountain Stream
Or bird

Then farewell to the warriors deeds farewell
                    [?once] & [?oft]
All hope which once was mine to fill
    An
~~The~~ [?hourless] trumpet with the Muses
                            breath
Yet in this peaceful vale we will not
                        spend
                            [?wanting]
Inglorious days though [?loving] peaceful
                            thoughts
A Voice shall speak & what will be
                            the theme

            or living men
    Dead things— or ~~worse than dead~~
                    ~~with swarms of~~ [?li]
                        ~~life~~
            ~~creatures oft~~
    ~~His fellow men that are~~ to him no
                        more
    ~~Unless belike he scorn them or despise~~

The two lines at the top of the page are a jotting related to l. 936. In the gap are some faintly penciled numbers whose significance is not clear. The lines in the middle of the page follow on from the drafts on 47ᵛ and 48ʳ, toward 953–958. The lines at the foot of the page revise ll. 812–814. Another draft of these lines, probably later, occurs on 45ᵛ (see note for ll. 812–814); neither revision was incorporated in MS. D.

MS. D: Transcriptions with
Selected Photographic Reproductions

MS. D (DC MS. 76) is a notebook originally without covers and of home manufacture, probably Mary Wordsworth's work. Twenty-eight leaves survive intact: 1–3, 5–15, and 17–30; two have been removed, leaving only stubs: 4 and 16. All leaves are sewn together in conjugate pairs except 3 and 25, which were added singly. Leaves 5–15 alone survive from the original version of MS. D, dating from 1812–1814; the paper of these leaves and of stub 4 is white laid, trimmed quarto, watermarked with the monogram P and countermarked 1810; that of leaves 1–3, stub 16, and leaves 17–30 is blue-tinted laid, trimmed quarto, watermarked with a coat of arms surmounted by a crown and countermarked HARRIS 1828.

Before the renumbering of the Dove Cottage manuscripts in 1972, MS. D was loosely sewn into the account book which contains MS. RV of *The Prelude* (DC MS. 21); some late revisions of *Home at Grasmere* appear penciled in Wordsworth's hand on blank leaves in the account book. Except for these revisions and a few others in MS. D itself, text and revisions throughout are in Mary's hand. (Concerning the late revisions, however, especially the punctuation, there is some uncertainty as to whether the hand is Wordsworth's or Mary's.) Using the revised MS. B as her copy in 1812–1814, Mary wrote out the original text of MS. D on white laid paper countermarked 1810. Whether she completed this transcript is problematic; the ink on 14^r of the 1810 paper appears to change between l. 258 and l. 259, and the new ink seems to proceed continuously in the manuscript after the transition to 1828 paper. This evidence alone cannot be taken as proof, but would suggest that Mary abandoned her 1812–1814 copying at l. 258 and resumed it at l. 259 nearly twenty years later. To incorporate extensive revisions by Wordsworth in 1831–1832 she removed the initial leaves (probably three) and—if any indeed existed—the concluding leaves of the earlier version, retaining only leaves 5–15. The conclusion to the poem she wrote out on the blue-tinted leaves countermarked 1828, which she sewed to the central section of the original version of MS. D. She seems to have copied nineteen lines per page on the 1810 paper; revisions in MS. B indicate that the lost opening on 1810 paper contained about fifty-seven lines, which would have filled three leaves: two leaves now entirely destroyed and one formerly attached to the stub of leaf 4. Before leaf 5 Mary sewed the present leaves 1 and 2 and copied a revised opening section on 1^r, 1^v, and 2^r. The lines at the foot of 2^r were then revised anew, deleted, and recopied on 2^v; the text on 2^v was further revised along with that on the top of 5^r. Subsequently leaf 3 was sewn onto 2^v, and the lines on 2^v were crossed out. On 3^r Mary transcribed ll. 46–59; at the foot of this page she very likely continued her text as it stood on the crossed-out 2^v. With the decision to incorporate ll. 60–70—which she had left out in her transcription, or which she had perhaps not yet reached—she cut off l. 71 at the foot of the page and perhaps several lines following, up to l. 76. She then continued her transcription on 3^v.

Probably at about the same time as the addition of leaf 3 Mary sewed in a piece of 1828 paper as leaf 25 and stuck on a piece of the same paper carrying ll. 384–402 to 19^r. (Leaves 3 and 25 are unnumbered; the other pages, therefore, were numbered before they were added. The numbering probably dates from 1831–1832.) After this Mary attached a piece of unmarked, gilt-edged, white wove paper to 21^v, containing ll. 474–483; and a piece of similar though not identical paper to 26^r, containing ll. 609–622. These revisions may carry Wordsworth's work on the poem beyond 1832, but it is impossible to date them with precision. In transcription, the stuck-on sheets are designated by the letter "a" following the leaf number, and the order of composition is preserved: thus the original lines on 19^r precede the lines on the stuck-over sheet, 19^{r}a.

Because this manuscript is primarily late fair copy, photographs have not been provided for the entire transcription, but only for the opening pages which bear complex revisions.

The Recluse — Part first   1
    Book first
    Home at Grasmere

Once to the verge of yon steep barrier came
A roving School-boy & what the Adventurer's age
Hath now escaped his memory— but the hour,
One of a golden summer's holiday,
He well remembers, though the year be gone.
Alone & devious from afar he came;
And, with a sudden influx overpowered
At sight of this seclusion, he forgot
His haste, for hasty had his footsteps been
As boyish his pursuits; & sighing said,
"What happy fortune were it here to live!
And, if a thought of dying, if a thought
Of mortal separation, could intrude,

I

The <u>Recluse</u>—<u>Part first</u>
<u>Book first</u>

Home at Grasmere

1   *Once to the verge of yon steep barrier came*

2   *A roving School-boy { —what the Adventurer's age*

3   *Hath now escaped his memory—but the hour,*

4   *One of a golden summers holiday,*

5   *He well remembers, though the year be gone.*

6   *Alone & devious from afar he came*

7   *And, with a sudden influx overpowered*

8   *At sight of this seclusion, he forgot*

9   *His haste, for hasty had his footsteps been*

10   *As boyish his pursuits; &, sighing said,* *10*

11   *"What happy fortune were it here to live?*

12   *And, if a thought of dying, if a thought*

13   *Of mortal separation, could intrude,*

Titles   The titles, like the text, are in the hand of MW, as are the page numbers in corners.
10   Line numbers throughout are in pencil, probably in MW's hand.

2

With paradise ~~before~~ him, here to die!
No Prophet was he, had not even a hope,
Scarcely a wish, but one bright pleasing thought,
A fancy in the heart of what might be
The lot of others, never could be his.

    The Station whence he look'd was soft
                                       + green,
Not giddy yet aerial, with a depth
Of Vale below, a height of hills above.
For rest of body, perfect was the spot +
All that luxurious nature could desire,
But stirring to the Spirit; who could gaze
And not feel motions there? He thought of
                                   clouds
That sail on winds; of breezes that delight
To play on water, or in endless chase
Pursue each other thro' the yeelding plain
Of grass or corn, over + through + through,
In billow after billow, evermore
                                  36

2

14   *With paradise before him, here to die!*
15   *No Prophet was he, had not even a hope,*

16   *Scarcely a wish, but one bright pleasing thought,*
17   *A fancy in the heart of what might be*

18   *The lot of others* ⎰ *never could be his* ⎱
19   *The Station whence he look'd was soft*
                               & green,

               ye⎱
20 20 *Not giddy bu*⎰*t aerial, with a depth*
21   *Of Vale below, a height of hills above.*
                            ⎰*s* ⎰*ot,*
22   *For rest of body, perfect was the* ⎱*p*⎱*lace*
23   *All that luxurious nature could desire,*
24   *But stirring to the Spirit; who could gaze*
25   *And not feel motions there? He thought of*
                                clouds

                     ⎰*of* ⎰*B*
26   *That sail on winds;* ⎱*with* ⎱*breezes that delight*
27   *To play on water, or in endless chase*
28   *Pursue each other thro' the yielding plain*

                    ⎰ *v*
29   *Of grass or corn, o*⎱*[?]er & through & through,*
           i⎱
30   *In be*⎰*llow after billow, evermore*   *30*

---

14 The apparent deletion line in "before" has soaked through from the blot on the recto.

16 In this manuscript it is not always possible to tell whether punctuation is original or added later; hence some discriminations are conjectural. Here the comma at the end of the line is lost in the gutter, and another one has clearly been added.

3

Disporting,
~~He sported~~, ~~Like~~ companion ~~ship, his fancy~~
         Nor unmindful ~~was~~ the Boy
Of sunbeams, shadows, butterflies & birds;
Of fluttering
~~Or~~ ~~aery~~ Sylphs, & softly-gliding Fays
Genii, & winged Angels that are Lords
Without restraint, of all which they behold.
The illusion strengthening as he gazed, he felt
That such unfettered liberty was his,
Such power & joy; but only for this end,
To flit from field to rock, from rock to field,
From shore to island, & from isle to shore,
                ground
From open ~~place~~ to covert, from a bed ~~to~~
Of meadow-flowers into a tuft of wood;
From high to low, from low to high, yet still
Within the bound of this huge Concave; here
thus
~~Should~~ be his Home, this Valley be his World.
~~Rejoice that bright day, Rejoice that blest day~~
~~Rejoice, that hour, joyless was the place to him~~
~~for I who live to register the bounty~~
To me, ~~for I thence hand now pens the tale~~
                                              thence forth
~~his that once young & happy Being, the place~~

3

Disporting.

31   ~~He sported~~ ⎰L⎱ ~~like Companions~~⎰hip⎱⎰his⎱⎰ancy⎱
     ⎰?often⎱⎰?he ?f⎱⎰ound⎱
     Nor unmindful was the Boy

32   ⎰Of⎱
     ⎰In sunbeams, shadows, butterflies & birds;⎱
     Of fluttering

33   ~~In aery~~ₐSylphs ⎱ & softly-gliding Fays

34   Genii ⎱ & winged Angels that are Lords

35   Without restraint ⎱ of all which they behold ⎱
36   The illusion strengthening as he gazed, he felt

37   That such unfettered liberty was his ⎱

38   Such power & joy; but only for this end ⎱

39   To flit from field to rock, from rock to field ⎱

40   From shore to island, & from isle to shore ⎱ 40
     ground
41   From open ~~place~~ to covert, from a bed

42   Of meadow-flowers into a tuft of wood ⎱
43   From high to low, from low to high, yet still
     ⎰C   c⎱
44   Within the bound of this huge ⎰conv⎱ave; here
     Must
45   ~~Should~~ be his Home, this Valley be his World ⎱
     ~~Since that bright day~~   ~~Since that blest day~~
     ⎰th⎱
     ~~From that time for~~⎰ward was~~ₐthe Place to him
                                          ~~to me:~~
     ~~For I who live to register the Truth~~
     ⎰F⎱
     ~~To me,~~ ⎰for I whose hand now pens the Tale~~
                                    ~~stood forth~~
     ⎰t   ⎰place
     ~~Was that same young & happy Being,~~ ⎰he⎰me

14

~~contained to exist~~

~~How~~ ~~that time forth~~ ~~the features of the place~~

~~As~~ Beautiful in ~~my~~ thought as ~~they~~ had been

When present to ~~the~~ bodily ~~sense~~ eye; of haunt

Of ~~my~~ pure affections shedding upon joy

A brighter joy & through such damp & gloom

oftimes, splenetic
Of the gay mind as ~~the gay~~ youth ~~dedectiones~~

Mistakes for
~~calmeries~~ sorrow darting beams of light

That no self-cherished sadness could withstand

And now 'tis mine perchance for life, dear Vale
Beloved Grasmere (let the wandering streams
Take up their cloud-ward / cloud-born ~~hills~~ ~~&c~~ their
The of thy lowly Dwellings is my home.
name)

— On Nature's invitation do I come

By Reason sanctioned. Can the choice mislead

That made the calmest, fairest spot of earth

dearest
With all its unappropriated ~~bliss~~

~~of not mine only for~~ ~~with me~~ ~~& wonders in~~
~~My own; entrenched at in you humble lot~~
~~and reconciled unto your dear circle~~
~~tended by the Orchard where with me~~
~~the younger brother of a long extinct~~
~~the only daughter of my parents died its.~~

My own; & not mine only, for with me
Entrenched — say rather peacefully embowered

4

continued to exist

From that time forth the feat\itres of the place
    ⎧tt
As ⎰B ⎱   ⎱   it
Were ⎩beautiful in∧thought ⎰ as they had been
           ⎰the   eye,
When present to ⎩my bodily sense, a haunt
   pure
Of my affections shedding upon joy
A brighter joy & through such damp & gloom
          ofttimes splenetic
Of the gay mind as to my∧Youth did stand
  Mistakes for
Instead of sorrow darting beams of light
That no self-cherished sadness could withstand.
And now tis mine perchance for life, dear Vale
  Beloved Grasmere (let the wandering Streams
            ⎰H
  Take up—the cloud capt ⎩hills repeat the
One of thy lowly Dwellings is my Home!
             name),
———On Nature's invitation do I come
By reason sanctioned. Can the choice mislead
That made the calmest, fairest spot of earth
          good
With all its unappropriated bliss
  & not mine only for with me   humble Cot
            within yon low abode humble cot
My own; entrenched us in yon humble Cot
[——?——?——?——]——yon low abode
  Say rather
Under its rocky Orchard, where with me
  A younger Orphan of a home extinct
The only daughter of my Parents dwells.
  My own; & not mine only, for with me
  Entrenched—say rather peacefully embowered

humble Cot.

Since that ~~blessed~~ day, ^forth the Place to him_ ~~to me~~
(For I who live to register the truth)
Was that same young & happy Being) ~~Cloud forth~~ ^became
As beautiful ~~to~~ thought, as it had been,
When present, to the bodily ~~eyes~~ sense; a haunt   5
Of pure affections, shedding upon joy
A brighter joy; & through such damp & gloom
Of the gay mind, as ofttimes splenetic Youth
Mistakes for sorrow darting beams of light
That no self-cherished sadness ^could withstand:
And now 'tis mine, perchance for life, dear Vale
Beloved Grasmere (let the Wandering Streams
Take up, & the cloud-capt hills repeat, the name)
One of thy lowly Dwellings is my home.

46 *Since that* ~~*bless'd*~~ *day*_∧*the Place to him——to me*
    forth (above line)
47 *(For I who live to register the truth)*

48 *Was that same young & happy Being——*} ~~*stood forth*~~
    became / appeared [?&]

49 *As beautiful to thought* } *as it had been,*

50 *When present* } *to the bodily* ~~*eye*~~ *; a haunt 50*
    sense;

51 *Of pure affections* } *shedding upon joy*

52 *A brighter joy,* } *& through such damp & gloom*

53 *Of the gay mind, as ofttimes splenetic Youth*
54 *Mistakes for sorrow darting beams of light*

55 *That no self-cherished sadness*_∧*withstand :*
    could
56 *And now 'tis mine, perchance for life, dear Vale*
57 *Beloved Grasmere (let the Wandering streams*

58 *Take up* { —*the cloud-capt hills repeat* } *the name)*
    ,
59 *One of thy lowly Dwellings is my Home.*

---

48 "appeared [?&]" is written in pencil.
59 Below this line the page has been cut off. It is probable that MW began copying the lines at the foot of 2ᵛ and the top of 5ʳ here (later MS. D, ll. 71–79), cut off the page to delete them, and then used the verso to insert ll. 60–70.

And was the cost so great? & would it seem   60
An act of courage, & the thing itself,
A conquest? who must bear the blame? sage man
Thy prudence, thy experience — thy desires
Thy apprehensions — blush thou for them all.

Yes the realities of life so cold
So cowardly so ready to betray
So stinted in the measure of their grace
As we pronounce them doing them much wrong
Have been to me more bountiful than hope
Less timid than desire — but that is passed.   70

On Natures invitation do I come
By Reason sanctioned. Can the choice mislead
That made the calmest, fairest spot of earth
With all its unappropriated good,
My own; & not mine only, for with me
Entrenched — say rather peacefully embowered,
Under yon Orchard, in yon humble Cot,
A younger Orphan of a Home extinct,
The only Daughter of my Parents dwells,
Aye we. Entrenched we in this ....

60   *And was the cost so great? & could it seem* {6 / 50}

61   *An act of courage*} *& the thing itself*

62   *A conquest* {? / —who must bear the blame} {? ge / —say} {M / man}
63   *Thy prudence, thy experience—thy desires*
64   *Thy apprehensions—blush thou for them all.*
65   *Yes the realities of life so cold*
66   *So cowardly so ready to betray*
67   *So stinted in the measure of their grace*
68   *As we pronounce them doing them much wrong*

69   *Have been to me more b*{o / eauntiful than hope}

70   *Less* {tim / [?]id than desire—but that is passed.} 70
71   *On Natures invitation do I come*
72   *By Reason sanctioned. Can the choice mislead*
                                    fairest
                            fair}
73   *That made the calmest, pur*{est spot of earth*

74   *With all its unappropriated good*}

75   *My own; & not mine only,* —} *for with me*

76   *Entrenched* {, / —say rather peacefully embowered,*
77   *Under yon Orchard, in yon humble Cot,*
78   *A younger orphan of a Home extinct,*
79   *The only Daughter of my Parents, dwells.*

65–70   The reason for the bracketing of these lines is unclear. WW may have considered revising or deleting them. They were deleted in MS. B and were not included in the text of MS. D on 2ᵛ and 5ʳ.

Under yon Orchard, in yon humble Cot,
A younger Orphan of a home extinct,
~~The~~ only Daughter of my Parents dwells   5
~~the more Association do some~~

My Reason stoothurned. Can the choice misteut
~~That made the utmost~~ ~~fairest~~ ~~on earth~~
~~with all its unappropriated blefs~~
~~took the object of my daily fight~~
My own,
~~through every change of Season, my Abode~~
Yon Cottage ~~where with me, my Emma dwells~~

O Aye think on that my Heart and cease to stir,
Pause upon that and let the breathing frame
No longer breathe, but all be satisfied.
Oh if such silence be not thanks to God
For what hath been bestowed, then where, where then
Shall gratitude find rest? Mine eyes did ne'er
fix ~~fix~~ on a lovely object nor my mind
Take pleasure in the midst of happy thoughts,
But either She whom now I have, who now
Divides with me this loved Abode, was there,
Or not far off. Where'er my footsteps turned,
Her Voice was like a hidden Bird that sang
The thought of her was like a flash of light

5

~~Under yon Orchard, in yon humble Cot,~~
~~A younger Orphan of a home extinct,~~
~~The only Daughter of my~~ Parents dwells
~~—On Nature's invitation do I come~~
~~By Reason sanctioned. Can the choice mislead~~
       [?fairest] ~~fairest~~   ~~on earth~~
~~That made the calmest purest spot~~
  ~~With all its unappropriated bliss~~
~~On earth the object of my daily sight~~
  My own,
~~Through every change of season; my Abode~~
~~Yon Cottage where with me my Emma dwells~~

                           stir,⎱
80 *80*   *Aye think on that my Heart and cease to* [?beat]⎰

81   *Pause upon that and let the breathing frame*
82   *No longer breathe, but all be satisfied.*
83   *—Oh if such silence be not thanks to God*
84   *For what hath been bestowed, then where where then*
85   *Shall gratitude find rest? Mine eyes did ne'er*
              Fix
86   ~~*Rest*~~ *on a lovely object nor my mind*

87   *Take pleasure in the midst of happy thoughts* ⎰
88   *But either She whom now I have, who now*

89   *Divides with me this loved Abode, was there* ⎰
90 *90* *Or not far off. Where'er my footsteps turned,* 60
91   *Her Voice was like a hidden Bird that sang,*
92   *The thought of her was like a flash of light*

   Here begins the paper countermarked 1810. The lines at the top of the page antedate those at the foot of 3^v. In these lines, "[?fairest]" above "calmest" was written in pencil; this line was originally short, and "on earth" was added in pencil, then overwritten in ink. "With . . . bliss" and "My own," were similarly written in pencil and overwritten in ink.

   90   MW wrote 60 for 90 here, perhaps misreading 80 for 50 above, but the error is corrected in the left margin.

[6ʳ]

6

93	Or an <u>unseen</u> companionship ⌡ a breath
94	Or fragrance independent of the wind.
95	In all my goings ⌡ in the new and old
96	Of all my meditations ⌡ and in this
97	Favorite of all, in this the most of all ⌡
98	——What Being, therefore ⌡ since the birth of Man
99	Had ever more abundant cause to speak

100   *favours of the heavenly Muse*
Thanks, and if ~~music and the power of song~~ *100*

101   *verse*
Make him more thankful, then to call on ~~these~~

102   *in*   *song*
To aid him ⌡ and ~~with these~~ resound his joy ⌡

103 The boon is absolute, ⌡ surpassing grace
104 To me hath been vouchsafed; among the bowers
105 Of blisful Eden this was neither given

106 Nor could be given ⌡ possession of the good

107 Which had been sighed for ⌡ ancient thought

108   *fulfilled*
And dear Imaginations reallized ⌡| ~~fulfilled~~
109 Up to their highest measure, yea and more.

110   Embrace me then ye Hills ⌡ and close me in ⌡ *110*
111 Now in the clear and open day I feel

[7ʳ]

7

112 Your guardianship; I take it to my heart ⌡

113 'Tis like the solemn shelter of the night ⌡

114 But I would call thee beautiful, for mild ⌡

115   ⌠gay;
And soft ⌡ and ⌡fair and beautiful thou art

116   ⌠y fa⌡
Dear Valley ⌡ having in th⌡ine⌡ce a smile

---

93 The underlining below "unseen" appears to be a later addition.
  107–108 MW appears to have initially believed that "fulfilled" concluded l. 108. The line tying the word into l. 107 is in pencil.

117   Though peaceful⟩ full of gladness. Thou art pleased⟩

118   Pleased with thy crags⟩ and woody steeps⟩ thy Lake

119   Its one green Island and its winding shores⟩

120   The multitude of little rocky hills⟩ *120*
121   Thy Church and Cottages of mountain stone—

122   Clustered like stars some few⟩ but single most⟩

123   And lurking dimly in their shy retreats⟩
124   Or glancing at each other chearful looks

125   Like separated stars with clouds between⟩

126   What want we? have we not perpetual streams⟩

127   Warm woods⟩ and s⟨[?]nny hills⟩ and fresh green
                                                    fields⟩

128   And mountains not less green⟩ and flocks & herds⟩

129   And thickets full of songsters⟩ and the voice
130   Of lordly birds an unexpected sound *130*

[8ʳ]

                                             8

131   Heard now and then from morn to latest eve⟩
132   Admonishing the man who walks below
133   Of solitude & silence in the sky.

134   These have we⟩ and a thousand ⟨n ⟨o
                                     ⟨ro⟨cks of earth

135   Have also these⟩ but <u>no</u> where else is found⟩
136   No where (or is it fancy) <u>can</u> be found

137   The one sensation that is here; 'tis here⟩
138   Here as it found its way into my heart

139   In childhood, here as it abides by day⟩
140   By night, here only; or in chosen minds *140*

141   That take it with them hence⟩ where'er they go.⟩

142   —'Tis⟩ but I cannot name it⟩ 'tis the sense

143   Of majesty, and beauty⟩ and repose⟩

144   *A blended holiness of earth and sky*

[?Scene]

145   *Something that makes this individu⟨a⟩il Spot*

146   *This small Abiding-place of many Men*

147   *A termination and a last retreat*

148   *A Centre, come from wheresoe'er you will*

149   *A Whole without dependence or defect*

[9ʳ]   9

150   *Made for itself and happy in itself* 150
151   *Perfect Contentment Unity entire.*

152   *Bleak season was it turbulent and bleak*

came

When Emma journeyed with me from afar
To this appointed Covert we advanced

153   *When hitherward we journeyed side by side*
154   *Through burst of sunshine and through flying*

⟨h   e⟩rs ;
s ⟨nows⟩

showers

ac
155   *P⟨[?aic]ed the long Vales how long they were⟩ and yet*

was left
156   *How fast we left that length of way∧behind*
157   *Wensley's rich Vale & Sedbergh's naked heights.*

Each vale far winding and each naked height

158   *The frosty wind as if to make amends*

steps
159   *For its keen breath was aiding to our course*

on   S
160   *And drove us forward like two ⟨ships at sea⟩* 160
161   *Or like two Birds companions in mid air*

162   *Parted and reunited by the blast*
Stern
163   *—Mean∧was the face of Nature, we rejoiced*

---

145   The revision is in pencil.
152/153   The word "came" is in pencil.
154   The word "showers" above "were" in l. 155 is in pencil.

                    countenance
164   *In that stern visage for our Souls thence drew*

165   *A feeling of their strength. The naked Trees* }

166   *The icy brooks* }   *as on we passed* } *appeared*
167   *To question us. "Whence come ye, to what end"?*

[10ʳ]

                                                10

168   *They seemed to say* } *"What would ye said the shower*
                    whither   *?* }
169   *Wild Wanderers*ᴧ*through my dark domain* }

170   *The sunbeam said* } *be happy." When this Vale 170*
                    { *e*
171   *We entered, bright and sol* { *mmn was the sky*
                              e } *,* }
172   *That faced us with a pasionate welcom* { *ing* }
                              { *D*
173   *And led us to our threshold.* { *daylight failed*

174   *Insensibly* } *and* ∂*round us gently fell*

175   *Composing darkness* } *with a quiet load*

176   *Of full contentment* } *in a little Shed*

177   *Disturbed* } *uneasy in itself as seemed* }

178   *And wondering at its new inhabitants* }

179   *It loves us now* } *this Vale so beautiful 180*
                    ! }   *,* }
180   *Begins to love us* } *by a sullen storm* }
                                        , }
18:        *Two months unwearied of severest storm* }
182   *It put the temper of our minds to proof*
                                        , }
183   *And found us faithful through the gloom* } *and*
                                        heard
184   *The Poet mutter his preclusive songs*
                    , }   { *voice*
185   *With chearful heart* } *an unknown* { *sound of joy*
                                        ; }
186   *Among the silence of the woods and hills* }
187   *Silent to any gladsomeness of sound*

---

169   The correction appears to have been made in transcription.
181   This line was inadvertently omitted in transcription; it is included in MS. B.

[11ʳ]

188   *With all their Shepherds*}

                      But the gates of Spring

189   *Are opened; churlish Winter hath given leave*

190   *That she should entertain for this one day*}

191   *Perhaps for many genial days to come*} *190*

192   *His guests*} *and make them jocund. They are pleased*}

193   *But most of all the Birds that haunt the flood*

194   *With the mild summons*} *inmates though they be*

                           keep festival

195   *Of Winter's household:* } *they* ~~*are jubilant*~~

196   *This day*} *who drooped*} *or seemed to droop*} *so long*}

197   *They shew their pleasure, and shall I do less*}

198   *Happier of happy though I be, like them*

199   *I cannot take possession of the sky*}

200   *Mount with a thoughtless impulse and wheel*

                                there

201   *One of a mighty multitude*} *whose way* *200*

    Is a perpetual

202   ~~*And motion is a*~~ *harmony and dance*

                 {*, how with a grace*

203   *Magnificent.*✗*Behold* { ~~*them how they shape*~~

    ~~*Orb after orb their course still round and round*~~

204   *Of ceasless motion, that might scarcely seem*

205   *Inferior to angelical, they prolong*

[11ᵛ]

213   ✗*Hundreds of curves & circlets, to & fro*

[214]   *Upwards &*

[12ʳ]

206   *Their curious pastime, shaping in mid air,*

               s}

207   *And sometime* } *with ambitious wing that soars*

---

191   MW may have reached 190 here by failing to count the inserted l. 181, or more probably by counting it as 180 by mistake.

203   The X marks the beginning of the lines WW published in 1823, later known as *Water-fowl*.

213   The X indicates that this line is an insertion at ll. 212/214 on 12ʳ.

207   The added "s" is in pencil.

208   ~~Above the area of the Lake their own~~
       High as the level of the mountain tops,
       ~~Adopted region girding it about meanwhile~~

209   A circuit ampler than the lake beneath ⌡
       ~~In wanton repetition yet therewith~~
210   Their own domain;—but ever, while intent
       ~~With that large circle evermore renewed~~

                                     ⌠2
211   On tracing & retracing that large round, ⌡130
       ~~Hundreds of curves and circlets high and low~~
212   Their jubilant activity evolves⤬ˌ
       ~~Backwards and forwards progress intricate~~

                         ⌠p
                         ⌊ₐrogress intricate
214   Upwards & downwards
       ~~As if one spirit dwelt in all and swayed~~
215   Yet unperplexed, as if one spirit swayed

216   Their indefatigable flight. 'Tis done ⌡

                or ⌉
217   Ten times and ⌡ more I fancied it had ceased ⌡
         But
218   ~~And~~ lo! the vanished company again
            ⌠,—   they approach—
219   Ascending ⌡   ~~list again~~ I hear their wings
                         ;⌉
220   Faint, faint at first ⌡ and then an eager sound
                                         !⌉
221   Passed in a moment—& as faint again ⌡ 140
                                               ;⌉
222   They tempt the sun to sport among their plumes ⌡
       ⌠T   smooth   ,⌉   or
223   ~~They~~ ⌊tempt theₐwater ⌡ ~~and~~ the gleaming ice ⌡
                                  ⌠,—
224   To shew them a fair image ⌡ 'tis themselves ⌡
                             ,⌉   ,⌉
225   Their own fair forms ⌡ upon the glimmering plain ⌡
                                             ,⌉
226   Painted more soft and fair as they descend ⌡
                     ⌠,   ,⌉
227   Almost to touch ⌊;—then up again aloft ⌡

[13ʳ]

                     13

                                       ,⌉
228   Up with a sally and a flash of speed ⌡
                                            !⌉
229   As if they scorned both resting-place and rest ⌡

208/209   The inclusion of "meanwhile" at the end of the line is an error in transcription; the word was deleted in pencil and ink before the whole line was deleted. In MS. B it is an alternative reading for "therewith."

211   MW errs doubly in her line count here; according to her earlier numbering, this line should be 210. She later corrected her 130 to 230, but her count remains inaccurate.

212   The X and caret signal the insertion of l. 213 on 11ᵛ.

221   MW wrote 140 for 240 here.

230   —This day {is / it a thanksgiving} 'tis a day

231   Of glad emotion and deep quietness} 250

232   Not upon me alone hath been bestowed}
233   Me rich in many onward-looking thoughts

234   The penetrating bliss; }{O / oh surely these have felt
                                                    it

235   Have felt it} not the happy {Q / quires of spring
236   Her own peculiar family of love

237   That sport among green leaves} so blithe {a / r / a train

238   But two are missing two} a lonely pair
                    [?oh] wherefore

239   Of milk-white Swans} why are they not seen
            Partaking
240   To share in this day's pleasure? From afar
        They came like Emma and myself to live
241   to sojourn to live They came, to sojourn here in

        Together here in peace and solitude} 260
            to sojourn here
242   Chusing this Valley, they who had the choice

243   Of the whole world} {W / we saw them day by day}

244   Through those two months of unrelenting storm}

245   Conspicuous {at / in the centre of the Lake

246   Their safe retreat} we knew them well} I guess

247   That the whole Valley knew them} but to us

248   They were more dear th{a / en may be well believed}
249   Not only for their beauty and their still
                            constant
250   And placid way of life and faithful love

251   Inseparable} not for these alone} 270

---

234   The line was corrected in transcription.

252   But that _their_ state so much resembled our's ⎱
253   They having also chosen this abode;

254   They strangers' ⎱ and we strangers ⎱ they a pair ⎱

255   And we a solitary pair like them ⎱

256   They should not have departed: ⎱ many days
     ~~Have I~~   Did I look forth
    Ha⎱   {th
257   I '⎱ ve ⋏looked for ⎰ them ⋏in vain ⎱ nor on the wing
    Could see
258   ~~Have seen~~ ⋏them, nor in that small open space
                         {odged,
259   Of blue unfrozen water, where they l⎰ived ~~so long~~
                         {ide
260   And lived so long in quiet, s⎰ilent by side ⎱
261   Shall we behold them, consecrated friends, _280_
262   Faithful Companions, yet another year
          {ing;
263   Surviv⎰iving they for us, & we for them,
          be   {broken
264   And neither pair [?~~being~~] ⎰[?divided]—nay perchance
265   It is too late already for such hope

[14ᵛ]

               generous
269   Recal my song the ~~ungenial~~ thought; forgive,
        {T
270   ~~Forgive~~ ⎰thrice favoured Region, the conjecture harsh
271   Of such inhospitable penalty _290_
272   Inflicted upon confidence so pure.
[273]   Ah,

[15ʳ]

                                 _15_

    Dalesmen
266   The ~~shepherd~~ may have aimed the deadly tube ⎱
    ~~And parted them incited by a prize~~
    ~~Which for the sake of her he loves at home~~
    And parted them
267   ~~He should have spared~~; or haply both are gone
268   One death, & that were mercy given to both.
    ^ ~~And could a Poet harbour such a thought,~~

---

252   The underlining below "their" appears to be a later addition.
269–272   The caret on 15ʳ at ll. 268/273 signals the insertion of these lines in the main text on 15ʳ. All revisions were made in pencil and subsequently overwritten in ink.
268/273   The caret indicates that the lines on 14ᵛ are to be inserted here.

Imagine such unworthy recompence
Of confidence so pure? more natural were it
  Ah if I wished to follow
273 *To follow without scruple*‸*where the sight*
   ⎰*my*
274 *Of all that is before* ⎰*his eyes, the voice*
  from?
275 *Which speaks*‸*a presiding Spirit here*
   me *I should whisper to myself*
276 *Would lead him — & not wronging what he sees*
  They who are
277 *Whisper "the dwellers in this holy place,*
278 *Must needs themselves be hallowed, they require*
279 *No benediction from the Stranger's lips,*
280 *For they are bles'd already ; none would give*
281 *The greeting "peace be with you" unto them 300*
282 *For* peace *they have, it cannot but be theirs,*
283 *And mercy, & forbearance—nay—not these*

[15ᵛ]

  16

  Their healing Offices Benevolence
  There is no call for these ; that office Love
284   *Their healing Offices a pure good-will*
   ⎰*recludes,*
285 *[?P*⎰*erforms,] & charity beyond the bounds*
286 *Of charity—an overflowing love,:*
287 *Not for the Creatures only, but for all*
  That
288 *Which is around them ; love for every thing*
289 *Which in this happy Region they behold!*
290   *Thus do we soothe ourselves, & when the*
        thought
291 *Is pass'd we blame it not for having come 310*
   ⎰*I*
292 *——What if* ⎰*we floated down a pleasant Stream*
   ⎰*m* ⎰*a d*⎱ *t*⎱
293 *And now a* ⎰*re landed,* ⎰*in* ⎰ *a*⎰*he motion gone*
  ⎰*I* ⎰*myself* *,*⎱
294 *Shall* ⎰*we reprove* ⎰*ourselves? Ah no,*⎰ *the stream*
   ⎰*never* ⎰*cease*
295 *Is flowing, & will* ⎰*ever* ⎰ *flow to flow,*
   ⎰*I*
296 *And* ⎰*we shall float upon that stream again.*
297 *By such forgetfulness the soul becomes,*
298 *Words cannot say, how beautiful : then hail,*
299 *Hail to the visible Presence, hail to thee*
300 *Delightful Valley, habitation fair!*

---

275 The "from" and the caret are in pencil.

301   *And to whatever else of outward form* *320*
302   *Can give us inward help can purify,*
303   *And elevate, & harmonize, & soothe,*

[17ʳ]

17

304   *And steal away, & for a while deceive*
305   *And lap in pleasing rest, & bear us on*
306   *Without desire in full complacency,*
307   *Contemplating perfection absolute*
308   *And entertained as in a placid sleep.*
309   *But not betrayed by tenderness of mind*
310   *That feared, or wholly overlook'd, the truth*
              ⊢ we
311   *Did ~~we~~ come hither, with romantic hope* *330*

312   *To find in midst of so much loveliness* '}
313   *Love, perfect love; of so much majesty*
314   *A like majestic frame of mind, in those*
315   *Who here abide, the persons like the place.*
316   *Not from such hope, or aught of such belief*
317   *Hath issued any portion of the joy*
318   *Which I have felt this day. An awful voice*
              hath   been
319   *'Tis true ~~I~~ in my walks ~~have~~ often heard*
320   *Sent from the mountains or the sheltered*
                                      fields

[17ᵛ]

18

321   *Shout after shout—reiterated whoop* *340*
322   *In manner of a bird that takes delight*
323   *In answering to itself; or like a hound*
324   *Single at chase among the lonely woods,*
325   *His yell repeating; yet it was in truth*
326   *A human voice = a Spirit of coming night;*
327   *How solemn when the sky is dark, & earth*
              r}
328   *Not dark, not{ yet enlightened, but by snow*
329   *Made visible, amid a noise of winds*
330   *And bleatings manifold of mountain sheep,*
331   *Which in that iteration recognize* *350*

The later paper, countermarked 1828, resumes on 17ʳ.

332   *Their summons, & are gathering round for food*⌐

              eer

333   *Devoured with keenness ~~when~~ to grove or bank*

            ⌐*y*   ⌐*with*

334   *Or rock⌐ey bield ⌐in patience they retire.*

335   *That very voice, which, in some timid mood*

336   *Of superstitious fancy, might have seemed*

337   *Awful as ever stray Demoniac uttered,*

338   *His steps to govern in the wilderness;*

339   *Or⌐ as the Norman Curfew's regular beat*

340   *To hearths when first they darkened at the knell:*

[18ʳ]

                       19

341   *That Shepheard's voice it may have reached mine ear* 360

342   *Debased & under profanation, made*

343   *The ready Organ of articulate sounds*

344   *From ribaldry impiety or wrath*

        Issuing,

345   *When shame hath ceased to check the brawls*

346   *Of some abused Festivity—so be it⌐*

347   *I came not dreaming of unruffled life*

348   *Untainted manners; born among the hills*

                       ⌐*a*

349   *Bred also there⌐ I wanted not a sc⌐hle*

350   *To regulate my hopes; pleased with the good*

351   *I shrink not from the evil with disgust⌐* 370

352   *Or with immoderate pain. I look for Man*

353   *The common Creature of the brotherhood*

354   *Differing but little from the Man elsewhere,*

355   *For selfishness & envy, & revenge*

356   *Ill neighbourhood, pity that this should be,*

357   *Flattery & double dealing, strife & wrong.*

358   *Yet is it something gained, it is in truth*

359   *A mighty gain, that Labour here preserves*

360   *His rosy face a Servant only here*

361   *Of the fire-side or of the open field* 380

362   *A Freeman therefore sound & unimpaired*

334–340   These lines and ll. 341–346 on 18ʳ are squeezed into a space left by MW in transcription. The lines expand MS. B ll. 420–427, which had been revised to six lines, and the space MW left would have accommodated six lines without cramping.

345   The word "Issuing" was omitted in transcription and added later.

[18ᵛ]

20

363	*That extreme penury is here unknown*
364	*And cold & hunger's abject wretchedness*
365	*Mortal to body & the heaven-born mind.*

363 *That extreme penury is here unknown*
364 *And cold & hunger's abject wretchedness*
365 *Mortal to body & the heaven-born mind.*

366 *That they who want*⎰'⎱ *are not too great a weight*
367 *For those who can relieve; here may the heart*
368 *Breathe in the air of fellow-suffering*

369 *Dreadless, as in a kind of fresher* ⎰*breeze*⎱ *[[?air]*
370 *Of her own native element, the hand*
371 *Be ready & unwearied without plea* 390

372 *From tasks too frequent*⎰,⎱ ⁰ʳ *& beyond its powers* +
373 *For languor or indifference or despair.*
374 *And as these lofty barriers break the force*
375 *Of winds,—this deep Vale, as it doth in part*
376 *Conceal us from the Storm, so here abides*
377 +*A Power & a protection for the mind*
378 *Dispensed indeed to other Solitudes*

[19ʳ]

21

379 *Favored by noble privilege like this*
380 *Where kindred independance of estate*
381 *Is prevalent, where he who tills the field* 400
382 *He, happy Man! is Master of the field*

383 *And treads the mountain* ⎰ˢ⎱ *which his Fathers*
                                                      trod

Not less than half way up yon ⎰ᵐ⎱ *[[?]ountain's side*
                        ~~little~~

*Behold a dusky spot, a*ᴧ*grove of firs*
        That
Which seems still smaller than it is, this grove
            ⎰younger   h⎱ ⎰r ⎰eldest
Just six weeks⎰older than th⎱e⎱ ⎰[[?young] child
            I learned, ⎰dwells
*As from the Dame*ᴧ*who* ⎱lives below,
                        [?]
Was planted by her Husband & herself
                from pelting
For a convenient shelter which ~~in~~ *storm*

372–378   The significance of the X at l. 372 and that at ll. 377/378 is unclear.

Their sheep might draw to, "& they knew it well"
S⎰ai⎱hed she, "for thither d⎰id⎱o we ⎰bear⎱draw them food
  ⎱S⎰
In time of heavy snow." She then began
In fond obedience to her private thoughts
To speak of her dead Husband: is there not
An art, a music, & a strain of words

[19ʳa]

384	*Not less than half way up yon mountain's*
	side
385	*Behold a dusky spot, a grove of Firs*
386	*That seems still smaller than it is; this grove*
387	*Is haunted—by what ghost?—a gentle spirit*
388	*Of memory faithful to the call of love*
389	*For, as reports the Dame, whose fire sends up*
390	*Yon curling smoke from the grey cot below,*
391	*The trees (her b⎰f⎱irst-born Child being then a babe) 410*
392	*Were planted by her husband & herself*
393	*That ranging [?]⎰o⎱er the high & houseless ground*
	~~There to become a Covert for the sheep~~
394	*Their sheep might neither want, (from perilous storm*
	~~From heat or tempest; & they knew it well~~
395	*Of winter, nor from summer's sultry heat)*
	~~Said she "for thither did we bear them food~~
396	*A friendly Covert, "& they knew it well"*
	~~In time of heavy snow." She then began~~
397	*Said she, "for thither as the trees grew up—*
	~~In fond obedience to her private thoughts~~
398	*We to the patient creatures carried food*
	~~To speak of her dead Husband; is there~~
	~~not~~
399	*In times of heavy snow" She then began*
	~~An art, a music, & a strain of words~~
400	*In fond obedience to her private thoughts*
401	*To speak of her dead Husband: is there not 420*
402	*An art, a music, & a strain of words*

[19ᵛ]

22

403	*That shall be life the acknowledged voice of life;*
404	*Shall speak of what is done among the fields*
405	*Done truly there, or felt, of solid good*
406	⎰[—?—] And⎱ *real evil, yet be sweet withal*
407	*More grateful, more harmonious than the breath*
408	*The idle breath of s⎰oft⎱weetest pipe attuned*
409	*To pastoral fancies? Is there such a stream*

384–402   This pasted-on sheet extends beyond the foot of 19ʳ and was folded in at l. 394/395.

410   *Pure & unsullied flowing from the heart*
411   *With motions of true dignity & grace.* *430*
            that stream
412   *Or must we seek* ~~*these things*~~ *where Man is not.*
413   *Methinks I could repeat in tuneful verse*
414   *Delicious as the gentlest breeze that sounds*
415   *Through that aerial fir-grove—could preserve*
416   *Some portion of its human history*
            the
417   *As gathered from* ~~*that*~~ *Matron's lips, & tell*
418   *Of tears that have been shed at sight of it*
419   *And moving dialogues between this Pair*

[20ʳ]

                                            23

420   *Who in their prime of wedlock, with joint hands*
                                    ⌠*w*
421   *Did plant the grove, now flourishing,* ⎰*While they* *440*
422   *No longer flourish, he entirely gone*
423   *She withering in her loneliness. Be this*
424   *A task above my skill: the silent mind*
            her
425   *Has* ~~*its*~~ *own treasures, & I think of these*
                            ⌠*ur*
426   *Love what I see, & hono*⎰*r humankind.*
427   *No, we are not alone, we do not stand*
            ⌠*S*
428   *My* ⎰*sister here misplaced & desolate*
429   *Loving what no one cares for but ourselves*
430   *We shall not scatter thro' the plains & rocks*
                            ⌠*'er*
431   *Of this fair Vale, & o*⎰*[?] its spacious heights* *450*
                        ⌠*liness*
432   *Unprofitable kind*⎰*ness, bestowed*
433   *On objects unaccustomed to the gifts*
434   *Of feeling which were cheerless & forlorn*
435   *But few weeks past, & would be so again*
            Were we not here
        ⌠*W* ⌠*re*   *;*⌉
436   ~~*If*~~ ⎰*we*⎰~~*were not*~~⌡ *we do not tend a lamp*

[20ᵛ]

        24

437   *Whose lustre we alone participate*
            shines
438   *Which* ~~*is*~~ *dependant upon us alone*

---

425   The revision was made in pencil and overwritten in ink.
438   The revision is in pencil.

439   *Mortal though bright, a dying, dying flame.*
440   *Look where we will, some human hand has been*
441   *Before us with its offering; not a tree 460*
442   *Sprinkles these little pastures but the same*
443   *Hath furnished matter for a thought; perchance*

444   *For some one serves⎰ as a familiar friend⎱*
445   *Joy spreads & sorrow spreads; & this whole Vale*
446   *Home of untutored Shepherds as it is*
447   *Swarms with sensation, as with gleams of sunshine*
448   *Shadows or breezes, scents or sounds. Nor deem*
449   *These feelings though subservient more than ours*
450   *To every day's demand for daily bread*
451   *And borrowing more their spirit, & their shape 470*
452   *From self-respecting interests; deem them not*
453   *Unworthy therefore, & unhallowed—no,*

[21ʳ]

25

454   *They lift the animal being, do themselves*
455   *By nature's kind & ever-present aid*
456   *Refine the selfishness from which they spring*
457   *Redeem by love the individual sense*
458   *Of anxiousness with which they are combined*
459   *And thus it is that fitly they become*
460   *Associates in the joy of purest minds*
461   *They blend therewith congenially : meanwhile 480*
462   *Calmly they breathe their own undying life*

463   *Thro' this their mountain sanctuary, ;—⎰ long*
464   *Oh long may it remain inviolate,*
465   *Diffusing health & sober chearfulness*
466   *And giving to the moments as they pass*

467   *Their little boons of animating though⎰t ⎱ts*
468   *That sweeten labour, make it seen & felt*
469   *To be no arbitrary weight imposed*
470   *But a glad function natural to Man.*

[21ᵛ]

26

[?] [?²]   [?fresh] [?well] [?being]
471   *Fair proof of this, Newcomer, tho' I be, 460*

---

463   The added punctuation is in pencil.
467   The deletion is in pencil.
471   The revisions above the line are in pencil. MW again errs in her line count here; according to her earlier reckoning, this should be l. 490. She apparently misread her 480 at l. 461 as 450.

                          gained
                      gained⎱
472   *Already have I   seen*⎰ *; the inward frame*
473   *Though slowly opening, opens every day*
                I   ~~with the spectacle amused~~
        ~~Nor am I less delighted with the shew~~
              a pensive With process not unlike to that which [? cheared]
              ~~Less than a~~ Stranger journeying at his leisure
        As [?] ~~unfolds itself; now here, now there,~~
              Through some Helvetian Vale
        ~~Than is the passing Traveller when his way~~
              Along ~~a glen~~ some
        ~~Lies thro' some unknown Vale, when low-hung~~
                                              mists
              Through some Helvetian Vale
        Break up & are beginning to recede
        How pleased he is to hear the murmuring streams
        The many voices whence he knows not, pleased

[21ᵛa]

474   *With process not unlike to that which chears*
475   *A pensive Stranger journeying at his leisure*
                                                ;⎱
476   *Through some Helvetian Dell* ⎰ *when low-hung mists*
                                         ;⎱
477   *Break up, & are beginning to recede* ⎰
                              where thin & thinner grows
478   *How pleased he is* ~~to greet the rocks & lawns~~
479   *The veil, or where it parts at once, to spy*
                                      ⎰ *k*
        ~~As they put off their Veil; the spi~~⎰[?n]~~y Pines~~
                                      ⎱*spiky*
480   *The dark pines thrusting forth their* ⎰[?] *heads ;*
        ~~As they thrust forth their heads; the scattered Huts~~
481   *To* ~~watched~~ *the spreading lawns with cattle grazed 470*
        ~~As they shine out; & see the Streams whose murmur~~
                                          ⎰*huts*
482   *Then to be greeted by the scattered* ⎰[?]ᴀ
                              ⎰ *ear*
        ~~Had soothed him⎰while they yet were hidden; pleased~~
483   *As they shine out; & see the streams whose*
                                          murmur

[21ᵛ]

484   *Had soothed his ear while* ~~while~~ *they were hidden: how pleased*
                                      ⎰*ay*
485   *To have about him which* w⎰*e e'er he goes*

In the unnumbered lines under the flap on 21ᵛ, the words in WW's hand are in pencil, and
"Through some Helvetian Vale" between "As . . . there" and "Than . . . way" was originally
written by WW in pencil, then overwritten by MW in ink.
    474–483   The back of the pasted-on flap bears part of an address; MW apparently used a
scrap of an old letter.
    482   The caret signals that l. 481/482 was to follow this line. As this backtracking was confusing,
MW deleted the caret and rewrote the line as l. 483.

486   *Something on every side concealed from view*
487   *In every quarter something visible*
488   *Half-seen or wholly, lost & found again*

489   *Alternate pro{gr{ss*
         spe}ct & impediment
         And yet a prospect

         Yet in the main a prospect spread & spreading
490   *And yet a growing prospect in the main.*

[22^r]

                    fresh objects
                    [?bright] [?landscapes]
                                        {albeit
491 *480* *Such pleasure now is mine, {& if I forced,*
492   *Herein less happy than the Traveller*
493   *To cast from time to time a painful look*
494   *Upon unwelcome things which unawares*
495   *Reveal themselves, not therefore is my heart*
496   *Depressed nor does it fear what is to come*
497   *But confident, enriched at every glance*

                                 l}
498   *The more I see the more det{ight my mind*
                        create   .}
499   *Receives, or by reflexion can extract}*
500   *Truth justifies herself, & as she dwells*
501 *490* *With Hope, who would not follow where she*
                                              leads
                            other
502   *Nor let me pass unheeded{loves*
503   *Where no fear is, & humbler sympathies.*
                    hath sprung up within
         {Already is inscribed upon
504   *{Of this sublime retirement my heart*
505   *A liking for the small grey horse that*
                                        bears
                     {M
506   *The paralytic{man, & for the brute*
                   sancti
507   *In scripture glorifyed—the patient brute*

[22^v]

508   *On which the Cripple, in the Quarry maim'd,*
509   *Rides to & fro: I know them & their ways.*

---

491   WW's revisions above the line are in pencil, and are probably an extension of the revisions across the top of 21^v, facing.

510   *The famous Sheep-dog, first in all the Vale*

                              {5

511   *Tho' yet to me a Stranger, will not be* {400

512   *A Stranger long; nor will the blind-man's*

                                   guide

513   *Meek & neglected thing, of no renown!*

514   *Soon will peep forth the primrose, ere it fades*

        ~~*Ere fades the primrose I shall have my Thrush*~~

515   *Friends shall I have at dawn, blackbird & thrush*

516   *To rouse me, & a hundred Warblers more;*

           Eagles to their ancient Hold

               {ose

517   *And if th*{*e ~~banished Eagle Pair return~~*

518   *Return, Helvellyns Eagles! with the Pair*

        ~~*Helvellyns Eagles, to their ancient Hold*~~

            {From

519   {*With my own door I shall be free to claim*

                       {*with those*

        ~~*Then duly shall I claim,*~~ {~~*acquaintance two birds*~~

                       sweep from cloud to cloud.

520   *Acquaintance as they* ~~*soar amid the heaven.*~~

521   *The Owl that gives the name to owlet-crag* 510

           whooping

522   *Have I heard* ~~*shouting*~~*, & he soon will be*

523   *A chosen one of my regards. See there.*

524   *The Heifer in yon little Croft belongs*

[23ʳ]

                                     29

525   *To one who holds it dear:*{ *with duteous care*

526   *She reared it*{ *& in speaking of her Charge*

527   *I heard her scatter some endearing words*

528   *Domestic, & in spirit* ~~*in spirit*~~ *motherly*

                   {Beast

529   *She being herself a Mother, happy* {Pair

530   *If the caresses of a human voice*

531   *Can make it so*{ *& care of human hands.* 520

532   *And Ye as happy under Nature's care*

533   *Strangers to me & all men, or at least*

534   *Strangers to all particular amity*

535   *All intercourse of knowledge or of love*

536   *That parts the individual from his kind.*

537   *Whether in large communities ye keep*

538   *From year to year not shunning man's abode*

539   *A settled residence or be from far*

---

530   MW errs inexplicably in her line count here. According to her earlier reckoning, this should be l. 519.

540   *Wild creatures, & of many homes, that come* 530
541   *The gift of winds, & whom the winds again*

[23ᵛ]

30

542   *Take from us at your pleasure; yet shall ye*

543   *Not want} for this, your own subordinate place*

544   *In my affections} {witness the delight*

545   *With which erewhile I saw that multi{tude*

546   *Wheel through the sky, & see them now at rest}*

547   *Yet not at rest} upon the glassy lake}*

548   *They cannot rest } they gambol like young whelps;*
549   *Active as lambs, & overcome with joy*
550   *They try all frolic motions; flutter, plunge* 540

551   *And beat the passive wa{ve with their wings.*
552   *Too distant are they for plain view, but lo!*

553   *Those little fountains} sparkling in the sun}*
       Betray   silver spout
554   *D̶e̶c̶l̶a̶r̶e̶ their occupation, rising up*
       rising up
555   *First one & then another silver spout*
556   *As one or other takes the fit of glee*
       somewhat
557   *Fountains & spouts, yet r̶a̶t̶h̶e̶r̶ in the guise*

[24ʳ]

31

{that
{that
558   *Of plaything fire-works, w̶h̶i̶c̶h̶ on festal nights*
559   *Sparkle about the feet of wanton boys.*

560   *{ How vast the compass of this theatre* 550
561   *Yet nothing to be seen but lovely pomp*

---

543   The added comma is in pencil.
544, 547–548, 553   The revisions were made in pencil, then overwritten in ink.
554–555   The tentative transposition of the final phrases is in pencil.
558   The revision was made in pencil, then overwritten in ink.
560   The dash was added in pencil.

562 *And silent majesty; the birch-tree woods*
563 *Are hung with thousand thousand diamond drops*
564 *Of melted hoar-frost, every tiny knot*
565 *In the bare twigs, each little budding-place*
566 *Cased with its several bead; what myriads there*
567 *Upon one tree while all the distant grove*
568 *That rises to the summit of the steep*
569 *Shows like a mountain built of silver light:*
570 *See yonder the same pageant, & again 560*
571 *Behold the universal imagery*
572 *Inverted, all its sun-bright features touched*
573 *As with the varnish, & the gloss of dreams;*
           also, of the whole
574 *Dreamlike the blending too ; along the shore*

[24ᵛ]

    32

            Landscape
575 *Harmonious Lands vision [?;] all along the shore*
576 *The landmark lost—the line invisible*
      boundary
577 *That parts the image from reality;*
578 *And the clear hills, as high as they ascend*
579 *Heavenward, so deep piercing the lake below.*
580 *Admonished of the days of love to come 570*
581 *The raven croaks, & fills the upper air*
582 *With a strange sound of genial harmony;*
583 *And in & all about that playful band,*
584 *Incapable altho' they be of rest*
585 *And in their fashion very rioters,*
        re
586 *The{ir is a stillness; & they seem to make*
                     .}
587 *Calm revelry in that their calm abode{*
     {L {ing {T   leaving, haste we on
   I {leav{e {them to their pleasure I pass on
     {T
588 *{Shem leaving to their joyous hours I pass,*
589 *Pass with a thought the life of the whole year*
                    woodland
590 *That is to come: the throngs of mountain flowers 580*
      will   s}
591 *And lillies that dance upon the wave }.*
       there is no
     Then boldly say that solitude is not

---

587 The period is in pencil.

[25^{v}]

596   With objects, wanting life—repelling love ,;⎱
597   He by the vast Metropolis immured,
598   Where pity shrinks from unremitting calls,
599   Where numbers overwhelm humanity,
600   And neighbourhood serves rather to divide
                          O What sighs more deep than
                                              his,⎱
601   Than to unite ⎰,. ⎰Y   yes, yes, there is a weight 590
       Of loneliness, he can report of it
602   Whose nobler will hath long been sacrificed. ,;⎱
       ⎰W must   ,⎱
603   He ⎰who inhabits⎱ under a black sky⎱
           world   to disgust
       city ⎰—   A city   ,⎱
604   A world ⎱ ∧ where, if indifference ⎰ do not yield
       Yield not, to scorn, or s
605   To scorn, disgust, or sorrow, living Men
606   Are ofttimes to their fellow-men no more
       Than to the Forest Hermit∧

[26^{r}]

                                              33

592   Say boldly then that solitude is not
593   Where these things are: he truly is alone
                          ⎰d
594   He of the multi⎱tude whose eyes are doomed
595   To hold a vacant commerce day by day∧
           objects, wanting life — repelling love
           With that which he can neither know nor love
           With objects
           Dead things, or living men to him no more
607   Than to the Forest Hermit are the leaves
608   That hang aloft in myriads, nay far less,

596–606   The carets at the beginning and conclusion of this passage, which is copied onto an unnumbered tipped-in-leaf, indicate that it is to be inserted on the facing page, 26^{r}, at ll. 595/607.
596   The added comma, in pencil, was overwritten by the semicolon.
601   After "unite" the dash seems to have been replaced first with a comma then with a period; "is" has been underlined in pencil, "o . . . his" written in pencil, and "What . . . his" subsequently overwritten in ink. MW seems to have written her line number in the wrong place; her count remains consistent.
601/602   The penciled bracket may have been intended to query the inclusion of this line prior to its deletion.
604   The word "world" above the caret and the revision at the end of the line are in pencil, overwritten in ink. The comma added after "indifference" is in pencil.
605   The first four words of revision were written in pencil, then overwritten in ink.
595–607   The carets here signal the insertion of ll. 596–606 on 25^{v}.
608–612   WW drafted these lines in pencil on an otherwise blank leaf of Prelude MS. RV, which was formerly attached to MS. D of Home at Grasmere. The draft reads:

                     Nay far less
               [?Him] [?his ?walk]
       For they protect from the sun & shower

                              { *defends*

Far less for aught that comforts or { [?]

                    { *F*   *noisy*

                    { [?]*rom* ~~*crowded*~~ *streets remote*

Or lulls or chears.∧   ~~*Society is here*~~ :

             Far from the living & dead wilderness

    Far

           Of the ~~*thronged*~~ *World, Society is here :*

The true community the ~~*noblest*~~ *Frame*

                    genuine

Of many into one incorporate

That must be looked for here ; paternal sway

One household, under God, for high & low,

One family & one mansion ; to themselves

Appropriate, & divided from the world

As if it were a cave, a multitude

Human & brute, possessors undisturbed

       For they protect him with their shade & [?lull]

               with whisper [?soft]

[26ʳa]

609	*For they protect his walk from sun & shower*
610 *600*	*Swell his devotions with their voice in storms*
611	*And whisper while the stars twinkle among them*
612	*His lullaby. From crowded streets remote*
613	*Far from the living & dead wilderness*
	{ *World*
614	*Of the thronged* { [?*City*], *Society is here*
	en
615	*A true Community—a* g[?*u*]*uine frame*
616	*Of many into one incorporate*
617	*That must be looked-for here ; paternal sway*
618	*One household, under God, for high & low,*
619	*One family & one mansion ; to themselves*
620 *610*	*Appropriate, & divided from the world*
621	*As if it were a cave, a multitude*
622	*Human & brute, possessors undisturbed*

[26ᵛ]

     34

623	*Of this Recess their legislative Hall*
624	*Their Temple & their glorious Dwelling-place*
	i
625	*D*[?]*smissing therefore all Arcadian dreams*
626	*All golden fancies of the golden Age*

     Swell his devotions with their voice in storms

     & whisper while the stars twinkle among them

                 [?Nay]

     His lullaby

MS. RV has now been separated from MS. D of *Home at Grasmere*; in the new numbering of the DC papers, it is DC MS. 21.

     In the unnumbered lines under the flap on 26ʳ, WW's revisions are in pencil; "here" in "Society is here" was underlined in pencil and the underlining reinforced in ink.

     621/622   There is a penciled X under "multitude"; its significance is unclear.

627   *The bright array of shadowy thoughts from times*
                                                  is
628   *That were before all time, or ~~are~~ to be*
              Ere time expire,
629   *~~When time is not~~ the pageantry that stirs*
                                              {*ed*
630   *And will be stirring when our eyes are fix*{*t 620*
631   *On lovely objects & we wish to part*

632   *With all remembrance of a jarring world*[?]}

633   *—Take we at once this one sufficient hope*}
634   *What need of more? that we shall neither droop*
635   *Nor pine for want of pleasure in the life*
              Scattered
636   *~~Which is~~ about us, nor thro' dearth of aught*

637   *That keeps in health the insatiable mind*}
638   *—That we shall have for knowledge & for love*

[27ʳ]

                                                  35

639   *Abundance, & that, feeling as we do*
640   *How goodly, how exceeding fair, how pure 630*
641   *From all reproach is yon etherial vault*
642   *And this deep Vale, its earthly counterpart*
643   *By which, & under which, we are enclosed*
644   *To breathe in peace; we shall moreover find*
645   *(If sound, & what we ought to be ourselves*
646   *If rightly we observe & justly weigh)*
647   *The Inmates not unworthy of their home*
648   *The Dwellers of their Dwelling.*
                              And if this
              otherwise
649   *Were ~~not~~, we have ~~enough~~ within ourselves*
650   *Enough to fill the present day with joy 640*
651   *And overspread the future years with hope,*
652   *Our beautiful & quiet home, enriched*
653   *Already with a Stranger whom we love*

[27ᵛ]

       36

654   *Deeply, a Stranger of our Father's House*
655   *A never-resting Pilgrim of the Sea,*
656   *Who finds at last an hour to his content*
657   *Beneath our roof. And others whom we love*

---

649   The revisions are in pencil.

658   *Will se⎰ᵉₖₖ us also, Sisters of our hearts*
659   *And One, like them, a Brother of our hearts*
660   *Philosopher & Poet in whose sight 650*
661   *These Mountains will rejoice with open joy*
662   *—Such is our wealth; O Vale of Peace we are*
663   *And must be, with God's will, a happy Band*

664   *Yet ⎰'ᵗₜₜ is not to enjoy, ⎰ᵗʰᵃᵗ ⎰ʷᵉ [? for ? that] exist*
665   *For that end only; something must be done*
666   *I must not walk in unreproved delight*
667   *These narrow bounds, & think of nothing more*

[28ʳ]

37

668   *No duty that looks further, & no care*
669   *Each Being has his office, lowly some*
670   *And common, yet all worthy if fulfilled 660*
671   *With zeal, acknowledgment that with the gift*
672   *Keeps pace, a harvest answering to the seed.*
673   *Of ill-advised Ambition, & of Pride*
            and or but ?
674   *I would stand clear, yet to me I feel*
675   *That an internal brightness is vouchsafed*
676   *That must not die, that must not pass away.*
677   *Why does this inward lustre fondly seek*
678   *And gladly blend with outward fellowship*
679   *Why do ⎰ᵀthey shine around me whom I love*
680   *Why do they teach me whom I thus revere? 670*
681   *Strange question yet it answers not itself.*
682   *That humble Roof embowered among the trees*

[28ᵛ]

38

683   *That calm fire-side it is not even in them*
684   *Blest as they are, to furnish a reply*
685   *That satisfies & ends in perfect rest.*
686   *Possessions have I that are solely mine*
687   *Something within which yet is shared by none*
688   *Not even the nearest to me & most dear.*
689   *Something which power & effort may impart*

---

669   The underlining is in pencil, reinforced in ink.
674   There is a penciled X in the right-hand margin, probably associated with the alternative reading, also in pencil.

690 *I would impart it, I would spread it wide* ⌉ *680*
691 *Immortal in the world which is to come.*
692 *Forgive me if I add another claim*
693 *And would not wholly perish even in this*
694 *Lie down & be forgotten in the dust*
695 *I & the modest Partners of my days*
696 *Making a silent company in death.*

697 *Love, Knowledge, a*⌈*ll*⌉*n my manifold delights*

[29ʳ]

39

698 *All buried with me without monument*
699 *Or profit unto any b*[*?*]⌈*ut*⌉ *ourselves.*
700 *It must not be, if I divinely taught 690*
701 *Be privileged to speak as I have felt*
702 *Of what in man is human or divine.*
703   *While yet an innocent Little-one, with a heart*
704 *That doubtless wanted not its tender moods*
705 *I breathed (for this I better recollect)*
706 *Among wild appetites & blind desires*
707 *Motions of savage instinct my delight*
708 *And exaltation. Nothing at that time*
709 *So welcome, no temptation half so dear*
710 *As that which urged me to a daring feat 700*
711 *Deep pools, tall trees, black chasms & dizzy crags*
712 *And tottering towers; I loved to stand & read*

[29ᵛ]

40

713 *Their looks forbidding, read & disobe*[*?*]⌈*y,*⌉
714 *Sometimes in act, & evermore in thought.*
715 *With impulses that scarcely were by these*
716 *Surpassed in strength, I heard of danger, met*
717 *Or sought with courage; enterprize forlorn*
718 *By one, sole keeper of his own intent,*
719 *Or by a resolute few who for the sake*
720 *Of glory fronted multitudes in arms. 710*
       hour I cannot read a Tale
721 *Yea to this ~~day I swell with like desire,~~*
    ~~can I~~
    ⌈*to*   ~~*even*~~
    Nor⌊*at this moment*⌊*read a tale*
722 *Of two brave Vessels matched in deadly fight*
723 *And fighting to the death, but I am pleased*
724 *More than a wise man ought to be; I wish,*

725   ~~I burn,~~ Fret, {& {I struggle, & in soul am there,}

[30ʳ]

41

726   But me hath Nature tamed & bade ~~me~~ to seek
727   For other agitations or be calm
728   Hath dealt with me as with a turbulent stream
729   Some nursling of the mountains which she leads
730   Through quiet meadows after he has learnt 720
731   His strength & had ~~its~~ his triumph & {his {its joy
732   His desperate course of tumult & of {[?]lee
733   That which in stealth by Nature was performed
734   Hath Reason sanctioned: her deliberate Voice
735   Hath said} , be mild & ~~love all~~ cleave to gentle things
736   Thy glory & thy happiness be there.
737   Nor fear, though thou confide in me, a want
738   Of ass} s pirations that _have_ been—of foes
739   To wrestle with, & victory to complete
740   Bounds to be ~~lept~~ leapt, [?] darkness to be explored} 730

[30ᵛ]

42

741   All that inflames} d thy infant heart, the love,
742   The longing, the contempt, the undaunted quest
743   All shall survive though changed their office, all
744   Shall live—it is not in their power to die.
745   Then farewell to the Warriors ~~shield~~ schemes, farewell
746   The forwardness of Soul which looks that way
747   Upon a less incitement than the cause

---

726   The revision is in pencil.
730   MW miswrote "quiet."
735   The revision was made in pencil, then overwritten in ink.
738   The underlining was initially done in pencil, then reinforced in ink.
740   The original correction of "lept" was made in pencil. The period at the end of the line was added in pencil.
741   The revision was made in pencil.
743   The "all" added to fill out a short line is in pencil.

748   *Of Liberty endangered, & farewell*
749   *That other hope, long mine, the hope to fill*
750   *The heroic trumpet with the Muse's breath!* 730

751   *Yet in this pl⎰aceful Vale we will not spend*
752   *Unheard-of days, though loving peaceful thoughts*
753   *A Voice shall speak, & what will be the Theme?*
754   *On Man, on Nature, & on Human Life*
            Musing
[755]   ~~Thinking~~ *in Solitude (see Preface to the Excursion*
                        to its conclusion)

---

750   Instead of 740 MW mistakenly entered another 730.

Appendixes

Appendix I

Publication and Reception of *Home at Grasmere*

The first edition of *Home at Grasmere*, a slender green volume of fifty-six pages published by Macmillan in 1888, bears no editor's name, nor any explanation for its appearance.[1] The Globe Edition, published simultaneously—a collected edition of Wordsworth's poems in one volume—carried an introduction by John Morley, but again no editor is named.[2] For lack of any better explanation Wordsworthians have assumed that William Knight was responsible for publication of the poem: he had access to Wordsworth's manuscripts at the time, and was also associated with the Macmillan firm. The assumption, however, is incorrect. Although Knight played a role in its publication, he was not the mysterious editor of *Home at Grasmere*. Indeed, he was profoundly distressed when the two volumes arrived on booksellers' shelves in 1888.

A professor at the University of St. Andrews, Knight was the most active Wordsworth scholar of the 1880's and 1890's. His energy and enthusiasm lay behind the founding of the Wordsworth Society in 1880, and he remained its secretary and staunchest supporter for the duration of its life. In 1882 the first volume of his heavily annotated eight-volume edition of Wordsworth's poetry appeared, published by Paterson of Edinburgh. He was the first editor to study the extensive collection of Wordsworth manuscripts—poems, family letters, and journals—most of which were then at the Stepping Stones, Ambleside. In his researches among these papers Knight discovered, or was shown, the manuscripts of *Home at Grasmere*. His knowledge of the poem dates from at least 1885, and perhaps earlier. In July of that year he read extracts

---

[1] Macmillan struck off two thousand copies of this edition in foolscap octavo; the volume sold for 2s. 6d. For a full bibliographical description, see T. J. Wise's *Bibliography of the Writings in Prose and Verse of William Wordsworth* (London, 1916), pp. 174–177. In March, 1891, fifty copies of a second edition, in medium octavo, were issued, bound in gray boards. The introduction and text reproduce those of 1888 exactly, although the title page is new; again no editor is cited, and no explanation for the publication offered.

[2] Correspondence in the Macmillan Archive indicates that Justice John Duke Coleridge was first asked to write this introduction (some of the Coleridge-Macmillan letters are extant in BL Add. MS. 55259; two are published in *Letters to Macmillan*, ed. Simon Nowell-Smith [London, 1967], pp. 204–206). When Coleridge declined, the task was passed to Morley, who was editor of Macmillan's English Men of Letters Series, and from 1883 to 1885 editor of *Macmillan's Magazine*. Morley's introduction was criticized as lacking in sensibility; see the unsigned "Mr. Morley on Wordsworth," *The Spectator*, LXI (22 December 1888), 1807–1808, and Edward Dowden's review in *The Academy*, XXXV (12 January 1889), 17–18.

from it at a meeting of the Wordsworth Society in London.[3] The wealth of his discoveries among the manuscripts persuaded Knight to undertake a life of the poet, and for it William Wordsworth, Jr., and Gordon Wordsworth gave him permission to publish *Home at Grasmere*, as he records in his Prefatory Note to Volume VIII of his edition. Initially conceived as a one-volume project, the life swelled to three; and this growth postponed the intended date of publication. Paterson's impending bankruptcy caused additional delays. Volume I, however, had been printed, though not yet published, when Macmillan produced its text on 14 December 1888. In Volume I, Knight seemed proud to announce his presentation of "the hitherto unpublished canto of *The Recluse*, entitled Home at Grasmere, given in full" (p. 208). But in his preface, dated 1889 and printed after the rest of the volume, Knight ruefully acknowledged that *Home at Grasmere* "was intended to appear first in this work," but had now "already [been] published by itself."[4]

One can patch together the story of how Knight's first edition of the poem became the third edition by examining the Macmillan Archive in the British Library.[5] Chance and accident, rather than any sleight-of-hand machinations, led to Macmillan's apparent coup in beating Knight into print. Knight's scholarly eight-volume edition (1882–1886) presents the poems in sequence of composition, so far as he could ascertain it. Macmillan's requested permission to follow this order and print his chronology in the firm's new Globe Edition, and for that privilege paid Knight twenty-five pounds.[6] On 31 March

---

[3] This reading is not mentioned in the minutes of the sixth annual meeting printed in *Transactions of the Wordsworth Society*, VII (n.p., n.d.), 7–33. But in his preface to *Wordsworthiana: A Selection of Papers Read to the Wordsworth Society* (London, 1889), Knight records that the sixth annual meeting was held at the residence of Lord Houghton in London on 8 July 1885, and that after the address by Lord Houghton, the society's president, "some portions of the unpublished canto of the Recluse were then read by the Secretary" (p. 12; the manuscript of these minutes, in the D.C. papers, additionally notes that the canto was "entitled 'Home in Grasmere'"). In the Preface Knight also includes a report of the first meeting of the society, originally printed in *The Spectator* for 16 October 1880. It notes: "Professor Knight stated that he had an unpublished MS. poem of Wordsworth's, and two poems of his sister Dorothy" (p. xvi). Whether the former refers to *Home at Grasmere* is uncertain. The Preface is dated December, 1888.

[4] *The Life of William Wordsworth* (3 vols.; Edinburgh, 1889), I, vi. A letter from Knight to Macmillan dated 31 March 1888 acknowledges that the life was "not yet through the press; although my part of the work was finished a year ago" (BL Add. MS. 55031). The Preface further reveals (p. v) that "although the first of the volumes has been printed for more than a year, the issue of the work has been postponed from causes too numerous to mention."

[5] In 1967 the BL purchased Macmillan's major correspondence from about 1855 to 1939. The archive has been catalogued and contains about 1250 volumes. For a brief history of the sale of these manuscripts see William E. Fredeman's "The Bibliographical Significance of a Publisher's Archive: The Macmillan Papers," *Studies in Bibliography*, XXIII (1970), 183–191. Simon Nowell-Smith's *Letters to Macmillan* prints a sampling of the correspondence. In my quotations from the Macmillan papers I have occasionally corrected punctuation where the original is confusing; otherwise I have quoted the letters without alteration.

[6] I am grateful to Simon Nowell-Smith for this information about payments. It derives from a manuscript note in an interleaved copy of the *Bibliographical Catalogue of Macmillan & Company's Publications, 1843–1889* (London, 1891), p. 546, which is in his possession.

1888 Knight wrote Macmillan, "I think you are wise in adopting this order of the Poems I have given, and I have pleasure in giving the permission to you to use it, on the conditions you annex. If you look to my more carefully supplemented 'order,' in a paper in *Transactions* of 'The Wordsworth Society,' you will find several important changes."[7] Five months later, in response to a query from the firm, Knight advised Macmillan not to print two extracts from *Home at Grasmere*—"On Nature's invitation . . . ." and "Bleak season was it . . ."—along with the full text of the poem.[8] He then proceeded to discuss the correct position of *Home at Grasmere*—briefly in that letter of 31 August, more extensively on 25 September:

> I think the canto of the Recluse "Home at Grasmere" should *follow* the Prelude, as a sort of appendix to it. We do not know the date of its composition; its chronological place could be half-way on, so to say, in the Prelude: but it would not do to disturb the order of the Books, in a work that has become a classic in English Literature, (as the *Prelude* has,) by the insertion of new matter between any of its fourteen Books. I therefore advise that you should publish it *as an appendix to the Prelude*.

Throughout this correspondence Knight's tone is cordial and helpful, and he appears to be genuinely concerned with getting the chronology right in this new edition. There is no reference to a separate issue of *Home at Grasmere*. But with the publication of the two Macmillan volumes, after Knight's own publisher had gone bankrupt, his disappointment was patent. On 20 December 1888 he wrote Macmillan:

> *The Recluse*—as you have issued it—is a beautiful Book: and I think I can rejoice that the world of English readers, or lovers of poetry, is the richer for its existence in this form, although I wish its publication had been subsequent to the issue of the Life of the Poet. Doubtless fewer copies of the latter will be sold, when people can say they have read this before, or can obtain it by itself. Gordon Wordsworth tells me he did not forsee the issue of it by itself, nor did he know that a considerable payment had been made eight years ago to his father, for the use, (and as Paterson understood the first use) of it in the Biography.
>
> But I am quite aware that the long delay in the issue of this work, (a delay over which I have had no control,) has enabled you to issue the Recluse now.
>
> I must be glad, although the interest of my Biography is diminished. [BL Add. MS. 55031]

Knight's largess of spirit is impressive, and touching too; he remarked before closing his letter: "The other matter of the omission of a note about the order of the Poems is a trifle of no consequence."

Macmillan's failure to acknowledge his assistance added but one more irony to a long string spun out of Knight's ill luck, not only with *Home at*

---

[7] BL Add. MS. 55031. *Transactions of the Wordsworth Society*, VII, 53–117, contains Knight's chronology; *The Recluse* is not listed.

[8] BL Add. MS. 55031. These two extracts were published by Christopher Wordsworth in *Memoirs*.

Grasmere, but also with other editorial projects. Early in 1888 D. C. Heath in Boston, Massachusetts, published a version of *The Prelude* edited by A. J. George. George sent Knight a copy, now preserved at the Wordsworth Library. The flyleaf bears the following annotation in Knight's hand:

> In all Literature there can scarcely ever have been anything more audacious, in its barefaced effrontry, than the thefts in the Notes to this volume. The author asked me if he might make use of some of my Notes. I granted him permission provided he made due acknowledgment. He has stolen 150, acknowledging only 8, and incorrectly quoting 7 of these 8.—It is the *ne plus ultra* of audacity.

Knight later reported that he allowed Edward Dowden to study his transcripts of previously unpublished Wordsworth materials "in a fit of generosity," and was appalled when Dowden "incorporate[d] *everything* which I had disinterred from oblivion" in the Aldine Edition of 1892–1893 (BL Add. MS. 55031). When Thomas Hutchinson asked for similar favors in 1895, as Knight was preparing his own Eversley Edition for Macmillan, he emphatically refused; later, however, he yielded. Predictably, Hutchinson's Oxford Edition beat Knight's own into print.

The final irony involved the text of *Home at Grasmere* itself. One observation in a letter implies that Knight had provided Macmillan with a transcript in advance of its official copy. "The *text* of this canto, 'Home at Grasmere,'" he cautioned, "should be carefully revised" (BL Add. MS. 55031). It was, before Macmillan published it, and it sharply pointed up the inaccuracies of Knight's own earlier text published in the following year.

Lacking a formal editor, Macmillan's Globe Edition of Wordsworth was a product of combined resources, and the firm's records spell out whose resources they were. Two hundred and fifty pounds were paid to Ward, Lock and Company for permission to reproduce its texts of the poems; twenty-five to Knight for his chronology; one-hundred to John Morley for his introduction; and, finally, one hundred pounds to Gordon Wordsworth for the copyright of *Home at Grasmere*.[9] The firm's traffickings with Ward, Lock and Company and with Morley need not concern us here, but those with Gordon Wordsworth affected the future history of *Home at Grasmere*. When Macmillan first approached Wordsworth's heirs for permission to publish *The Recluse*, securing it seemed impossible. On 11 April 1888 Gordon Wordsworth informed the publisher:

> The fragment of the 'Recluse,' which is all that exists of it, is, to the best of my recollection, not more than 650 lines long of which no small portion has been previously

---

[9] The record of these fees comes from Simon Nowell-Smith, as cited in note 6. Ward, Lock and Company absorbed Moxon's properties when Moxon went out of business, and the text used for the Globe Edition was that of Moxon's 1857 edition. J. R. Tutin contributed a signed bibliography to the Globe Edition, but I have found no correspondence or record of payments regarding it.

published, and arrangements have been made for it to be printed in toto in Professor Knight's forthcoming life of my Grandfather. We are much obliged to you for your kind proposal but under the circumstances it would hardly seem worth while for you to entertain the matter. [BL Add. MS. 55259]

A mere two days after this firm dismissal, however, Gordon Wordsworth wrote Macmillan in a much more encouraging tone, and at the end of six weeks the question to be resolved was no longer whether Macmillan might publish the poem but whether it should, as Gordon Wordsworth put it, "have the exclusive right (excepting Knight's memoir) of publication, or simply the right." Exclusive right was granted. In mid-August Gordon Wordsworth sent off a carefully edited transcript of the poem, volunteering himself and his cousin William Wordsworth, of Bombay, as proofreaders of the printed copy (BL Add. MS. 55259). There is no evidence of continuing concern about infringement upon the rights of Knight.

The granting of exclusive copyright to Macmillan kept *Home at Grasmere* from appearing in collections of Wordsworth's poems edited by Edward Dowden (the Aldine Edition, 1892–1893), by Thomas Hutchinson (the Oxford Edition, 1895), and by Nowell Charles Smith (3 vols., 1908). It did appear in A. J. George's Cambridge Edition, published in 1904 by the Houghton Mifflin Company in Boston; the firm has no record of any correspondence with Macmillan about publication rights, and may not have realized that the poem was not in the public domain. Macmillan's copyright was good for thirty years, then ran for another twenty (until 1938) as "restricted copyright." Before it expired E. E. Reynolds was able to include *Home at Grasmere* as an appendix to his edition of *The Excursion* for the Macmillan Golden Treasury Series.

The family's willingness to grant exclusive copyright in 1888 may have grown out of their solicitude to preserve the poet's reputation. Unlike the somewhat Gothic *Somersetshire Tragedy*, *Home at Grasmere* would not tarnish Wordsworth's image, but they believed that its incompleteness demanded some explanation or justification.[10] Only a few days before publication Gordon Wordsworth expressed the family's uneasiness to Macmillan:

I see you have 'the Recluse' nearly ready for publication. I do not know whether you are publishing it with any introduction or explanation of its circumstances—but as it seems to me that my Grand Father's probable reason for not publishing it during his life time was its exceedingly fragmentary condition, I am writing to ask whether you agree with me that it would be fairer to his reputation to advertise it as a fragment than as 'a poem'—and if so, if you could see your way to making the alteration? The lines if described as a poem seem to be open to charge of formlessness.

---

[10] For a discussion of *The Somersetshire Tragedy* and Gordon Wordsworth's destruction of its manuscript in 1931, see Jonathan Wordsworth, "A Wordsworth Tragedy," *Times Literary Supplement*, 21 July 1966, p. 642.

You will excuse my troubling you on this point. It is one to which I am rather sensitive as we have been accused in certain quarters (but I quite think unjustly) of disrespect to his wishes in giving the fragment to the world at all. To which I consider the best answer to be that he withheld it owing to its fragmentariness, hoping to complete it—a defence which is weakened by its being called a poem. But of course I base my request on the broader ground of justice to his reputation in poetical construction—if I may use the term. [BL Add. MS 55259]

Examination of a copy of the published *Recluse* quieted Gordon Wordsworth's fears, as he noted in a letter to Macmillan on 12 December 1888:

I have hardly had a moment to myself today or yesterday in which to thank you for your letter and for kindly sending me a copy of the 'Recluse.' It makes a most delightful little volume, and now I see it in print I am more than ever convinced we have not done wrong in publishing it. Your note of introduction is quite explicit and should obviate any disappointment caused by the advertisement. [BL Add. MS. 55259]

The brief introduction, following the title page of Macmillan's *Recluse*, reads: "In the prefatory advertisement to the First Edition of the Prelude, 1850, it is stated that that poem was designed to be introductory to the Recluse, and that the Recluse, if completed, would have consisted of three parts. The second part is the Excursion. The third part was only planned. The first book of the first part was left in manuscript by Wordsworth. It is now (1888) published for the first time *in extenso*."

Thus some ninety years after Wordsworth and Coleridge had formed their grandest scheme, the long-slumbering *Recluse* awakened. Only a few critics noticed the event, and then indifferently. Examining the reviews, one cannot avoid comparing them with the responses Wordsworth's earlier publications had aroused. Not always complimentary, they had nonetheless displayed intensity of feeling; "This will never do," Jeffrey had thundered after perusing *The Excursion*. The reviews of the late 1880's are notable only for their blandness or pettiness. The *Saturday Review* anonymously and rather noncommittally ventured, "In the prolonged absence of good new poetry there is a pleasure in welcoming a little volume by Mr. Wordsworth," and, daring to praise the one section of the poem Wordsworth had himself published in his collected works (*Water-fowl*), concluded, "It only remains to thank the representatives of Mr. Wordsworth for this addition to the treasures of his poetry, and to remark that the booksellers present it with a modesty and elegance not unworthy of the verse."[11] *The Spectator*'s reviewer fussed a bit over the poem's "many instances of those little egotistical condescensions which make one frequently smile and shrink in all Wordsworth's longer poems," and hedged: "*The Recluse*, then, though it is too inconsiderable an addition to his highest work, to exalt appreciably Wordsworth's fame, will amply sustain it";

---

[11] *Saturday Review*, LXVII (12 January 1889), 43–44.

"it is a new and beautiful exemplification of his chief sources of inspiration, and that is all."[12]

Astonished by that "all," one turns with some relief to the positive opening of Edward Dowden's review in *The Academy*. The appearance of *The Recluse*, he averred, "is a very important event for all who love the poetry of Wordsworth. I do not know that there are seven hundred consecutive lines to be found anywhere in his writings of greater interest than these." This introduction would seem to augur a thoughtful and thorough consideration of the poem, but Dowden continued, "With this word I dismiss the fragment of 'The Recluse,' for I must speak somewhat fully of the edition of the 'Complete Poetical Works' now put forth, with no editor's name, but seemingly with the authority of Wordsworth's representatives."[13] That is all we hear of Dowden's appreciation.

Three other reviews announced the publication of the poem, but discussed it in only the most superficial terms. An anonymous notice in *The Athenaeum* merely observed that the first part of *The Recluse* had now been published and invited the reader to compare passages in it with Wordsworth's other poems. Rowland Prothero's unsigned review in the *Edinburgh Review* set out to show the beauties of Wordsworth's poetry, particularly in *The Recluse*, but it soon lapsed into a summary of *The Prelude* and *Home at Grasmere*. George Charles Moore Smith's review in *The Eagle: A Magazine supported by Members of St. John's College* (Cambridge) was full of high praise, and found lines 703–744 (from MS. D) "so noble in spirit and so magnificent in expression that it is scarcely to be surpassed, as I think, in English poetry." Despite the encomia, however, and obvious pride in the achievement of a member of the college, Smith's review is vague and disappointing.[14]

Finally, in September, 1889, the *Nineteenth Century* carried a brilliant seventeen-page article on *The Recluse* by William Minto: "Wordsworth's Great Failure."[15] More biographical than critical, it remains the finest discussion to date of the poem's history. Minto's perceptive admiration of *Home at Grasmere* stands in marked contrast to Knight's patronizing dismissal in his brief preface to the text in his 1889 biography:

The introduction to *The Recluse* was not only kept back by him [Wordsworth] during his lifetime, but was omitted by his representatives—with what must be regarded as true critical insight—when *The Prelude* was published in 1850. As a whole, it is not equal to *The Prelude*; certain passages are very inferior, but there are others, that posterity

---

[12] *The Spectator*, LXI (29 December 1888), 1852–1853.

[13] *The Academy*, XXXV (12 January 1889), 17.

[14] *The Athenaeum*, No. 3196 (26 January 1889), 109–110; *Edinburgh Review*, CLXIX (April, 1889), 415–447; *The Eagle*, XV (1889), 461–468.

[15] XXVI, 435–451. Minto also wrote the entry on WW for the *Encyclopedia Britannica*, 9th ed., XXIV (Edinburgh, 1888), where he stressed the role of *The Recluse* in WW's poetic career.

will cherish, and cannot willingly let die. It was probably a conviction of its inequality and inferiority that led Wordsworth to give selected extracts from this canto to the world in his own lifetime.[16]

This view Minto sharply countered: "I cannot agree with the opinion that this canto of the Recluse's Home and his aspirations, is inferior to *The Prelude*. It is really a fragment of that impassioned history, written throughout in the same exalted vein; the verse is of the poet's prime, and the feeling is more whole-hearted and buoyant, being crossed by no disturbing currents of regret or misgiving" (p. 439). Minto showed that he did understand why other admirers of Wordsworth paid the poem so little heed. He argued that the popular conception of the poet's character had been so firmly shaped that "people were not disposed to accept Wordsworth as a poet of unfulfilled ambition—a self dissatisfied poet whose achievement in one great particular fell short of his aspiration. On the contrary, he had become fixed in the public mind as a very type of self-confidence, not to say self-complacency" (p. 443). This image, Minto knew, was false. He had studied the letters available in Knight's newly published life, and with keen psychological insight he was the first scholar to assess correctly the importance of *The Recluse* in Wordsworth's long career:

The history of the unfinished *Recluse* is the history of Wordsworth's poetic life: his conception of this grand purpose and lifelong striving to fulfill it being the central line that gives unity and dramatic interest to his career. It was this project that brought him to Grasmere, and the failure of it tortured many hours and days and weeks of his fifty years' residence in the Lake Country. [p. 436]

For all his emphasis on "failure," Minto knew as well as we know today that *Home at Grasmere* was not a failure but a triumphant success, and that its publication at long last, after many dormant years, was a major literary event. His essay has deservedly been brought back into circulation by its inclusion, in somewhat shortened form, in the anthology of criticism edited by A. W. Thomson, *Wordsworth's Mind and Art* (Edinburgh, 1969), pp. 10–27.

---

[16] *Life*, I, 231–232.

Appendix II

PREFACE.
[to *The Excursion*, 1814][1]

The Title-page announces that this is only a Portion of a Poem; and the Reader must be here apprized that it belongs to the second part of a long and laborious Work, which is to consist of three parts.—The Author will candidly acknowledge that, if the first of these had been completed, and in such a manner as to satisfy his own mind, he should have preferred the natural order of publication, and have given that to the World first; but, as the second division of the Work was designed to refer more to passing events, and to an existing state of things, than the others were meant to do, more continuous exertion was naturally bestowed upon it, and greater progress made here than in the rest of the Poem; and as this part does not depend upon the preceding, to a degree which will materially injure its own peculiar interest, the Author, complying with the earnest entreaties of some valued Friends, presents the following Pages to the Public.

It may be proper to state whence the Poem, of which The Excursion is a part, derives its Title of THE RECLUSE.[2]—Several years ago, when the Author retired to his native Mountains, with the hope of being enabled to construct a literary Work that might live, it was a reasonable thing that he should take a review of his own Mind, and examine how far Nature and Education had qualified him for such employment. As subsidiary to this preparation, he undertook to record, in Verse, the origin and progress of his own powers, as far as he was acquainted with them. That Work, addressed to a dear Friend, most distinguished for his knowledge and genius, and to whom the Author's Intellect is deeply indebted, has been long finished;[3] and the result of the investigation which gave rise to it was a determination to compose a philosophical Poem, containing views of Man, Nature, and Society; and to be entitled, The Recluse; as having for its principal subject the sensations and opinions of a Poet living in retirement.—The preparatory Poem is biographical, and conducts the history of the Author's mind to the point when he was

---

[1] For fuller information about WW's allusions here, see *Prose*, III, 10–12.

[2] The account which follows slightly distorts the facts; see *Prel.*, pp. xxxiii–xxxix, and *PW*, V, 363.

[3] This work is *The Prelude*; the friend is STC.

463

emboldened to hope that his faculties were sufficiently matured for entering upon the arduous labour which he had proposed to himself; and the two Works have the same kind of relation to each other, if he may so express himself, as the Anti-chapel has to the body of a gothic Church. Continuing this allusion, he may be permitted to add, that his minor Pieces, which have been long before the Public, when they shall be properly arranged, will be found by the attentive Reader to have such connection with the main Work as may give them claim to be likened to the little Cells, Oratories, and sepulchral Recesses, ordinally included in those Edifices.

The Author would not have deemed himself justified in saying, upon this occasion, so much of performances either unfinished, or unpublished, if he had not thought that the labour bestowed by him upon what he has heretofore and now laid before the Public, entitled him to candid attention for such a statement as he thinks necessary to throw light upon his endeavours to please, and he would hope, to benefit his countrymen.—Nothing further need be added, than that the first and third parts of the Recluse will consist chiefly of meditations in the Author's own Person;[4] and that in the intermediate part (The Excursion) the intervention of Characters speaking is employed, and something of a dramatic form adopted.

It is not the Author's intention formally to announce a system: it was more animating to him to proceed in a different course; and if he shall succeed in conveying to the mind clear thoughts, lively images, and strong feelings, the Reader will have no difficulty in extracting the system for himself. And in the mean time the following passage, taken from the conclusion of the first Book of the Recluse, may be acceptable as a kind of *Prospectus* of the design and scope of the whole Poem.[5]

---

[4] *Home at Grasmere* is the first Book of the first Part of *The Recluse*; the rest of Part I was never completed. What the third Part might have been remains a mystery, as, apparently, none of it was ever composed. See the Introduction, above. The Advertisement to *The Prelude* (London, 1850) announces that "the materials of which it [Part III] would have been formed have . . . been incorporated, for the most part, in the Author's other Publications, written subsequently to the Excursion" (p. vii). One supposes that these were mainly sonnets.

[5] The lines which follow are reprinted above in the Reading Text of *Home at Grasmere*, MS. D, ll. 754–860; punctuation has been modernized.

Home at Grasmere

Designed by R. E. Rosenbaum.
Composed by Syntax International Pte. Ltd.
in 8 and 10 point Monophoto Baskerville 169,
with display lines in Monophoto Baskerville.
Printed offset by Vail-Ballou Press, Inc.
on Warren's Olde Style Wove, 60 pound basis.
Bound by Vail-Ballou Press in
Joanna Arrestox B book cloth,
with stamping in All Purpose Gold foil.